Z E R O
DANCES

ZERO DANCES

A BIOGRAPHY OF
ZERO MOSTEL

ARTHUR SAINER

LIMELIGHT EDITIONS   NEW YORK

First Limelight Edition September 1998

Library of Congress Cataloging-in-Publication Data

Sainer, Arthur.
    Zero dances : a biography of Zero Mostel / Arthur Sainer.
        p. cm.
    Includes index.
    ISBN 0-87910-096-6
    1. Mostel, Zero, 1915-1977. 2. Actors—United States—Biography.
I. Title.
PN2287.M77S25 1998
792'.028'092—dc21
[B]   98-37793
                                                            CIP

This work is dedicated to my beloved wife, Maryjane Treloar, who kept after me during the many months that no publisher seemed ready to transform this manuscript from a secret known only to our friends into a public event. I kept telling Maryjane to stop badgering me, to cease kvetching, but she paid little attention. Perhaps she was right to insist.

*"Do you think it is possible to write a life of anyone?
I doubt it; because people are all over the place."*

—*Virginia Woolf*

The art of biography? This art, traditionally the written history of a life, presumes that one can chart the journey of a human being from one place, one condition, to another place, another condition. But Ulysses wanted only to return to the place where he had started when the Greeks set out to reclaim Helen. And perhaps all journeys, of people, salmon, viruses, monarch butterflies, all journeys presage a movement home. So in a sense this "art of biography" is looking at a movement which unconsciously wants to undo itself, which wants to be no movement at all, which wants to return to itself.

The journey of a child of immigrant parents, who came to be known as Zero Mostel, can be seen as the story of one who wanted to find his way home, even as this aggressively-labeled Zero took on the role, in *Ulysses in Nighttown*, of Joyce's Leopold Bloom. That Bloomsday Odysseus, an assimilated Jew in Catholic Ireland, spends unsupportable hours in search of the key that will re-center him; he believes his loss is simply that of the latchkey that will admit him to the familiar domicile he

1

shares with Molly Bloom and from which he has been absent one long Dublin day and night. Did Zero believe he was absent from where he wanted to be? That he had lost or misplaced or simply thrown away the key that would readmit him to that better part of himself? One is hard put to evoke a simple yes or no; there is only the attempted charting of this awkward, often painful, sometimes hilarious journey.

An apocryphal tale: The theatrical agent, evaluating the prospective client in his office, asks the latter to demonstrate his prowess. "Do something funny," he encourages Zero. The latter, never one to shy away from the pleasures of overkill, lifts the agent's typewriter and flings it out the window. A dubious tale, but symptomatic of how legends adhere to this legendary fat man.

Another story: Zero stops at an art-supply shop on Manhattan's East Side. The dealer, with whom he has had a long and affectionate relationship, holds out a new drawing pen. "It's a fine-quality item, take it to your studio, it's a gift, I'd like you to have one." Zero reaches across the counter, grabs the dealer by the collar and growls, "What about my discount?"

Zero won several Tony Awards for acting. One of his acceptance speeches, we're told, was delivered in Yiddish. He would break into a rapid Yiddish with actor Sam Jaffe, with the painter Herbie Kallem, and once with a gentleman studiously peeing at the adjoining urinal in a rest stop on the Jersey Turnpike. As the story goes, the gentleman's urine was indiscriminately splashing around that of adjourning urinals. "You piss," Zero is said to have commented in plain Yiddish, "like Chagall paints." The latter is said to have responded in similar Yiddish, "I am Chagall." Having established identities in such a forthright manner, the two continued comfortably urinating and discoursing in that East European *mamaloschen* so dear to the heart of Sholom Aleichem.

The obstreperous, noisy Mostel also had a history of settling into long silences. The boorish Mostel could quickly convert to the introspective Mostel; the public performer shed his glistening skin and dived into the interior mode of the private painter.

These facets almost take on a sense of inevitability; in hindsight they seem predictable. One is tempted to say, of course. I always saw him that way." But who ever saw him, or saw any of us, for that matter?

(Toby Mostel, Zero's younger son, told me, "Years after the Tip Toe Inn ceased to exist, I'd run into people who ate there. They'd tell me they used to frequent the Inn so they could watch the Mostel family battling at supper.")

What about a life? Does a life ever add up?

Middlebury College in Northern Vermont bestowed honorary degrees on David Rockefeller and Zero Mostel. Rockefeller confided to the graduating class that among his collections he was particularly proud of some fifty thousand rare insects. Zero, no slouch at acquiring pre-Columbian art, quickly let it be known that he himself was curating a sizable collection of cockroaches. Did Zero have a favorite? Yes, the common garden variety, the proletarian roach, not a picky eater in the least.

Zero is said to have shaved his friend Sam Jaffe one night at Lindy's restaurant, recruiting the whipped cream from Jaffe's beloved strawberry shortcake. Everything within Zero's reach—poodles, tablecloths, other humans—everything was a potential prop, a tempting foil.

We like to intimate that we are on better terms with art than life, the former seems to us more manageable, it can be erased, redrafted, you can presumably say anything, write anything, paint anything. Who can tell you different?

Tevye and Zero, two legendary creatures reaching across time, encounter one another. Each manifests an idiosyncratic Jewishness: Tevye's is a nineteenth-century peasant wisdom; Zero's is a twentieth-century urban wisdom of the street; its possessor knows the score. Through *Fiddler on the Roof*, the exploits of Tevye are to occupy Zero's attention night after incalculable night over a span of thirteen years. But from where has this gentle, obstinate Tevye emerged in the first place? We are going to digress briefly, moving from the journey of Zero to that of the fictional Tevye.[1]

It's early in the twentieth century, shortly before the Great War. Sholom Aleichem, already an emigre to and from an America he has abandoned as unworkable, is convalescing from a life-threatening bout with tuberculosis. He writes from Lausanne, Switzerland, to Yiddish theatre impresario Jacob Adler (father of Celia, Stella and Luther) in New York.

> In my play, you will find none of the effects on which the Jewish public has for so many years been nourished . . . no soul-tearing scenes, no corpses in cribs, no demented women . . . no transient

4

borders seducing innocent maidens, and no vulgar jokes. You will find only a simple Jew, father of five daughters, an honest, clean, wholesome, and greatly suffering character who, with all his misfortunes, will make the public laugh from beginning to the end. . . . My present title,

he informs Adler,

is *Family Pictures in Four Acts.*

Adler and his theatrical rival, the equally-renowned Boris Thomashevsky, have each mounted one earlier play by Sholom Aleichem. Adler's production of *Pasternak* opened on the same night, February 8th, 1907, as Thomashevsky's staging of *Stempenyu,* in order to preclude a nasty race between the impresarios. Unfortunately, both plays quickly shut down. The sudden demise of two major productions had left Sholom Aleichem, desperate for cash to meet family medical bills, more than a little disheartened and less than sanguine about the golden opportunities open to him along Second Avenue, the Yiddish theatrical mainstream. But here is Sholom Aleichem, irrepressible, his body healing slowly, once more offering a new, heartfelt work for the theatre. It turns out that Adler has no particular interest in this father of five daughters, in Sholom Aleichem's wholesome, suffering character, though he is canny enough to keep the lines open, and he encourages the author to keep cranking out new plays.

But the commercial theatre is not about to bestir itself for Sholom Aleichem during his lifetime, and Tevye's career in show business, decades before the emergence of Zero and *Fiddler,* first comes to light on a movie screen. In April, 1919, the silent Yiddish film *Khavah,* or *Broken Barriers,* opens in New York, dramatizing that heartrending sequence in which Tevye declares his daughter Khavah dead after he learns that she has married a Gentile. It is a critical moment uncomfortably close to that which will haunt Zero during the last three decades of his own life, even as he himself is performing as the Tevye who disowns his daughter for marrying outside the faith. The shtetl for *Khavah* has been constructed in Leonia, New Jersey, where the film is shot, but only four months later, on August 29th, Tevye and the fictional Kasrilevke finally materialize onstage at the Irving Place Theatre on Manhattan's Lower East Side. *Family Pictures in Four Acts* has been renamed *Tevye der Milkhiker (Tevye the Dairyman)*, and the title role is now in the hands of the young impresario Maurice Schwartz.

Sholom Aleichem based his Tevye on an actual dairyman named Tevyeh who delivered milk and cheese to summer residents at Boyarka, "an hour's train ride from Kiev." In his stories, Sholom Aleichem kept changing the number of daughters that Tevye fathers, but the actual Tevyeh, curiously like the actual Zero Mostel, had no daughters at all. Sholom Aleichem had nicknamed the real-life Tevyeh *Der Milkhiger*, the Milky One, and some quality of innocent cunning, of a clown-like transparency, was henceforth to adhere to the images of the real and fictional Tevyehs.

But by the time Tevye reached the stage and the silent screen, Sholom Aleichem had been dead for three years. For two days in May of 1916, the Yiddish Mark Twain, as he had come to be known, lay in state in a Bronx apartment at 968 Kelly Street.[2] His daughter Marie Waife-Goldberg recalls the "changing guard of all the Jewish writers in the city . . . a continuous stream of people kept passing the bier all through the night, the line outside, even at night, stretching for blocks around the house." Sholom Aleichem was only fifty-seven when he died. The fictional Tevye was now on his own. But by the 1920's there was no stopping this Tevye; he had gotten a taste for fame and he liked it.

Between Sholom Aleichem's second arrival in America in 1914 and his death a year and a half later, the family of Yisroel and Tzina Mostel produced the fourth of their five sons. There were to be seven children in all, including two daughters. Simcha Yoel Mostel, or as he was called in English, Samuel Joel, was born on February 29th, 1915, though he publicly leaned toward February 28th, a more bountiful date since it produced three more birthdays every four years.[3] Several decades later, Sammy, now known as Zero, finds his way after much wandering to the persistent Tevye. *Fiddler on the Roof* is a hit beyond the wildest dreams of its backers; our wise and foolish Tevye is a Broadway star; and Zero Mostel, already internationally acclaimed for his portrayal of fools and servants of fools, takes on the persona of a superstitious, warmhearted, kvetching Jew living precariously within the confines of the Pale of Settlement in the Western part of Czarist Russia that is generally known as the Ukraine.

With Tevye, Zero makes a journey back to that principally impoverished region of Eastern Europe, that odd mixture of urban sophistication and rural piety that nurtured his own parents and Tevye's creator some seventy years earlier, the land of Galicia, Poland, and of the Pale. It is a recurrent story of abandonment and return, of Jews migrating to America or Palestine, and of the offspring making a largely symbolic turning to the Old Country: through painting and music, through the novel, through the theatre and film, essentially through the inheritance and reformation of memory.

Under the proscenium arch, Zero becomes nakedly Jewish, the archetypal Orthodox Yid. Even as one knows Zero is an actor playing a role, one "knows" the opposite, that he *is* the Jew of the Old Country, his own ancestor. In some inexplicable fashion which we seem to understand very well, the mask and the man merge into one identity. It is an age-old interchange, a transaction never disturbed by any other reality. There are to be other turnings for Zero; Tevye is not the final word. But we are beginning our journey back to that vanished world from which Yisroel and Tzina Mostel emerged onto another kind of stage.

A vanished world. Are the Mostels Polish, Russian, Rumanian, Hungarian? On their first walk together in 1942, the newest comic sensation at Cafe Society Downtown confides to Kate Harkin, later his second wife, that his name is really a pseudonym for Remo Feruggio, an Italian Catholic from . . . pick a town, let's call it Naples or Parma. Clara Baker, formerly Clara Sverd Mostel, Zero's childhood sweetheart and first wife, recalls that "he always told me that his parents were Italian. But what did I know? I believed everything he told me." In fact, a Remo Feruggio certainly existed, but he was hardly a Mostel of any kind. Remo was a painter, much like his friend Zero, and a veteran of the famous Mostel Thursday-night poker games. It's likely that the spontaneous if temporary exchange of Zero for Remo, the cadence and the sense of a romanticized full-bodied ethnicity that was present in "Remo" pleased young Samuel Joel.

No one that this writer initially queried seemed to have any notion of the Mostel ancestry, not Ben Raeburn, the retired editor-publisher of Horizon Press who considered himself Zero's oldest friend, and neither of the Mostel children, Josh and Toby. Raeburn could only tell me that Zero spoke Yiddish to his mother. "He would call her from my office. There were times he just didn't want to go up to the Bronx for the Friday night meal. He would tell her he was out of town, that he was calling from Pittsburgh." That was as much documentation as Raeburn could provide: there had existed a Yiddish-speaking mother who apparently could be cozened into believing that a local call from Manhattan was coming from Pittsburgh. But did Neopolitan Jewish mothers speak Yiddish? According to Raeburn, "The question never came up."

I had to assume that it had come up somewhere and broached the matter to Josh Mostel, the elder of the two sons. "Italian Jews?" I asked. Josh shrugged: "I've no idea." By the time I was making these inquiries, Kate Mostel had lost her lifelong battle with asthma; she could tell me nothing. It appeared that no one close to the Mostels had any notion as to where these Yiddish-speaking parents, only one generation back, had migrated from. But was it possible that no one had seriously inquired?

I finally reached a fruitful source and was rewarded with a frontal attack of fact and opinion on many matters pertaining to the Mostel lineage. Aaron Mostel, one of Zero's surviving brothers in 1988, shouted into the phone: "Lvov! Lemberg! Stanislow! Where did you hear Italian? Somebody is *meshugah*?"

Lvov, also known as Lwow, also Lemberg, now in 1998 renamed Lviv, still lives, along with Stanislow, Kiev, Bialystok, Brody, Vilna, Tarnopol, all part of the historic life of East European

Jewry. The Mostels—Yisroel Mostel, his first wife Esther, and his second wife Tzina Druchs—can be traced back to that uncertain, militant and sometimes murderous world of Eastern Europe. While various contingents were attacking, intermarrying or carving each other up, the energetic and highly-inventive Jewish communities were sometimes taking sides, sometimes battling one another, usually maintaining some degree of uneasy and precarious neutrality. The Jews were alternately protected and then oppressed by the East European nobility, often by the same forces from one decade to the next. They might at one moment be living in peace with their Gentile neighbors, only to find themselves in the next moment under seige by these very neighbors for whom Jewish overseers or tax collectors, employed by local barons and princes, constituted the visible enemy, the presumptive agents for an oppressive elite.

From 1340 on, when Casimir III of Poland invaded, German and Bohemian Jews comprised a significant element of the populace of Galicia and its principal city, Lvov. The city changed hands numerous times over the next centuries. In the sixteenth century, Lvov was part of an independent Galicia. Then the Poles absorbed Lvov once again and it became Lwow. Lvov or Lwow (or in more recent times, Lemberg) came to be considered a major cultural center, "the Vienna of the East," with a university, a medical center, museums and concert halls.

The Jews, intermittently under the protection of the Crown, were seen as an all but indispensable factor in trade, for the city was a transit point between the West and the Orient. But its Jewish population was also at the mercy of vengeful forces. In 1648–49, the Chmielnicki massacres terrorized Lwow, and Jews were high-priority victims. A staggering percentage of Lwow's Jews were wiped out; it was largely the Gentile populace's refusal to turn over the surviving Jews to those laying seige that prevented the Jewish death toll from escalating further.

Towards the close of the eighteenth century, the Poles lost Lwow to the Austro-Hungarian Empire and the city was renamed Lemberg. In 1919 Lemberg became part of a newly redrafted Poland; for the Jews this meant a semi-autonomus existence which lasted until the Soviet invasion of 1939 when some ten thousand Jews were deported eastward. The Nazi invasion in June of 1941 sent thousands more fleeing east with the retreat of Stalin's forces, and the several thousand Jews who remained were, with the exception of six people, wiped out overnight. The Nazi massacres continued over the next years, as new prisoners moved into the Lemberg ghetto. A handful of men, women, children and infants hid in the sewers for months, and some of these survived. Terror, with the enthusiastic support of many local Ukrainians, was chronic, but a righteous Christian, at the risk of his own life, saved many in the sewers. In July of 1944 the Red Army liberated and absorbed, for the tender mercies of Joseph Stalin, both the city and all of the Ukraine except for the westernmost part of Galicia. Now we find, once again, a "liberated" city with its new name of Lviv in the newly-independent territory of Ukraine. But this liberated Lviv, which once nourished the father of Samuel Joel Mostel, has to a large extent been emptied of its Jews.

Yisroel (Israel) Mostel spent his early years in a shtetl nestled close to Lemberg. It was the middle of the nineteenth century; the Mostels were vintners and Yisroel was trained in the family business. Notes Aaron Mostel, "The family sent father to school to learn how to manage and develop vineyards." Yisroel was to be instructed in the chemistry of wines. The Mostels cultivated vineyards in Hungary, then part of the Austro-Hungarian Empire, and Zero and Aaron's grandfather supervised the shipment of Mostel wines in railroad tank cars across Central and Eastern Europe.

Herman Mostel, son of Esther and Yisroel, would tell his half-brothers and sisters how their father could produce white wine from red, that Yisroel was an expert at coloring ingredients. "If he'd become a bootlegger," says Aaron Mostel, "he'd have been a rich guy. But he wouldn't do it. In America father sold only sacramental wines."

Yisroel Mostel married Esther in Europe. They had four children. In the late 1880s, Yisroel came to America, perhaps preceding the family, as many Jewish husbands did who were trying to establish a base in the New World. Esther died in America, at a comparatively early age. Then Yisroel took a second wife.

Tzina (Celia) Druchs, who would give birth to Zero in 1915, was the last of eleven children, and came from the province of Stanislow in East Galicia. She was orphaned at the age of six and sent to live with wealthy relatives. As a young adult she enrolled at the University of Vienna. She could speak many languages, and was particularly versed in Polish, German, and Yiddish. Later, in New York, she would utilize her prodigious language skills to write letters for illiterate immigrants who wished to correspond with family and neighbors left behind in the Old Country. Nine brothers and sisters who stayed behind were eventually murdered by the Third Reich.

Tzina's name is derived from *Tsena Urena*, a seventeenth century work of literature, composed in Yiddish by Jacob ben Isaac Ashkenazi. It is popularly referred to as *Tzinarina*, and was meant to be read to women who had themselves never been taught to read. The novelist Cynthia Ozick remarks that the *Tsena Urena*, purveying translations of weekly Torah readings together with a variety of folktales, "is the work of a single teeming, twinkling, original, joyfully pious mind, combining scriptural stories . . . legend, myth, tale, homily, and a vivid storyteller's style. . . . A fitting name then for this Tzina Druchs Mostel, a woman of learning, piety and wit who, far from the expansive educational centers of *Mitteleurope*, transported to the ferments and instabilities of the New World, fortified herself each day with a Yiddish newspaper and the *New York Times*, and engaged in the task of helping to unravel the mysteries of English for women deprived of the benefits of formal learning. "She believed in America," Aaron Mostel recalls, "she wanted her children to think, to be well-read. She especially cherished Sammy [Zero]. He was one of the most brilliant kids on the Lower East Side. He had great intellectual capacity. He could talk on any subject in the world."

In the early days of their marriage, Yisroel and Tzina Mostel lived in the Brownsville section of Brooklyn. Zero was born in the two-family house the Mostels rented on Strauss Street. By the turn of the century, Brownsville was home to some fifty thousand Jews. Irving Howe notes that Brownsville was regarded as "a pastoral village in which [quoting Elias Tcherikower] 'Jews could live as in the old country, without any rush or excessive worries. Jews there didn't work on the Sabbath, and they went to *shul* three times a day.'" But in 1917, Strauss Street and its immediate environs had no *shul*, Yisroel's response was to transform the Mostels' downstairs living room into a house of prayer for Shabbat and he himself functioned as rabbi. But a year later the Mostels abandoned Brownsville, the pastoral village—today a paradise for crack dealers—and moved their brood to the teeming ghetto of Manhattan's Lower East Side, specifically to another two-family house at 140 Columbia Street.

The Columbia Street residence had five rooms and six occupants, with Zero and Aaron sharing a bedroom. The Mostels also had the first private telephone in the neighborhood. Like many New York families well into the Thirties, the Mostels acted as a kind of informal switchboard, alerting neighbors that they were wanted on the phone or taking messages for them. The house on Columbia Street, like the ghetto neighborhood of which it was an integral part, was alive with humanity. "There were a lot of us," Aaron remembers, "always lots of visitors, always food, plenty of food. Nobody went hungry when they came to our house." Tzina Mostel was an accomplished baker, and there was a sister-in-law who spent much hands-on time making kosher magic in the Mostel kitchen. "Whatever one of them didn't know how to cook, the other one knew and would take over."

In those early years of the century, Yisroel was employed by a relative, a Delancey Street vintner named Isaac Wirklich. The bottled wine they produced was labeled I. Wirklich and Sons. When Isaac Wirklich suffered a stroke, Yisroel, together with Isaac's son Nathan, took over the various Wirklich enterprises. Eventually, Yisroel added a small kosher wine of his own. As Aaron Mostel puts it, "A little side business."

Though he chose to make his living in the world of shopkeepers, Yisroel was, like his brother, a Judaic scholar. The two Mostel brothers undertook the training of rabbinical students on the Lower East Side, at a time when New York City offered few opportunities for advanced Jewish study. It's Aaron's contention that the work of the Mostels helped develop what eventually became Yeshiva University in New York, but I've found nothing to support this claim. There were already two existing yeshiva colleges by the turn of the century; they later merged to form Yeshiva University.

The Mostels had a spiritual grounding that fostered an acute sense of justice, a sense of what the needy immigrant in that teeming Yiddish ghetto was undergoing. Aaron recalls that "there was no such thing as welfare in the early part of the century. When they developed it they called it 'home relief,' or just plain 'relief.' But in those early years there was no relief." In the eyes of the Mostel children there was Yisroel, the just man, and Tzina, the just woman, traditional defenders of widows and orphans. Yisroel was known for walking into the *shul* and collecting money to purchase shoes for a needy child; he was known for soliciting funds so that neighborhood children might have milk every day. Tzina founded an organization known as *Kimpe-turem Fabank* [Woman Who Has a Child]; groups of women would gather in the Mostel living room for the purpose of sewing shirts and diapers for impoverished children. The Mostels were not only equipped with one of the rare telephones in the neighborhood, they also could boast of a sturdy sewing machine. And Aaron, when we spoke in the late Eighties, suspected the *Kimpe-turem Fabank* might still be in operation.

When Zero was a child, Tzina and Yisroel found another pastoral village. The Mostels began to spend much of the year on a farm in Moodus, Connecticut. Recalling Moodus in later years, Zero would reminisce about the livestock; in language touching on the cadences of Wordsworth with a little dusting of Blake, he would call up images of clucking chickens, grazing cows and gamboling lambs. The family would reside in Moodus from Passover, usually in April, through the High Holy Days of Rosh Hashanah and Yom Kippur, in September or early October. Ever on the lookout for a *shul*, Yisroel purchased a church building that was up for auction and effected the interior conversions necessary for the worship of Adonai.

Within a few years, the Mostels made yet another move, back full-time to Manhattan, quite likely for practical reasons. The farm was turned over to Yisroel's sister and her husband, "practically given away," Aaron Mostel notes bitterly, "to our uncle, Sam Banner." But Banner was unable to meet the mortgage payments and the inevitable foreclosure ensued. In later years the property became a well-known resort called Banner Lodge.

Like many Jewish immigrant families, the Mostels spoke a mixture of English and Yiddish, often switching tongues in mid-sentence. But the nuances of English could prove difficult. There is the case of Tzina's brother Chaim, who changed his name from Chaim Druchs to Charles W. Schwartz and operated a toy and stationery store known as H. Schwartz on Ludlow Street. Uncle Chaim was a Talmudic scholar, but it appears that he had a tenuous connection to the English language, at least to its articulation. According to Aaron Mostel, Chaim or Charles struggled mightily with his adopted tongue. Herman, the oldest of the Mostel children, would make an effort to bring Uncle Chaim and spoken English face to face, to place them on speaking terms. But Herman's proclamation that "a chair is a chair" brought Chaim's response that "a cheh is a cheh." Certainly an intelligible utterance, spiced with a sweet overlay of Yiddish dialect, if not exactly the tones of an Anglo-Saxon to the manor born.

If many Jewish households struggled with the language of their adopted land, they brought with them from Europe that centuries-old preoccupation with and reverence for learning, that determination to further their children's education. The Mostel household placed a premium on learning; Yisroel and Tzina presided over a home where serious literature mattered, where ideas circulated, where art was respected, where the Laws of Moses, Biblical prophecy and Rabbinic teachings were nurtured, and where the Sabbath was faithfully observed.

Sammy, named for prophet Samuel who was given to God's service at birth, who was later renamed a reductive Zero, took it all in. Sammy listened to his father reading Yiddish from the comic tales of Sholom Aleichem; he became well-versed in Hebrew and Yiddish, and made significant inroads into the study of Torah and later into the Talmud. He was proficient in many areas; it seemed that whatever Samuel Joel put his hand to he mastered. Not only could Sammy read several languages with speed and intelligence, he had a marked facility for drawing and also a grasp of comic improvisation that harked back to the mode of commedia dell'arte. In a very real sense, the Mostels were harboring an impish and highly-charged Renaissance child.

Aaron Mostel recounts that while an undergraduate at City College, Sammy also attended classes at the Jewish Theological Seminary, one of this country's principal centers of Conservative Jewish thought. (The JTS's records, going back many decades, could neither confirm nor deny Sammy's attendance.) In fact, Sammy's proficiency in all matters of Jewish learning led his father Yisroel to have reasonable expectations that his brilliant offspring would eventually become an ordained rabbi. But one day Sammy turned to his father and announced, *"Trom mir vaint nisht zein kine rav."* ["From me no manner of rabbi will emerge."] And that was the last of Sammy's formal investigations into the worlds of Torah and Talmud. Although as it turned out, he had already drunk deeper from those springs of Judaic thought than perhaps he was ever to realize.

3

In June, 1931, the Seward Park High School yearbook prints a rhapsodic notice alongside the headshot of chubby young Samuel Joel Mostel. "A future Rembrandt, or perhaps a comedian?" There is no mention of a rabbinical calling.

Nineteen thirty-one finds the country moving deeper into what is to become the Great Depression. Sam is sixteen years old. He has been painting for some time; perhaps he will never attain "future Rembrandt" status, but he is by all accounts a young man with some gift for rendering visual images. And he is certainly regaling his teenaged friends; the comic impulse his second nature, Sam is already the acknowledged life of whatever party happens to be in progress. Sammy's gang consists predominantly of working-class Jewish adolescents, offspring of East European immigrants, "Jews without money," to borrow Mike Gold's title—young, generally noisy and feisty teenagers tasting a degree of freedom, but at this juncture not venturing far from the secure if often oppressive sanctuary of Old World custom. Most of these teenagers want to break away; the seductions of the assimilated life already beckon to them through the dynamics of the street, through public discourse, secular institutions of learning, English-language newspapers, and through radio and the first awkward sound tracks of talking pictures. Sam is unique among his friends; he already has a familiarity with the local art museums and galleries, but popular and symphonic music are now reaching into every home that can boast of a Philco or Stuart Warner radio.

While the Mostels dwelt at 140 Columbia Street, the family of Clara Sverd lived nearby at 286 East Broadway. Clara, her sister Norma, her friends Nettie Crosley, Rose Ripps, and Eeta Linden, Natey the apprentice butcher, and Jenkins, apparently the family name of the lone Gentile to grace the group, all lived in close proximity. By the turn of the century, East Broadway had become one of the educational strongholds for East European Jewry. It nourished old World traditions even as it paradoxically helped uproot many observant Jews from their observance. Even as these East Broadway institutions labored to sustain Jews in the faith of their fathers, they encouraged assimilation into the very culture that understood little about that faith and judged it an anachronism.

The *Daily Forward*, comfortably rooted in its imposing, multistoried headquarters on East Broadway, came to represent a kind of ongoing guidance counselor, principally through editor Abraham Cahan's brainchild, the "Bintel Brief." Cahan was marked by a certain overbearing genius. Despite the fact that several competing Yiddish-language dailies more accurately reflected Jewish political and religious issues, Cahan and his "Bintel Brief" promoted the sense that the *Forward* more directly addressed the concerns of these new Americans. The heartfelt plaints embedded in letters-to-the-editor, some of which Zero Mostel would perform on long-playing records years later, came from Russian mothers whose daughters had the ill grace to marry "modern" Hungarians and were now taunting their old parents for their backward ways, from laborers painting stressful situations in sweatshops, from offspring who had left impoverished elders in the Old Country, from wives who could not tolerate their husbands and from husbands who had an equal aversion to their wives. E.g.; "She is first-class Hungarian, she laughs at the way I talk." "One of the workers in our shop is a miserly fellow. His whole life is wrapped up in his bank book. . . . He hates music, the theater, and socialism. . . . I am convinced that worker will be a boss." "So I married him . . . living with him a short time, I learned to hate him." "A novel could be made out of my life." "My wife . . . is a great preacher of women's rights. . . . She has a big mouth, cries easily, and hates to listen to anyone." Cahan, who may well have been the principal composer for these bitter litanies, caught the struggle of half-literate immigrants trying to accommodate themselves to English syntax and New World custom, to survive disorientation, to ameliorate hatred for fellow immigrants and the entrenched social and political powers, and to give voice to an often extended grieving for the lost European home.

If the *Forward* popularized social and political issues, public libraries like Seward Park, directly across the street from the *Forward* building, offered the immigrant family the vast new worlds of secular literature, philosophy, art, and the social sciences. And at 197 East Broadway, the five-story armory of learning known as the Educational Alliance provided untold thousands, the young Sam Mostel among them, with their first formal training in the visual arts. At the Seward Park Library, even into the Thirties, Sam could encounter socialists, Buddhists, Zionists, and anarchists; at the Alliance he could encounter an "Americanization" agenda in its waning days that, to some critical extent, reflected negatively on the background and deep-rooted values of his own family. "By the turn of the century," social historian Irving Howe writes in *World of Our Fathers*,[4]

> the tension between the established German Jews and the insecure East European Jews had become severe, indeed rather nasty. . . . The Germans found it hard to understand what could better serve their ill-mannered cousins than rapid lessons in civics, English, and the uses of soap. . . . One focus of this struggle was the Educational Alliance, curious mixture of night school, settlement house, day-care center, gymnasium and public

forum. The Alliance represented a tangible embodiment of the German Jews' desire to help, to uplift, to clean up and quiet down their "coreligionists". . . . Throughout its life the Alliance was wracked by the question: to what extent should it try to "Americanize" the greenhorns?

And to what extent should it work toward the preservation of Old World custom, the maintenance of a way of life that struck the more genteel Germans as rude, hopelessly out-of-date and yet, for all that, of authentic value as an anchor to ancient tradition? In their later years Clara, Nettie, and Sam conjured up visions of the Alliance as a magical conveyance that transported them to the brilliant interior of a culture to which they had previously been strangers. But as it opened its doors to the mysteries of secular America, the Alliance, perhaps unconsciously, began to shut its doors to an orthodoxy that had nourished the elders of these hungry children. And paradoxically, even as the Alliance fed the hunger of these young Jews impatient to distance themselves from the parochial aspects of the culture of the ghetto, in the eyes of mainstream America the Alliance itself represented many of the negative connotations of that very ghetto life it had been intent upon counteracting.

Orthodoxy versus secularism—the children of the Lower East Side were confronting issues of belief they were hardly prepared to deal with. Eeta Linden, whose family also lived at 286 East Broadway, has the impression that the Sverd children, Clara and Norma, were "brought up not Orthodox in any possible way." It's likely that the forward-looking Sverds considered their Orthodox neighbors vestigial models of a superstitious culture one could pity, disparage, or mercifully avoid. Clara Baker notes that her parents were agnostics.

"My father wanted to be Americanized. He'd had *enough* in Russia. Judaism didn't mean a thing to my parents. But," she insists, "we were Jewish." One "vestigial" cell, where Judaism maintained its dynamic force, was certainly the Mostel home, where food and dishes had to meet the exacting standards of kashrut, where Yisroel kept up his Judaic studies, and where the father anticipated, even as Tzina noted with interest the burgeoning artist, that Sam would enter the rabbinate. Not only did Sam not embrace the rabbinical calling, he began dating a Jewish girl from down the block whose parents, had deliberately cut themselves off from any religious observance. And apparently it never occurred to Yisroel and Tzina Mostel to inquire of Sam just what *kind* of Jewish girl Clara Sverd was.

"Clara," Aaron Mostel remembers, "was not a stranger. She was welcomed into our household. We always *knew* Clara. She would sit on my father's lap as a kid. Poppa and momma both called her affectionate names. She was like part of our family. She was not like Kate who was from a different atmosphere." (For "different," read Gentile.) And Linden remembers that "when Sammy and Clara got married and they moved to Brooklyn, Clara learned to keep a kosher home."

Was the kosher home to please Sam? A nagging thread of ambivalence will run through both the public and private life of Zero Mostel. He needs to break away from the constraints of Orthodoxy; the very crudeness of his humor, the focus on sexual drive, the obsessive attention to physical appetite, all conspire to draw him from and often to violate Judaic practice which views the physical life as a responsibility and not an indulgence. And yet there are moments when the burden of *mitsva* (Divine commandment) is seen as a priceless heritage. We are face to face with a striven being who, throughout his adult life, attempts in his own lunatic way to juggle two seemingly irreconcilable values.

4

Zero the celebrity came to be known as a kind of Low Priest of Eros; his resistance to the physical charms of young women and those acknowledging forty-plus was distressingly low. Painter Frances Kornbluth, a neighbor of Zero and Kate's on Monhegan Island, indicates it was common knowledge that Maria Karnilova, who created the role of Tevye's wife Golde in *Fiddler on the Roof*, had to smack Zero's straying fingers whenever the two performers found themselves together in a taxi. But in the early Thirties young Sam Mostel seemed to his own peers very much of a romantic and somewhat of an idealist, if hardly a proselytizer for the straight and narrow. Nettie Crosley, Sam's girlfriend before he turned his attentions to Clara, remembers a gallant adolescent. "I was always buying Kotex, and Sammy insisted not only on walking me home but on carrying my Kotex box for me." Clara Baker's recollections are of Sam as courtly suitor. He would call at her house every day; not only would he accompany her to the subway during her undergraduate years at Hunter College but would wait outside the station for her return so that the ever-faithful knight might carry her books home.

21

"I was a kid when we met," Clara recalls. "I thought Sammy was cute. We began to see each other every day for four and a half years. At first I didn't take him seriously as a beau. I was young. I wanted to date other people. I dated somebody else *once* during all that time, and Sammy followed us down the street. He was wearing a black slicker and making all kinds of grimaces behind my back, and I finally said to him, 'Go home, Sammy, I want to kiss this guy goodnight so please go home.' Well what happened? *We*, me and this other fellow, go to the movies. So *Sammy* goes to the movies! He sits behind us, all through the double feature. It seems he just can't leave me alone with *anybody*."

One has to wonder how much of Sam Mostel's synthesis of desperate lover and private eye in trenchcoat was sheer clowning. Clara's impression? Her young suitor was stricken, consumed with jealousy. She sees herself in retrospect, some half-century later (we first spoke in January of 1988) as a desired being insensitive to her suitor's wounds. The suitor's response was to dog his Jewish princess, to pretend the hurt was make-believe but simultaneously to pile guilt upon the beloved, to crowd her with the knowledge of his own irrepressible needs. In short, clowning Sam had the capacity to make the adored Clara a little miserable. At a remarkably early period in this teenaged courtship the air was already thin.

But if Clara was smothered by needful Sam, she clearly enjoyed being treasured by her boyfriend and by the elder Mostels. "And I liked the family a lot. The father was a very Orthodox Jew with a long beard, and very sweet." The Orthodoxy was not offputting. "It was a very observant family, and Sam's mother wore a *sheitel*," a wig traditionally donned by Orthodox Jewish women.

The young Sam of early courtship days had not yet developed the Falstaffian girth that lent to the later Mostel that blissful aura of piling up calories. "When we were going together, and even when we got married, Sammy was thin. Not *very* thin, but thin. Of course he was already a bit ample on the bottom. But he was very handsome when he had his hair. Losing his hair was one of the worst things that could have happened to him. Oh he was thin and gorgeous, with big brown eyes."

In some fashion, everyone in the group "went" with Sam, a situation that generated a grievance Baker could still invoke and even nurse half a century later. "The minute he started to date me everybody turned against me. Sam was the life of the party, and if anybody took him away from the group, if he became interested in a girl—me, let's say—*they* were antagonistic. *They* wanted him. Natey, for instance, hated me with a passion." Natey was not a female rival but a male butcher. "And Natey was really angry because I was taking Sam away from the party, and without Sam the party was nothing."

The Jewish ghetto of the Lower East Side, circa 1936, was characterized by a tribal ingathering of parents, grandparents, aunts, uncles and their multifarious offspring. The tribe could provide a comforting, perpetual babble of Yiddish and English as well as a constant flow of borscht, *shav*, matzo ball soup and gefilte fish. The tribal adolescents derived material, psychological, at times spiritual support from this ingathering, but the elders could also be tyrannical and tedious. Often they struck the younger generation as so out-of-date one couldn't even try to explain the modern world to them. Sammy Mostel and his teenage friends would seek release from the suffocation of the ghetto through the development of informal groups, social and political clubs, constant dating, partying, and that time-honored custom we now call "hanging out." They would meet on the sidewalk, at corner candy stores, in hallways, in the kitchens and parlors of the disciplining and loving elders of the tribe, particularly when the latter had gone off to the movies or to visit relatives who rarely had phones. Nettie Crosley saw her home as a stifling fortress, a safe, overprotective jail, a kind of Jewish Alcatraz with a benevolent warden dispensing chicken soup. The inner circle of the group crowded about the hearth to conceive of projects that seemed to them openings both to the public world and to that inner world which they had hardly begun to decipher.

"Saturday nights we'd sit in the kitchen at my house,"

Nettie recalls, "discussing whatever Rose Ripps was dreaming up." While the girls schemed and gossiped in the kitchen, the boys would be lounging, albeit with some tension, in the living room, wondering what the inner circle, ensconced by stove and icebox, was up to. The radio brought in the sounds of Arturo Toscanini conducting the NBC Symphony Orchestra, and Sam would be yelling over the measures of Beethoven, Debussy, and Mahler that Rose Ripps and the other conspirators were having another bureau (communist cell) meeting. And Sam would accuse Rose of masterminding this infamous bureau which operated close to Nettie's parents' icebox.

So the Saturday night date often had to do with the measures streaming out of the Philco or Stuart Warner. Individually and collectively, the group also spent countless hours on the street or at the settlement houses: the Henry Street Settlement, the Educational Alliance, and Madison House. These institutions, geared to encourage learning among immigrant families, spoke to them of the great world of art and philosophic thought. Miraculously, the intelligence of modern humanism had already touched Sam. Nettie Crosley speaks of those days as ". . . a golden era. We had culture pushed down our throats. My own father had a pushcart on Orchard Street. The culture we absorbed came from other people. A lot of it came from Sammy who was a fund of information, even as a kid."

Clara Baker cannot say enough about her former husband. "Sammy was brilliant. He enriched my life. What did we know from art? At sixteen Sammy took me to every art gallery in Manhattan, and he'd lecture to me. I didn't know *anything* before this. I had a natural affinity for art but no background. Most of our friends had no education in art, but Sammy already knew."

Sam had graduated from Seward Park High School in 1931, a time when the country was moving deeper into the Great Depression. By 1935, with Sam's graduation from City College, the economy had just about come to a standstill. Sam managed to begin graduate school at NYU, studying and painting at night. During the day "I went to work turning sleeves in an overcoat shop belonging to one of my brothers-in-law. I quit after four weeks." Employment was difficult to come by, and for Sam, if one is to believe Clara's testimony, finding employment was equivalent to coming down with the measles, an experience of sheer misery. After his brief affair with the sleeves of overcoats, Sam, according to his own account, found work on the docks. Aaron also recalls Sam the undergraduate ushering at Lewisohn Stadium,[5] and earning a little pocket money handing out sheet music for the Goldman Band concerts in the city parks and at the Hall of Fame on NYU's Bronx campus.

Sam the artist "didn't want to be a comedian." Clara is emphatic about that, but there is little doubt that if the rendering of a visual image was second nature to him, so was the penchant for taking center stage. The summer of 1936 brought on a moment of triumph, of unexcelled glory for this twenty-one-year-old unemployed college graduate, the acclaimed favorite of hundreds on Columbia Street and certain East Broadway tenements. One of Nettie Crosley's uncles managed a resort hotel in the Catskills, the Hotel Balfour, and Clara and Nettie were given reduced rates. For sixteen dollars a week, the young women had at their disposal three ample meals, a daily pre-breakfast "snack" (most likely pickled herring, potatoes and hot tea), an occasional midnight supper, as well as whatever went under the rubric of "entertainment."

Sam, who could snack with the best of them, became a significant if idiosyncratic force, a veritable whirlwind within the confines of the Balfour that summer. The women planned a three-week vacation. Sam the wunderkind, with no cash to speak of and hard put to scrape up enough to find his way into Sullivan County, nevertheless managed to join the women during their final week. He geared up for what would prove to be an astonishing run through the heart of the borscht belt by firing off sixty-six letters to Clara in the course of nine days. On the envelopes Sam drew storks with tears, a tender if ominous note. Legend has it that midway through the Mostel postal siege, the local South Fallsburg mail-carrier, by now well instructed in the image of grieving stork, no longer needed to check the addressee's location.

Sam's presence at the Balfour made itself known rapidly. The communal shower on the floor the young women occupied set off an operatic detonation which pleased a certain Mrs. Perlmutter down the hall. Sam's repertoire, unfolding within a venue of cascading hot and cold water, tended toward classical golden oldies, including bits from Mozart's *Marriage of Figaro* that seemed particularly to dazzle Mrs. Perlmutter, whose musical standards were perhaps weakened by a surfeit of fresh country air, even though her own offspring would in future years become an acclaimed Metropolitan Opera star named Jan Peerce. "I can tell you," the prescient Mrs. Perlmutter confided to the young women, "he's gonna be a famous singer some day."

Clara's view is that her frantic young lover's voice was nothing to write home about, but the Balfour's purveyor of opera, grand and relentlessly Italian, shortly unveiled another of his musical attributes. Nettie Crosley remembers with much affection that "on Friday night when the guests discovered that Sam could more than hold his own *davening* [praying] in a *minyan* [Orthodox practice requires a minimum of ten Jewish men for prayers], Sammy became the greatest attraction in the history of the Balfour. He led it all."

But we are hardly finished with the Mostel arsenal. The Balfour, unlike many Catskill resorts in the Thirties, lacked the services of a social director, although there was a social hall and a small dance band, probably made up of trumpet, drums, sax and clarinet. Needless to say, Sam took over directing duties during his week-long invasion. The result was a musical work which bore some resemblance to Bizet's *Carmen*.

"Sammy ended up being the social director," Crosley remembers, "and we did *Carmen*."

Clara has no memory of this event. "I didn't," she protests.

Nettie is adamant. "You did. My God, we were hysterical. We were in the chorus. It all took place in the social hall."

Nettie paints a picture of Sam Mostel as Bizet's femme fatale. "He wore Clara's multicolored sweater, and then he grabbed the drummer's fan, you know those little teeny fans, they have a hook at the end? And he did a fan dance with the drummer's fan, except that the hook got caught in the sweater."

The hook jogs Clara's memory. "And he *ruined* my sweater, that was the problem." But for Nettie it remains an exquisite remembrance of lunacies past. "That was his *Carmen* outfit. And we ended up collapsing on the platform with laughter. The people in the audience—the seats were benches—those people were no longer sitting up. They were flat down. Everybody was convulsed. And then the Spanish gypsies came on . . . well, by this time the place was coming apart."

There is an odd note concerning Sam's *Carmen* ensemble. The summer of 1936 was the time of the official Olympic games, held that year in the Berlin of Hitler's Third Reich. Concurrent with these games, which many of us now remember best through the Leni Riefenstahl documentary film, *Olympiad*—a fraudulent if beautiful mythologizing of the perfection of form—a counter event known as the Protest Olympics was unfolding in Barcelona. That very month, July of 1936, the Spanish Civil War also broke out. Some of the participants on hand for the protest in Barcelona stayed on to join one of the disparate groups formed to battle the rebel columns; they included a number of Americans whose fighting unit came to be known as the Lincoln Brigade.

The young Jenkins, a member of Sam's Lower East Side gang, apparently went directly from wartime Barcelona to peacetime South Fallsburg, still five years away from World War Two. From Jenkins's Protest Olympics garb, Sam borrowed the sash that had been holding up his sweatpants. The sash thus found itself engaged to support the wiggling midriff of the borscht belt's newest Carmen, its political character transformed to that of farcical costume draped over fledgling comedian, many of whose ancestors would soon be wiped out by the goose-stepping heroes of Riefenstahl's other paean to Aryan purity, *The Triumph of the Will*.

All who knew the early Sam Mostel seem to be of one mind: Sam was not only naturally inventive, there was about him that sense of broad intellectual inquiry and hands-on reshaping of

material phenomenon under the banner of Art that characterized the movement we've come to think of as the Renaissance.
Sam had the ability to realize his perceptions in a variety of aesthetic modes. If the Carmen portrayal may have owed much to
the tired gestures and stereotyped shtick of veteran stand-up
comics, and one can only guess at that years later, Sam's animated vision of a percolating coffeepot, one of the highlights of
his early performances at Cafe Society Downtown, demonstrated an ability to compose a kind of sweatshop sonata from
the sounds and contours of household objects hardly prepos-
sessing in their own right. His drawings of children, cows, rabbinical scholars, and nude young women attest to that sense of
delight in the sometimes humble but often bold parameters of
living flesh. There is the testimony of his scholarly pursuits,
advanced enough so that he was considered a candidate for the
rabbinate, the development of an extraordinary friendship with
Albert Einstein—more on this later—and his possession of a
mind so retentive that by the opening read-through of Arnold
Wesker's play, *The Merchant*, the last play in which the aging
Mostel would ever perform, Sam had already memorized the
formidable number of lines assigned to the character of Shylock.

"He could read a page of Latin"—again the testimony of
Aaron Mostel—"then hand you the book and read all the Latin
back at you. Once, early in his career, he's preparing for a radio
show; the director hands Sammy this big script, Sammy looks at
it and throws it on the floor. 'Zero,' the director says, 'how come
you threw the script on the floor?' So Sammy tells him the truth.
'I already memorized the script.' And he had, he already knew
it by heart. So why shouldn't it be on the floor?"

The precocity and energy of the young Sam Mostel had the
driving force of a gadfly let loose among comparatively quies-
cent teenagers, even as the later Zero would prove to be both
driving and driven in more sophisticated circles. The Lower
East Side group had several haunts, one of which was a recently
constructed tenement building on East Broadway which housed
Regina Lang and her parents, across the street from P.S. 147, the
elementary school Baker and many of the others had attended.

The teenagers spent hours in similar tenement apartments, listening to the radio, playing cards, and entertaining one another.

Obviously the Thirties was not a time to be spending money; no one on the Lower East Side had cash to spare; the radio cost only the few bulbs and electrical current needed to operate it; and neighborhood movie houses charged ten or fifteen cents. Some weeknights the management of these houses enticed audiences by offering a premium of dishes; some nights they offered a version of Bingo, sometimes called Lucky, and sometimes a seductive ice-cream cone supplemented the children's matinee. But Regina Lang was also associated with a magical day at Radio City Music Hall, and Nettie Crosley, half a century later, still cherishes the event that left both her and Sam Mostel "mesmerized."

"Regina Lang's brother belonged to a social club and he got a few of us jobs addressing envelopes, a thousand envelopes for a dollar and a half. So Sammy and I sat one whole day addressing envelopes. The Radio City Music Hall had just opened up, so Sammy and I took our money, got on the subway and went uptown. They were playing *Nana* and we were totally mesmerized by it. [The film version of Emile Zola's novel opened at the Music Hall on February 1st, 1934.] Then we took the subway back down to Broome Street. Where we even got the damned carfare to get home I don't know. We're in my house and momma says, 'Sammy, you hungry?' Momma fed everybody. Of course he was hungry, we were both hungry, but we're so stunned by this movie we barely say anything. So momma made supper and not a word was said—totally mesmerized, we'd been to the Music Hall! You gotta remember we spent every penny we earned, a day's work that we put in and we just blew every penny. And a stage show too, featuring Mrs. Perlmutter's son Jan Peerce singing 'The Bluebird of Happiness.'"

The Music Hall had been planned as a theatre for live performance and the feature film was an afterthought, added when it became evident that live entertainment wasn't drawing a large enough audience to keep the theatre afloat. What the cavernous, other-worldly interior of the Music Hall offered was that sense of being enveloped within some Eastern architectural fantasy. For Nettie Crosley and Sam, Zola's grimly realistic and in certain ways fantastic tale of Nana, the beautiful prostitute from the wrong side of the tracks who reduces grown men to tears, may have conjured up a kind of miraculous terror, a perverse Cinderella story in which unadulterated eroticism penetrates the taboos of a fixed social order, a story in which the privileged male, protected by wealth, puffed up by status, lies prostrate before a naked bosom and foot. Beauty, in Zola's tale, becomes an arbitrary weapon, a loose cannon, so-called moral values lose their footing; a sexual prowling which in an ironic fashion is almost disembodied comes to haunt the souls of the staid bourgeoisie of late nineteenth-century Paris. One can only speculate that the narrative of this loose sexual cannon was to a young man impatient with the constraints of religious orthodoxy a shocking depiction of how far the liberation from bourgeois constraints might lead him.

Clara Sverd's parents had concerns about the young man constantly dancing attendance on if not literally prowling after their precious offspring. Clara at this time was eighteen. Perhaps it was not sexual license that worried the Sverds, nevertheless something that had the character of an unfocused persistency was taking place and, as they saw it, going nowhere. Thus after a courtship of four and-a-half years, the threat of matrimony began to loom before Sam. As Clara tells it, "Once I had my tonsils out, and Sam meets my father at the hospital. My father wants to know what his intentions are." Sam was already agitated over the routine tonsilectomy. Clara recalls that "You never saw anybody so upset, Sam didn't want anybody to disturb me." But now the disturbed one was Sam, who may not have had conscious intentions at all. "My mother had been pushing my father to push Sammy, but then my father stopped. My father wasn't a pusher. Sam was very sensitive, and much more sensitive than I was at the time. But he couldn't be pushed; it wasn't right."

Clara's father, even in the heart of the Depression, made a comfortable living running an ice-cream parlor in Lower

Manhattan. As Clara puts it, "I was the poor little rich girl of the Lower East Side tenements." But sometime after the parental pressuring of Sam, the father dies. The household is devastated; overnight its traditional head and sole breadwinner is gone. The remaining Sverds despite their avowed agnosticism, now follow the time-honored tradition of sitting *shivah*. (The first week of mourning, literally the number seven, is spent at the home of the departed one. The mourners sit on low stools and all the mirrors are covered.) Sam, never one for half measures, moves in with Nettie Crosley's family for an entire week, he takes his meals with the Crosley's, he shares a bed with Nettie's brother, he is anxious to be in as close proximity as he can to the mourners. He runs each morning to the Sverds and participates in the solemn ritual of grief.

Clara graduates from Hunter College in June of 1939. Shortly after, she and Sam are joined in what each hopes will be that state of happy wedlock one has heard rumors about. But Baker remembers the wedding as a day in which an undercurrent of previously submerged troubles manages to surface, and familiar problems are intensified.

"The day started all wrong. My father had died, so we had a small wedding. I didn't want to strap my mother." The widowed mother is recalled as "very shy, peculiar," even "neurotic," a poor housekeeper and particularly anxious this day about the condition of the apartment where they were all to meet before going on to the wedding. "She doesn't want Sammy's mother to come with Sam because the house isn't clean enough. Normally I go down on my hands and knees and clean the place. Well, my mother says it's a *shanda* [a shame] the house doesn't look good. But there's no phone in our house because my mother had such an inferiority complex she thought she couldn't use a telephone." Clara makes three trips to the neighborhood candy store to use the public phone. "First call I tell Sammy to come alone. But back home my mother's thinking maybe they'll be insulted, better tell them to come. Back I go to the store. 'Bring your mother,' I tell Sam. Back home my mother has changed her mind again, so I'm back at the candy store a third time. 'Better she shouldn't come,' I tell him. I just wanted to be agreeable, I'm trying to please everybody.

"Well, some time later Sam walks in with his brother. My uncle had just arrived from California with his new fiancée, they're here for my wedding. I haven't seen this uncle in years. So when Sam walks in I say, 'Where's your mother, Sammy?' And he's yelling at me, 'Where the hell do you *think* my mother is? *I think I'll go, I think I'll stay, I think I'll go.*' In front of my uncle he's yelling all this. I was so embarrassed, so upset, I ran into the bedroom. I had never seen Sam like this, he was definitely not sympathetic and I was just trying to appease my mother. I had to get *her* dressed, get *myself* dressed, there was no one to help *me*, and then he gets angry. Well of course he was annoyed at my mother, not me. When we broke up he wrote in the newspaper that I was a spoiled child of a doting mother."

The wedding took place at a kosher hotel, on which occasion the sense of timing of the normally unflappable Tzina Mostel went awry. Clara's recollection is vivid. At the conclusion of the ceremony, after Sam broke the traditional wineglass, Tzina came bounding down the aisle prepared to kiss the groom. "And I said to myself, if he kisses *her* before he kisses *me* I'm leaving. And I would have. But he stops—he says, 'Wait, Mother, I haven't kissed the bride yet!' He saved the day, he had the presence of mind to do the right thing, he could have gotten bewildered." Nettie's impression is that Sam and bewilderment were not on a first-name basis, that Sam was always in control, but Clara is focusing on what she perceives as a reprieve from marital disaster. "When his mother came to kiss him, I was subconsciously ready to turn on my heel and leave. I really didn't want to go to that wedding. But we got married. Then the fun began."

The fun involved, among other events, a honeymoon. "To our apartment in Brooklyn." "They lived," Eeta Linden remembers, "near Prospect Park, a nice neighborhood." The venue for honeymoon night was Coney Island. "We went with Rose and her husband Pete Ripps." recalls Clara. "I won everything that night. I hit all the balloons. Rose and Pete came for breakfast the next morning. Then later Sammy's family descended on us. His brothers were kidding me, they put a pillow under me, it was a symbol that I was this devirginated virgin. His father took Sam into a separate room to find out if I, the bride, had been a virgin the night before, and if the marriage was now consummated. Sam had put some red blood on the bedsheet—or ink, I believe—to show him. It was all silly. As for me, I minded absolutely nothing, I was a happy-go-lucky twenty year-old. I thought it was all funny."

There are treasured memories of Sam as the playful *idiot savante*, as the inspired wunderkind of comedy. On one occasion the newlyweds, together with Rose and Pete Ripps, take the Hudson River Dayline excursion boat upstate. Sam, for whom all the world's a stage, begins to "carry on," passengers quickly get wind of a delightful spectacle at one of the railings, and there is major jostling to catch the merriment. Sam is like a magnet. He draws such a crowd that the alarmed captain pleads with his passengers to disperse; the weight on one side of the now unbalanced vessel is such that the entire boat is tipping to a precipitous angle.

The issue of Sam's lapse from traditional Judaic practice will prove a wrenching one when it surfaces a few years down the road, and will take its place as one of the haunting themes of his life. At the time of this first marriage the elder Mostels are devoted to Clara. Believing that Sam has settled on a model Old World Jewish bride, it never occurs to them that, kosher home notwithstanding, Clara is remote from all the religious customs that have shaped their own lives.

Clara smiles over the memory of a Yom Kippur spent with her in-laws in their Bronx synagogue. Orthodox synagogues customarily separate the sexes during services. Women traditionally sit either upstairs or to the rear of the men; in the latter case they are shrouded from male eyes by a curtain. "So there I sat, upstairs," Clara notes, "and Sam's mother is going around bragging that her daughter-in-law is praying away. The truth is I didn't know one word of Hebrew." And what was Sam doing? "Running in and out of the *shul* to get some air." Not unusual during the marathon Yom Kippur service, but Nettie Crosley is at pains to correct what she perceives as a misapprehension. "Air? Sam was running out so he could smoke his cigar." Nettie builds on cigar-smoking as pivotal event. "That Yom Kippur day is when Sammy started breaking with tradition." Sensual pleasures are seen overriding the concerns of the most solemn day of the Jewish year. "That was his ruination, the cigar and his marrying a *shiksah*." The *shiksah* reference of course is to the one who doesn't know "one word of Hebrew." "But the cigar was the worst, it started him down the road."

Clara and Nettie both deny that Sam even observed the Sabbath. "He did try to please his parents," Clara recalls. "Once during our marriage we stayed overnight in the Bronx. They wouldn't let us sleep in the same room, just in case I might be unclean [in the midst of her monthly period]. Sam was usually an observant Jew *only* when he was home in the Bronx." But Clara also notes that when she and Sam were on vacation, and thus further from parental scrutiny, Sam paradoxically would don *tefillin*, the small leather straps and the two tiny boxes within which lie certain scriptural passages. The practice of donning *tefillin*, rarely observed by most Conservative or Reform Jews, takes on a gratuitous perversity when a Jew whose connection to Judaic practice is largely indifferent all year long seeks out this age-old, neglected rite during what is essentially a secular moment in the sun. But if Sam was consistent in seeking center stage, he also had a thirst for upsetting everyone's expectations, including perhaps his own.

There is the issue of money. Sam was the life of any party he happened to be a guest at, but performing was hardly conceived of as a calling, even when he was formally onstage. By 1936 the word had gone out among left-wingers that Sam could more than hold his own onstage and he began entertaining at union halls, at benefits for the beleaguered members of the Lincoln Brigade and for left-wing causes in general. But after all, he had spent his young life being "the life of the party" in numerous tenement kitchens, occasional ferryboats and borscht belt palaces. What payment might there be other than the laughter and psychological support of guests, bystanders and political comrades? As Clara tells it, "We were married and poor as church mice, and every time he went to entertain for nothing I had to launder a new shirt, and every penny counted. I said, 'Why don't you ask for five dollars?'"

It was difficult for Sam—that Sam who in later years , during contract renewal talks for *Fiddler on the Roof*, would demand the use of a chauffeured limousine, to make the most marginal demands of people with whom he was in political sympathy. But Clara was suffering, and no doubt Sam understood this suffering but needed to disengage himself from it. And so the issue of money, even as both Clara and Sam could hardly avoid its presence, was never adequately addressed. The issue pressed on Clara, and it pressed on Sam who felt the need to nourish political causes like antifascism and the fight against racism, and whose horror of gainful employment in the world of commerce was already legendary. Clara's mother also became a troubling factor, doling out cash in an erratic manner that the young bride considered maddening. "Our problem was always poverty. Sam and I started with absolutely no furniture. I told my mother I needed three thousand dollars. I was going to furnish our little apartment. Well she gave me eventually maybe ten thousand, but she would not give it to me in a lump sum. I wasn't going to waste that money. Sam got very angry. He felt she was dictating to us. If she had let me handle the money as an adult, and if Sam had talked to me like an adult instead of like I was two years old, maybe we would have stayed married."

It is Aaron Mostel's contention that his brother "worked his ass off," but Clara and Nettie have vivid recollections of the celebrated Mostel ass in a reclining position when employment threatened. "He was so artistic," Clara notes, "that he couldn't take an ordinary job. There were jobs starting to open up in '39." The Abraham and Strauss adventure remains an exemplary moment in the Mostel campaign against nine-to-fiveism. The battleground upon which Sam withstood the latest threat of gainful employment took place in the wilds of Brooklyn. Sam moved into the very teeth of enemy fire, hopping on the

Brighton Beach subway line along with those eager partisans of labor, Clara and Nettie. Sam's pretense was that he was seriously testing the job market. The department store was offering three dollars a day for salespeople. Clara: "Three dollars was pretty good money for those days." Nettie's observation is that "Sam made sure they wouldn't hire him. He carried on pretty good."

One has to conjure up what the nature of "carrying on pretty good" might be in 1939; suffice it to say that personnel at Abraham and Strauss, to the relief of our unscathed warrior, deduced that Sam's talents were not in line with their image of a sales staff. Though A&S passed up the opportunity to employ the husband, it did employ the wife. Clara's wages became the sole steady support of the family, periodically supplemented by money from Clara's mother, and the one-sidedness of the arrangement added to the strain of the marriage and eventually drove a further wedge into it.

Of course it was the "carrying on pretty good" that was to catapult this reluctant wage-earner into the limelight for some three decades. The picture that emerges is of a brash, highly-sensitive, extraordinarily intelligent young man stranded in a world that had no way of transacting day-to-day business with him. As far as the world could see, Sam was a brilliant, graceful klutz with an enormous appetite for learning, for sheer experience, for contact with the developing modes of creativity—his love of Picasso's many phases, his engagement with Joyce's *Ulysses* which he read over and over while an undergraduate at City College. But the world had no way of usefully employing these gifts. Sam was like some churning mechanism that needed constant tending, that needed to vent what appeared to be an inexhaustible supply of its own energy. Throughout his life he was viewed as an unmanageable force that was constantly "on," as one who needed to be thrusting forth some attitude, some opinion, some physical display meant to shock the locals, to dislocate the recipient. Many of these recipients drew back; some took offense, believing that the onrushing stream, the hot venting of Mostelisms, represented a gratuitous act, an unwarranted intrusion into one's privacy.

Others were deeply touched, even when what Sam Mostel was offering struck them as unnegotiable.

"He was able," Nettie observes, "to make a comedy out of everything." Clara's lament is that she had been raised as a poor little rich girl on what she deemed the Park Avenue of the Lower East Side, "and suddenly to be poor with somebody who couldn't earn a living, well the magic was going out of this marriage. Sam made magic wherever he went, and suddenly there was no more magic. The bills had to be paid. I didn't mind working, I didn't mind that, but we'd have friends over, we'd be sitting there having coffee and suddenly the lights would go out. He'd forgotten to pay the light bill, or he used the money for something else. The marriage was no fun anymore. I blame myself sometimes as well as him. He was so artistic he couldn't take an ordinary job. And I should have been more sympathetic."

There is the portrait of Sam the ingenious chef, making an onion sandwich on a roll, using the light inside the refrigerator so that he might save on the electric bill. Against this image there is the portrait of Clara's mother, the intrepid supplier of homely necessities, a kind of walking CARE package. Clara: "She would take the subway out to Brooklyn to clean my house while I was at A & S's. She'd cook my dinner and leave food and go back on the train before I came home. She was very sweet about it. She didn't like to get in our way."

But to Aaron Mostel, Mrs. Sverd had not the first sense of how to manage a home, nor did her daughter. "They'd come to my parents' home, that's where they got a good meal. Sammy came from a Jewish home, he was used to eating a *steak*, a *latke* [potato pancake]. The Sverds didn't know from those things. The mother would go out and buy some cold cuts and put them on the table. Or she'd invite them to dinner and say, 'I'll give you four dollars. Go out and eat.' She was not a *ballabusta* [first-class homemaker] where if you come to her home she prepares a proper meal. And my brother was brought up in a household where they set a *table*, with linen napkins, with real silverware."

For a time the sense of mutual affection fortified the marriage, regardless of the cuisine, the dietary concerns, and the oppressive if not grinding poverty. But there is another outburst, similiar to the one that took place the day of the wedding, and Clara experiences it as another rude awakening. "He had this artist friend named Alex Maltz. One day—Sam is supposed to be out looking for a job—I stop at Alex's studio on Twenty-eighth Street to rest, and who's there but Sam. I say, 'Hi Sammy,' meaning nothing other than I'm glad to see him. I had no anger in me. I don't think twice about it. Well he turns around to me in front of all the people there. I'd never seen him angry like that since our wedding day, and he says, 'What are you doing, checking up on me?' I was stunned, is this how he feels about me, the man who called at my house every day, who carried my schoolbooks every day? I rushed out of Alex's studio and started for home, but he followed me on the subway. I didn't ever want to talk to him again, that was enough for me never to see him again, that's how hurt I was, this ugliness coming out of him. *When did I ever check up on him?*" After some reflection, Clara adds: "I couldn't believe this was the same loving, sweet person. I should have understood he's young, he's suffering from the same thing I was, a responsibility he was not ready for."

Alex Maltz, a fragile and yet surprisingly vigorous ninety-eight-year-old painter in 1995, recalls that Sammy began studying with him in the heart of the Depression. "He came to my class out of City College. My studio was at Forty-nine West Twenty-eighth Street. Sammy took classes in etching, lithography and woodcuts. In a sense, this kid followed me around." When asked whether he considered Sam a serious student, Maltz allows himself a conservative shrug. The image of Sam as painter turned showbusiness celebrity seems to cloud Maltz's earlier recollections, but it struck this writer that Maltz nevertheless nourished the memory of his wayward student and that he hardly played the role of a distant professional in Sam Mostel's life. "I helped Clara and Sammy furnish their apartment in Flatbush when they got married," a statement somewhat at odds with Clara's recollection of starting married life with no furniture—but we are addressing events half a century later.

There are interesting connections between the Maltzes and the Mostels. Alex Maltz, born in 1897, is descended from Russian Jews. His father comes from Old Constantine, a Ukrainian town near the city of Kiev. Alex's passion for the written word embraces not only the writings of Dostoevsky and Maxim Gorki but that of the Mostels' beloved Sholom Aleichem. Many years ago Alex and his wife Amy Blaisdell, a poet and public relations director for Helena Rubenstein, rented quarters adjoining those of Albert Bigelow Payne, early biographer of that Mark Twain known affectionately in Yiddish quarters as the American Sholom Aleichem. Alex, now a widower, is also an elder relative to Albert Maltz, one of the unfriendly witnesses called before the House Un-American Activities Committee. Both Albert Maltz and Zero found themselves blacklisted during HUAC's rampage through the Bill of Rights. Alex Maltz was also close to another suspect American, Barney Josephson, who would play a crucial role in establishing Sam Mostel as Zero the performer, a turn of events which, though he might always play it down, would ultimately distance Zero from Alex's primary world of painting and graphic arts.

As for the struggles of the newlyweds, Eeta Linden remembers that the marriage seemed to be going well. "They would take time to go swimming at Manhattan Beach. Sam would constantly be doing his wonderful routines which he shared with all of us. He was sensitive and patient and taught me how to ride a bike." The stress appeared to be no more than what other couples were experiencing during the waning days of the Depression. "I liked Sammy," Eeta remarks, "he was very nice, very amusing. And they seemed to love each other. But then all at once I didn't see Sammy around."

The breakup takes place in 1941. According to Clara, it was not planned as a formal breakup. "I loved him but I needed to get away from that marriage. I just couldn't take the poverty of it any more. We couldn't pay the rent, I was tired of asking my mother for money, so we decided he would go to his parents' house in the Bronx and I would go to my mother's house in Manhattan. But he didn't go to the Bronx, he went to that small studio at Alex Maltz's on Twenty-eighth Street and slept on a cot. He couldn't bear to tell his mother."

Tzina Mostel, when she learns of the separation, tries her hand at mediation. In metaphorical cadences, she advises Sammy that "A wife is not like a pretzel—you take a bite and throw the rest away." And in fact the bridegroom tries to effect a reconciliation. One day, when Sam has already taken Cafe Society audiences by storm, he spots Clara on Fourteenth Street. "He was having his shoes shined—he was making *money*, see? He knocks on the window of the bootblack parlor and comes running out, and he says, 'Maybe the vacation did us both good.' He says, 'Let's get together again.' So I said, 'There was no vacation.' I was very snippy. I always covered up what I really felt. He never understood that part of me."

Later, Clara and a date witness Sammy's performance at Cafe Society Downtown. "Sam was very upset to see me there with another man. The way Sammy saw things, he was now earning a living. We could make a go of it. Well he does a skit on me right there at Cafe Society. He says, 'Doctor Agony—remember Doctor Anthony on radio?—'what should I do? My wife took my books and my pictures and everything I own.' Of course I was hysterical sitting there listening to all this."

What *had* Clara taken? Certainly Sam's peace of mind, his sense of well-being. And perhaps a sense of wholeness had been badly shaken. The Doctor Agony plaint is comedy stirred with much bitterness, with a taste of humiliation; it is vintage Mostel. With his own children and at times with both wives, Sam's anger would drive him into a fierce, morbid lunacy. But too often the morbidity is layered over with comic lunacy. Pain would sit beneath an overlay of slapstick, beneath a perverse, hysterical merriment. Sam's merriment had an aggressiveness to it that discomfited many audience members over the years; perhaps the signals weren't clear. One suspects we aren't that far from the adolescent in a black raincoat stalking his sixteen-year-old girlfriend and her date down the street, scowling comically but genuinely intent on making his beloved miserable.

The estranged couple would occasionally see one another, but less and less as time went on. Clara reiterates that the separation "wasn't breaking up the marriage," but she is forced to admit that "of course it was." Did she envision their marriage as still being intact? "Yes. We would try to see how it was when we were both working steadily. We never really broke up, it just faded away. And then one day I decided I wanted a divorce. Why? I wanted the magic. I was very childish; I didn't have the magic of the four-and-a-half years when he absolutely idolized me. Suddenly this relationship was too down-to-earth, too real. I wanted some show of tremendous affection and it wasn't forthcoming. And I didn't want the marriage to get ugly."

Aaron Mostel says of the breakup, "Sammy told me the story later. None of us knew it at the time. He comes home one day to Clara—even the chandelier is taken out of the ceiling, everything is cleaned out of the house. She took all his clothing and threw it on the floor. She acted viciously. But he doesn't say anything to any of us in the family. He was ashamed, embarrassed. Did they have a fight? I don't know what the hell it was. He used to come up for meals. We're living in Kelly Street, but he says nothing and there's no Clara. So once I visit him in the studio on Twenty-eighth Street where he paints, it's Alex Maltz's place, and I said to him, 'Sammy, what's wrong, you're not living with Clara?' He says, 'I don't want to tell momma and poppa that I'm separated, that I'm sleeping here on a cot.' So I said to him, 'You know, Sam, you gotta be honest. With poppa and momma you got a home. Come home with me.' We get in my car and we drive home and he tells momma the story. So my mother says to him, 'Sammy, you're my child. What happened between you and Clara, that's your business. You got married legally, maybe the two of you can work it out.'"

It was not to be worked out. Quite likely for all the reasons one can imagine. Both Sam and Clara were prideful. Both had been sheltered, if in different ways. Marriage is too often a trauma. It demands a "growing up" that isn't conducive to making magic. And there is the age-old issue of the artist who constructs an agenda at odds with the mainstream.

Enter Kate Harkin. A curious business, this recurring vision of the one who has replaced you. Clara Baker sees Kate once on TV and is unable to fathom what this woman has to do with Sam Mostel. "She seemed so devoid of a sense of what this unusual man was really like—the pathos and sensitivity and his fight for humanity—that I couldn't believe she was married to him. She met him when we were separated and he had been very ill and she took care of him. I bumped into him uptown during that period and I said, 'Sam, how are you? How's the family?' And he says, 'Not as healthy as *you* look.' I found out later he had been very ill [Clara believes it was colitis] and he was angry that I wasn't there to have taken care of him. I didn't know he'd been ill, none of my good friends would tell me anything, except Rose. They all wanted Sam for themselves."

But Sam was no longer for any of them. The old gang, the struggling cadre nurtured by East Broadway institutions, was coming apart. Eeta Linden meets Sam near the Forty-third Street Paramount Theatre one day. "He was already famous, already at Cafe Society. I said to him, 'Sammy, how are you?' And he looked at me as if he didn't know me." One night Eeta is invited to a fund-raising party, one of the numerous benefits for left-wing causes that are endemic to cities like New York, Chicago, and Los Angeles. "Top floor, you ring the downstairs bell, the elevator doesn't work. It's around Forty-sixth Street, between Fifth and Sixth Avenues." The occupants of the top-floor apartment are Sam now-Zero Mostel and, as Eeta puts it, "his new wife." Shortly after the fundraiser Eeta is visiting her aunt. "And she introduces me to Sammy's aunt. So I say, 'I was just at a party at Sammy's house and met his new wife.' Well Sammy's aunt gives me a look, and she says to me, '*They're* not married.' Well what does 'they're not married' mean? In his aunt's eyes it means that Sammy's new wife isn't Jewish."

Years later Eeta would come upon Sam—"Now everybody calls him Zero"—at the Tip Toe Inn, a restaurant at Eighty-sixth Street and Broadway, across the street from the Mostel apartment building. The Tip Toe Inn was a Mostel family hangout and other customers recall that the verbal assaults the Mostels heaped on one another were of epic weight, yet so habitual that they seemed part of the nightly fare. As Eata puts it, "Zero would be holding court. I would see him there often. But we never spoke."

Throughout this journey to uncover the person who was Sam-Zero Mostel, I will hear about the anger of Kate. I will repeatedly hear about Kate cutting Sam off from his past life. But one has to ask, which of these two people is using the other and for what purposes? It's likely that Kate was an unwitting buffer who kept Sam from having to confront issues he was reluctant to address: his life with Clara, his relation to his parents and to Judaic thought and practice.

Nettie Crosley is rueful about the manner in which Sam cut himself off from his old life. "There was Kate and we were all shut out." To Clara it is understandable; it was simply that "he didn't want her anger. Kate met my sister at one of these parties—my sister Norma was in the theatre—and she's talking to my sister and they're having a lovely conversation, and when she finds out who my sister is she runs away from her. Zero could not cope with her anger towards *me*. He was giving me *money*." Nettie is persuaded that "no one could blame her. The second wife always resents money going to the first wife." "That," Clara counters, "was *her* problem. She married him knowing what the situation was." And Nettie assents, but adds, "She thought she knew, but then reality set in."

Money in the form of alimony has a nasty habit of reducing finer values, it locks people into adversarial positions at a time when they are emotionally vulnerable. According to Aaron Mostel, the breakup devastated Sam, but at some later point in the disintegrating marriage the trauma was layered over by the emotional issue of alimony. "She sued. She made a whole business. He was already a movie star. He made a lot of money in Hollywood, and she picked up every buck he had. She'd make legal claims on him, because he traveled in the nightclubs she'd say he was out of marital reach. He didn't have *eating* money. If it wasn't for his brothers he couldn't eat. She really gave him the business but good when she sued him."

This is Clara's side of the story: "I felt that my mother had given us so much, and I cut down the alimony thousands of dollars because he kept crying poverty. If he'd spoken to me like a man to a woman, or man to man as they say, I might have listened. But he meets me one day and says, 'Let's have lunch.' We go to some place on Forty-second Street, and the lunch turns out to be we should have the same lawyer so it wouldn't be so expensive. So I said, 'What about *my* lawyer? I always knew you thought I was stupid, but *how* stupid I didn't know!' By this time I was so fed up with being the naive little girl I started out of the restaurant, and of course here again in this fancy restaurant he's yelling, *'Clara, come back!'* You know how he can do— he knew no shame—and I walked out of there so fast. All of these events were little hurts to me. And then I got angry. I thought, 'I'm not going to do any more for you, why should I?' I didn't care then, I wanted my money."

The divorce takes place. But there is also the *get*, the religious divorce ceremony at which an Orthodox rabbi officiates. Clara and Sam are thus divorced twice, once in the domain of New York State and once in the domain of the Lord.

The early winter days of 1988 were bitterly cold. I took the subway out to Forest Hills to spend several hours with Aaron Mostel. At this writing, in 1997, Aaron is no longer alive, but in 1988 he is recovering from a stroke, his wife is in a home (a victim of Alzheimer's disease), his parents Yisroel and Tzina are long since dead, and Zero has been dead eleven years. With the exception of Bill (Velvel), all of Aaron's brothers are gone. There is one sister still living in '88, but she's in Jersey and it's a trip. Aaron has a daughter he dotes on. He has nephews and nieces he rarely sees but with whom he maintains periodic phone contact. A young Jamaican woman arrives each morning, prepares his lunch and sees to his general needs.

Aaron buys the *New York Post* and a Yiddish paper. Radio and TV keep him in touch, so to speak, with the outside world—he is interested in the doings of Reagan, Bush, Gorbachev and of the ongoing Israeli–Palestinian conflict. But by mid-afternoon this aging Mostel is usually alone with the past. He exercises each morning according to doctor's orders, on fine days he sits in the park, and when he can physically negotiate the trip he attends services at the local *shul*. "One day a guy—a fellow Jew, mind you—steals my *tallis* [prayer shawl]. I seen him with it on. I says to this character, this criminal, 'Nice tallis you got there.' He says to me, "So?' Like he's telling me 'So, what's it your business?'"

Time hangs heavy for Aaron. Born in 1912, by 1988 he is treading cautiously through his seventies. An active representative much of his life for the Northeastern district of the United Jewish Appeal, he was constantly on the road, constantly at the wheel of his car. Not unlike the mythical Willy Loman, Aaron opened up the New England territory for the UJA; in fact, he criss-crossed much of the country. Now he moves from the living room to the deep recesses of this modestly-sized apartment with care; lifting himself from the seductive sponginess of the upholstered chair requires a bit of engineering, some judicious hoisting with his aging arms, but he performs under his own steam, and once on his feet he becomes an unsteady but sprightly and eager adolescent anxious to share with me old family photographs and other memories. I am someone he comes to trust, with a touch of caution.

"Sammy," Aaron wants me to understand, "was not the kind of guy who would go to work in the borscht belt. We were not borscht belt people, we had summer homes, we lived on Long Beach, we had a farm in Moodus, Connecticut, we were not children who worked as busboys in the Catskills."

I suggest that Zero labored at fashioning the image of aggressive borscht belt comic. Aaron agrees. "Later on when he needed money—he was already famous—he would get booked at Grossinger's, the Concord, and some smaller hotels on the same trip."

Aaron's recollections of his younger brother literally glow— with praise, warmth, affection. "He was a very productive guy. He was winning awards for his art very early. During the time he was married to Clara I used to drive him out to Long Island. I had an old Chevy—I was the first guy in our family to own a car—and Sammy and I would load the Chevy up with paintings and drive out to the Island where he'd sell his work for fifty, seventy-five dollars. There's probably a couple hundred paintings all over Long Island that Sam Mostel painted as a kid."

Over the next year or two, there will be periodic phone calls between Aaron Mostel and myself. His voice is strident and charming, a propulsive voice, and a wonderful gift to me, a "resource" as we now say, a cornucopia of information. Perhaps some of this information is a little biased; perhaps clarity is not always its strong suit. Nevertheless it comes from the heart and has helped give this story a degree of warmth that moderates against the icy blasts of recrimination that will issue now and then from other sources as they, too, remember Zero in their way.

The WPA, founded in 1935, was never a solution to the Great Depression, but it mobilized energies at a time when the country was an economic basketcase. It brought a measure of hope; perhaps it even encouraged a sense of dignity during a long, dispiriting decade. The idea for the WPA's Federal Art Project, which produced some ten thousand works (sculpture, drawings and paintings, a number of them by Sam Mostel) seems to have been largely inspired by the monumental figure of Diego Rivera.

Rivera came up from Mexico at the beginning of the Thirties and set off a singular explosion, in San Francisco, in Chicago, and in Henry Ford's Detroit. Rivera's peasants, workers, revolutionary armies, and complex industrial machines, laid out in searing colors before the plaster had a chance to dry, did for the mural what Whitman's *Leaves of Grass* did for American poetry. The giants of industry were caught up in Rivera fever.

In 1931, Nelson Rockefeller commissioned Rivera to paint the modern era as Rivera saw it, the theme was to be "Man at the Crossroads." The Rockefellers were planning the world's largest office complex, to be known as Rockefeller center, and they conceived of Rivera's giant fresco, spanning much of the lobby of their principal structure, as a tribute to the genius of industrial enterprise. But by 1933, in the midst of what Rivera construed as positive labors, the artist collided head-on with the Rockefellers. What Rivera saw in the midst of his peasants and workers was the face of Lenin; it was not exactly the face the Rockefellers had envisioned.

A well-publicized struggle ensued. Rivera, as a conciliatory gesture, offered to balance Lenin with Lincoln, but for the distressed Rockefellers not even the figure of Honest Abe could mitigate this Bolshevik eyesore. For the Rockefellers, Lenin had to be wiped out. Rivera was intransigent. The art community, largely in Rivera's camp, was up in arms, and the Communist press demanded that Rivera sever ties with the capitalist enemies of the people. The impasse ended when Rivera abandoned first the mural and then the United States, and the unhappy Rockefellers, publicly assuring everyone that the unfinished work minus the offending image would not be damaged, did the simplest thing anyone could conceive of; they destroyed not only the worrisome Lenin but Rivera's entire mural.

However, Rivera was now part of our consciousness. The sense of his militancy, the sheer abundance, complexity, scale and daring juxtaposition of images had imprinted itself on the architects of Franklin Roosevelt's New Deal. Rivera's labors pointed a way for the Roosevelt Brain Trust to battle the financial and emotional doldrums which had taken hold of so much of the culture. If it was a time for the Left to pressure the New Deal into an understanding of the need to implement forceful social programs, it was equally a time for a socially-conscious arts community to collaborate with the New Deal in buoying up an uneasy, largely traumatized society. It was now socially permissible for serious artists to be government employees. In the wake of Rivera's experience, artists like Ben Shahn, Arshile Gorky, Jackson Pollock, Michael Loew and his protegee William de Kooning, as well as hundreds of other men and women, began to render colorful images of a people striving through sheer labor to build a better world. One of Rivera's students, according to Aaron Mostel, was the latter's brother Sam, who traveled to Mexico to seek out the master. Rivera's struggle had touched everyone; his oversized hands had deepened the social consciousness of an age. If Sam Mostel's painting took a decidedly abstract turn, Rivera nevertheless reached Sam in that place where he saw himself allied with the brotherhood of the oppressed.

One senses that the young Sam Mostel wanted to confront the capitalist dragons just as Rivera had done, that he wanted to wake the masses from its bourgeois dreams and lead the struggle from darkness into the Socialist sunlight. But the radical Zero Mostel at left-wing rallies from the Thirties well into the Fifties was partially displaced in ensuing years; the Zero Mostel of the Sixties onward found himself making difficult accommodations. If many of his theatre and film vehicles showed evidence of Marxist leanings or were produced in conjunction with Leftist sympathizers, a meretricious commercialism that was very distant from the Rivera ideal nevertheless informed much of Zero's later work. The reasons are complex, not the least of which was the need to earn a dollar, but the results were simple. The capitalist engines of industry may not have found a new ally but at the very least they neutralized the strength of a potential adversary. Zero Mostel the painter had difficulties but they were not primarily those of the marketplace, except insofar as paying performances would pull him away from the artist's studio time and again.

Tales of the serape and the shallek. It is Aaron Mostel's recollection that Clara accompanied Sam to Mexico City so that the novice could learn at the feet of the master and that the couple returned with a serape for Tzina. Aaron's comment: "My mother needed a serape like a *luch in kup* [a hole in the head]." But Clara insists she never visited Rivera and has no knowledge of Zero's studying with him. "As for the serape, Sam and I had it in our apartment. One day it turns up on his mother's couch. Don't ask me how it got there."

However it got there, the serape's transfer from Brooklyn to the Bronx is worth a moment's reflection. Whether the serape was purchased in Mexico or a flea market in Manhattan, Sam apparently had second thoughts about its placement. Since the serape's function, partially decorative, is also to clothe, in a sense to embrace, one might reasonably inquire why such nurturing is deemed more appropriate in the household of one's parents than in the small apartment the young newlyweds had been trying to furnish. Add to this the fact that Sam never bothered to consult Clara as to whether she would even mind the loss of the serape and one has an incident, on its face of little consequence, that is nonetheless troubling.

The story of the muffler, the *shallek*, intensifies the issue of nurturing. During one of our meetings in Forest Hills, Aaron is expounding on his brother's brilliance in elementary school and adds that the mature Zero became a friend of Albert Einstein's and would travel to Princeton to visit the physicist. At this point I can't quite comprehend what I'm hearing.

"Visiting him? At the Institute?"

"At the . . . where he lived, in New Jersey."

"In Princeton? He's visiting *Einstein*?"

"At Princeton. And when he comes in—"

"How does he get to come in?"

Aaron is growing impatient; again he spells out the rudimentary facts. "I'm telling you he went to visit him in Princeton, what's wrong with you? He used to be a friend of Einstein's, so when he comes there he's wearing a—"

"You don't happen to have a picture of the two of them together?"

"No."

But Aaron tells the story of the muffler. "So Einstein touches this beautiful muffler that Sammy's wearing and he says to him, 'Zero, where'd you get that muffler?' He says, 'My mother knitted it for me.' Einstein says, 'That's a beautiful muffler.' So when Sammy comes to visit us—at the time we're living on One Hundred and Seventy-second Street and Ward Avenue in the Bronx; it's across from James Monroe High School—Sammy says to my mother, 'You know, Einstein liked this shawl, he fell in love with it.' You know my mother, the great lady, she went out and bought wool and she made Einstein a nice muffler.

Sammy comes to us the next time—he used to come about every second week; my father had a heart condition at that time—and she gives him the muffler for Einstein. A couple of weeks later, in the evening, my mother gets a phone call from Princeton. This man spoke German. Zero had told him my mother spoke good German. *'Das ist Frau Mostel? Ich bin Albert Einstein. Ichull eena badanken fur dem shallek.'* The muffler was this nice color, green. Einstein tells her she has a wonderful son. My father is listening to all this, so when she hangs up she says, 'You know who that was?' She tells him and he nods and says, 'I know you made the *shallek* for Einstein,'"

What a strange creature this Sam-Zero is. An outrageous buffoon on the Hudson River Dayline and a sober comrade to one of the world's most original minds. His intellectual capacities have been hinted at. The movement of the world in all its manifestations engaged him, and apparently leading figures along the spectrum of thought were drawn to him. Bertolt Brecht sought him out; Charlie Chaplin embraced him as a peer; he became a member of Henry Wallace's inner circle during the latter's run for the presidency in '48; Clifford Odets and Ring Lardner Jr. valued him as a comrade. And there is the luminous figure of Albert Einstein opening his door to him. We may well be tracking the journey of a sometime lunatic, but if so we are tracking an inspired sometime lunatic.

But what of Tzina Mostel's reaching out to knit this comforting, in the best sense of the word, nurturing, garment for Albert Einstein? It's in keeping with a lifetime of nurturing that encompasses countless hours spent with illiterate immigrants on the Lower East Side and countless years devoted to her own children. That in just a few years after the incident of the *shallek*, Tzina is to turn a remorseless face against "the wonderful son," as Einstein characterized Zero, to pronounce her beloved son dead to Judaism, offers us another facet, a chilling view of this strong-willed, resilient, loving, and ultimately unbending creature.

The Federal Art Project, even as it supports Sam the painter, does him a fearful unkindness—it puts him "to work." This at a time when Sam and Clara are still together. At the Museum of Modern Art, Sam is one of a number of artists hired to deliver "chalk talks," to expound on the aesthetics and historical background of various works in the MOMA galleries. At the 92nd Street YMHA, Sam instructs students in painting and drawing. It comes as no surprise that the exhibitionist in Sam never pales, nor does Sam resist cutting corners when opportunity winks its eye. Perhaps the unbridled respectability of institutions brings out those delicious impulses toward subversion. At the Y, an Art Project supervisor, making a routine inspection, discovers Sam far from the site of instruction, in the Y swimming pool, and upon demanding to know what the delinquent instructor is doing in such a submerged fashion, is told that "I'm teaching water color." At MOMA, the story is told of Sam the gallery lecturer receiving word of a transfer to some other facility. Sam's relief is of such magnitude that he suspends his lecture in midsentence, and having induced one unsuspecting gallery auditor to stand on his head—let us not reason why—walks off the premises with the visitor still upended.

Through the Federal Art Project and his studies at the Art Students League, Sam makes a number of life-long friends. An emotional network is thus constructed that extends from West Twenty-eighth Street to a lobster-fishing village off the southern coast of Maine known as Monhegan Island. The League provided Sam and generations of painters with a sense of discipline; the WPA's Art Project helped direct that discipline towards a social purpose. Together they gave a cohesion, a sense of bonding to a number of disparate painters, some of whom built studios in or near the same factory building at Forty-five West Twenty-eighth Street and some years later also constructed or renovated summer homes on Monhegan Island.

If we like to say that as humans who partake of genetic and personal memory and inhabit layers of history, we carry our lives with us, then Sam-Zero's impulse was to nurture and transport many of his ongoing relationships from city to country and back again. Both Twenty-eighth Street and this tiny Monhegan Island became venues for Thursday-night poker games, for weekly sessions with hired models, for kibbitzing, one-upmanship and for the tireless art of sheer hanging out. People, events and places take on an interchangeability; they become surrogates for a Mostel home. They replace Clara; effectively shut out Kate; and comfort a quietly grieving Mostel who can find no way "back home" after his parents pronounce him dead to their world.

In 1941, some time after his separation from Clara, Sam abandons the cot at Alex Maltz's and moves into one of Poppa Strunsky's apartments in Greenwich Village. Poppa Albert Strunsky was the proprietor of a series of buildings just south of Washington Square Park, one fronting West Third Street, and two others on MacDougal and Sullivan Streets. Strunsky was considered a benevolent Village character. According to his son English Strunsky, Poppa was notorious for being a casual collector of rents. "When a tenant couldn't pay," English recalls, "my father might simply transfer him to a less desirable apartment." The tenants characterized these structures affectionately as Strunsky's Stables.

The Strunskys had come to Greenwich Village in 1917, to a neighborhood which daughter Emily remembers as "quiet and charming." Mother Mascha Strunsky opened a restaurant on Eighth Street and when the laundry beneath it closed its doors, Mother Strunsky announced that "people down here in the Village don't have enough money. I'm going to open a cafeteria." After giving repeated warnings to visitors that the new premises were three steps down and they had better watch their footing lest they descend too rapidly, Mother Strunsky named her cafeteria Three Steps Down.

There was an engaging sense of a caring, like-minded community looking out for all its members in those Village years from World War One to the attack on Pearl Harbor. There were modest dining places whose proprietors were solicitous of the network of impoverished artists, of those who had come to identify themselves with the New Bohemia. There were artists, hangers-on, and the people the artists slept with. There were self-styled geniuses, some of whom produced imaginative work, but all seemed hard-pressed to finance the nightly supper. Three Steps Down, Alex's Borscht Bowl, Romany Marie's, these and other Village restaurants were intent on feeding people. My cousin Chig Kugel, whose father Sam Roth ran the Poetry Book Shop in the Twenties, recalls that Romany Marie's specialty was *chorba*, a Rumanian vegetable soup with little meatballs. My own recollection of Alex's Borscht Bowl in the Fifties is of a congenial nest, no fuss, no hype, a hideaway of comfort and plentiful borscht [beet as opposed to cabbage soup] and sour cream. Occasionally a boiled potato would find its way into the borscht.

One assumes that Sam-Zero was drawn to that as-yet-undiminished sense of a cohesive art community, although the Village of the Provincetown Players, of Maxwell Bodenheim, e.e. cummings, and Djuna Barnes (before she became a recluse) was gone by the Forties. It's likely that Strunsky's charitable house of the delinquent tenant and the chronic master of insolvency found one another through the good offices of an actor who had been a Broadway and Hollywood fixture for many years. Sam Jaffe, whose image as elder medical man in the TV series *Ben Casey* brought him acclaim from a generation growing up in the Fifties, was best known to earlier generations as Kipling's selfless Hindu boy in the movie *Gunga Din*, and as the venerable elder of Shangri-la in Frank Capra's adaptation of James Hilton's *Lost Horizon*. The actress Bettye Jaffe, Sam Jaffe's widow, recalls that "Zero came into Sam's life right after Lillian, Sam's first wife, died in 1941" and that Zero, himself a dispirited husband after the breakup with Clara, nevertheless helped Sam Jaffe through a difficult time.

When I met with her in 1988, Emily Strunsky Paley, a woman of quiet strength in her nineties, retained vivid memories of Zero, Kate Harkin, and Sam Jaffe. "I've known Sam Jaffe almost all my life. It was Sam who introduced me to Zero. But in fact I was closer to Kate at first." And Kate believed that everybody, in one fashion or another, fell in love with Emily. If Poppa Strunsky provided shelter and Momma Strunsky delivered protein and wayward calories, their daughter Emily offered emotional sustenance.

In the early Twenties, Emily and Lou Paley were living at Fifteen West Eighth Street in Greenwich Village. They had been brought up to entertain at home, and on Saturday nights it was understood by intimate friends, casual acquaintances, and gate-crashers that the party was at the Paleys. On a given Saturday night, songwriters would turn up to drink, exchange gossip and make music. Buddy Da Silva, Howard Dietz and the Gershwin brothers were frequent visitors. Ira would eventually marry Emily's sister Leonore. A frenetic group of siblings, developing a hilarious comedy act and calling themselves the Marx Brothers, helped to keep Saturday nights somewhat hysterical.

English Strunsky, ten years younger than his sister Emily, recalls that a typical repast for boisterous Saturday night visitors would consist of cream cheese and Fig Newtons. And like many urban and rural households, whether guests were enspirited with Scotch, Moxie, or the juice of various fruits, there would be the inevitable congregating around the baby grand. Howard Dietz tells of some noisy goings-on one night in the apartment over his own; when he investigated he was invited in but cautioned to be quiet, for the fellow at the keyboard, George Gershwin, was just warming up, and English Strunsky recalls with pleasure, "When George sat down to play, everybody listened, and he could play for hours." It was not unusual for Gershwin, after playing at home, to make his way to the Paleys and immediately settle down to their baby grand.

Emily Strunsky Paley and Sam Jaffe were of the same generation, but Sam Mostel grew up some two decades after them. While the Mostels, the Sverds, the Crosleys, and the Lindens were Lower East Side immigrants, living among the pushcarts clogging Orchard and Hester Streets, and while the tenements teemed with the impoverished—there might be one toilet, often an outhouse in the backyard, for an entire six-story house—the young marrieds, Emily and Lou Paley, were members of a comfortable, privileged Bohemian circle in which secular art was a way of life. While Sam fought to distance himself from Torah and find his place as a visual artist, while he was the one to introduce fine art to his classmates at Seward Park High School, the younger Paleys were as to the manor born; they had grown up around accomplished painters and musicians. While Sam, Clara, Nettie, and Rose met on the sidewalk or huddled around the radio to pick up a Toscanini broadcast, the Paleys, intimately caught up in the lives of Tin Pan Alley's mainstream composers, were also at home in the concert halls and at the Metropolitan Opera house.

But we are now with Sam Mostel; it's 1941 and Sam is a Villager. Among his assets: the use of an art studio; old and new friends encouraging his creativity; high visibility at benefits for left-wing causes; and a salaried stint with the Federal Art Project. But he also has, by the measurements with which Western society evaluates its citizens—no money to speak of, no career—and, in the crassest possible terms, no foreseeable future.

Early in the winter of 1942 Sam Mostel's life takes a decisive turn. Sam is discovered—as if prior to this event he had been leading the cloistered existence of a latter-day Emily Dickinson. There is considerable confusion, distortion, and sheer fabrication about just how this coming out came about. The discoverer is usually Himan Brown but on occasion it's Barney Josephson. The event is usually a benefit performance for some progressive cause—Spanish, Chinese, or Russian relief. In one version Himan Brown discovers Sam at a benefit for victims of the Sino-Japanese War in 1941. Another version has Barney Josephson coming upon Sam's chalk-talk performance at an artists' ball. In an interview with *Esquire* magazine, Sam proclaims that he auditioned for Josephson six times in six months. And these declarations go on and on, to no particular purpose.

One thing is clear. Sam Mostel was discovered, recognized, uncovered, found. "*I* found him," the writer Sig Miller tells me. "I found him at a bar mitzvah." Miller had been writing radio dramas, and one Saturday in the waning days of 1941, "I don't know how it happened, but I was at this bar mitzvah." Miller attests to this being a rare occasion. "I don't go to them ordinarily. But there was this guy, Sam Mostel, he was just doing some little comic routines for ten, eleven dollars a shot. I thought he was just super-talented. I don't know what *he* was doing there. He was obviously too good to be wasted on bar mitzvahs."

Sig Miller wrote for producer-director Himan Brown and he brought Sam to Brown's broadcasting studio. "There was nothing in it for me, I just thought Himan should see this guy." Sam auditioned for Brown, whose impression was that he was in the presence of a special talent but that Sam "wasn't an actor. His strength was not in creating roles—at least not before Tevye." Brown saw him as a performer in the larger sense of the word. "He needed to be seen 'live' and in ways that would not hem in his talents."

Brown himself is a legend in broadcasting. In 1929, while still in college, Brown sold what today we would call a sitcom, to the embryonic radio network, NBC. The program was initially named *The Rise of the Goldbergs*; its writer was Gertrude Berg who herself took on the role of Molly Goldberg, matriarch of an immigrant Jewish family. Himan Brown performed as the husband Jake and survived six months before Berg fired him from the program he had sold for her. Some two decades later, during the infamous blacklist of the Fifties, Berg would again fire, this time involuntarily, another Jake, the actor Philip Loeb, one of Sam-Zero's cherished friends. That firing, as we will come to see, represents one of the darkest moments both in the history of broadcasting and of this country.

The precocious Himan Brown developed into one of broadcasting's most prolific producer-directors; he guided such enterprises as the early Thirties horror program, *The Witch's Tale*, the much-loved *Inner Sanctum* with its creaking door, and Arch Oboler's mystery series, *Lights Out*. He was also an integral part of that fecund Catskill network, the borscht belt, but seems to have missed Sam Mostel's epic *Carmen* production. When I met with Brown in June of 1988, he still operated out of the Himan Brown Studios on West Twenty-sixth Street. CBS was broadcasting its *Guiding Light* soap opera out of that complex, and at one time the studios provided interior sequences for Mel Brooks's film, *The Producers*, which starred a now world-famous actor named Zero Mostel. Sam's audition led Brown to assume a responsibility for the performer's immediate future. Echoing Sig Miller, Brown recalls that "there was nothing in it for me, I just liked him, I wanted to see him get started." Brown took Sam on as a personal project. The first step was an audition at La Martinique, a smart nightclub enjoying much popularity. "They weren't interested. He wasn't what they wanted. I took him to a number of places. Nothing happened. Nobody took an interest. Until I brought him to Barney Josephson."

Barney Josephson began operating what he liked to call, in street parlance, "a saloon" at Two Sheridan Square in Greenwich Village. It was 1938. "I wanted a club where blacks and whites worked together and sat together out front. There wasn't, so far as I know, a place like it in New York or in the whole country." Even in Harlem's Cotton Club, "blacks were limited to the back one-third of the club, behind columns and partitions. It infuriated me that even in their own ghetto they had to take this." And in other clubs where blacks entertained, no black audiences were permitted. With six thousand dollars of borrowed money, Josephson rented the basement of what in recent years has been home base for the late Charles Ludlum's Theatre of the Ridiculous. Josephson had to come up with two hundred dollars a month. The painter Charlie Martin, a colleague of Sam's on the Federal Art Project,[6] recalls that he helped carry a pile of chairs down for the first audiences, and Josephson invited a number of other Village artists, including William Gropper, Ad Reinhardt, and Syd Hoff, to paint murals on the walls in return for $125 and "a due bill for another $125 so they could come in and eat and drink any time."

Cafe Society, which Alex Maltz tells me got its name from the actress-playwright Clare Booth, later Clare Booth Luce, was packed every night, but for the first two years Josephson kept losing money. He remembers that nobody in the Village had any money and that "I should have opened where the money was." He planned a second club, Cafe Society Uptown, at 128-30 East

Fifty-eighth Street. According to music critic John Wilson,[7] the press agent Ivan Black who had been a schoolmate of Josephson's in Trenton, New Jersey, sent out a press release declaring with traditional hyperbole that Cafe Society had been such a success in Greenwich Village it was opening an uptown branch. This item, picked up by the daily papers, brought people from midtown and uptown flocking downtown to find out what was going on. Suddenly Cafe Society Downtown was a financial success, and when Cafe Society Uptown opened in October, 1940, it was making money within three months.

Jack Gilford, who according to Wilson, "had been a stooge for Milton Berle," and was to become an intimate of Zero's, opened the downtown branch as comedian-emcee. The club saw other comics over the next few years, like Jimmy Savo and Imogene Coca, jazz musicians like Teddy Wilson, Art Tatum and Hazel Scott, blues singers like Lena Horne and Sarah Vaughan, and folk artists like Susan Reed and Josh White. And a largely unknown blues singer from the deep south, Billic Holliday, who had already cut a record with Artie Shaw's band, performed at Cafe Society Downtown's opening with Jack Gilford and sang on for the next nine months.

The historic encounter between the saloon keeper and the man who "carried on pretty good" takes place on a Wednesday afternoon, February 10th, 1942. It will lead to events not dissimilar to the farcical chase scenes and sweaty bedroom antics that characterized many of the vehicles Zero made common cause with in the ensuing years. Josh Mostel believes that celebrityhood made his father more than a little crazy. Sig Miller reflects that Zero's manner of moving through the century "put Barney in tears." Something untoward would damage what starts out as a benign arrangement between impresario and prima comic.

Himan Brown's impression is that Zero and Barney quarreled over money. Zero himself announced that his start at Cafe Society Downtown netted him forty dollars a week and that his salary rose to one hundred dollars when he took the act uptown. "Zee stayed with Barney for a year," Himan Brown reports, "then suddenly quit him. He didn't need him any more.

I never thought that was very nice of Zero." I ask Sig Miller if the quarrel was over money, but too many years have gone by. "I can't remember what it had to do with," Miller notes, "but I know Barney was given to tears on a number of occasions because of Zero."

On a blistering hot summer afternoon in July of 1988, I meet Barney Josephson. He is a slight, smiling, energetic man, eighty-six years old, who greets patrons at the door of his restaurant. B.B.Q. is situated at the corner of University Place and Eighth Street. At this site years before, Josephson operated a prior restaurant, The Cookery, well-known to Village habitues, where artists like Mary Lou Williams and Mabel Mercer performed. As Wilson reports, the postwar hysteria over Communists had wiped out both of Josephson's Cafe Societies in 1947, and soon after he opened the modest Cookery.

John Wilson, who wrote Josephson's obituary for the *New York Times*, notes that Leon, Barney's brother, was held in contempt of Congress after refusing to answer any questions before HUAC. Barney, the brother of an admitted Communist, is then hounded by a number of gossip columnists from major syndicates that include the Hearst press. The attackers: Walter Winchell, Westbrook Pegler, Dorothy Kilgallen, Lee Mortimer, and other self-proclaimed patriots. The war on Barney Josephson is a quick triumph; gross earnings at both Cafe Societies drop precipitously. Within a year, after a loss of $90,000, Barney Josephson is finished as a night-club entrepreneur; the clubs are sold, presumably to more upright Americans.

Now, forty years after the close of his legendary nightclubs, and less than three months before Josephson's death at St. Vincent's Hospital on September 29th, we converse. We sit at a front table where Josephson can still direct incoming traffic and remain in close proximity to the cash register. He seems to me very able, alert, in touch with all aspects of a complicated and bustling enterprise. We chat for some two hours, and he prefaces our conversation by warning me that there are areas he will not cover since his own memoirs, which include that far-off period when Barney and Zero worked closely together, are to be published in the next few years. I hope these stories, the ones he keeps from me that afternoon, materialize in book form; the ones he does *not* keep from me have an exquisitely painful lunacy.

The Sam Mostel audition took place in midafternoon that February day in 1942 in the all-but-deserted premises of Cafe Society Uptown. The Fifty-eighth Street location consisted of four stories and a basement. Everyone concerned had the luxury of a private dressing room, "Hazel Scott, the orchestra guys, even the waiters." At the beginning of the audition no one but Barney Josephson was in attendance. "He did a couple of turns and then I cut him short. That was enough for me. I said, 'Mostel, that's enough, come over here.'" Josephson confesses that "when you're auditioning that's the worst thing for a performer, to have the so-called producer cut you short. It sounds like he's telling you he's had it."

But by the time Josephson broke off the audition, the two men were no longer alone. "I had a very nice young man named Ivan Black who was my press agent. He was coming in to work around the time of the audition. Midafternoon is when press agents start when you're doing clubs. Ivan sits down quietly beside me to listen to this guy. Then I ask Mostel, 'How much of this material have you got?' The first thing you have to worry about with comic guys is material. They can come in with some pieces that are hilarious, then they do those pieces for five or six weeks, *then* what are you gonna do with them? In my clubs, customers come *back*."

Sam informs Josephson that he has *loads* of "stuff," and in response to Josephson's query as to who's knocking out this stuff, Sam tells him in no uncertain terms, "*Writers?* I knock out my own stuff." Josephson believes he has uncovered a gold mine. "I think, 'Here's a funny guy. He writes his own material and he says he's got lots of it.'"

Sam Mostel is hired. "We're all booked here Uptown," Josephson tells him, "but I can work you in Downtown." The audition has taken place on a Wednesday and Sam is told "You're opening next Tuesday." Josephson tells me that six days is pretty short notice, but I say aloud what Josephson must have believed—Sam could have opened on the spot. But what was it that Sig Miller, Himan Brown, and now Barney Josephson saw in this new recruit? What was it that made Sam of the Lower East Side, and Sam of the Hotel Balfour, and Sam of Poppa Strunsky's Stables the life of any party he happened to be at?

Josephson exclaims that "*Nobody* ever had that quality, *nobody*. I started Jack Gilford when I opened Cafe Society Downtown. I always loved him. He's wonderful. *Today* he's wonderful—but he's different than Zero." Josephson is never able to articulate for me exactly what this Mostel quality is, only that "I saw right away, right away, what I saw in nobody else."

A delicate issue surfaces that afternoon and it has to do with anti-Semitism. Josephson confides in his young charge, who admits to being Jewish, that show business is hardly innocent of racism and anti-Jewish sentiments. He tells Sam that "there are many Jewish artists working who everybody *knows* are Jewish, but their names are not Jewish." Josephson mentions that Jack Gilford is a stage name for Jacob Gehlman, that everyone knows Danny Kaye is Jewish but that the pseudonyms seem to placate the anti-Semites. Josephson is drawing a bead, not too delicately, on Sam Mostel's name. "'Now Mostel could be anything. You got a little nose'—he had that little button nose—'you could be anything. Italian, what the hell. But with Sam—do you need it? Suppose we change your first name?'" Josephson can feel that "this guy wants to work. Now Ivan Black is sitting beside me all this time, he hasn't opened his mouth, he's just watching, listening."

Josephson interrupts his narrative to explain why "I changed lots of names. It wasn't a nice show business name, or it was too long. My ads are one-column wide and I can't use a name that's long because then they gotta break it up on two lines. Or the name is too difficult to say, too difficult to remember. In this business you want people to remember your name."

Aaron Mostel will tell me that "They could have changed it to Chaim Shmuel Dreck," and Sam, as Josephson recalls, cries out, "You can call me Shit. I want to work!" And at this point

Ivan Black utters the fateful words. "'Barney, why don't you call him Zero? He's starting from nothing."

Josephson is particularly animated, remembering this moment. He is playing all the voices, his own, Ivan Black's and Sam Mostel's. "As soon as Ivan said that, Zero went 'That's it! That's my name! People gonna ask how I got my name, I'm gonna say it's from the marks on my report card.' He reeled off five or six other whys for this name. To this day there are intimates who never questioned that Sam's given name wasn't Zero." Or that it was Zero because of the condition of his bank account, or due to his tightly-defended position at the foot of the academic ladder.

In the early days of the Second World War, blacks could easily be recruited as cannon fodder in Europe or the Pacific, but as Josephson recalls, in the presumed non-racist north "a black couldn't walk into *anyplace* except Cafe Society and get a cup of coffee, or into the cheapest bar to get a beer. So a W.E. duBois, a Paul Robeson, Langston Hughes, Dick Wright, they had no place to go, they came to my place. Eleanor Roosevelt came to my place because Franklin Jr. had come and liked it and dragged his momma down. She was never in a nightclub in her life before she came to Cafe Society, and never was in another one."

By 1942 Josephson had a good rating with the critics. John Wilson of the *New York Times* and Whitney Balliett of the *New Yorker* came to believe that Josephson's trumpeting of fresh talent was more than windy rhetoric. "If I had my guy send out a press release saying, 'Tuesday night Barney Josephson will present a new comic discovery named Zero Mostel,' that's all I had to say. People would come to see the new star that was gonna be made *that night*. If I said, Lena Horne is opening tonight, nobody ever heard of her but they would come to see a new star rising." Josephson's roster of discoveries as well as talent fallen on hard times was impressive. "At one point I took the whole Downtown show—it included Hazel Scott and Teddy Wilson—and moved it uptown. Let me tell you, some agent had persuaded Teddy Wilson to leave Benny Goodman and form his own band, but that new band never made it. It didn't go, so Teddy began working at Cafe Society as a soloist. And it was something like a fresh start for him."

Sam Mostel or rather the newly-minted Zero Mostel, debuted at nine p.m. on Tuesday, February 16th, 1942. The press turned out as Josephson had expected. "Everybody was there as usual and Zero came on—and all I can tell you is that if you want to use the expression 'a star is born'—it happened *like that!* He was a star— *in a second! Incredible! That was it!"*

I ask whether Zero was nervous. Josephson dismisses the possibility. It is his sense that the new comic had absolute self-confidence. The negative side of this self-confidence would land Zero in hot water throughout his life. Josephson is emphatic; "He could not discipline himself, nor could anyone *help* him. *Nobody* could, not even his wife as far as I know. Oh I could go on with stories about him." There is no need to go on with such stories; everyone else is ready to supply me with anecdotes concerning the undisciplined one. But the connection between lack of discipline and self-confidence? Isn't the undisciplined being the one who lacks confidence, whereas the confident being would be centered, therefore self-disciplined, not addicted to center stage?

By all accounts a new star rose to the heavens that February night in Greenwich Village. "In two weeks people were comparing him with Charlie Chaplin." And what of his social awareness? "That's where you have an edge, you're a comedian with a brain, with a direction." One has to remember we're talking about an era when nightclub and radio comics operate either in stand-up fashion, scattering one innocuous funny line after another, or perform as characters in situation comedies focusing on generalized domestic behavior—Jack Benny's legendary stinginess, Fibber McGee's boyish enthusiasm for outlandish tales, the Great Gildersleeve's endearing pomposity. Social criticism is a rarity; it comes from a pioneer like Henry Morgan on WOR in New York who snipes repeatedly at the absurd elements of the capitalist system—"you may have to pay a little more for bread, but look at what you save on battleships"—and from Fred Allen who highlights a southern bigot named Senator Claghorn on network radio. The Left always seems embattled, but Zero becomes part of a minority in what will come to seem the golden age of social criticism. By 1948, the political center and the Right will so dominate the airwaves that Henry Morgan's Sunday radio show will have one sponsor left, the comedian Fred Allen.

Some segment of Cafe Society's audience in 1942 was in harmony with Josephson's own political consciousness, but too often "the Left didn't have the dollar and a quarter needed to come into my place and pay for their beer. They could stand at the bar the whole night, order a bottle of beer for a quarter, and dance too. But they had to have the quarter and the dollar. I had three shows, at nine, twelve and two, and anybody could stay and dance the whole night." Too often the people who had the dollar and a quarter were not in tune with Josephson's creed; perhaps they came to be amused.

Customers who caught Zero's act during the nine o'clock show might remain for the midnight performances, which meant that Zero's second show had to have enough fresh material to please those who had already caught the earlier act. "He'd mix it up. Now for the late show, most of those early people are gone, so he can repeat. The late show begins at two, but by the time Zero gets on it's 2:30 in the morning. He was the closing act."

Josephson never had the impression that Zero actually planned any night's work. There were no pre-written monologues or bits. "He was free. Free. He just went out and did what he wanted to do, off the cuff, like he was appearing at a house party." Which was confirmed by everyone who knew him. Cafe Society was simply an extension of Lower East Side living rooms, union halls and various venues for bar mitzvahs. Josephson also remembers that in contrast to performers of the Milton Berle stamp, Zero was not given to verbal exchanges with his audience, though spectators were never free from that anxious sense that they might be sucked into the jaws of some Mostel happening.

What was it that Zero's audiences saw? An obituary notice in the *New York Times* speaks to a quality that stayed with the performer throughout his adult life. Robert McFadden notes on September 9th, 1977, the morning after Zero's death, that he "could look like a pile of tires or an elephant tiptoeing across a stage with pants on. He had sagging jowls and a throbbing paunch, but his movements could be as elegant as a dancer's, and his face seemed to be made of rubber, flexing from toothy grin to terrible grimace."

Whether or not the 1942 Sam-turned-Zero gave off that image of aforementioned elephant, everyone agrees that sense of graceful, enchanting klutziness was apparent early. As was the perception that the figure in the performance space reverberated with what Zero usually but not always repressed. That is, there was a palpable undercurrent, an imminent sense of explosive possibility. One could simply not be sure that decorum would be observed, that Zero would maintain the discretion that separates self from spectator. In a very literal sense, Zero was shameless, willing to exploit any weakness in himself or in those watching. Given the usual absence of confrontation, the air was nonetheless charged with a not-always-comic menace.

Sam-Zero's principal stock-in-trade were portraits, short cameo renderings of homely household objects: kitchen utensils, mother's inanimate helpers and the like; and of real or mythical people, as well as animated portraits of other species along the evolutionary chain. There is Senator Polltax T. Pellegra, spiritual cousin to Fred Allen's Senator Claghorn. Polltax T. Pellegra's views concerning U.S. military action in the Pacific are forthright if slightly skewed. "What the hell was Hawaii doing in the Pacific in the first place?" There is the Charles Boyer turn—"Hedy [Lamarr], let me run through your hair—barefoot." On a given night the spectator might be treated to Zero's transformation into a percolating coffee pot or Zero's taking on the essential aspects of a butterfly at rest. The depiction of this butterfly at rest would constitute an odd and precious moment at a HUAC hearing some darkening years down the road.

Viola Harris (my cousin) who was a young actress in 1942, recalls her first encounter with Zero. "I always felt that to be in show business one had to be very—what shall I say?—very svelte. What Zero looked like that night at Cafe Society surprised me. He was plain fat, with the hair very sloppy. I thought he was very off-beat, considering the kind of comedy I had known, which was mostly stand-up stuff. I knew young comics like Philly Foster, what they did was mostly gags. Zero didn't do gags. I remember there were lots of different sounds that he made, all very amusing and clever. He was highly successful with the audience. . . . Zero [was] very different from anyone I'd seen before.

"I remember that Sam Jaffe was there that night, and I had had a crush on Sam Jaffe ever since I was a theatre student. Bob and I [Viola's husband was the actor Robert H. Harris] were introduced to Zero by Sam, but that meant very little to Zero because everyone wanted to speak to him. He wasn't a *big* name, but he was up-and-coming, and Cafe Society was the kind of place where they would have up-and-coming and off-beat performers."

Viola Harris recalls the trip home that night. "Bob and I walked home through Central Park. It was three or four in the morning—you could still do that kind of late-night walk in those days—and Zero and Sam Jaffe were walking with us and carrying on absolutely madly, jumping and screaming and trying to climb trees and pushing each other like two kids, and I just thought they were absolutely adorable. It was just very amusing, and there was a kind of zany freedom that they had that I thought was lovely."

I ask Viola whether Zero was, to some extent, putting on a show for her benefit. "Possibly. I think it was more because of Sam. They both had the same kind of sense of humor, and they were very old friends. It was just fun to watch. They seemed to me a great deal older than I, and I thought how interesting that supposedly adult people behaved in this way."

Bettye Jaffe also remembers these "supposedly adult people." "Sam and Zero did a show together at the beginning of the war, promoting War Bonds. In 1942, Sam would catch Zero's act at Cafe Society. I believe he'd catch it all night long. Then they'd go out on the town, which for them meant shooing pigeons off church steeples." One night Zero was climbing a telephone pole; a policeman came along and said, 'What are you doing?' And Zero said, 'Somebody left a message for me.' After a while the police just got used to them and I suppose they could just do anything. Sam had been in this period of deep mourning after Lillian, his first wife, died, and Zero really pulled him out of it. I believe all these hijinks, all this kind of craziness was what made it possible for Sam to go on living."

Kate Cecilia Harkin was also in that world we refer to with good-humored indulgence as show business. She had already been "in the business" for much of her young life. Like the mass of entertainers for whom employment signifies a continual hustle, Kate found her working life always erratic and usually sluggish. She was of Irish-Catholic stock, one of eight children in a Philadelphia household. The only girl in the pack, at twelve she lost her father whose trade was stone-cutting. Kate tapdanced, studied ballet, performed in a ballet troupe, and eventually became number-sixteen-from-the-left on the Rockettes line at Radio City Music Hall, that palace of glitz and fantasy where Sam and Nettie had once blown a day's wages. Kate was eager, attractive, and intent on developing her theatrical strengths. But the meeting with Zero at Cafe Society led to some unforeseen and troublesome consequences. Much of what was to unfold over the ensuing years would see her displaced or diverted onto a new course, a course she addressed responsibly according to her own lights but with much ambivalence.

After giving birth to Josh, Kate sought out an acting teacher. She began lessons with Don Richardson, which permitted her, as she tells journalist Marilyn Funt,[8] to identify herself on her passport as "actress" rather than "housewife." Kate also confides to Funt that during her stretch as "housewife," she had considered identifying herself as "quartermaster," the dispenser of toothpaste, toilet paper, and other basic necessities. As for the liberated Zero, the battler for racial equality (e.g., the admission of Jackie Robinson to Major League Baseball), Kate is blunt: Zero would raise the roof if his spouse wasn't on hand every night to prepare supper.

Kate's account of the fateful night she is introduced to Zero at Cafe Society: Zero walks her home; he invites her out for dinner the next night; he in turn is invited into her apartment and winds up, fully clothed, in her shower; he never materializes for the dinner date. Zero later tells Kate the dinner slipped his mind. The champion snacker is forgiven and the relationship develops apace.

Alex Maltz plays a key role in this fateful night. "I saw her sitting at a table. I'm at the bar with Barney and I spot this pretty young woman, so I point her out to Sammy. I have no idea who this young thing is. But Sammy didn't need to know anything more. He moved in right away."

Within a short time, the estranged but still legally wed husband of Clara Mostel moves in with Rockette-number-sixteen-from-the-left. Did the Mostel parents, Yisroel and Tzina, have any idea that their once-hoped-for rabbinical scholar was not only living, in the parlance of the pre-Kinseyan age, out of wedlock, but with a Gentile at that? English Strunsky is persuaded that the parents were in the dark about Zero's domestic arrangements, that Zero "didn't want to insult them." Events were now moving rapidly. The hottest new attraction in show business had a producer, a press agent, and a love nest, and within a few short months he would be touching various entertainment bases. Broadway reaches out for this latest find and casts Zero in a revue called *Keep 'Em Laughing*. The Paramount Theatre brings him onto its world-famous stage. And radio, the medium for which Sig Miller had brought Zero to Himan Brown in the first place, discovers that Zero is a valuable resource.

The radio show, *The Chamber Music Society of Lower Basin Street*, broadcast over WJZ, flagship station for what was then NBC's Blue Network, proclaimed that its specialties were "the three b's: barrelhouse, boogie woogie and blues." Its host was Milton Cross, emcee for the Saturday afternoon Metropolitan Opera broadcasts; its musicians, well-known jazzmen of the Forties, and torch and blues singers like Dinah Shore and Jane Pickens; and its comedian, first heard in April of 1942, Zero

Mostel, who would broadcast intermittently until *Lower Basin Street's* demise in 1944.

Keep 'Em Laughing opens April 24th at the Forty-fourth Street Theatre. Its stars are Victor Moore and William Gaxton. Moore, a venerable and low-keyed character actor, may best be remembered as Alexander Throttlebottom, the shy and forgotten vice president of the United States in the 1931 Gershwin-Kaufman-Ryskind musical, *Of Thee I Sing*. Zero's Broadway debut finds the young comedian sharing featured billing with perennial supper-club chanteuse Hildegarde, with the dance team of Paul and Grace Hartman, and with choreographer Jack Cole and his dance ensemble. Several weeks later the revue is overhauled, renamed *Top-Notchers*, England's beloved Gracie Fields takes over top billing, and Zero continues as a holdover.

Cafe Society's press agent, Ivan Black, takes Zero on as a personal account for the next three and a half decades, functioning as a kind of solicitous Boswell to Zero's epileptic version of Doctor Johnson. Black is constantly feeding antic items to gossip columnists like Leonard Lyons, Earl Wilson, and the veteran Walter Winchell. I ask Sig Miller, "How much of Ivan Black's prose can be taken as gospel?" and Miller smiles wryly and quietly announces, "Not too much." There is an enchanting exuberance to Black's broadsheets; he marks 1942 as a golden year in the life of the one who is "starting from nothing." In later years he recalls 1942 as the time when Zero was featured in forty-six national magazines, broke all records ever held by comedians at the Paramount, was chosen by six hundred radio editors as the season's "greatest new male star," and won the Newspaper Guild's Page One award.

Zero's Paramount engagement begins July 21st. The film, perhaps mercifully obscure four decades later, is called *Priorities on Parade*. Zero shares the stage with MGM's Ann Miller, the long-limbed dancer and perennial screen buddy to one ingenue after another, and with Jack Benny's redneck foil, bandleader Phil Harris and his orchestra. On the night of August 4th, the syrupy Crosby-Astaire vehicle, *Holiday Inn*, is screened. Zero is on the bill as part of a Paramount gala that features composer

Irving Berlin, Mrs. Perlmutter's world-renowned offspring Jan Peerce, singers Connee Boswell and Betty Hutton, movie star Alice Faye, and the bands of Benny Goodman, Phil Spitalny, Xavier Cugat, and Skinnay Ennis.

Shortly thereafter, barely six months following his astonishing debut at Cafe Society, Zero boards the cross-country train out of Grand Central Station for the first of several encounters with the Hollywood dream factory. He has been signed to appear in a Hollywood extravaganza, MGM's version of a hit Broadway musical that had featured Ethel Merman and Bert Lahr. Cole Porter's *DuBarry Was a Lady* makes much ado about a nightclub men's room attendant who takes a nap and dreams he is Louis XV. The dream engineers a convenient transformation of the club star idolized by the attendant as the lady becomes Louis's favorite mistress, Madame DuBarry.

MGM options this reverie as a vehicle for Red Skelton and Lucille Ball, and imports comedians Zero Mostel and Rags Ragland from New York to inject *DuBarry* with extra shots of titillation. Aaron Mostel tells me this event hardly marks the Mostel clan's initial foray into motion pictures, for Aaron himself has appeared years earlier as a member of a choir in a Yiddish film produced by the pioneer Vitagraph Pictures company. But by 1942, despite the preponderance of Jewish impresarios, the plenitude of lox, bagels, and colorful expletives, there is hardly a trace of authentic *Yiddishkeit* in the City of Angels.

Shortly after his arrival in Hollywood, Zero settles into a poolside cottage within a housing complex known as the Garden of Allah[9] and is shooting righteous missiles back east, principally to Tzina. He has discovered, presumably to his disgust, that Hollywood is awash in alcohol. In these letters, he singles out British performers who are not only deep into their cups but snorting and mainlining as well. In contrast to this dissolute colony of Brits, our clean-living Zero extols the virtues of sobriety and steadfast labor.

"What do I do when we're not filming?" asks Zero in correspondence remembered half a century later by Aaron Mostel. "I take a car. I go out near Hollywood or into the desert, and I paint, I sketch. These other guys, before they get up in the morning they have to be treated for hangovers, they've got to be given rubdowns. Why couldn't they hire some good Jewish guys, these Jewish bastards?" Aaron notes that Zero liked to label MGM Mayer's *Gonsa Mishpucheh*, literally all of Mayer's relatives. Whether this meant that Mayer did hire some "Jewish guys" is not clear, but if he did they were evidently in need of rubdowns and caffeine.

But something goes awry in Hollywood. Zero's career takes an inexplicable, seemingly undocumented turn about which there is much silence. What happens between *DuBarry*, shot in the summer of '42, and *Panic in the Streets*, Zero's next film, which goes into production in 1949? There are seven unaccountable years. Kate Mostel's book, *170 Years of Show Business*,[9] is remarkably vague on this period, to the extent that there is any mention of Hollywood at all. Sig Miller doesn't know the whole story—perhaps Barney Josephson does—but Miller informs me that Zero was fired from *DuBarry*. I press him for details. "He insulted Louis B. Mayer. Zero talked to him as if Mayer was one of the errand boys. You don't do that to Mr. Mayer. They had him on contract and they dropped him. He talked to Louis B. Mayer as if he was an idiot." I venture the thought that very likely Mayer *was* an idiot, and Miller responds: "Yeah, but you don't tell that to the man who runs one of the largest studios in Hollywood. Not a good idea."

But it's from Barney Josephson that I learn what took place. To begin with, when Zero was booked into Cafe Society he asked Josephson to function as his manager. They agreed to work together, but the arrangement survived about a year and a half. "When you're at a job you have to have some self-discipline and Zero was devoid of it *completely*. Now I arranged the movie deal over the telephone. I never saw the completed film but I was on the lot with him every day."

I ask Josephson, "You went *out* with him?"

"I was his manager. I had to be there watching this guy because I knew he needed somebody to hold him."

I ask if Kate went as well and Josephson responds reluctantly. "They weren't married then. He brought Kate out against my wishes. He had a wife that I never knew about when he started working for me. She initiated a court action for support, claiming she never was supported by him. When he went to Hollywood to make the picture and I then knew about the problems he was having with his wife, I said, 'I hear Katie's going out there with you.' I said, 'You shouldn't do this because there's such a thing as the Mann Act, taking a woman out-of-state for immoral purposes. And you still got a wife hanging around and she's been after you for some money. She claims you're making ten times the money you're making and so on. All these years she says she never got a penny and she wants some of it now. And I can't fault her for that, but you're my boy and she isn't.' Well, when I get out to Hollywood, Kate's already there, in a motel. I took a cottage where only one city in the world would have such a name—the Garden of Allah.[10] There are cottages around a pool, and Zero is supposed to be there *with* me, but he's sleeping with Kate at the motel outside Hollywood. And he took her out to dinner, the *three* of us went nightclubbing, dancing around, and he's making a spectacle of himself."

"Was it fun for you?"

"It was *no fun* for me! It was all grief for Barney."

I ask how Zero fared in terms of discipline.

"Discipline? It's a surprise to me they kept him on as long as they did. But they did. You know how hot he was? When the deal was made, all of Hollywood was after him, every goddamned studio, and MGM particularly wanted him for this film. If you know how a studio works—they don't take a newcomer for one picture, they take you on a seven-year contract. I said *no*. I managed Hazel Scott for seven and a half years, they had to buy her per film. I made the contracts out telling what the producers could and couldn't do. They couldn't change her hair, they couldn't change her color, they couldn't put an apron on her, they couldn't make her a kitchen maid. And I got her ten times as much money as any black artist ever got. So what I got for Zero was incredible. They wanted him to come out so they could screen him—I said, 'No, Zero Mostel doesn't screen for anybody in this world. You saw him in the Cafe? That's Mostel, that's what you're buying.'"

"So they bought it."

"They bought it. The contract was for one film. They want to tie him up over a period for two films? I said no. I said, 'After the first picture you can have him for one more picture the same year. If you want him for the next year, we'll consider that, but he's free, he can go anywhere. If you make a deal for the second year, you can have him for two pictures only—that's it—after that you have to bid with everybody else.' I tell you *nobody* ever went to Hollywood like this."

I tell Josephson, "You're a tough act to follow."

"Right. So when you're out there, like always, they give you a call date. So I'm out there with him but they're not ready to shoot, not for weeks. But he's on salary from the day he arrives. So now they've got the right to have him come out to the studio on some days, and they're screen-testing him. They're having Zero do all his club routines on film. So there's a story going around the MGM lot after awhile—when Mr. L.B. Mayer, otherwise known as The Boss, comes to the studio in a bad humor, which was often, and he's got this movie screen in his office, they would project these screen tests of Zero onto The Boss's private screen, and that was the only thing that could put L.B. in a good mood for the day. I was told this by Arthur Freed who ran the studio."

At this point Barney Josephson, sitting beside me in his B.B.Q. restaurant near the front door and cash register on this hot July afternoon in 1988, nearly a half century after the Zero-in-Hollywood-saga, refreshes us both with an imitation of Zero Mostel doing his version of an old Jimmy Durante routine as a sample of what might put Louis B. Mayer, otherwise known as The Boss, in a good mood in July of 1942. Josephson erupts into Durante's old patter routine: a-one tooth, a-half-a-tooth, a-whole tooth and no tooth. . .

"Only Zero did it even better than Durante. Anyway, at some point I am just fed up with Zero's shenanigans. I said, 'Zero, I've got two saloons to run in New York. You're not paying any attention to me.' The Kate business was already too late to change. But this guy is hot, *hot*, even Chaplin wants to meet him. One night he's at Chaplin's house. It's described to me, the terrace, lawns and all, and it's now two thirty in the morning and Chaplin will not let him go. Zero's got to be at the studio at seven and Chaplin is following him out onto the terrace and begging him for more routines. I'm sorry I didn't witness this. More, more, more. Chaplin couldn't get enough of him. He'd do the isolationist Southern senator, he'd make a string tie of his necktie, he'd say, 'Mah friends,' and he'd *bark*. Now who the hell would think of that? And he'd wind up saying, 'What the hell was Hawaii doing in the Pacific anyway?' People used to fall off their *chairs* in the Café."

I press Josephson. "So he had Kate with him, so he wasn't the most disciplined guy on earth. *Chaplin* loved him, Louis B. *Mayer* loved him, at least in his private screening room. *So what happened?*"

"What happened?" Josephson echoes my plaint. "MGM blacklisted Zero Mostel way before the days of the blacklist."

Again Zero is ahead of his time.

"Zero was a Left guy, like I was. I told him, 'You're going out to Hollywood, you're going to work for MGM, they're the most reactionary studio in the business.' I have knowledge that Mayer has spies in every progressive organization in Hollywood. They go to all the meetings, they go to all the fund-raisers, for Spain, for Russia, reporting back on anyone who's connected to the studio that they were *there*, at this meeting, at this or that fund-raiser."

I protest to Josephson, "It's '42, the war is on, the USSR is our ally, Warner's is making *Mission to Moscow*."

"I know, but this ain't Warner's. I have to tell you, MGM had big plans for Zero. They called me in, showed me a script they were preparing for him. A second film. They were going to make him a star. But it was not to be."

Why was it not to be?

"Louis B. Mayer, The Boss, is having some get-together at his country club one evening. It's an exclusive, posh joint, and there's gonna be this swell affair or whatever. So L.B.'s got it in his head he wants Zero to entertain."

"Entertain? He's paying him?"

"What paying him? The Boss says entertain, you smile, maybe you don't run, but *you get there, and you entertain.*"

"Like in Mayer's private screening room."

"Only live this time."

"But Zero doesn't buy it."

"Zero says to me, 'Who the fuck does this guy, this *shmegegeh,* think he is?' I say, 'He's the head of the studio, he pays your salary.' So Zero is grumbling but I'm laying it on the line. I say to him, 'The Boss is sending a studio limo out here to the Garden of Allah to pick you up and take you to the country club. So you're expected to be here, and Kate is expected to be nowhere in sight, and you're expected to make The Boss happy tonight cause it's a special night or whatever the hell it is. Get it?'"

"Did he get it?"

"Do you have to ask? Comes late afternoon, no Zero. I'm waiting at the Garden of Allah, I'm hoping against hope. Comes early evening, no Zero at the Garden of Allah. Comes finally the studio limo, all nice and shiny and everybody in it smiling—"

"Who was in it?"

"Probably the chauffeur, maybe a PR guy. But need I add, no Zero Mostel appears to get into this limo to be driven out to the swell event."

"And The Boss?"

"Fit to be tied. Pissed."

"So Zero is out dancing with Kate, or they're in the sack?"

"No. He's at a fund-raiser."

This stops me cold. And Josephson explains.

"There's a man, a very dear friend of mine at that time, named Harry Bridges. He's head of the International Longshoremen on the West Coast and the government's trying to deport him. They claim he's a Red and he makes them uncomfortable. So they want to kick him out of the country."

"Back to Australia."

"So there's this big Left bash in Hollywood, to raise money

for Harry's legal expenses fighting the government. And my client and L.B.'s employee, Zero Mostel, is busy entertaining at this bash."

"Right."

"And of course L.B. Mayer has his spy at the fund-raiser so it's not gonna take very long for word to get back to the studio where Mostel was when he's supposed to be clowning for The Boss's privileged guests at the country club."

"Doesn't look good."

"I'm on the *DuBarry* set early the next morning, and Zero is there ready for work. And suddenly through one door onto the set waltzes Arthur Freed and Zero is down near the other end, and Freed has this awful smile on his face. Then Freed calls to Zero, clear across the room so everybody can hear, 'Good morning, Comrade,' and at the same time Freed is raising his arm and giving Zero the Bolshevik salute. Zero blanches. He knows things are bad, but *how* bad he doesn't yet know. But he's soon to find out."

"How bad?"

"The orders go out. Zero is taken off the picture. The editors are told to cut as much Zero out of *DuBarry* as they possibly can, and the contract is torn up. He's *finished* as far as MGM is concerned, but that's not even the worst. Word goes out to *every other studio in town* that Mostel *doesn't work*."

"The blacklist early."

"As far as Hollywood is concerned, Mostel is finished. *Finished*."

"Until Kazan," I put in hopefully, "calls him back seven years later."

"And then a couple of years after that he's finished *again*."

Josephson looks at me over the table, still smiling genially. "So he goes back to New York and picks up the pieces and we book him back into Cafe Society and then he goes on to other clubs, La Martinique, places like that. But as I told you, I stopped being his manager. I'd had it."

The Western consensus tells us that World War Two involved a moral imperative, though in recent years that war, now technologically-outmoded—the art of mass murder can be beautifully engineered in the Eighties and Nineties—has taken on a somewhat tarnished image. Questions abound that speak to the internment of Japanese-Americans; the firebombing of Dresden and Hamburg; the gratuitous horrors of Hiroshima and Nagasaki; the Allied unpreparedness even as Hitler mounted what came to be known as the Battle of the Bulge; and our refusal to blow up rail lines the Nazis used to transport millions to labor and death camps. And the Western home front had its undiminished stock of racism and anti-Semitism. It had its Senator Bilbos, its Father Coughlins. It had its Nazi sympathizers in Britain, primarily housed in Oswald Moseley's fascist movement. It had a deeply divided French nation, with enthusiastic collaborators both in Vichy and in "Free France." And throughout the Thirties it had its Charles Lindberghs in the United States, people deeply sympathetic to the Nazi cause. And it also had curious figures such as the inimitable Louis B.

Mayer who on one occasion reportedly advised other film industry moguls not to portray the Nazis as bad fellows since the Third Reich, without a doubt, would conquer Europe and probably take over the United States before they were finished redrawing the map of the world.

Nevertheless Zero Mostel's generation and the generation that came to maturity in the 1940s believed that options were closed to them after Pearl Harbor, the rancorous fighting within a Left which had been united against Franco and the Fascists in 1936 and badly split after the Hitler-Stalin pact, came to an abrupt end with the Japanese attack. "The last good war" had, despite the courageous resistance of conscientious objectors, the overwhelming support of the Allied countries, even in a Stalinist Soviet Union where many of the oppressed initially welcomed the Nazis as liberators.

To use a Brechtian locution, this last good war was a long time coming but once it had gotten a head of steam it proved to be a pisser. By the beginning of 1939, having already digested the Sudetenland, a delicious appetizer, Hitler proceeded to the main course and polished off the remainder of Czechoslovakia, then turned his appetite eastward—to the Old Country of the Mostels and of Sholom Aleichem's Tevyeh *Der Milkhiger*. On August 23rd, 1939, sensing that the next meal perforce needed a dining partner, Hitler along with Joseph Stalin astonished the Western allies by the formation of the nonaggression pact that gave the Third Reich freedom to move on Poland. Poland, that unfortunate territory or state of mind, was to be carved up yet again. Hitler's forces attacked on the first of September, clearly upsetting the Poles who had themselves been eyeing a juicy morsel known as Lithuania, particularly the city of Vilna. Warsaw residents recall the Luftwaffe over the skies of their city on September 1st. On September 3rd, Britain and France finally abandoned the notion that Hitler's appetite had limits and issued a formal declaration that World War Two, in rehearsal since the Japanese invasion of Manchuria and the Fascist rebellion in Spain, had finally opened. It was to have a long run over a vast stage and would consume much of the earth's resources.

After an initial period of what came to be known as the Phony War, the Germans made their move; they swiftly overran Western Europe, making a mockery of France's seemingly unassailable Maginot Line, and on June 13th, 1940, Paris, which was to be defended to the last French citizen, simply fell—and shortly after that Hitler himself arrived in Gay Paree and did a little dance. In no time the Nazis were at the English Channel; what was left of the British Army had already been evacuated at Dunkirk. By that summer of 1940, with Goering's Luftwaffe and Britain's RAF battling over the skies of England, much of this world was either overrun by one army or another or was doing battle as a contingent of the Allies or Axis powers. On the 22nd of June, Nazi troops crossed eastward into areas of Poland that Stalin had occupied as part of the nonaggression pact. So much for the shared dinner party.

We understand that Zero kept up with political events, but what he could not possibly have known was the extent of the massacre taking place in Eastern Europe—to vast populations, to Leftist resistance, and particularly to the Jews, to the very *landsleit* (townspeople from the place where one has emigrated) and surviving relatives of the Mostels. For at eleven in the morning on June 22nd, several hours after the Soviet army had evacuated the city, Nazi troops entered Lvov or Lemberg, a town which had only recently become part of the Soviet Ukraine.

Joseph Tenenbaum, one of the few survivors of the Lvov-Lemberg carnage, records that

> In a matter of hours large posters appeared on the walls inciting the population to wreak vengeance on the Jews "responsible for the war and the killing of several thousand Poles and Ukrainians." The slaughter started immediately. The "new order" was inaugurated with "unrestrained plunder, violence, torture, mass shootings and murders of the civilian" (Special Commission Report on German Atrocities).
>
> The hunt for Jewish men and women went on unabatedly. Several thousand were herded into the prison on Kazimier-zowska. . . . The captives were unmercifully tortured and many shot. After two days of massacre, only six individuals out of several thousand returned home. [11]

It was only the beginning of a terror that was to devastate the Jewish population of Europe, both those who perished and the survivors. By the end of this last good war, after the ghettoes, the cattle cars, the labor and extermination camps, Lvov-Lemberg was a city for all practical purposes liberated of Jews. And it was the same with Sholom Aleichem's Kiev. For the Jews, Eastern Europe was, to borrow the title of Roman Vishniac's book of photographs, a vanished world.

The Japanese decimated the U.S. fleet at Pearl Harbor with what is believed to be the very scrap iron we had sold them when New York's Sixth Avenue El was dismantled. The probability is that the Sixth Avenue El had transported Zero and Nettie Crosley to the Fiftieth Street stop and the screening of *Nana* at Radio City Music Hall that magical winter's day in 1934. The return of the El in such hostile fashion precipitated wartime conscription—peacetime conscription had been initiated in 1940—and such a rush to marry and avoid the draft that bandleader Vaughan Monroe was singing "Is it love or is it conscription?" It also meant a surge in enlistments, the breakup of families, the beginning of rationing (coffee, tea, cigarettes, gasoline), the development of a wartime economy, the vast movement of women into factories, the creation of the entertainment industries' morale-building project out of which developed the USO and which made the Stage Door Canteen a second home to G.I. Joe. And it meant staggering fatalities on every battlefront, and for those who stayed behind it meant the growing reality of "our boys" coming home in boxes.

The United States had been living an isolationist dream: we were going to steer clear of foreign entanglements. FDR's third presidential campaign was built on the understanding that he was keeping us out of European conflicts. Eddie Cantor had popularized a song about fools fighting on "some foreign soil," in which American mothers exhorted the powers-that-be to "Let 'em keep it over there." The isolationist dream collapsed, we went, we almost segued from the Great Depression into the new Great War which had no name when we got into it. Keep it over there? By the end of '41 there wasn't even an over there.

"Over here" the home front turned its lights down—usually brownouts, occasionally blackouts—saved tin, grew victory gardens, caught victory measles, watched Lucky Strike's green package "go to war" and transform itself at home to white, buttoned its lip because no one knew when the enemy might be eavesdropping, invented leg makeup to replace nylons, and gave up cuffs and two-trouser vented suits, even though the "zoot suit with pegged pants and a reat pleat" hung around long enough for a race riot in Detroit to be named after it. The boys were going off and the Crosbys and Sinatras and Comos and Eberles and the Jo Staffords and Peggy Lees and Helen O'Connells and Dinah Shores were musing about the boys coming home and the lights going on again "all over the world," with a particular nod to the white cliffs of Dover. And the Andrews Sisters and Ernie Pyle and Bill Mauldin were fashioning new legends about G.I. Joe and Sad Sack, and word was filtering back regarding a German fraulein named Lili Marlene. Terms like *snafu* and *ruptured duck* were entering the language, as was the family name of somebody, always said to have just been here, they called Kilroy.

On March 5th, 1943, Zero Mostel was, to use the title of a Bob Hope-Eddie Bracken movie of that period, caught in the draft. There is every indication that Zero supported this last good war, but after a short time as Infantry Private Samuel J. Mostel, service number 32816776, the pleasures of military service rapidly palled. Zero's short-lived Army career took him first to Camp Upton, later to Camp Croft, and finally to Fort George Meade in Maryland. A number of his friends in show business, among them actors Martin Gabel and Alfred Ryder, were at Camp Upton, but in short order this congenial gathering dispersed.

Kate believes Zero wanted to join the Special Services in order to entertain troops overseas. "You had to be pretty dangerous," she tells interviewer Marilyn Funt years later, "if they wouldn't let you go. . . ." Zero had signed a petition urging the inclusion of black baseball players in the major leagues, that and his "too-early" general anti-Fascist stance made him suspect in the eyes of the military. Very quickly Zero wanted out of the armed forces, but Kate had decided she wanted in. She speaks of it as a moment of "pure insanity"; despite Zero's conviction that she would loathe Army life, Kate joined the WACS. When Zero obtained his discharge—the unofficial word is that once again he "carried on pretty good"—Kate who throughout her life was plagued with asthma, was able to obtain a medical discharge. "I never even had a uniform," she notes, "and he was in about nine months and then we got married."

Some four months before his Army discharge, Zero's film remnants, the frames that hadn't been transformed into outtakes (functionally, garbage on the cutting room floor) opened with whatever else was left of *DuBarry Was a Lady* at the Capitol Theatre in New York. The date was August 19th, 1943. Many of the gaudy movie palaces, the Paramount, the Strand, the Roxy, the Music Hall, sometimes Loew's State and Loew's Paradise, offered stage shows while the reels were being rewound. It was still the heyday of the big swing bands of Benny Goodman, Artie Shaw, Tommy and Jimmy Dorsey, Glenn Miller, Count Basie, Duke Ellington, Charlie Barnet, Erskine Hawkins, Gene Krupa, and others, and of the "sweet" music of Kay Kyser, Fred Waring, Guy Lombardo, Orrin Tucker, and Sammy Kaye. The Capitol featured one of the sweet ensembles, Horace Heidt and His Musical Knights.

The Capitol's printed program for August 19th promised immediate delivery of war stamps and bonds. Heidt's sweet and jolly Knights gave way rapidly to the frenzied brass of the Tommy Dorsey band and the general noise, fast patter, and leaden humor of *DuBarry*. Employing the Forties-musical formula, *DuBarry* saturation-bombed its customers, theorizing that not only is more better but that with an impressive array of talent, one has to hit the mark occasionally. The gifts abundantly unfolding included new Cole Porter songs and skillful performers like Red Skelton, Lucille Ball, Gene Kelly, Donald Meek, Douglass Dumbrille and old-time comic George Givot. And the two new recruits, Zero Mostel, and Rags Ragland.

The local New York press had no wonderful words for

DuBarry, for its stars, or for the debuting Zero Mostel. Otis Guernsey, reviewing the film on August 20th for the *New York Herald-Tribune*, refers to Zero as "the Broadway nightclub star who has zoomed to popularity via his impersonations of various well-known characters. In [*DuBarry*] he touches on the style of Charles Boyer." But Guernsey hardly seems to be recognizing the next Charlie Chaplin; perhaps that next Chaplin was embedded in the outtakes no one was going to observe except the cleaning women, or if Metro thought to preserve the excised footage, the maintenance staff responsible for general storage. The *New Yorker's* terse comment in its issue of August 21st that the change from Bert Lahr, star of the Broadway production, to the film and radio comic Red Skelton was an idea whose time never should have come.

I recall Skelton's radio shows—I was an adolescent in the early Forties and my buddies and I were knocked out by Skelton's oft-repeated "guzzler's gin, a smooooooth drink." But apparently Skelton's *DuBarry* shtick does not come across as particularly smoooooooth or engaging to the major film critics. Both Skelton and costar Lucille Ball do nothing but weary the *New Yorker's* correspondent: we are given to understand that Red Skelton "is not the man to wrest any comedy from . . . a king's being pierced in the rear by an arrow." Neither Skelton nor Lucille Ball is a match for the likes of Bert Lahr and that professional belter, Ethel Merman. As for Zero, we're told that he has more or less been "rung in," as if he were a sprig of parsley or a clove of garlic intruding on the morning oatmeal.

With the press seriously underwhelmed, it became evident that the *DuBarry* that finally staggered into the Capitol was not going to do great things for Zero Mostel, with or without L.B. Mayer's voodoo act. It would take a call from Elia Kazan some seven years later to bring Zero back to the movies. But by the time Zero appeared in *Panic in the Streets* under Kazan's direction, Hollywood had become an even more polarized community, the cold war had settled in, HUAC (House Committee on Un-American Activities) was on the prowl, writers, directors, performers, editors, and producers had all been set against each other, careers were being destroyed, and a political chill was felt throughout the country. And Richard Nixon and Senator Joseph McCarthy hadn't as yet taken center stage.

The Harkin-Mostel wedding took place in the office of the mayor of Long Branch, New Jersey, on Sunday morning, July 2nd, 1944. In preparation for this event, Kate was a weeklong guest of the Paleys at their summer house in Allenhurst, New Jersey. On Friday night, after Lou Paley and Mother Mascha Strunsky had gone to bed, Kate and Emily Paley sat waiting on the front porch for the male wedding participants to arrive from Manhattan. Emily finally turned in and Kate sat alone waiting for "The Prince." Prince Zero, Sam Jaffe and Zero's friend Tully Flaumenhauft arrived early Saturday morning; they had driven up in Tully's car and there had been an argument on the way. The nature of the dispute was withheld from Kate for the time being.

Sunday morning came fast on the heels of Saturday. Does Kate remember wedding bells? She remembers Sam Jaffe's "running commentary in Yiddish"; she remembers that Zero didn't remember to bring the wedding ring; she remembers that Emily Paley struggled to dislodge her own wedding ring so that Kate might wear it for the ceremony; and she remembers the wedding breakfast at the Paleys: lox, herring, chopped liver, whitefish and cream cheese, while Kate pined for "good old [American?] waffles and sausages." Then, she remembers, the men went off to play golf while the ladies napped or went to the beach. The honeymoon, vintage Mostel, was in full swing.

As for the Friday night altercation, it had to do with Kate Harkin's religion. Tully Flaumenhauft, an importer of some means, had tried to persuade Zero either not to wed Kate Harkin or to exhort the bride to convert to Judaism. Whether such conversion was ever an issue between Zero and Kate, and there seems little likelihood of it, both bride and groom were aware that mixed marriages, as late as the Forties, were considered calamities by Orthodox Jewish families and that this wedding might lead to untold misery. But it was summertime, and bride and groom were young; perhaps a life of bliss awaited them. We can't know what was going on in Tully Flaumenhauft's mind; could it have mattered that in the time of the ovens of Auschwitz and Treblinka, one more convert might be added to the world's stock of surviving Jews? The newlyweds, energetic, hopeful, moving in what they perceived of as an up-to-date if cynical, often cowardly and unjust world, had little patience with archaic tribal-based custom. One needed only a good heart, ample courage, and a strong sense of justice.

But in too short a time the unthinkable and yet perfectly predictable happens. The news reaches the Bronx. The repercussions are worse than anyone might have anticipated. For Zero, what ensues is catastrophe, the dimensions of which minimize the trauma of the shut door of L.B. Mayer's *Gonsa Mishpucheh.* According to Nettie Crosley, "The family sat *shivah* when Zero married Kate." The father, Yisroel Mostel, the immigrant rabbi for whom the wedding of Torah and Judaic practice was not only a way of life, it *was* life, who had envisioned his offspring as a spiritual mentor to fellow Jews—Yisroel goes into mourning. The twenty-nine-year-old Samuel Joel Mostel is pro-

Young boy from Tzina
Mostel's family in Poland.
Presumed murdered in
Holocaust. Courtesy:
Aaron Mostel.

Holocaust victim, likely one
of Tzina Mostel's cousins.
Courtesy: Aaron Mostel.

Holocaust victim, likely
Tzina Mostel's uncle or
granduncle. Courtesy:
Aaron Mostel.

Likely husband and wife,
Tzina Mostel's Polish rela-
tives, Holocaust victims.
Courtesy: Aaron Mostel.

Bottom row: Zero's brothers, Aaron (left) and Milton. Top, from left: Tzina's sister-in-law Stella, brother Chaim (Charles), Tzina, sister-in-law Simma (Celia). In Tzina's lap, Zero in reflective mode. Circa 1916. Courtesy: Aaron Mostel.

The Mostel boys. Top row: Milton (left), Zero, Aaron. Bottom: Velvel (Bill). Circa 1925. Courtesy: Aaron Mostel.

Tzina (right) holding unidentified niece. Left: probably two sisters-in-law. Circa 1925. Courtesy: Aaron Mostel.

Drawing of Yisroel Mostel (rendered by 13-year-old Zero in 1928). Courtesy: Josh and Toby Mostel.

Zero as a young, nicely groomed artist. Circa 1930.
Courtesy: Seward Park High School Alumni Association.

Clara Baker, born Clara
Sverd, then Clara Mostel,
Zero's first wife. Circa 1960.
Courtesy: Clara Baker.

Zero doing his badminton number. Monroe, New York. Circa 1935. Courtesy: Rose Ripps.

Zero in hitchhiker mode. Monroe, New York. Circa 1935. Courtesy: Rose Ripps.

Zero (left) and Pete Ripps. A tender moment in high grass. Monroe, New York. Circa 1935. Courtesy: Rose Ripps.

Pastoral setting featuring Pete Ripps (left) and Zero. Monroe, New York. Circa 1935. Courtesy: Rose Ripps.

Philip Loeb, driven to suicide by the blacklist. 1948.

Barney Josephson, founder of Cafe Society and namer of Zero Mostel. 1982.

Zero, comfortably attired in wool jacket and attractive tie. Circa 1940.

Zero at work in his Twenty-eighth Street studio,
circa 1970. And some samples of his art.
Courtesy: Josh and Toby Mostel.

Zero (left) in serendipitous moment from film version of *Rhinoceros*. 1973.

Zero and Gene Wilder listening to Kenneth Mars's rendition of "Springtime for Hitler" in *The Producers*. 1967.

A distraught Zero in *The Angel Levine*. 1970.

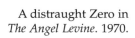

nounced dead. And Tzina? On hearing the news, the mother prays for her son's "departed" soul and turns an icy countenance on the living, anguished soul who tries in vain to find a path back to her during the remaining ten years of her life. Not only will Tzina never lay eyes on her new daughter-in-law, she will refuse to admit the existence of two grandchildren. Toby, the younger grandchild, will never see his grandmother, and Josh, the elder grandchild, the firstborn of Zero and Kate, will visit his grandmother once—on her deathbed at the hospital—and she will refuse to look at him. To Tzina, these grandchildren are the effects of a spiritual calamity; it is as if they had never been properly born.

Marilyn Funt, interviewing Kate, touches on the rift that was never healed, and there's a curious glibness to Kate's response: "I never even met Zero's mother, and she never saw her grandchildren. His mother had said since he married a Gentile they [Zero's parents] would have to kill themselves."

Zero, like the character of Leopold Bloom, a role he will assume in the play *Ulysses in Nighttown*, also cannot find his way home. But whereas Joyce's Ulysses envisions the bosom of wife Molly Bloom (a role Kate at one time performs in *Nighttown*) as the center of the hearth, and Homer envisions Penelope's long-patient bosom as the home Odysseus seeks, Zero will come to see that Kate is neither Molly nor Penelope but rather an unmitigated nuisance, a creature who cares for him deeply in her fashion, but it is a fashion that brings him no solace. If Zero has a home, it is probably behind the door he shuts each night so that he can find a moment of solitude. There is another door, but that Mostel door is shut to him.

There is a dilemma that Orthodox Jewry has never resolved. It has to do with Jews living within their history. The Pentateuch, the five books of Moses, speaks of the mixed marriage of Moses to "the Cushite woman" who might be Sudanese or Ethiopian. Miriam and Aaron speak contemptuously of the Cushite woman and Torah instructs us that *they*, brother and sister, transgress because they disparage Moses's attachment to his beloved. God turns Miriam into a leper for this disparagement, even though

Moses has indeed wed outside the faith. But there is another concern that addresses the cohering of a Jewish community, for the Jewish community by definition is a bonding together in faith and observance and is strengthened by the observance of God's *mitzvot*, God's Commandments, and they are not only to "love thy neighbor as thyself" but to keep the Lord's Sabbath and to instruct one's children in Jewish history, belief, and custom. To what extent are an embracing of one's neighbor and cherishing the custom of one's neighbor a diminution of the bonds of the Jewish community? At what point does liberation begin to undermine and ultimately transform the very nature of community?

Certain liberal elements of Conservative, Reform and Reconstructionist Judaism hold that *mitzvot* implies a constant reevaluating of *Halachah* (Law), in order to address responsibly the constant unfolding of life. Thus one can make out a case for *mitzvot* as simply and truly to love all beings, to understand that no human is alien to God, but that all humans are God's children. And yet a community also defines itself by its differences, by the ways in which it is not a generalized lumping together of all peoples. When Zero assumes the role of Tevye in *Fiddler on the Roof*, he plays out the terrible dilemma his own mother and father played out years before. But unlike Tevye, Tzina and Yisroel Mostel are never to be reconciled to the events of July 2nd.

The Jewish concept of *shivah* brings us to magic or to magic-thinking. Sitting *shivah* is not only an act of mourning, but among the *frum* (the holders to strict Orthodox custom) a positive effort towards aiding the departed soul on its journey. This soul, this *neshumeh*, is considered to have started off on its final journey from earth. The grieving family sits at home on low stools and visitors sit with them. All mirrors are covered because the departed, or departing, soul may not even have left the house. The soul is trying to find its way to its eternal resting place and in stumbling around the house might inadvertently come up against its own image in an uncovered mirror, an image that might so frighten it it would sicken, faint, never find its way out of the house and thus never find its way to the Lord. For many non-Orthodox Jews, *shivah* is a practice steeped in magic or superstition. Most of us believe we are liberated from magic-thinking, but we still knock on wood, treasure wish-bones, and utter good-bye (God be with you) every day. If Tzina and Yisroel Mostel are playing out rituals many of us consider primitive and outmoded, that consideration reflects our own thinking at a certain moment in the development of thought.

It's a day or so after the wedding. Kate and Zero are renting an apartment at Forty-nine West Forty-sixth Street. Kate discovers Zero in the act of leaving the apartment. Where was he off to? He was going to paint, in the studio on West Twenty-eighth Street—as usual. And the honeymoon?

"My big resentment from the beginning," Kate tells Marilyn Funt, "was how little time we spent together. I went to the movies or theater with friends, and he went to his art studio. He had a life by himself, and it was hard for me to adjust to it."

Funt asks whether Kate continued to work and Kate tells her, "We were traveling so much, with Zero in nightclubs all over, and after two years we had Josh. When you have children you have to stay home forever and ever."

ixth Avenue in the upper Twenties has traditionally been the heart of the wholesale flower market. Merchants recall their parents operating from these few streets, selling flowers, plants, gardening equipment and the like. The flower district intersects a culture in which working hours appear to have no boundaries, workers have no set patterns of labor and their tools are often of an insubstantial nature. Of course the working tools of the painter and sculptor have solid weight, even if the completed substance, "the work," then floats within insubstantial constraints we call market value. The neighborhood, marked by old factory buildings in which the post-War years have seen light industry functioning in layered intimacy with painters, sculptors, potters, and set designers, is also home to dancers, actors, writers, and musicians who work, sleep and dine in odd blocks of time and whose tools range from nothing much at all to items of prodigious weight.

During the day, delivery trucks move merchandise through the clogged east-west canyons that comprise the side streets from Fifteenth to Thirty-ninth. At night these streets appear to be in states of repose or exhaustion; some of the residue of labor lies haphazardly in and out of garbage cans, in gloomy or garishly-lit doorways, and along the rims of gutters mercifully spared for a few hours the onslaught of grinding engines, brakes, iron conveyors, and rubber tires. Artists of one or another determined or tenuous persuasion can be seen leaving and entering the various buildings, and occasionally sounds of labor may be heard in the form of hammering, typing, tapping, or vocalizing. It's a busy, possessed, concentrated, sometimes fruitless, sometimes productive region. It has an anonymity not necessarily of its own doing; for every retiring or ultimately unredeemed artist, there is another obstinately primed for fame and fortune. There isn't anything that can't be formed, can't be dreamt, nothing to stop anyone except the limitations that stop us all, artists and other beings alike.

The Mostel headquarters comprised one cell in a cluster of like spaces, but into its confines through the years came various other painters, some of whom like Zero's painter friend Herbie Kallem had studios in the same building, the Thursday-night poker players, as well as a panoply of performers, press people, curious relatives, and obdurate bill collectors.

Himan Brown fondly recalls the occasion many years ago when a burglar, absorbed in lightening the inventory of a nearby shirt factory, found himself unexpectedly pursued by the local authorities. Perched on a roof overlooking the windows of the Mostel studio, the discouraged shirt thief began unloading several cartons of evidence, some of which floated fortuitously through the open Mostel window. When I interviewed Brown in his office some thirty years after the bungled shirt robbery, he indicated that the very shirt in which he was greeting me was none other than a member of that airborne lot of size fifteens which had sailed into Zero's embrace and which the otherwise concentrated painter had then generously distributed among an assortment of friendly shirt-wearers. If nothing enters our lives unbidden, then some aspect of this flying *largesse* speaks to a connection between Zero the painter and one of Raphael's luminous angels gracefully winging in charitable items for the downtrodden but incorrigibly hopeful.

Tin Pan Alley had flowered on these streets in the Twenties. Forty-five West Twenty-eighth Street had once housed the music firm which published the early Gershwin songs. I am told the firm had been housed in Zero's very studio. "Each one of these studios," Ian Hunter explained to me, "was structured as an L-shaped room. The small area was like a dining cove. In later years, when Zee got flush, he bought a building across the street, number Forty-two. It was four stories with a bar at the bottom. [Until the Nineties, when the bar lost its lease, the Beaubern Cafe, as it was known, displayed some Mostel memorabilia.] The space at Forty-two was quite ample. Forty-five had less room but I remained in the old building."

If Twenty-eighth Street during business hours had the air of a clogged, commercial thoroughfare, its night aspect as desolate backwater region from which the essential energy had displaced itself simply hid the fanciful, often hyperactive interior from the casual passersby. Into the Fifties, many of the artists who worked in Forty-five West Twenty-eighth Street lived on the premises. (Henry Kallem, Herbie's brother, had his own studio a block away, at Twenty-ninth Street; he was always to be the odd, third wheel of the Kallem-Mostel conveyance.) Rent at Forty-five West Twenty-eighth Street ran in the neighborhood of forty-five dollars a month, but there was a difficulty: the street was zoned exclusively for commercial use; transforming studio space into residence violated zoning regulations.

Ian Hunter recalls occasions when all his neighbors would suddenly converge on his studio, lugging with them their beds and bathtubs. It seems that city fire inspectors were about to make their periodic, unannounced search. "We would be tipped off. Everyone was at my door. My studio was considered safe because I had another address on West End Avenue and so I could always claim I wasn't living in my studio. [Did no one ever question Hunter's need for six bathtubs while he painted?] I tell you, this moving in and out, this back and forth with beds, tubs and whatnot could really screw up my morning's work. After the inspector left we would all have a sort of party, to celebrate the happy occasion. We'd come out of it unscathed once more."

The aura of the brotherhood of steadfast, down-at-the-heels artists permeated these structures. Chronic poverty worked its will, but so did the unreasoning optimism that prevails in the midst of flaking plaster and mounting bills, forever whispering that "something may turn up." Metakos, the Greek neighbor, might bring over freshly-brewed coffee, Mediterranean style. The furrier Oscar Rosen, one of the Thursday-night poker players, would annually fashion new hats for "the guys." On occasion, an artist might actually sell a work.

The painter Remo Feruggio, whose name Zero had temporarily appropriated at his initial encounter with Kate Harkin, once popped up in the uniform of a Naval officer. "Braids, cap, the works," the painter Bill McCartin recalls. "We were all floored to see Remo gussied up in this fancy stuff. Turns out he had gone on a two-week cruise to teach art and they gave him this uniform he had to wear. The boys all flipped over the uniform. None of these guys had a penny in those days. They were all hustlers; they'd knock you down to sell a painting."

Kate Mostel was ambivalent about the Twenty-eighth Street arrangement, realizing that the studio provided "an important creative outlet" during the years of the blacklist, that the unemployed Zero "didn't have to lie around the house moaning." But there was the other side of the coin. "In those early postnuptial days I felt about his leaving me for the studio the way some women feel about their husbands playing golf. But I got to accept the painting the way I got to accept Zero carrying on in restaurants. Like a friend once said, 'If I wanted someone who behaved like an accountant, I should have married an accountant.'"

Ian Hunter and Zero regularly painted together. "During painting days we worked almost religiously. We'd paint in Zero's studio on Saturdays, then we'd break for lunch, then come back to work and turn on the radio for the Metropolitan Opera broadcast. Zee would inevitably go into one of his imitations. Usually he'd be doing the diva."

Hunter recalls, "We'd begin with four or five minutes of working from the model, and Zero would get four or five figures onto his canvas. He'd use the lines of the model to get him started,

but representation wasn't the objective. He'd use the model's contours as negative or positive space. Also he'd get these enormous
canvases, already stretched and already with eighteen layers of
gesso on them. He loved using long bristle brushes. He'd hold his
brush way out and he'd start on the left side of the canvas." This
"painterly painter" liked a soft brush which he would load with
plenty of paint. "Normally we'd work for maybe twenty minutes,
then break. Sometimes it would be shorter periods. At times the
model would keep track of the time."

Zero during painting sessions: "Once he said to me, 'Don't
do anything more, just frame it.' Herbie had been behind me
and had signaled to Zero what I was doing. But mostly Zee
wouldn't comment; mostly we didn't discuss our work."

Zero loved to ferret out certain treasures in the city, to track
down suppliers who stocked particularly high-quality goods
and services. Zero referred to these treasures as "bunks," and
they ran the spectrum from food to art. Zero had a pastrami
bunk on the Lower East Side, a Jewish dairy bunk near Twenty-
eighth and Broadway, the old secondhand bookstore bunks on
Fourth Avenue, and further uptown he had a pre-Columbian-
art bunk. Ian remembers Zero taking him to Torchy's art-supply
shop on West Twenty-third Street. "Torchy was Zero's paper
bunk. I saw that Torchy had a remarkable supply of materials in
his cellar, he had marvelous quality paper. Zero could feel the
rag content, it was terrific paper, you could draw on it, you
could work with a dry brush. One of the things about Zee was
that he always loved good paper."

This penchant for knowing where the treasures are hidden,
this thirst for excellence backed by the ability to weigh the mer-
its of like substances is a joyous thing to hear about, but it also
raises the disquieting issue of the need to control through the
very categorizing of hierarchies of excellence, for the categorizing has within it the seeds of deadening or foreclosing life, of
apportioning and conversely denying merit. In its most benign
fashion, the search for excellence helps root excellence within its
own ground; at its most detrimental it creates fetishes and moves
toward an ossification of excellence.

Zero searched for a more essential treasure, one that Ian believes he never located. "He was always looking for his style, and I think he never found it. You would see him evolving. Something was happening, then a play would come along, or a film offer would pull him away—and the painting would suffer. Those worlds, of the painter and the actor, those worlds didn't mix. I always considered myself a close friend of the painter. If he had painted let's say for two years steady, *two years*, he might have come into a definitive style. But with all the performances? He just didn't have the energy."

But Zero had the energy for the psychic nourishing of a brotherhood of artists and performers. What he seemed unable to give to his own family he was able to offer to these relationships, to a brotherhood that included Herbie Kallem, Ian Hunter, Sam Jaffe, Jack Gilford, and Philip Loeb, a brotherhood that kept itself alive for several decades. And what finally did the brotherhood in was suicide, Alzheimer's, aneurysm—death in one fashion or another.

Herbie Kallem's daughter Gillis sees the Mostel-Kallem bonding as extraordinarily obsessive. "And they'd end up having lofts above each other when Zero bought that other building, at Forty-two West. My father moved over to Zero's new building, but he also kept his old studio at Forty-five across the street. Every Thursday night it was poker. Poker rain or shine. Thursday was my night to be with my father when my parents split up. I would go to his sculpting class, then across the street to the top floor where I'd fall asleep in this big chair and my father would play poker for a couple of hours."

According to Gillis, and confirmed by almost everyone who remembers him, in the presence of others, when he was not painting, the public Zero needed constant attention. "He might give all his concentration to the poker game for awhile, but then he'd go off and rant and rave."

Zero's sons were not part of the brotherhood. Ian Hunter recollects Toby Mostel as a teenager and is troubled as he recounts Zero's bull-in-a-china-shop mode of reaching out as a father. "Throughout his childhood, certainly through high school, Toby was drawing, messing around. But Zero was clumsy with his sons. He'd invite Toby up to the studio—come and draw with the old man, something like that. And the kid was seeking a basis for camaraderie. But Zee was never much good as a family man. Toby comes up once to draw at the studio. Now Zero hardly ever comments about any of our work, mine or Herbie's. But he starts in on the kid; he's being harsh, critical, and finally Toby just packs up his stuff and leaves."

If Zero never found his "style," did he have a vision of how he wanted to work as a painter? I ask Ian Hunter if Zero saw himself as part of a movement, was he drawn to social realism, to the message of the Left, as a sometime disciple of Diego Rivera? Ian is emphatic. "He despised the message. He thought the message had nothing to do with art." But he loved Picasso's *Guernica*. He had a reproduction of its several panels in his apartment.

The bunks, the brotherhood of art, the bungled strategies of fatherhood—and *Guernica*. Zero, what did you see in those panels? New strategies for collective slaughter? The ingenuity of the merchants of death? Picasso paints as witness to the sustained bombing of civilians. But Picasso is insidious. The move toward abstraction, toward a nonrepresentational depiction of agony, distances us. And this emotional distancing brings on an intensification of horror. We are quiet in the face of the recollection of a monstrous event. Evil becomes a poem of horror. We witness it in the terrible restraint of silence. Are we, moral beings in a cataclysmic world, reduced to judging excellence, and is that a moral judgment, and if so, by what power is it fashioned?

The journey and agony of Zero. Is painting a way to redeem weakness, a redemption of evil? Art as abstraction. Art permits the perception of what isn't there but is there in truth. I'll not only see you, I'll raise you. Raise you, Lazarus. Art redeems. Raised from the dead. Zero paints Yisroel, the father who mourns his loss.

The last good war ended in August of 1945. Hiroshima and Nagasaki were now fearful names and they would reverberate. But we have had Guernica, Coventry, Babi Yar, Kristalnacht, Pol Pot's Killing Fields, May Lai, Treblinka, Sarejevo, Rwanda, Haiti, the Shining Path, Sadam Hussein, to say nothing of pogroms throughout history, the genocidal attack on Armenians by the Turks early in this century . . . the list is endless.

How are death and destruction to be measured? We are left with unredeemed people; their lives diminish us.

The dead and the living. Josh Mostel, born in 1946, tells me, "My father was a child." Visiting destruction of a kind, this paternal terror is feeble when measured against today's weaponry, but terrible in its own right.

On June 1st, 1945, two months prior to V-J Day, Zero makes his second Broadway appearance. *Concert Varieties*, produced by Billy Rose at the Ziegfeld Theatre, is offered up as "an entertainment." Rose envisions a series of month-long entertainments, enlisting fresh performers for each of these diversions. The high-powered gathering of talent for the initial offering leaves the press indifferent; by and large the critics find themselves un-entertained. Zero is seen as a quaint engine, laboring at full throttle. Among his numbers: the now well-established isolationist senator who, several years after the attack on Pearl Harbor, is still musing on the presumption of Hawaii. What *was* it doing in the Pacific?

Some of the New York drama critics are puzzled as to what Zero was doing at the Ziegfeld. The *New York Times's* Lewis Nichols contends that Zero, along with Eddie Mayehoff and Imogene Coca, go on "a little too long for comfort." A less charitable, wearying view is registered by Robert Garland of the *Journal-American* who weighs in with a bit of leaden, predictable wise-guyism. "In my ignorance, Eddie Mayehoff is unedifying while Zero lives up to his name." A somewhat positive if grudging note is struck by Leo Mishkin of the *Morning Telegraph*, a much-consulted racing sheet. Mishkin would have opted for more Coca, Mostel, and Mayehoff; presumably it would have "lightened the load of culture no end." Could cultural overload have been induced by dancer Katherine Dunham, jazz drummer Sid Catlett, or boogie-woogie pianists Albert Ammons and Pete Johnson? Perhaps Mishkin was worn down by the dry elegance of emcee-raconteur Deems Taylor, a forerunner to Alistair Cooke. From the vantage point of half a century's distance, *Concert Varieties* now has the smell of late vaudeville or early television; either way it seems to have fallen between two stools. But perhaps it was wonderful in its own way.

The summer of 1945 also marks what Ivan Black claimed was Zero's "first appearance in a dramatic show." The play, *The Milky Way*, a staple of summer stock, is mounted at the Long Beach Theatre on Long Island's south shore. The title of Zero's first straight play not only directs our attention outward to constellations and stomachward to a favorite chocolate-covered confection, but also puts one in mind of that milky Tevye who would in time come to travel the long, dusty road with Zero.

By 1946 the last good war has given way to the cold war. Time-Life's Henry Luce has been in the vanguard of a conservative press stridently proclaiming America's need to rearm; Harry Truman, the pugnacious little give-'em-hell warrior, has been standing up to Uncle Joe Stalin cheek-to-jowl, for the Soviet bear, as usual, has been terrorizing its neighbors; and Winston Churchill, whose ministerial robes have been unceremoniously passed on to Labor's Clement Atlee, comes to Fulton, Missouri, and introduces the Iron Curtain metaphor, a phrase that Churchill himself first heard, according to his biographer Martin Gilbert, in a radio broadcast by the Reich's foreign minister on May 2nd, 1945. The Red Menace is having a reprieve, once again snaking its way through the country. Witch-hunts and loyalty oaths will soon become as familiar to us as Arthur Godfrey and Wheaties.

The birth of Joshua Mostel on December 21st, 1946, recalls the legendary heir who assumes the mantle of leadership from the dying Moses; armed with the Pentateuch, Joshua crosses the Jordan into the Promised Land. How is this latter-day Joshua armed, following his father's footsteps? "Use Desinex," advises his paternal elder, hardly one to allow any quip a moment's respite. Josh, as he comes to be known, ultimately takes to the stage; in his mature years he begins to rival his father pound for pound. He is the firstborn, his grandmother Anna Harkin will live side by side with him during her last years, his grandparents Yisroel and Tzina will never acknowledge his existence, much less embrace him or remember his birthdays. The firstborn, the child of joy, living among the agitated Mostels, grows himself. At this writing he seems to be making his way.

At the time of Josh's birth, Zero has been holding forth at the Embassy Club. Ivan Black announces that his client has been approached to play Goya in a Broadway musical; if true, nothing comes of it. But on December 26th, *Beggars' Holiday* opens on Broadway. Originally called *Twilight Alley*, it's a jazzed-up take-off on John Gay's 1728 musical, *The Beggars' Opera*. Pimps, prostitutes, and petty chiselers abound. Duke Ellington provides a score that's colored for back-alley sleaze. It's a starring vehicle for the popular Alfred Drake as Macheath, indomitable ladies' man and genial, archetypal pimp, but none of these savory elements ignite the fire we will see when the Brecht-Weill *Threepenny Opera* opens at the Theatre de Lys Off-Broadway a few seasons later.

Nicholas Ray is credited with direction of the book, but the *Morning Telegraph's* George Freedley tells readers that John Houseman originally mounted the work, or at least got it underway, and that then George Abbott "did a job of slicing the production down to an evening's entertainment." On the whole, Freedley has positive things to say, noting that playwright-librettist John Latouche "has written scenes which are extremely funny, especially those for Zero Mostel" who is cast as Hamilton Peachum, a conniving ward politician. Zero, it turns out, is "The joy of the evening," his clowning "inspired," a view not challenged by the *Daily News's* John Chapman who writes in backhanded fashion that "Zero Mostel is in there for laughs, and quite surprisingly gets some."

But not everyone is enchanted. Richard Watts in the *New York Post* notes that there is "a lot of praise . . . I would even include Zero Mostel, as a comic scoundrel, if he didn't work with such fatiguing effort." And Howard Barnes in the *Herald-Tribune* records that "when Zero Mostel takes over, as the chief interpreter of the so-called wit in the piece, it emphasizes the generally low level of the musical. . . . Mostel appears to be improvising in most of his scenes and the individual encounters are as dreary as the sagging libretto deserved them to be." In the *New York Times*, Brooks Atkinson, dean of Broadway drama critics, finds that "Zero Mostel's grotesque and sweaty posturing . . . is no substitute for comic skylarking." And Louis Kronenberger in *PM* (an extraordinary, innovative New York daily, it never ran advertising and it lived through most of the Forties) writes that *Beggars Holiday*, without putting [*Beggars' Opera*] to real use, has not quite disposed of it either. . . . Scoundrelly Peachum, for example, became a mere zany who Zero Mostel absolutely mauled with his intemperate practices."

Intemperate, sweaty, fatiguing? Hardly the reception Zero had been used to during his Cafe Society days, or during his youth in kitchens, Catskills, and ferryboats. But it's likely that such negative feedback struck Zero as the carping of fools and that he dismissed all of it. When did a Mostel not know better than tight-assed Philistines affecting wisdom in aisle seats?

In March of 1947 despite mixed notices, *Beggars' Holiday* adds a Sunday night performance. Zero has still been doubling at the Embassy Club but the new schedule sets up a conflict and he does his final Embassy performance the night of March 3rd. At the same time he is seeing a doctor about his throat; quite likely he is on for too many hours, night after night.

At midnight on March 29th, Zero, according to another Ivan Black press release, is scheduled to auction paintings—his own?—for the Artists League of America at Webster Hall. Black also announces that Zero is finishing a book on Daumier. Is there such a manuscript? No one I've spoken to has any knowledge of it.

Following Zero's employment in *Beggars' Holiday*, the Mostels were apparently back in California. Frances Chaney, Ring Lardner Jr.'s wife, recalls that some time in 1947 Zero and Kate were living in Los Angeles. "I'd run into them in the supermarket." But she has no remembrance of what they were doing to make ends meet. Certainly Zero was not working for any of the film studios; there was to be no movement against Louis B. Mayer's edict until Elia Kazan hires Zero for *Panic in the Streets*, a movie that was shot in 1949 on location in New Orleans. Kazan is credited with first breaking the blacklist against the Comrade who was largely chopped out of *DuBarry*, but we are getting ahead of ourselves.

In the fall of 1947, the House Committee on Un-American Activities subpoenaed a series of both "friendly" and "unfriendly" witnesses to appear before it in Washington, D.C. The witnesses were members of an industry which had seen a number of bruising battles within its several guilds and even a major strike in 1945 that involved Warner Brothers and sympathetic guild members from other studios. The battle lines between Left-Wing-Liberals and Right-Wing-Conservative forces, between cold warriors and Progressives were drawn some time before HUAC began its inquiries into what it suspected was the subversion of the Hollywood product. But the lines were fuzzy; there were additional designations and overlapping concepts: middle-of-the-roaders, parlor pinks, capitalist goons, fellow travelers, neo-Fascists, Communist dupes. And there was reality which follows no line and infers the insubstantiality of designations.

For all those who lived through the days of the HUAC inquisitions, of the ensuing blacklists, the growing power of Congressional figures like Richard Nixon and Joseph McCarthy, the naming of, damning of, and clearing of names, the loyalty

oaths, the taking of the Fifth and First Amendments, the impris-
onments, the wrecked careers, the suicides—in Hollywood, in
Washington, in New York—for all those it was a time that might
better not have been. And yet it is certainly our past. A past with
heroes and villains? One supposes heroes and villains, but to
break with judgments (the painting with broad strokes, the
drawing up of battle lines, which satisfy something in us), one
might speak of the courageous and of those who could not sum-
mon up good courage.

The probings of HUAC, initiated in the late Forties and
pushing well into the Fifties as if feeding on itself, and the
extent to which first Hollywood and then the burgeoning TV
industry caved in to the appetites of the Committee and its sympathizers, were to have a profound bearing on the course of
Zero Mostel's life. They were to mark Zero as they marked so
many others. They were to intensify traits, some of which can be
seen in a positive light—I am thinking of Zero's loyalty to beleaguered comrades—and some of which cast him in a light that
made a number of colleagues wonder just who this chap was.
Ironically, the oppressive blacklist that effectively shut the studio doors to a political spectrum that ran from the radical Left to
middle-of-the-road Liberals and even to the apolitical Center,
acted in Zero's case, though in circuitous fashion, to foster an
opportunity to create one of the most celebrated roles in theatrical history, that of Tevye in the initial Broadway production of
Fiddler on the Roof.

The House Committee's so-called friendly witnesses included
Walt Disney, Jack Warner, Robert Taylor, Adolphe Menjou, and
the mother of Ginger Rogers.[12] During the last good war Taylor
had starred in *Song of Russia,* an idealized depiction of Soviet citizens and Red Army heroes. With the benefit of hindsight Taylor
could clearly recognize Marxist propaganda and could spot
Screen Actors Guild (SAG) members "who seem to sort of dis-
rupt things once in a while. Whether or not they are Communists
I don't know." One particular actor who seemed "to sort of dis-
rupt things" at SAG meetings was "Mr. Howard Da Silva. He

always seems to have something to say at the wrong time." It's likely that the militant Da Silva had much to say, whether always at the wrong time is open to question.

Howard Da Silva was one of the administrative heads of the Actor's Lab, a professional theatre company that was considered the most prominent and energetic theatre school in Hollywood. The Lab's political sympathies were quite openly with the Left, and by the start of the Fifties the Lab was simply wiped out, a victim of the blacklist. The major studios, representing the theatre school's financial support base, had ceased to send their starlets to the Lab's acting workshops.

The dissolution of the Actor's Lab and the return to New York of blacklisted personnel, like Da Silva, Morris Carnovsky, Phoebe Brand, Mary Tarcai who ran the acting school along with her assistants Joe Papirofsky (later, as the founder of New York's Public Theater, Joe Papp) and Bernie Gersten, would eventually encourage the portrayal of liberal values in the only performance media not closed to the Left, theatre and dance. It's not possible to overstate the importance of these liberal activities, even if it seemed during the years of the inquisition that every liberal statement was hardly more than a rearguard action in the face of the flag-waving army of the Right.

Lela Rogers, mother of Ginger, had already testified how a line of dialogue from Dalton Trumbo's screenplay for *Tender Comrade* had much aggrieved her daughter. Ginger Rogers had been forced to say, "Share and share alike—that's democracy." We are to presume that the younger Rogers was able to recover from this assault on her sensibilities, but Mother Rogers, the avenging angel, was in Washington to offer further insight into the menace of Socialist doctrine.

The embattled Left and its liberal colleagues mobilized quickly against the militant fervor of the Right. Producers, directors, cinematographers, writers, editors and performers vowed that they would stand together. The reality is that in too many cases they fell apart, singly and together. Members of the newly-formed Committee for the First Amendment, which included Humphrey Bogart, Lauren Bacall, Frank Sinatra and Groucho Marx, flew to

Washington to provide moral support for the unfriendly witnesses. Nineteen unfriendlies, including Charlie Chaplin and Bertolt Brecht, were subpoenaed, but only eleven were actually called. The eleven were all writers or writer-directors.

On the witness stand ten declined to discuss presumed Communist Party–affiliation, citing First Amendment guarantees of free speech. The eleventh was Bertolt Brecht, whose only visible contribution to the Hollywood dream factory was the product of his unhappy labors on an anti-Nazi melodrama called *Hangmen Also Die*. Brecht "adopted the role of a wag"— this from Klaus Volker's *Brecht: A Biography*[13]—he "attributed any possible revolutionary statements in his songs and plays to wrong translations, and whittled himself down to being the author of 'historical plays' against Hitler." The remaining ten, to be known shortly as the Hollywood Ten, came with prepared statements, each accusing the Committee of infringing on his constitutional rights, though only Albert Maltz was allowed to deliver his statement. All ten were charged with contempt.

After his moment of disingenuous feinting before HUAC, Brecht drove back to New York with producer T. Edward Hambleton and Joseph Losey, who was directing *Galileo* for a Broadway run. It was the 30th of October, 1947. That evening, as Volker recounts it,

> Brecht laughed as he listened to parts of his interrogation on the radio at Hermann Budzislawski's. The headlines he feared never materialized. When Brecht said good-bye to Charles Laughton the following morning, the latter was evidently very relieved that it now required no particular courage to act in *Galileo* [which Laughton had translated and Losey directed at the Coronet Theatre in Beverly Hills, July of 1947]—its author had not exhibited any courage either.

On October 31st, Brecht was en route to Paris. He was finished not only with HUAC but with America, and would never return. He was not one to bare his soul to the benign or hostile probings of any government.

Among the Ten who would stay to do battle was John Howard Lawson, a founder of the Screen Writers Guild and by all accounts the Hollywood writers' Marxist theologian. Albert Maltz, another of the Ten, had endured a humiliating public struggle: one of his theoretical essays for the Marxist periodical, *The New Masses*, had advocated a less ideological approach to literature. The essay had caused dissension within Party ranks; Maltz had been called on the carpet and after an agonizing debate had recanted his modest plea. The most well-known of the Ten was Dalton Trumbo, particularly for *Johnny Got His Gun*, a novel situated in the consciousness of a World War One veteran whose combat injuries have literally left him a basket case. All in all, the unfriendly Ten and the bureaucratic witch-hunters supported by taxpayer dollars had nothing useful to exchange except diatribe.

One member of the Ten was destined to join the Mostel brotherhood in the next few years. Zero was obviously aware of Ring Lardner Jr. during, if not prior to, the hearings, and as Frances Chaney suggested to her husband when I met with them both during the summer of 1988, "Ring, don't you think that Zero had a *big* feeling about your political involvement? I think that meant a lot to him." Lardner was one of the sons and the namesake of the famous humorist, and by the mid-Thirties he had become a Hollywood writer. And by 1950 he would be in the penitentiary in Danbury, Connecticut.

A film branch of the Communist Party was organized in 1936 with the idea that film, as a mass-market entertainment, should in some manner be enlisted in the cause of Marxism-Leninism, although as Victor Navasky relates John Howard Lawson's thinking about it,[14]

> "the collective process of moviemaking precluded the screenwriter, low man on the creative totem pole, from influencing the content of movies." As the Party's national chairman, William Z. Foster, told the faithful in a secret meeting at Dalton Trumbo's house in 1946, "We can't expect to put any propaganda in the films, but we can try to keep anti-Soviet agitprop out."

Ring Lardner Jr., together with Lawson,

> did run a writer's clinic that tried to analyze scripts from the viewpoint of a Marxist aesthetic, but submission and compliance were mostly voluntary, and the project never got very far.

After Lawson's death, Lardner wrote to the *New York Times* in response to an article that saw Larson as the mentor who "used to give his colleagues tips on how to get the Party viewpoint across in his dialogue." Such "tips," Lardner noted, or any "approach to the politicization of screenwriting" would be construed by Lawson as "puerile."

HUAC's questioning of Lardner during the initial set of hearings in 1947 illustrates the combative flavor that permeated the discourse. There is a quality of insane reasonableness that is all but maddening, even some four decades after the fact.

> Chairman: All right, then, answer the question.
> Lardner: All right, sir. I think I have to consider why the question is asked.
> Chairman: *We* will determine why the question was asked! We want to know whether you are a member of the Screen Writers Guild.
>
> • • • • • •
>
> Lardner: . . . if you can make me answer this question, tomorrow, it seems to me, you could ask somebody whether he believed in spiritualism.
> Chairman: There is no chance of our asking anyone whether they believed in spiritualism, and you know it.
>
> • • • • • •
>
> Lardner: I am also concerned, as an American, with the question of whether this Committee has the right to ask me—
> Chairman: Well, we *have* got the right, and until you prove we *haven't* got the right, you have to answer that question.
>
> • • • • • •
>
> Investigator: Now, are you, or have you ever been, a member of the Communist Party?
>
> • • • • • •
>
> Lardner: I am trying to answer the question by stating, first, what I feel about the purpose of the question which, as I say, is to discredit the whole motion-picture industry.

> Chairman: You won't say anything "first." You are refusing to answer this question.
> Lardner: My understanding is, as an American resident—
> Chairman: Never mind your understanding!

HUAC, irritated by but conceivably also satisfied with the heels-dug-in position of the Ten, charged each with contempt. On November 24th, 1947, Congress voted the contempt citations. The Ten appealed; three years later the U.S. Supreme Court refused to consider the case. The convictions could not be overturned. The Ten, already victims of the blacklist, unable to find work in the film industry, now faced the looming prospect of lengthy prison terms.

Navasky writes that at the time of the Congressional citations

> fifty top Hollywood executives met for two days at the Waldorf-Astoria Hotel in New York to consider what their positions toward the Ten should be. Eric Johnston, president of the Motion Picture Association of America, who had earlier promised, "As long as I live I will never be party to anything as un-American as a blacklist," announced after the meeting that the Ten would be suspended without pay, and that thereafter no Communists or subversives would "knowingly" be employed in Hollywood. Liberal Hollywood, which had been with the Ten on arrival in the East, abandoned them as they left—partly out of shock at the confrontation with the Committee, partly in reaction to the indictment for contempt of Congress, and partly out of fear, after the Waldorf meeting, that they themselves would be tainted. The Committee for the First Amendment, which had announced a major propaganda campaign on behalf of the Ten, folded almost as fast as it had formed.

We moved without grace from the terrible last good war to that uneasy peace we named the cold war. Events were in the saddle, it was no time for comedy. But when in this bitter century was it ever a time for comedy, conversely a time not for comedy? What *was* Hawaii doing in the Pacific? Are comedies, Mozart's *Don Giovanni*, Moliere's *Misanthrope*, Chekhov's *Uncle Vanya*, a way of apprehending the surface of events? Do comedies discomfort the spectator less than *Hamlet, Woyzeck, Madame Bovary,* or *The Idiot*? Zero shamelessly rends the curtain and there is The Thinker squatting on the chamber pot; Zero blinks brightly at the unfolding comedy of HUAC, of its chariman J. Parnell Thomas, of Ring Lardner Jr., who while serving his prison term in Danbury one day greeted the former HUAC chairman himself, who had been caught taking kickbacks from staff members. In this comedy, where the cynicism of Zero Mostel is too often corroborated, people sometimes go to prison, careers are wrecked, marriages die, parents divorce children, the gas chamber and new countries flower and wither, a fiddler is seen and not seen. Comedy? Kierkegaard understood it, as did that incandescent madman Nietzsche, as did Dante and Shakespeare. As did Thursday-night poker players on West Twenty-eighth Street, and perhaps Ring Lardner Jr., in prison, understood it.

On September 29th, 1949, Kate Mostel gives birth to a second son. He is given the name of Tobias. The family, in a sense, is complete. "Child of my loins," Zero will proclaim. Some forty years later Toby is still recovering from drug-addiction and from a childhood under the roof of volatile, egocentric, raging parents.

"Those parents," it is Emily Paley's judgment, "did not understand their children." Emily nevertheless believes there was genuine love in the household but that Kate and Zero were incapable of expressing it. For all that, she is convinced that the children "came out remarkably well."

English Strunsky's view is that Kate and Zero, very simply, "were lousy parents." Emily reflects: "They were so important to themselves. But Kate was very pretty; she was charming and bright, a wonderful woman. That terrible asthma killed her." Strunsky wants it understood that "the relationship between Josh and Toby has also been strained." Brother and sister agree that, as Emily notes, "They are just now beginning to get together." "Now," Strunsky adds, "that they are six hundred miles apart they'll probably do even better."

At the time of this writing, Josh Mostel is living in Manhattan; Toby in Florida, having previously returned to Portland, Maine, after several years further up the Maine coast, in Eastport. Strunsky believes the parents were so caught up in their own concerns that there simply wasn't the psychic space needed to give parental attention to the boys. And whatever attention was forthcoming, whatever reaching out did exist was usually clumsy and layered with negative criticism. Ian Hunter has already recalled for us Zero's bungling attempts to reach out to Toby the painter.

Emily Paley remembers a painful instance of Zero responding to one of Josh's acting stints. "Zero wasn't obvious about it, but Josh certainly picked up what his father wasn't overtly saying, that Zero would have done the role differently—and better. Zero was simply more interested in himself at the moment." And in so many other moments, apparently the painter-performer needed all the space he could command; some part of him didn't want offspring muscling in on serious turf.

But her own criticism is painful to Emily Paley. "So many people say things about Zero that are destroying. So he wasn't a terrific father. I was crazy about Zero. I loved him and I think he was a remarkable man."

Frances Chaney notes that Zero's parents, Yisroel and Tzina, behaved as if their daughter-in-law and the grandchildren, Josh and Toby, simply did not exist. "They really followed the old tradition," like the archetypal Tevye. "You've also got to remember that blacklist or no blacklist, good times or bad, Zero and Kate's household was a place where there was an awful lot of *tummeling* [agitation, rowdiness] going on constantly. There wasn't any *time* to miss the old grandparents, whom the two boys had never even met. I mean, when you've got a father and mother who were as *big* as Zero and Kate . . . they were both enormous, fantastic personalities." These personalities, parenting as best they could, had now to face a time when the liberal, much less the Left, honeymoon was over.

Southern California, 1948. Blacklists, witch-hunts, widening polarization. There is a presidential campaign in progress; aspirants include the current office-holder Harry Truman, the Republicans' Thomas Dewey, the Progressive Party's Henry Wallace, and Strom Thurmond who represents the breakaway right wing of the Democratic Party, known in '48 as the Dixiecrats. The Hollywood Ten are awaiting a higher court ruling on their appeals; the cold war deepens week by week; there is a blight across the political landscape that runs from Washington to Moscow.

But the days were not wholly grey. Just as comedy also embraces darkness, one's dark vision encounters its own luminosity. We were certainly living through ugly times, bleak, absurd, foul, corrupt—and for all that, joyful. Even in the worst of times we come upon a silent laughter.

The embattled Left had its sanctuaries, its support groups, and for theatre people in Hollywood the Actor's Lab provided a home within which the issues of justice and the corruptive bent of capitalism were given voice. I was an interested observer and a writer working in the Lab's little known playwriting workshop. Its view of justice hardly embraced the anti-Communist struggle, a decade after the Moscow purge trials and the disappearance of millions into Stalin's Gulag, nor to the best of my knowledge, did it show the least concern for the attempt to create a Jewish state in Palestine. But many of its original dramas did address the struggles of the working class, and it did highlight the battles of minorites fighting to make it in the economic jungles of urban America. Arnold Manoff's *All You Need Is One Good Break* typified the Lab's judgment of the capitalist art of hustling, its hero convinced of his capacity to manipulate the system of laissez-faire. The Lab is important in our story because it provides a direct line that goes back to the Group Theatre and culminates with the Actor's Studio, and because its demise ultimately sets the stage for the birth of Zero Mostel's Tevye.

The Lab was fed by Group Theatre veterans: not only the aforementioned Da Silva, Carnovsky, and Brand, but by Walter Coy, J. Edward Bromberg, Curt and Bert Conway, Roman Bohnen, and Will Lee. Frances Chaney, Pamela Coy, and Ellie Pine became part of the Lab; young writers like Les Pine and Oliver Crawford were among its prominent playwrights.

Roman "Bud" Bohnen never made it past the blacklist. Arthur Miller had considered the veteran performer for Willy Loman in the Broadway premiere of *Death of a Salesman*, but Bohnen is best remembered for another death. One night during the 1948–49 season, Bohnen himself died while onstage. For Bud Bohnen it was a literal death; for the Actor's Lab it was a disquieting symbol. In the next few years the Lab itself would be "put away," a casualty of the country's insatiable hunt for Reds. During its comparatively short life the Actor's Lab was a thriving force: it was combative, narrow-minded as befits an ideological approach to art; it saw itself as heir to the thinking of

Stanislavsky and of the Group Theatre; and it had the kind of largeness of soul, reinforced by its ideology, that sought to make itself color-blind by casting blacks not according to skin pigment but theatrical prowess.

HUAC, in consort with the Hollywood studios, which included the worst- and best-intentioned of people, most of whom eventually made deals in order to save their careers, was out to expose anyone who was not right of center. Many Leftist writers were able to keep working—under assumed names, or hidden by their "fronts," and paid but a small fraction of their earlier wages. Some went to prison, like the Hollywood Ten; some to England where they could work under their own names, like Lardner after his release from Danbury, like Joseph Losey, like Sig Miller who had discovered Zero at a bar mitzvah; some to Greece like Jules Dassin; and many came to New York where before long they ran into a thriving new blacklist as television came of age.

Performers of the Left, unlike writers, had no recourse to fronts; no one could front for Zero Mostel's face, or for Lionel Stander's expansive nose and gravelly voice. Hundreds of performers came east to find work, as writers and directors were also doing. but television, the new game in town, would prove to be a momentary sanctuary; it would not be able to hold out against the pressures of the witch hunt. What would be left? The theatre? Europe? Driving a cab? A suicide note?

Here is Conrad Bromberg, J. Edward's son, recalling to Victor Navasky what the early years of the blacklist felt like to an adolescent: [15]

> For the first three years of it, all I got were snatches in Beverly Hills at the dinner table. He'd report conversations with his agent. "He thinks I'm in trouble with Metro." This was the period of the graylist. There was no great discussion at home that the children were privy to. There were meetings, but I think the decision was made to protect the children. We didn't even know the testimony was happening until it broke on the front page. They may have wanted to protect my nine-year-old brother or they may have wanted to get it over and done with and not bother anybody. We were very middle-class children. We were

all very sun-tanned, going to the beach every day, kind of living out the Hollywood dream, and I don't think they wanted to explode it. By 1949 my father hadn't worked in a year, and it had become palpably clear that he wasn't wanted. After that we came back to New York and then it was out on the table. There was an FBI car parked outside every morning and he was ducking subpoenas. It became like the reign of terror with everybody naming everybody.

A haunting image that Conrad Bromberg recalls:

All I can remember is his sitting, waiting for a phone call, with the FBI guys mysteriously appearing or waiting across the street.

Toby Mostel remembers how his parents, hardly concerned about protecting him in the face of their own political problems, hid in their apartment and sent him, a child, to the front door when the FBI came calling. But in the late Forties Zero had not yet been touched by the witch hunt.

Work, however, was scarce. Until 1949, with the filming of *Panic in the Streets*, Zero had an occasional Broadway role, and in '49 he performed in a TV special on the DuMont Network in New York. The Mostels shuttled between New York and Hollywood, Zero worked at whatever was available to him, and sometimes during those grim days he recieved word that his beloved father, Yisroel Mostel, had, as we like to say, passed on to the next and hopefully better world. And Zero's grief had to be one of silence; in his mother's house, where the family again sat *shivah*, he was not welcome.

By the early Fifties New York City was crowded with the displaced from Hollywood. Actors did what they could during those early years of Uncle Miltie and Caesar and Coca and Steve Allen and Jackie Gleason and Arthur Godfrey and Lucy and Desi and Ozzie and Harriet. Then in 1953, a handful of the blacklisted from the Actor's Lab joined forces with others of the Left to produce a labor of love Off-Broadway. They called it *The World of Sholom Aleichem*, and it was blatantly a love song to Yiddish culture, to Yiddish writers, to the Yiddish theatre, to the vanished world of the East European Jew. They saw this production also as theatre of protest; the issues were familiar ones: the downtrodden, the humiliated, all those crying for a moment in the sun. *The World of Sholom Aleichem* was to prove a landmark event in the history of the American theatre. And was to lead eventually to our milky friend Tevye, and to his new, grubby companion, Zero Mostel.

ig Miller: "One of Zero's nightclub acts was to ask if anybody in the audience had a handkerchief. So this guy gives Zero his handkerchief. Zero takes a match and sets fire to the handkerchief and watches it burn. Then he hands the remains back and he says to the guy, 'Sorry, it didn't work.'"

Abner Symonds, former *Village Voice* photographer: "I met him once at a party. I had on this tie that I liked a lot; it was reasonably expensive this tie, and Zero comes over and cuts it in half. Like that."

Media developer Dunya Cilliers: "My father and mother knew Zero and told how during the 1960 presidential campaign Zero is out in the street in front of a Broadway theatre and suddenly he seems to go into an epileptic fit. He's down on the ground, thrashing around, foaming, moaning, and then an instant later he jumps to his feet and announces to anyone who will listen, and by this time a nice crowd has gathered: 'Vote for Nixon!'"

Kate Mostel: "On one occasion he boarded a [subway] train with a cane, pretending to be blind. But crazy blind. He walked down the aisle, his arms groping, idly slapping people in the face, and made his way to his target—a section where an old lady was standing while an able-bodied man sat comfortably. Finally, because he was so ostentatiously handicapped, the man gave up his seat to Zero, who made a big production of reading the *Times* with his fingers as if it were in Braille. Then, at the perfect moment, Zero got up and, with a cavalier bow, gave the old lady his seat. At the next stop he grandly got off the train."

June Gitlin, administrator with *The World of Sholom Aleichem*: "In the Forties he was trying to lose weight. Dr. Langrock was in obstetrics at New York Hospital. Zero would turn up in Langrock's waiting room among the other patients, all of them women, and he would lie down on the floor. He had the women in hysterics."

Actor Lou Peterson: "He was the kind of a man who would see you across the street and he would yell, 'Lou, baby!' and he'd run across the street and unbutton your fly—which would embarrass me no end."

Actor Gerald Hiken: "My wife and I are sitting in the garden at the Museum of Modern Art. Zero's nearby and he's being pestered for his autograph, so he comes to sit with us. We make the mistake of telling him that one of my wife's relatives is one of the wheels at MOMA but that we never hear from him. At that moment the relative appears; he's crossing into the garden. Zero? You can guess. He shouts across the width of the garden at this guy, 'Asshole, how come you never call your family?'"

Sig Miller: "We're walking on Fifth Avenue and Zero's hat blows off in the wind. Behind him, in the direction the hat is taking, I see several Helen Hokinson-type matrons. [Portly, proper matrons, made famous in Hokinson's *New Yorker* cartoons.] It's a new hat he'd just bought. He turns around and says to these ladies, 'Why do you hate me? Because I'm Jewish? You have no right to hate people because they're Jewish. I'm a perfectly nice guy.' I mean he's berating these poor women for four or five blocks."

"Were they terribly embarrassed?"

"They were laughing in an embarrassed way, but they were laughing."

"Anything would set him off."

"Anything. Meanwhile the hat disappears completely."

But the Mostel flamboyance won't disappear; the declamatory, opinionated, sensitive, ogling, prideful, righteous, God-fearing pain-in-the-ass never tires, is never at wit's end, is always prepared to bounce back, to make his statement.

But he has to scramble for work. Money and politics weigh heavily. It's as if we're back to the days of Clara and her mother, the days of Abraham and Strauss. Zero gives of himself—if not to his wife and sons, then certainly to public causes—tirelessly. He performs at various benefits: for the Police Athletic League, the National Foundation for Infantile Paralysis, the Israel Orphan Asylum. Jared Brown in his biography, *Zero Mostel*,[16] notes that Zero performed at Progressive Party rallies for Henry Wallace in 1948; a favorite song of that period speaks to the witch hunts: "Who's Going to Investigate the Man Who Investigates the Man Who Investigates Me?" Brown has the impression that, at some point in the campaign, Wallace actually considered the possibility of capturing the presidency. The scene that Brown paints is of a relaxed Henry Wallace indulging in a woolgathering session with Zero, Paul Robeson, and others close to the campaign.

As one who was energetically working for Wallace's election—I was a political organizer for the Progressive Party in Southern California—I remember that all of us running that campaign out of Los Angeles hoped beyond hope that Wallace would win the election, but we believed that Thomas Dewey would probably take the White House. The defeat of the Democratic Party hardly deterred us. We were trying to gather a strong protest vote against both major parties and simultaneously working to build a strong third party.

Wallace's question, directed to Robeson, Mostel, and whoever else was sitting around the room, as to what jobs they would like in the Wallace White House, seems sheer fantasy in retrospect, and yet I can understand the kind of ambiance that would generate such a question. Robeson's response, that he would like to be ambassador to Moscow, makes a lot of sense, but Zero's response, that he would like nothing but "a part in a play," seems peculiarly meager and modest. With Zero's imagination, one would have hoped that he might at least have sought to take over the directorship of the F.B.I., with Groucho or Harpo as first lieutenants.

The witch hunts were not kind; Louis B. Mayer still sat in Metro's catbird seat. Beyond Mayer there had come into being the ferreting moles of righteousness, the self-appointed guardians of the patriotic path. Zero had not yet been fingered directly, but he was uneasy. And the finger-pointers were proliferating. Some were political gossip columnists like Walter Winchell, Jack Lait, Lee Mortimer, George Sokolsky, Westbrook Pegler, Jack O'Brian, and Dorothy Kilgallen, and labor columnist Victor Reisel, who was later to be horribly maimed, blinded by acid through the courtesy of some vengeful element he had been castigating. Some were scandal sheets like *Confidential* magazine; some were institutional publications produced by organizations like the Catholic War Veterans, the American Legion and the Motion Picture Alliance for the Preservation of American Ideals; and some were newly-founded publishing houses like Aware, Inc. and American Business Consultants, the brainchild of several former FBI agents, cranking out *Counterattack*, a four-page weekly begun in May, 1947 and the book-length *Red Channels: The Report of Communist Influence in Radio and Television*. These publications cast a wide net: any connection with people, institutions, or events remotely touching on the Left at any time was sufficient reason to find oneself branded as a subversive. Jared Brown tells of one man whose name appeared on the list of those who ought not to be hired because he had presumably fought with the Loyalists in Spain. The man's claim that at the time of the Spanish Civil War he was barely old enough to walk, much less engage in battle against Franco, was not enough to free him from suspicion.

The *Red Channels* body count began in 1950: the first casualty was actress Jean Muir who had been performing as Henry

Aldrich's mother in *The Aldrich Family*. NBC Television dropped Muir because she belonged to organizations like the Southern Conference for Human Welfare, an institution whose members included Eleanor Roosevelt and Senator Estes Kefauver (the latter would be Adlai Stevenson's running mate in 1956). The roaming finger of *Red Channels* also lighted on Zero Mostel, and it lighted on his colleague Sam Jaffe as well. As time went on, the vigilante publications ironically took on an additional function: they began to be used to remove people from the blacklist, provided the one named would render important service, e.g. the naming of others.

By the early Fifties, Sam Jaffe was in despair; he could no longer find work. What brought a measure of relief was Jaffe's encounter with Thornton Wilder. The playwright suggested that Jaffe look into the Brattle Theatre in Cambridge, Massachusetts. If the Brattle offered nominal wages, it also provided a base for what was deemed to be serious work. In due time Jaffe was performing the title role in Molière's *Tartuffe*, a part he would repeat several years later at New York's 92nd Street Y. Jaffe's work also paved the way for Zero, who was cast in Molière's *Imaginary Invalid*. We're told that Zero liked the idea of working with an ensemble, and he had an abiding love for Molière that went back to his undergraduate days at City College. How did the Brattle ensemble take to the ebullient improviser? Producers Jerome Kilty and Albert Marre thought well enough of Zero to cast him in a second Molière comedy, *The Doctor in Spite of Himself*. Brian Halliday who performed in *Invalid* recalls opening night. Zero stopped in the middle of a scene, announced to the audience, "Now I'm going to do my impersonation of a whale," picked up a carafe of water, filled his mouth with water, spouted, then resumed the scene.

Several of Zero's friends also brought their special gifts to the Brattle. The word had gone out that Zero was depressed. David Burns, Jack Gilford, and three other Mostel fans bought front-row-center tickets for one of Zero's performances. The five sat with newspapers in front of their faces. At a certain point in the play the first of Zero's buddies lowered his paper, revealing his face to Zero. The face now had a beard. The paper was raised again, the second newspaper was lowered, and the beard had magically transported itself to the second face. In time the same beard skipped along from one face to the next.

One odd note concerning *The Imaginary Invalid*: Kate Mostel was also in that production and she received *two* salaries, the second as director. The dual compensation actually disguised the bulk of Zero's payment, the sleight-of-hand bookkeeping providing a method by which the combined Mostel wages could be hidden from Clara at a time when she and Zero were still at loggerheads over alimony.

Again we are examining difficult, turbulent, depressing moments in both a personal history and in the culture of the United States. But as always, these moments are broken by instances of brightness, of humor, even of a silliness, largely superficial, that loses its weight before the gloomy light of day.

There is Zero's confrontation with the new medium of television. Before *Red Channels* named him, Zero was able to perform on an occasional program, such as the special presented on the DuMont Network (WABD, Channel 5 in New York) in November of 1948, the very month in which Harry Truman turned back the combined efforts of Henry Wallace, Strom Thurmond, and the heavy favorite, the Republican Thomas E. Dewey to unseat him.

That November, TV was in its infancy; most programs which happened not to be old movies, cartoons, or syndicated films were performed "live," and the DuMont Network was an innovative force. Probably DuMont's most significant contribution was the support it gave to an experimental comic named Ernie Kovacs. Zero, in his own way, was potentially as inventive as Kovacs; Zero had the energy but there is little evidence that he had the will, the sustained interest, the sense of engagement. It may be that performing came too easily.

Everyone who saw him acknowledges Zero as a revolutionary force in Barney Josephson's Cafe Society, but unlike Keaton's or Chaplin's devotion to film, or Kovacs's to television, nothing suggests that Zero particularly respected any of these media or sought to develop their potential. Ultimately, and we've heard this before, Zero performed as he might have done at home or on the street. Nightclubs, TV, film, theatre, radio—all performance disciplines became vehicles for taking center stage. It's true that Zero often elected to share this center with social concerns, but whereas men like Kovacs and Keaton sought to comprehend and stretch the aesthetic potential of TV and film, Zero's response to performance media resembled that of an ill-clothed man rushing into a new overcoat. The medium became a kind of haphazard garment.

Zero's DuMont Special was called *Off the Record;* in one sequence comic Joey Faye and Metropolitan Opera star Mimi Benzell were embroiled in a parody on *Carmen,* that takes us back twelve years to that night in South Fallsburg at the Hotel Balfour. Two months later, in January of 1949, Zero appeared as the lunatic Banjo in a CBS production of the Kaufman and Hart comedy, *The Man Who Came to Dinner,* with Edward Everett Horton starring in the role of Sheridan Whiteside, the acerbic drama critic modeled after Alexander Woollcott. Banjo, a takeoff on Harpo Marx, was created by David Burns on Broadway and performed by Jimmy Durante in the Warner Bros. film adaptation. It's a role that seems tailored for Zero's amiable hysteria. Banjo's first entrance introduces us to an overheated thespian in the throes of a condition not unlike St. Vitus's dance. Banjo is carrying in his arms a thrashing, shrieking, sexually unprepossessing nurse, aptly named Miss Prim, whom he is deliriously kissing and to whom he is operatically proclaiming, "I love you madly. Don't be afraid of my passion. I can feel the hot blood pounding through your varicose veins." What in fact did Zero make of Banjo? Perhaps in some long-forgotten vault in some CBS storeroom sits a kinescope of the production. As for viewers, there were comparatively few in 1948 and '49 and most were obsessed with Uncle Miltie (Milton Berle). Hollywood was still the major game in town, and in the person of Ella Kazan would soon be calling Zero to New Orleans. The effect of *Red Channels* was still to be felt.

We sophisticated Westerners sometimes proclaim that we've grown past the need for heroes, even as we admonish those idols who disappoint. Joc Montana? Mother Teresa? Martin Luther King? The Dalai Lama? We can't grow past this need for heroes and role models. We're nourished by rumors of saints, prophets and visionaries, by people who rise from troubling conditions to effect some act of purity or generosity, some extraordinary physical feat, or some act of grace or genius.

When Zero is asked to work for Elia Kazan, it's not simply that the call has come after a seven-year drought, it's that the best and the brightest has sought him out. "What a director!" he will say of Kazan as actors and crew go to work on the streets of New Orleans and in Maritime Union headquarters where some interiors for *Panic in the Streets* are shot. The actors are nervous on the premises of the Maritime Union; Zero feels it's "full of tough characters," there's going to be trouble, somebody's going to get slugged. "Then Gadge [Kazan] comes in, starts ordering them around with curses. They think he is wonderful and do everything he says."

This Gadge, or Gadget, nickname for the nervy kid who worked in the Group Theatre with Luther and Stella Adler, with Jules Garfield, Morris Carnovsky, Frances Farmer, Bobby Lewis, Franchot Tone, J. Edward Bromberg, Philip Loeb, Sanford Meisner, Ruth Nelson, Phoebe Brand, with directors Harold Clurman, Cheryl Crawford, and Lee Strasberg, this Greek merchant's son, born in Turkey, who won't make serious inroads as an actor but helps put Clifford Odets and the Group on the map with his electrifying cry of "Strike!" at the conclusion of *Waiting for Lefty!*, this buddy of Odets, of Arthur Miller, of Tennessee Williams, this audacious director of Miller's *All My Sons* and *Death of a Salesman*, of Williams's *A Streetcar Named Desire*, this up-and-coming film director who has already made *A Tree Grows in Brooklyn*, *Gentlemen's Agreement* and the documentary-style *Boomerang*, this mercurial imp who in years to come will direct films like *Viva Zapata!*, *Baby Doll*, *East of Eden*, *On the Waterfront*, *The Last Tycoon*, as well as the film version of *Streetcar*, has tapped the blacklisted clown, Zero Mostel, to play a menacing, bumbling sidekick to a pathological gangster (performed by Walter, later Jack, Palance).

Not only does the occasion prove an emotional balm and of aesthetic import to Zero, for he's privileged to watch the uncompromising Gadge ply his art as if from the interior of the raw world of moviemaking, it also opens the gates to other film projects and to a steady income. The five other films Zero will appear in during 1950 and '51, for Warners, Columbia and Twentieth Century-Fox, are largely mass-market contrivances— two are minor disasters merchandised for Humphrey Bogart loyalists—but they help generate a multiyear contract with Fox, and offer Zero a second chance to reach for the illusory brass ring of stardom.

Zero is hardly a leading player in *Panic in the Streets*, and despite the drive he exhibits on screen, his portrayal of an anxious, minor hood is curiously subdued. Curiously because it suggests that he isn't comfortable in the role; he appears worried. Past the fact that the character of Fitch *is* worried, the actor portraying him is confronting his own anxieties. It appears that

Zero is wrestling with a discipline called acting, and in the course of this struggle he seems very self-conscious, so much so that the effort frames and molds the character.

For Kazan, *Panic* affords an opportunity to experiment with the rough-hewn texture of documentary he had applied to the earlier *Boomerang* where exteriors were shot in the streets of Stamford, Connecticut, and interiors in the county courthouse in White Plains, New York. Location shooting starts to come into its own at this time. For *Panic*, Kazan wanted actors "who looked like people . . . New Orleans would be my true star, that wonderful city where you can smell the river, the coffee, and the Creole cooking everywhere you go." All of this is wonderfully reminiscent of the *neo-realismo* films of Rossellini and DeSica in Italy during the last good war, but Kazan is good enough to remind us in his autobiography, *A Life*,[17] that the early comic two-reelers shot their outdoor scenes on location.

In his study *Kazan on Kazan*,[18] the film critic Michel Ciment records the director's thoughts.

> It is the first time I threw the script over. We had a property truck with a typewriter on the . . . tailgate. Every morning the writer [Richard Murphy, who also wrote *Boomerang*] came with me. . . . We [rewrote and] shot on the whorehouse streets, in the low bars, in the wharfs. . . . Nobody at the studio [Zanuck, Twentieth-Century Fox] checked our work. They did not know where I was going next. We shot all over the city and I had the crew and the cast crazy. Some of them complained I'd suddenly go on a boat or a train. . . . I picked up people in the street . . . I sort of felt liberated on that picture.

Did Zero feel liberated? Kazan doesn't seem to have helped dissipate the self-consciousness that fledgling actors often experience, but for sheer, end-run body mass, Zero, as Gadge saw him, was nothing short of heroic. "He was terrific," Kazan remembers. "He was comfortable with his body. He'd do *anything* physical you asked him to. I worked with Jack Palance and a handful of other rugged-looking guys, but Zee with his supposed flabbiness had a way of being at home with his body that was extraordinary."

What gets *Panic* moving is the bullet-ridden corpse of an illegal immigrant that the authorities fish out of the harbor. As *Life* magazine, citing *Panic* as its Movie of the Week, in its August 21st, 1950 issue, revealed to its readers:

> the dead man carried . . . pneumonic plague, the Black Death of the Middle Ages. The police must track down anybody who had contact with the dead man—his cronies and murderers—in order to inoculate them. They must work swiftly and secretly lest criminals get panicky, run out of town and spread plague through the country.

Kazan cast Richard Widmark as the young, courageous public health officer, his life on the line in the attempt to short-circuit the plague. Barbara Bel Geddes is the supportive wife, all daylight, health and clean-curtains wisdom. When Widmark isn't taking brief respites at home with Bel Geddes, he's out in dark, unhealthy neighborhoods tracking down the likes of Walter Palance and a sinister Zero Mostel. Zero seems to be running scared throughout the streets of New Orleans. He reports to Anna Mason in the *New York Times* of August 6th that "Every night I take a hot bath in ten pounds of Epsom salts. One day I run a hundred yards seventeen times before they got that scene right." Mason notes that Zero "ruefully surveyed his plump bulk. 'Before the picture is over my legs are taped. Three times I go to different doctors to make sure I do not have a bad heart.'"

The press is generally kind to *Panic in the Streets* (title courtesy of Twentieth Century's sales department). Hollis Alpert in the *Saturday Review of Literature*, September 2nd, is pleased with the manner in which "Walter Palance . . . as the murderer [projects] the craft and stupidity that add up to his particular quality of evilness, and Zero Mostel completely reverses his comic field as the weak pal." During the 1971 Kazan retrospective at MOMA, film curator Charles Silver writes that although "Kazan is not able to sustain the necessary tension that Hitchcock or genre masters like Don Siegel and Phil Karlson might have brought to this good basic material [nevertheless the film is] sufficiently rich in acutely-observed detail to make a genuine resurgence in Kazan's career" and that "The image of Zero Mostel

transformed into an overstuffed coffee sack is perceptive . . ."
Zero is always noticed, albeit not always with favor. He seems
ill-at-ease—would we could observe what L.B. Mayer saw in
those early screen tests—but even *Panic* suggests an undercurrent of daring; one senses that Zero will try anything, that if he
isn't in the role, he's consciously adjacent to it, connected to an
idea that we can neither readily identify nor discount.

With his work on *Panic* completed, Kazan learned from
Tennessee Williams that the plan to film *A Streetcar Named Desire*
was going forward. Knowing that Williams badly wanted him
to direct the movie, Kazan's initial reaction was one of distress:
what was he to bring to the film that he hadn't already brought
to the play? But after some hesitation, Kazan was not only filming *Streetcar*, he was also back in New Orleans, building on
what he had gleaned from *Panic* and its sense of *cinémá vérité*.
Zero meanwhile had gotten a fistful of work in Hollywood,
albeit none of it approaching the inspired levels of either Kazan
project. Might there have been a role for Zero in *Streetcar*? He
was surely a veteran of poker nights.

Of the five movies Zero performed in during the next
months, four had their New York openings between January and
August of 1951, and three opened within a month of each other,
in July and August. During this period, Zero signs a seven-year
contract with Fox; he is on loan to Columbia for their film version of Samuel Taylor's Broadway play, *The Happy Time*, but on
the first morning that Zero reports to Columbia the guard at the
gate, as if in a parable by Kafka, turns him away—with no explanation. Back at home, Zero waits for the phone to ring. It never
rings. No one at Columbia, or at Fox, or at any Hollywood studio
bothers to call him. Finally he reads in *Variety* that someone else
will be playing his role in *The Happy Time*. And then he learns
that Fox has torn up his contract. Obviously not a happy time,
and never an explanation. "I hated Hollywood," he will exclaim
later, ". . . the people, the climate, the business. Everything. My
wife hated it. The kids hated it." But if the films were nothing to
write home about, the money was good, as long as there was any
of it around.

The first of the five features to be released during that unhappy time of good money and lackluster scripts is a Bogart vehicle called *The Enforcer*, earlier known as *Murder, Inc.* and later, by the time it opens at London's Palladium, again known as *Murder, Inc.* No title can save it. The running time, when Warners releases the film at New York's Capitol on January 25th, 1951, is mercifully brief, eighty-seven minutes, giving way to Lionel Hampton's band onstage. The screen image of Senator Estes Kefauver, best known for his committee's investigation into crime syndicates and mobster Frank Costello, opens the film. "What follows," Kefauver instructs the audience, "is no social document, but a gory round of killings by ice pick, razor, butcher knife, and pistol." Into this venue of time-honored, blue-collar slaughter we find Bogart as a battling district attorney intent on bringing urban thugs to justice.

Location shooting is now sweeping Hollywood and many of the exteriors are filmed in the streets of Los Angeles, though the narrative wants to suggest the criminal life of Brooklyn's Murder, Inc. Zero, fresh from gang warfare in New Orleans, is cast as "Big Babe" Hazich, a glowering, downcast, shifty-eyed hulk strongly suspected of packing in recalcitrant citizens courtesy of ice pick. The *New York Times* film critic Bosley Crowther writes on January 26th that the menu of razors, butcher knives, and other death-inducing favorites is sending various audience members into the merciful land of Nod. He reports picking up derisive noises around him. Derisive? Could Zero, Herbie Kallem, and others of the Thursday-night brotherhood have been slouching in the orchestra? Crowther further informs us that plump, punky Zero is pushing to become part of the homicide crowd. Bretaigne Windust is given directorial credit, but apparently it also took the efforts of Raoul Walsh, another veteran of the Hollywood wars, to cook up this feature.[19]

On July 13th the Capitol is back with yet another Bogart vehicle. *Sirocco*, a Columbia release, also reunites Zero and Everett Sloane, both of whom slogged through *The Enforcer*. (Sloane is best remembered as the loyal, see-no-evil Mr. Bernstein, who oversees Orson Welles's press empire in *Citizen*

Kane.) Sirocco is set in Damascus, circa 1925. There is fighting between Syrian and French colonial forces, and Bogart plays a gun-runner who tangles with Lee J. Cobb as a Col. Feroud, while sinister black marketeers, Muslim fundamentalists, informers and generally ominous characters suggesting the underside of what we then called the "Third World" lurk about through several reels. Zero's career is taking a curious turn; in this malformed descendant of *Casablanca* he is seen once again as unredeemed thug, specifically an Arab merchant named Balukjian who manages to betray Bogart during the film's ninety-seven minutes. No ice pick is discernible. Onstage at the Capitol Theatre: the wonderful Ethel Waters, with Teddy Powell's orchestra. "There's a little cabin in the sky, baby . . ."

A third dreary feature is *The Guy Who Came Back*, also titled *The Guy Who Sank the Navy*, also *Humpty Dumpty, Just One More Chase, The Man Who Sank the Navy* and *The Man Who Came Back*. Paul Douglas, who played a tough police officer in *Panic in the Streets* and the original big-time operator, Harry Brock, in the Broadway production of *Born Yesterday*, is seen here as Harry Joplin, a former All-American fullback who has taken to the bottle. Zero plays Boots Mullin, a café owner who commiserates with Douglas from the service side of the bar. Like many alcoholics, Harry Joplin has seen his marriage dissolve; he's remorseful, pining for wife and kids and seeking a lift. The wife is Joan Bennett and the lift is Linda Darnell, a compensation thoughtfully provided by Fox studios to dispel a bit of the ninety-two minutes of gloom.

Also in July of 1951, Fox opens a Clifton Webb vehicle, *Mr. Belvedere Rings the Bell*. Zero is reprieved from swarthy, menacing antisocial types, but remains the second banana, a supporting character. In socioeconomic terms, Zero is still kicking around in the service level of society, alert either to the needs of gunrunners, assassins and alcoholics, or as in *Belvedere*, to a literate, caustic celebrity out slumming among the downtrodden—in this case elderly people lodged in a disheartening storage unit for "senior citizens." As Belvedere's sidekick, Zero is a sweet-faced gofer, but his work is still curiously subdued. At the

Roxy the film runs eighty-eight minutes and shares billing with "The Famous Ice Show" starring Carol Lynne and a "Gala Variety Revue" starring Florian Zabach.

The final Mostel release in the Fifties is a sweet, at times affecting movie which, after two earlier titles, *Kitty and the Marriage Broker* and *The Marriage Broker*, comes to be known as *The Model and the Marriage Broker*. It's Columbia's attempt to cash in on the genial I-see-the-world-for-what-it-is personality of Thelma Ritter and the girl-next-doorness of an attractive ingenue named Jeanne Crain. Ritter plays Mae Swazey, a hard-bitten marriage broker who, like so many of the tough-exterior sisterhood, is a soft touch for a bird with a broken wing. Crain, a pretty if somewhat insubstantial presence, is the wounded bird. Kazan directed Crain in *Pinky* and later noted "her inability to express much of anything." In *Model*, Crain affects the part of a stunning fashion model unhappily locked into the role of mistress to a man for whom she is nothing but a delicious after-dinner snack. Ritter, believing that homewrecking isn't for nice girls, decides to broker a love affair for Crain. Zero, Ritter's goodhearted optometrist neighbor, Mr. Wixted, is congenitally into bachelorhood, a condition Ritter deems to be marginal and an affront to social cohesion.

Here, Zero is sidling up neither to ice picks nor wedding bells; at best he provides a little sympathy as the movie reels pleasantly along. Crain's vacuous good looks, perfectly acceptable in the Rodgers and Hammerstein movie *State Fair*, here comes up against traditional old-world skepticism. Since the Ritter and Mostel roles are abundantly charged with "character," Crain's delicate country-meadow features are, in contrast, reduced to something close to absence of character. And since the film's principal worry is Crain and since there is almost no character to root worry in, we are left with a peculiar but hardly unusual problem in aesthetic balance. *Model* offers crumbs of humor, principally through Ritter's verbal byplay, with an occasional assist from Zero who assures a customer that "when a lady can wear glasses as well as [this lady] can, it is a pity that she does not wear them all the time . . ." Spoken like a true optometrist.

During the shooting of *Belvedere*, Harry Brandt's press office at Fox issued a release telling members of the industry that Zero is "set with a long-term contract," that "the entire Mostel family has settled in Hollywood," and that Zero was "in filmtown to stay for two reasons—the money, and because he was tired of nightclub tours away from his family." But that was before *The Happy Time* and the gatekeeper.

15

Out to sea, in more ways than one. Kazan holds out a life-
line; Zero is pulled toward the insubstantiality of the dream factory, then Fox and Columbia set him adrift once more. But Zero
could always swim.

Monhegan Island is ten miles off the coast of southern
Maine; Captain John Smith used it as a base from which to
explore Penobscot Bay in 1614. Zero settled in for the final three
decades of his life, for vacationing, painting, for a second home.
Monhegan becomes a sanctuary of sorts, but the interior life
can't be left in Manhattan.

How is rent to be paid, on either island? Kate has been
studying acting, she finds an occasional Broadway role, now
and then she is cast in a road company production; and Zero
takes whatever work is available, in nightclubs, in a play, sometimes along the borscht belt in the Catskills. The borscht belt is
still alive in the Fifties.

Frances Kornbluth, painter and veteran Monheganite of
many summers, recalls the Mostels in the Fifties "Kate was
working all those years Zero was blacklisted. He'd come up to

Monhegan with the kids and Kate would be on the road. Kate supported the family. They used to rent the Jay Connoway house and Zero would come up with a maid and the two little kids."

In 1953 Kate is on tour with the old domestic farce, *Three Men on a Horse*, supporting Wally Cox (of *Mr. Peepers* fame) and Walter Matthau. In 1954 Kate is on Broadway in the Dorothy Parker-Arnaud d'Assau comedy, *Ladies of the Corridor*. Zero is also on Broadway in 1954 with the short-lived *A Stone for Danny Fisher*.

Zero treated the idea that actors needed training with a contempt that was barely civil. He was bemused by the notion that performance called upon the development of something commonly known as "technique." After all, Raimu, the brilliant French film star Zero idolized, had absolutely no training. And there is something to be said for the natural, intuitive performer. And yet Zero did spend three years with an acting teacher. Kate had discovered Don Richardson; she took lessons with him and connived to bring Zero into Richardon's studio. Jared Brown relates the initial Mostel-Richardson encounter.[20]

The sight greeting Richardson? An individual of excessive weight enters his studio with "bangs, a torn umbrella and a torn raincoat." Kate introduces the two men and heads for the exit, instructing her husband not to "give [Don] any shit." Richardson proceeds to point out the stage; he then suggests that Zero "do something" on it. Zero has a counter suggestion; he reaches into the famed Mostel hostility zone—it's never a far reach—and announces that since Richardson is presumably the expert, the teacher should mount the stage and "do something." One imagines there is a stalemate at this juncture, but eventually Zero, seduced as usual by the possibilities of center stage, succumbs.

The improvisation Zero develops is oddly reminiscent of Bernard Malamud's novel, *The Assistant*, in which a poor tailor is visited by a strange little man who offers to burn his store down for the insurance money. In later years, Zero will perform in the film adaptation of Malamud's story, *The Angel Levine*, again as a poor tailor. Such tailors, as Zero well knows, were endemic to the life of East European Jewry. In the improvisation before Richardson, the tailor, all but destitute, decides to torch his property. With the store in flames, the man realizes that his small son is in the back room. Frantic, the tailor fights his way through heat and smoke and carries the child out into the street. But his child has succumbed to the devastation wrought by this already destitute father.

"He sat on the curb," Richardson remembers,

> at the edge of the stage, crying. I found myself very moved . . . he looked up at me and said, "Would you like to see it funny?". . . he did the same improvisation . . . with a kind of black humor . . . at the end . . . he had the kid out on the sidewalk [and] was trying to [revive him].

Richardson agrees to work with this mountain of challenging flesh, this hostile, amateur writer-director, who has demonstrated a natural ability to make up the role and then place himself in it.

It's not clear just what Zero, studying with Richardson, came away with, for there was always in Zero that conviction that he could do it better—the writing, the directing, certainly the performing—just as there was another facet that loved the collaborative process with artists like James Joyce, Samuel Beckett, Elia Kazan, Janos Kadar, and Burgess Meredith.

Monhegan has a fabled history. The late Alta Ashley, long the island's historian and once its physician, writes in her book *Under the Grey Gull's Wing*[21] of Stone Age tribes, "the Red Paint people," coming to Monhegan four thousand years ago to hunt and fish. "Monhegan was a stopping place for early Spanish and Portuguese explorers. Even Norsemen and Phoenicians are thought to have come ashore to replenish their water supplies and to feast on local berries." In the nineteenth century Monhegan had become a community for fishing, sheep-farming, and wool-working. The island has seen radical changes in recent years. Some two dozen families of lobstermen and women currently make up the year-round community, but lobster fishing is in trouble throughout New England; the seas have been over-fished.

On Monhegan, lobstering ends on June 25th. From late May on, the summer residents begin to drift in. The Island Spa, affectionately known to old-timers as Zimmy's, headquarters for coffee, newspapers, nicknacks, sneakers, island-photographs, dungarees, costume jewelry and gossip, is gone. Lorimer (Zimmy) Brackett, the old curmudgeon and former Arthur Murray dance instructor, died several years ago. Billy Payne's sober sweetness has replaced Zimmy's down-home irascability; the Island Spa has been shifted a few hundred feet up the main road and renamed Carina. Billy and his wife Jan Bailey stock gourmet food and serious poetry and fiction. Onto the premises of the original Spa, Billie Boynton and Jackie Bogel (Jackie was one of Zero's summer models) have set up their Lupin art and framing gallery. The brothers Doug and Harry Odom ran the Monhegan Store for many years; it stocked produce, beef, lobster, kerosene and more gossip. It burnt to the ground in 1964, was rebuilt, and has changed owners several times.

Nothing on Monhegan is as it was. Zero, Kate, Herbie, and Henry are gone. There are new tensions over property lines, waste disposal, fire hazards, water use, pollution control, and maintenance of woods and trails. Only the cats and the deer take things in stride. There used to be four telephones on the island; most of the populace lived by gas and kerosene, but now there are as many phones as there are deer, and electricity is becoming more prevalent. But, as islanders and summer people will tell you, there is always the sunset to put matters in perspective.

The physical beauty and serenity of Monhegan began to draw artists early in this century. Rockwell Kent first came in 1904. He supported himself through carpentry; the several houses he built are still standing. George Bellows began to summer in 1911. Edward Hopper came later; he and Bellows painted the Monhegan lighthouse a number of times. In 1932 Jay Connoway founded an informal art school which was maintained in one fashion or another until 1947. At the end of World

War Two a number of ex-GI's came to Monhegan to paint. "These painters didn't really enroll," notes painter Bill McCartin. "But the way Connoway had set it up allowed them to paint and qualify for tuition from the government. Herbie and Henry Kallem began to come up here, so did Joe DiMartini and Nick Luisi."

And so did Zero. He was introduced to Monhegan either by Herbie Kallem or Clifford Odets. Odets, with his second wife Betty and their two children, had come to Monhegan sometime in the late Forties. Herbie Kallem's second wife Sally had roots to fishermen going back several generations. Kallem met Sally on the island; he had heard of Monhegan from other painters in New York. Gillis Kallem tells me that her father came out after the war, that "some of the artists who met during the WPA re-met here on Monhegan. For some reason people from New York knew about Monhegan, that it was a beautiful place, and that in those days it was also cheap."

Clifford and Betty Odets rented their first house, now called the Don Stone house, from Jay Connoway. Later, Zero and Kate rented Connoway's house, while Odets and actor Karl Malden rented at different times what is now called the Bogdanove house. Today there are houses on Monhegan named for Mostel and Herbie Kallem. Though the owners are gone, the names persist and often resonate. There is also the Jamie Wyeth house, just off Lobster Cove.

In the summer of 1988 Gillis Kallem sits in the house her father built, a sturdy, two-story dwelling with a narrow porch on the second floor facing Lobster Cove (now screened in, it was built by Herbie as an open porch in the Seventies) and a wide deck that faces the house of the *New York Times* cultural correspondent Mel Gussow, his wife Anne, and his recently deceased brother Allen Gussow, a painter and art critic. Past it is the extension of the harbor and Manana Island and past that, on clear days, the mainland. "This house was built in the Fifties. My father borrowed money from Zero to buy the property and somehow between Herbie and Zero they got the money to buy the land where Herbie, my Uncle Henry and then Zero built houses." Doug Odom explains that "Harry and I sold them the land to build those houses. Zero's brother Milton, an accountant, handled the legal end."

Monhegan natives and summer folk always have tales to tell. They thrive on anecdotes, they weave yarns, spin twice-told tales and warm one another with fables old, new, and outlandish. This propensity for feeding on certain kinds of narrative may have something to do with the nature of islands, and of people who inhabit them. Like Zero, there is an "outlandishness" of sorts that seems to overcome the folk who are not inland. Here is one anecdote lovingly told to me one warm summer's day by Harry Odom:

"Odets's wife come in the store one day and she asked me was there a place her husband could rent where he could be by himself, away from the kids, so he could write. There used to be this place near Burnt Head, so Maynard takes her out there. She says, 'It's fine, but don't they have a bathroom?' 'Oh,' says Maynard, 'I'll show you the bathroom.' So he takes her out back and shows her the privy. She stares down this hole and sees this hornets' nest. She says, 'Sir, there's a hornets' nest down there.' So Maynard says, 'Oh if you sit down quick they can't get at you.'"

Unlike HUAC. Odom remembers HUAC. "Back when they called all those actors to Washington, when they said they were Reds? Odets and Zero had some differences over that." Odets was a belligerent "unfriendly" witness in 1952 who nevertheless named names. He named his fellow Group Theatre actor J. Edward Bromberg, then gave the eulogy at the memorial service after Bromberg's death.

I ask if Zero first visited Monhegan because of Odets, but Harry Odom doesn't know. Odets spent about three summers on Monhegan and Doug Odom connects those summers to the opening of *The Flowering Peach*, Odets's drama about Noah and the fabled ark. The mention of theatre stirs delicious recollections in Harry. "We had *beautiful* seats in Boston. We also had them for *The Country Girl*. Odets had me come backstage. He said to all these reporters hanging around him, 'Listen, I got a friend visiting me from where I go in the summer, so back off a little while.'"

Michael Loew, another of the painters who summered on Monhegan, had known Zero during the WPA days. Loew had been a supervisor for the Federal Art Project until he left to fulfill a commission to design murals for the American pavilion at the 1939 World's Fair. (For that project he hired a then-unknown painter named Willem de Kooning.) Loew spent the war years in the Pacific, working with the Nava} engineers, the Seabees. The Pacific war destroyed Loew's hearing, later partially restored by surgery. By 1949, through contact with fellow artist Joe DiMartini, Michael Loew and his wife Mildred were settling on Monhegan for their summers. Mildred Loew, now widowed, remembers one of the early encounters with the Mostels.

"We were living in Mike's studio on Twenty-eighth Street and Fifth Avenue. It was perishingly cold. We went to this party at Zero and Kate's; it was full of theatre people. They were living on West Eighty-sixth Street [the Belnord] and Kate talked about their place as if it was the pits. I thought it was rich and elegant. As for Mike and Zero, they had known each other *before* the WPA."

Mildred Loew's recollections of the Mostels are mixed. Mutual friends believe that she and Kate were unusually close, but something in her has never reconciled itself to Kate Mostel, and certain incidents still rankle. "We had a big old house on Monhegan, near the church. It was torn down years ago. Every night the gang would come to our house, we called it Fun and Games Night. We'd play charades, all kinds of games. I'd spend the day baking cookies—I was quite stupid about doing all that work—and we'd feed everybody cookies and tea. No liquor, remember it was a dry island in those years." Apparently Zero was able to discipline himself during charades, actually able to allow others a degree of psychic space. Kate joined in all the games, she had no particular favorites. Fun and Games Nights were relatively benign moments, but there were other moments. Mildred tells me Kate hated a lot of things and one of her pet hates was art. It isn't the first time I've heard this.

"She *hated* art, hated it when Zero would come home with art books, hated it when he would come home with actual works of art." E.g., pre-Columbian statuary. I inform Mildred that in her book Kate writes that Zero was always "shlepping her around to museums when they were away from home," and Mildred tells me, "I don't *ever* remember her going to a museum. He couldn't shlep her *anywhere!* She was a very strong person." While Zero would go to museums and galleries with Herbie, Kate might go to the theatre. "And she loved the Russian Tea Room. I would meet her on a Saturday evening. Museums? And she bought a lot of expensive clothing. Money was very important to her. Status was important. She'd been a very poor girl. Her mother had run a boarding house. They were lace-curtain Irish."

Mildred recalls that Kate would remark how she loved "the Jews." "Sure, the Jews gave her everything—money, power, prestige." I ask if Kate confided in her, and Mildred in her artfully aggressive manner assures me that *there is nothing to confide.* She'd say Zero was a killer. She blamed Zero for Toby's psychological difficulties. In his twenties, those summers on Monhegan, Toby was crazy as a kook."

Mildred has a wealth of bitter memories to unload. "Zero claimed to love the artist. With all his money, he never did a bloody thing for the artist. He says to Michael one day, 'I want you to do a portrait of yourself,' and pulls out a wad of bills. 'Here's a deposit,' he tells Michael and gives my husband two hundred dollars." Mildred remembers Michael as a perfectionist, a painter who labored four or five months before he completed the self-portrait to his own satisfaction. "So he gives this painting to Zero and then asks for the balance of the payment. 'You gave me a deposit,' he tells Zero, and Zero says, 'Oh no, I paid you the full amount.' That," Mildred emphasizes, "is how Zero supported other artists."

In the summer of 1952, Zero and Kate rented a house belonging to Ring Lardner's mother. It was in New Milford, Connecticut, and the Mostels, enroute to inspect the premises, stopped nearby to say hello to the younger Lardners. "They came into our house," Frances Chaney remembers, "and Zero was screaming and yelling about how he didn't want to be in the country at all, how he hated the country. But they rented the house, as we and they both knew they would. Kate and I and the kids were always down at the lake that summer."

Ian Hunter and Ring Lardner Jr., both blacklisted, had taken their families to Mexico after Lardner was released from Danbury Prison in 1951. The Lardners stayed in Mexico for only seven months, then returned to California and then spent two years in New Milford. When the Hunters returned from Mexico in 1954, both the Hunter and Mostel families began spending part of their summers in New Milford.

Ian Hunter's recollection of the blacklist years has certain bright aspects. "The blacklist period was a sort of coming together. You see, we [Ian, Ring, Zero] were mutually oppressed. The kids said they had a jolly good time those years. We'd rent this property in New Milford, the Mostels took the farmhouse and we took the barn. It was a few acres. There really wasn't space to work at your art, to draw, not like Monhegan. The women would go off with the kids during the day, so Zero and I had a lot of time together. We'd fish, we'd cook. Zero would make what he called 'rich man's herring.' He'd get the best herring, he'd use the best cream."

During the Fifties, the blacklisted Lardner and Hunter collaborated on a number of adventure programs for British television, including a series called *The Adventures of Robin Hood* whose legendary bandit tries, as we well know, to redress the economic ills of the poor. The secular idealism of this series may have helped in some measure to alleviate the spirit of two aggrieved writers who could not work at their craft in their own country. A closeness also developed between the members of the three oppressed families and by the early Fifties they were all settled in Manhattan, the Hunters and Mostels both inhabiting huge apartments at the Belnord on West Eighty-sixth Street and the Lardners at 607 West End Avenue, between Eighty-ninth and Ninetieth Streets.

Lardner recalls: "We used to meet at the Tiptoe Inn on Eighty-sixth Street." I mention that I've heard Zero would hold court at the Tiptoe Inn, and Frances Chaney declares that "wherever he was he *was* holding court. He was always on. He was funny and delicious."

Always on? Was Zero always on with the Lardners?

Frances Chaney reflects. "Most of the time. Oh, not *all* the time. But if there was any kind of public activity he'd be on. If he ran into you at the market he'd start chasing you around or doing something insane. That was his kind of energy. He'd be very serious if you'd go down to the studio, and he'd be very serious after finishing work at night because he was tired. He'd moan and complain about how tired he was."

Lardner recalls that "once I drove with Zero out to Long Beach [on the south shore of Long Island]. It was during the blacklist and the scene out there was like *The Front*. It was some kind of adult camp or summer hotel and he was there to do his act. And after we got there there was some dispute about the money. Most of these people took advantage of the blacklisted, they'd try to get you to work as cheaply as possible."

"I met Zero around 1938." Painter Charlie Martin reminisces about these early years half a century later. We're speaking in Martin's Monhegan studio one summer's day. "I'd see Zero at artists' parties. I already knew Herbie and Henry Kallem but we all got to know each other better during the WPA. I taught for a year on the Federal Art Project. Then they promoted me to a Brooklyn district where I was a supervisor. Then I got promoted to the East Side. I'd see Zero now and then, we'd shake hands, I'd see him on Twenty-eighth Street with his group, they'd be painting, playing poker. At that time I believe he was already sharing studio space with Herbie. They were very old friends."

I ask the obligatory question one asks Monhegan summer people. "How did you wind up on Monhegan?"

"Joe DiMartini was already on Monhegan, I'd never even heard of the place. It was a June day, the thermometer read one hundred degrees, my wife Florence and I were driving down the Maine coast and there's this sign. It says 'Port Clyde Ferry.' So we took a ferry and wound up on this little island. We stayed overnight in a rented room. The next day we're on the ferry to go back to Port Clyde when I hear these voices. A voice says, 'Hey Charlie, what are you doin'?' I look up, it's Herbie Kallem. I look up again, it's Moe Schulman. All these guys I worked with on the Federal Art Project—Joe Di, Mike Loew, Moe, Herbie. I said, 'My God, what are you guys doing here?' They said, 'Why don't you come back? It's a great place.' I said, 'Yeah, okay.' So Florence and I came back in August, and rented a place for the month. We walked around and I got in with these guys again. There was something about Monhegan—I felt reduced to a lovely age." As I understood this "lovely age," Charlie Martin, who also drew books for children, was speaking of a return to a more elemental life. "We've been coming here ever since. Now Herbie was building two houses. He was a helluva good carpenter—good in many directions. He did more carpentry than art. Then eventually Zero came up, to visit a couple of times. Then he decided *he'd* settle in here. The island has changed, of course, over the years. There's the money pressure, there's how you cut your hair. The artist believes times can't change him."

Charlie Martin and Zero Mostel spent much time together on Monhegan. "We saw each other a great deal. Now he was never a walker. He wouldn't do any walking on this island." I ask, "How do you exist on Monhegan without walking? You can't get anyplace." Charlie answers, "Well, he just wasn't an athletic man, he refused to be, he would walk back and forth along the road; that's about it. He had to walk up Horn Hill once to buy a house and he decided no. [Horn Hill is a steep dirt road, very rocky. It leads to the Burnt Head trail and eventually to Burnt Head, high over the ocean.] This house was a beautiful bargain, a great place. The lady wanted to get rid of it, in fact she had two houses, she wanted seventeen or eighteen thousand, it was a vast place on top of the hill. Ten years later that house brought something like one hundred and fifty thousand." And in 1995, probably another hundred thousand.

Charlie muses about the protocol of Monhegan carpenters. "The year we're building my studio, Zero started to build his house. He'd been renting up till then. When he started to build, just past Herbie's and Henry's, all the carpenters that had been working on other houses, on my studio for example, they all moved to Zero's house. Then when Zero finished, another rich man moved here, a fellow named Lothrup, and he decided to build by the ice pond. Well that took up another two years of the carpenters' work. So when I wanted the studio done I had to hire people from the mainland. Of course that was the wrong thing to do—if you're on Monhegan you're supposed to wait. But I couldn't wait, I needed a space to work in."

"Then Zero built his studio alongside his house."

"Right. He took delight in all this stuff, in the land, the carpentry, it was great. With his studio, we'd all go down there. There were many get-togethers—I wouldn't call them parties, just sitting around on the porch. Then we had Zero's sketch class. He loved to draw from the model, to work in what they called the fifteen-minute period. Some like to work for an hour with one pose. I prefer the Zero way. Mike Loew, myself, Herbie, Joe Di, some seven or eight guys, we'd go there and work with Zero. Zero paid the model, it was all free for us guys, he'd invite us and he'd insist on the fifteen-minute period. Zero built his house around 1963 or '64, we all had a lot of fun together, it was all very pleasant. Then he began to drift away, to do a lot of summer work."

Some years ago a number of Monhegan artists formed an association and opened their studios to the public during prescribed hours each week. Zero never opened his studio publicly. Neither did Jamie Wyeth. One who did was Arlene Simon.

"In the Fifties some of us were just out of art school. We'd have costume parties every year at the schoolhouse. I remember one year we were Teutonic knights out of *Alexander Nevsky* [Eisenstein's 1938 film] and Herbie carved our swords for us. We spent a week making costumes and we won a prize, we five Teutonic knights. Kate didn't go to the party that year but she wanted the kids to see our costumes. So we came up to where the Mostels were staying, with our swords, our shields and our crosses. Zero and Kate had come up with a black maid for the kids, and this woman took one look at our weapons and our crosses and she went *running!* We must have looked like the real thing, out to cut people up."

Arlene Simon remembers Kate: "She loved to play the piano, loved the popular songs, all the old Astaire movies. Once in their apartment on Central Park West—it was not too long before she died—she got hold of four or five Astaire movies. She invited a few of us over and screened all these movies. Remember, she had been a dancer. She loved the idea of dancing."

Kate dancing. Zero dancing. Was Zero not comfortable with his body, not an athletic man as Charlie Martin claims? But Kazan remembers that the Zero in *Panic in the Streets* "had a way with his body that was extraordinary." But perhaps the 1960 bus accident caused a radical change.

16

F *light into Egypt*, which opened on Broadway on March 8th, 1952, brought together several refugees and sons of immigrants in a time of continuing political and cultural turmoil. Elia Kazan, its director, was the offspring of an Anatolian rug merchant; Zero Mostel, of East European Jews; and playwright George Tabori and stars Paul Lukas and Gusti Huber were refugees from Central Europe. Thus those who created and mounted *Flight* came by and large from the embattled Left-Liberal-Jewish enclave that was seeing one door after another shut to it. Producing the play was Irene Mayer Selznick, whose first endeavor, *A Streetcar Named Desire*, was nothing less than one of the major events in the history of American theatre. Selznick, divorced from film magnate David O. Selznick, had fled the Hollywood that for the second time had shut its gates on Zero Mostel. She was also the daughter of Louis B. Mayer, the very mogul who had thrown Zero out the first time.

In *170 Years of Show Business*, Kate Mostel dismisses *Flight into Egypt* as a work of little merit. Her standard for success is based on the producer's ability to keep the show running.

Selznick, still a rookie at the game of break-even and building sufficient word-of-mouth for a grim subject, was unable to translate Tabori's play, which had a short life on Broadway, into a living wage for the company.

George Tabori's drama had inherent problems, but it was not without merit. In the Fifties, Tabori, Hungarian-born, was laboring in New York along with his wife, the actress Viveca Lindfors. Another Tabori play of the early Fifties, *The Emperor's Clothes*, produced at the Greenwich Mews in the West Village under Stella Holt's direction, portrays a politically liberal family resisting pressure from Hungary's Fascist government in the years prior to the collapse of the country in 1945. The family is reminiscent of the victimized characters in *Flight*. In both works, husband and wife are middle-class, well-educated, with an artistic bent; their young offspring are intellectually curious and fiercely loyal to the liberal views propagated by their elders.

In *Flight*, the parents, Austrian survivors of Hitler's Final Solution, having migrated from the postwar ugliness of Vienna, try to find their way to the United States. Momentarily stranded in Cairo, they are unable to come up with the funds or political connections needed. Not only are they mired down in a culture for which they have no sympathy, they are veritable prisoners in a public space, "hot and heavy, traplike," known as Glubb's Hotel. The proprietor of this graceless shelter for wayfarers is performed by Zero Mostel, fresh from movie roles as low-level henchmen and unsavory aliens. Tabori characterizes Glubb as "an Anglo-Levantine, dry, cold, matter-of-fact, with the simple logic of the greedy." In *The Emperor's Clothes*, the acquiescent slaves of Fascism manage the corruption, in *Flight*, the slaves of the marketplace, exemplified by Glubb, assume these burdens. In Tabori's eyes there is always dirty work to be accomplished in a society which envisions its citizens as so many interchangeable parts in a vast industrial complex where profit is the final arbiter.

Tabori's early plays found limited audiences in New York, by the Seventies Tabori had left both his wife, Viveca Lindfors, and the inhospitable United States. In recent years he has become artistic director of Der Kreis, Theater in der Porzellangasse in Wien (Vienna). It is another irony: some four decades after Franz and Lili Engel, the husband-and-wife survivors of *Flight into Egypt*, abandon the geriatric Vienna, a city that reeks of history, the waltz, psychoanalysis, marzipan, and the unholy marriage to Adolf Hitler, Tabori creates new theatre in its ruined entrails.

Broadway and Tabori got nowhere together. *Flight* found the Broadway press uncomfortably stirred, brought to a leaden despondency. The *Times's* Brooks Atkinson and the *Herald-Tribune's* Walter Kerr saw the play as harrowing, but neither claimed to have been moved. Zero, who managed to lift the human spirit at Cafe Society, seems to have conspired now to weigh it down. Act One finds Glubb crouching outside the Engels' room, peeping in on Lili who is hemming a black dress. Tabori calls his heroine "sweet and vulnerable, product of the charm, the music, the imperial death Vienna means to some." Glubb has his eye to the keyhole—vulnerable women are his meat, his linzer torte—two quick bites and he's digested Lili. But Glubb is also suspicious. The Engels are in arrears; Glubb is no Poppa Strunsky and it doesn't pay to get too get worked up over a little pastry.

Greed, Tabori tells us, has its logic, and Zero's Glubb, a disciple of bottom-line philosophy, lays out his credo to Tewfik Bey, neighborhood cop.

> No credit has been the principle of my life. Unenlightened self-interest has saved me from raging poverty, broken friendships, the bailiff's threat. I'm not my brother's keeper, I'm an [sic] hotel-keeper. I keep an hotel. It keeps me. but it's like a tiger. it's got to be fed with gas, electricity, taxes and wages.

The Engels have hardly room to maneuver. Franz's health has been broken; it's a serious question whether he can make it out of his chair, much less out of Cairo. And then there's the question of money—there isn't any. The Engels can't keep up with the rent, therefore they can't remain at Glubb's; but they can't pay their back rent, therefore they can't leave Glubb's. And though this tension leaves Glubb a little sweaty, its between a-rock-and-a-hard-place nature gives him pleasant shivers. In Act

Two, Glubb, ever the academician, is instructing Tewfik in the art of dealing with Lili. "Keep cool. You'll never be rich if you sweat. Money doesn't like nervous people." And later:

Ah, how to make people pay up? An art indeed. First, you must have indignation. (Bangs on the table) A royal conviction, it's an outrage what's been done to you. (Raging) Mrs. Engel, what do you think you're doing? You're undermining our whole social system. I'm your creditor, therefore your slave. If I let you stay, your debts will accrue. If I let you you go, I'll never see my money.

And a little later:

(Icy voice) Mrs. Engel, your grandmother, you say, is dying? What, may I ask, has the old lady's cardiac complaint to do with the ominous gap in your account?

The play makes no one comfortable. Its irony is dispiriting; we have entered an emotional Arctic region. The laceration of the spirit is a recurring sight in the Fifties; people want to get warm, to be reassured that things will come round, but Tabori's truth leaves one on edge.

In his autobiography Kazan devotes several lines to the play. During rehearsals he is distracted by his forthcoming HUAC testimony, by the needs of Tennessee Williams, Arthur Miller, the film studios, and his beleaguered friends on the Left. Kazan goes off to California where Tennessee Williams waits for him. The Warners' promotion staff believes that *Streetcar* will walk off with numerous Academy Awards. Meanwhile the *Flight* company, which includes David Opatoshu, Jo Van Fleet, Joseph Anthony, and Paul Mann, could think about their next project, or about unemployment insurance.

In a few months it will be summer, time for Monhegan, or the house in New Milford. And there are the weekly bills, and the monthly bills. Toby is three and a half; Josh a little over five.

Clifford Odets testifies before HUAC, and Kazan remembers that

a few weeks after his testimony, he, Molly [Kazan], and I were walking down Lexington Avenue one evening, when we were accosted by a group of young people, decent and well educated

they were, who began to jibe at Clifford, telling him how badly
he'd let them down. Clifford didn't defend himself; he was
silent. The encounter did not last long, and we were soon continuing down the avenue. He still wasn't speaking . . . [He] was distressed not because of hurting other people but because he'd
killed the self he valued most.

March 28th, 1988. I've been on the telephone with Elia
Kazan. He understands I'm working on a biography of Zero. He
suggests I pick him up at his home in the East Nineties. I had in
mind that we would converse in relative seclusion, in his study.
It is not to be. Instead we make a foray into the world of
peremptory traffic signals, anxious pedestrians, and overbearing public conveyances. In short, we converse amidst the
chronic upheavals endemic to a Manhattan afternoon.

I am several minutes late. Kazan is already on the sidewalk,
waiting, a man on the move. A wonderfully squashed Irish hat
is somewhat settled on his head. He seems to me an aging, boyish, loose-limbed fellow.

The questions come at me rapidly: Am I still writing for the
Village Voice? Why am I so thin?

In response to the first: Yes and no, I write occasional pieces,
they grow more occasional with time. To the second: Contrary
to the semi-cadaverous spectre I appear to be forcing on the
world, I do eat, I have a terrific appetite—but I burn it up. To
quote my wife: "It all goes to your head."

I've decided days before this meeting that the one issue I
won't pursue is the matter of Kazan's HUAC appearances.
Hadn't we all made our judgments years ago? Hasn't Kazan, in
highly publicized statements and in later interviews already
explained, then explained yet again his position, then again
rethought it? Was there a Party conspiracy to indoctrinate the
passive recipients of mass entertainment in the West? An
effective conspiracy at that? Ask Bertolt Brecht, Erwin Piscator,
Judith Malina, or Julian Beck how often art has stirred *anybody* to
political action. Ask John Howard Lawson who, as Hollywood's
designated Marxist theoretician, might have been pleased to
detect *some* leftward movement during World War Two.

But hasn't a true work of art the capacity to move something in us?

Was the naming of names reprehensible? Kazan was not Emile Zola exposing anti-Semitism in the French military; he was validating and feeding an invalid, inflammatory pack of Congressional hounds. These hounds were sniffing every which way, perhaps for their own edification, most likely to puff up some misguided sense of patriotism. But the price to a decent society has been far too great.

Enough. Kazan has chosen to be his own witness and judge. He has had ample occasion, just as Ibsen's John Gabriel Borkman had, to replay and reevaluate his actions. He does so again in his massive autobiography, *A Life*, which, during our walk, he mentions several times but which then had not yet been published.

We talk of many things, but barely of Zero "He was like a loaf of bread," Kazan tells me. "Nice man, very."

This nice man, incensed at his former idol's testimony, came to refer to Gadge as Loose Lips.

"I'm seeing you," Kazan tells me, "primarily because I liked Zero so much."

I ask myself, is he putting me on? Am I in some way a public receiver of the word, some witness to Kazan's declaration that it is all water under the bridge, that the past, to paraphrase a Yogism, is almost past? Is he informing me in his own amiable fashion that it is important for human beings to think well of one another? Zero's response to Hal Prince, when the producer suggested that Jerome Robbins be brought in to rework troubling moments of *A Funny Thing Happened on the Way to the Forum* during the critical tryout period, has almost been written in stone. Zero could hardly forget that Robbins had also named names, including that of Madeline Lee, Kate's close friend and the spouse of Jack Gilford. And Zero is reputed to have told Hal Prince to bring Robbins in if he could improve the show, that "We of the Left do not blacklist."

I don't believe Kazan is putting me on. He hardly needs me to help him launch a new trial balloon. He has the world's ear. Is he at peace with himself and with those who still remain his accusers, his righteous judges? I can't know that, I can only surmise that our walk through the streets of Manhattan tickles something in him, and in me. We are like teenagers together, giggling, exchanging stories, gossiping about our families, revealing some of our concerns about personal careers, about the Middle East, speculating about the world of painting, about literature, theatre, and film.

We are hurrying across Eighty-sixth Street in the face of rapidly changing traffic. He says, "I bet you were surprised I agreed to see you "

"Yes. Surprised."

This confession seems to please him. He has an idea. There is a new Dunkin Doughnuts on Lexington Avenue near Eighty-fifth Street and he wants to treat me. We survey the delicacies past the counter and place our orders. We settle against a narrow ledge at the rear, armed with our Styrofoam cups of hot coffee and our jellied-and-otherwise doughnuts and proceed to analyze the inordinate satisfaction of sugar. We agree that sugar is surely the worst assault imaginable short of other addictive substances but that it is also an indulgence that succors the aching heart. Kazan and I reach a consensus: if sugar is treacherous, it is nevertheless a disarmingly open-faced treachery which informs you: Don't worry, enjoy, let tomorrow care for itself; indulge now, pay later. Like a taxi ride.

Sugar is not the sole item under discussion. I ask about Kazan's production of *Flight into Egypt*, hoping that he will recount moments during rehearsals that will shed light on Zero at work. Kazan tells me he doesn't even remember what happens in Tabori's play. I find myself narrating the events in the play to its director, and again I wonder, even as I'm somewhat bemused, watching myself, sugar doughnut and coffee in hand, informing Kazan about the play, whether my host at this workers' palace of sweets, is putting me on. (Albeit it's well over thirty years since that Broadway production, surely he might recall something of the plot?) Kazan seems so pleased to be settled into his formica niche at Dunkin Doughnuts, his bashed

Irish hat nuzzled against the remains of his sugar delight, listening to his guest go on and on about Cairo and Vienna and about the displaced and about America as the presumed Land of Promise—a promise for Sholom Aleichem, for Zero's parents, for my own parents and for Kazan's, and for Tabori's distraught Engels family.

I mention that Tabori, whose plays never found their audience in New York, seems to have carved out a place for himself in the very Vienna his characters couldn't wait to get out of. We explore the fact that the early Tabori, who seemed emotionally tied to the sardonic vision of Brecht but whose aesthetic in the early Fifties was much closer to that of Arthur Miller and what we then considered the theatre of realism, never found understanding in the United States.

Kazan agrees that there was a heaviness, a sense of lost opportunities that didn't sit well with a culture for whom disappointment was hardly more than yesterday's news, a culture that came to proclaim in good Flower Child fashion that "today is the first day of the rest of your life." Not unlike the philosophy of Esmerelda, Tennessee Williams's young gypsy daughter in *Camino Real*, whose virginity after a night of prostitution is restored by daybreak. The early Tabori drama was weighted down with that Conradian sense, surely anti-American, that character is fate, that yesterday is also tomorrow. Who would want to cough up serious money for such dire news? Even those of us working within the marginal confines of the Caffe Cino, La Mama, and Judson Poets Theatre during the hysterical optimism of the early Sixties could not feed such a message to our peers, even if we believed it. Only the likes of Eugene O'Neill could get away with character-is-fate rumblings, and he had the decency to be pained by his insights, whereas Tabori seemed to take pleasure in inflicting the message on trusting spirits. The Brechtian play offered us a way out: change the system, wake up, take charge, throw the bums out. With Tabori, the system was internalized: there was nobody to throw out.

As we're navigating our way further downtown, Kazan lets me know he has a pressing agenda and it has to do with his kidneys. We're weaving in spiral-like fashion southward toward Central Park and I'm given to understand that Frederick Olmstead's wonderfully designed haven and the call of nature that is sending repeated signals to Gadge Kazan's bladder are about to converge.

Kismet! I don't believe this is happening but I find myself standing guard while Gadge is positioned behind a tree adjacent to the Mall, having the most blissful relief a man with a distended bladder can have. He occasionally peers around the harboring tree toward me with what appears to be a wink, as if to more fully confirm his appreciation at the sudden harmony of the universe. But it turns out he is also just the tiniest bit concerned about passersby. In fact a passerby materializes, a respectably-dressed, middle-aged male, who is not absolutely certain he is seeing what he is seeing, and is too studiously correct in demeanor to double-check. I in the meantime don't exactly know where to be looking or how to position myself. I am at once sentinel and detached observer. It's a moment which might have inspired Mozart, witnessing the ecstatic buffoonery of a colleague. A moment surely worthy of Zero—who might not have bothered with the tree.

In *A Life*, Kazan talks further about Zero.

> I thought him an extraordinary artist and a delightful companion, one of the funniest and most original men I'd ever met: I never knew what he was going to say next. I constantly sought his company. He liked me too—one reason being that he was one of three people whom I rescued from the 'industry's' blacklist, which was already in effect. . . . I got him in my film—and so earned increased admiration from 'outside.' I was a political hero as well.

Kazan provides a footnote, after his HUAC testimony.

> One winter's night, on Seventy-second Street near Columbus Avenue, I ran into Zero. By that time I'd hardened myself against the disapproval some old friends were giving me and didn't much care what people a good deal closer to me than Zero thought. But for some reason I did care what he thought. He stopped me and put an arm around my neck—a little too tight— and said in one of the most dolorous voices I've ever heard,

"Why did you do that? You shouldn't have done that." He took me into a bar and we had a drink and then another, but he didn't say much and I didn't say much. All he did was look at me once in a while, and his eyes were saying what his lips were not: "Why did you do that?" I never saw him again.

In August of 1988 I receive a letter from George Tabori; he's writing to me from Vienna concerning *Flight* and his memories of Zero.

I met him in the late 40ties [sic] in Hollywood at the Richard Contes who were friends of mine. We fell in love with each other but the relationship remained platonic. No, we had not worked together before *Flight into Egypt*. What did we talk about? That was 30 years ago . . . a time of McCarthy as you know and we were both more or less blacklisted. At least in TV and Radio, although I am not, I never have been. . . .

I was often in his apartment and also in his studio. I could not afford to buy one of his paintings, and he remained deaf to all my hints about hoping for a gift. What is interesting about Kazan's political schizophrenia was, that while he was under great pressure from the shits he tried to resist it by casting my play with some leftists like Paul Mann and Zero. On the other hand for the leading lady he cast a German actress who apparently had been slightly touched by the colour of brown [Nazi brownshirts] and was incidentally totally miscast. So that during rehearsals we had protests from some lunatics, both from the left as well as the right.

Zero seemed to me invariably friendly. If he was anxious he was hiding it, and was like all great clowns very serious. I remember visiting him in the hospital after he had been run down by a bus [in 1960]. We both joked that the critics at this time had gone too far.

A few days after the 'mixed reviews' [we were] standing backstage around the piano. The producer Irene Selznick came with a copy of the *New York Times* containing Kazan's paid advertisement, justifying his having turned fink. Irene, like all of us, was in a state of shock and she vomited into the piano, although she was a Republican.

I saw Zero a few times in the Fifties, I wanted him for the lead in my play *Brouhaha*, and he read for that other genius—director Peter Hall—who thought Zero was "too much" and instead of him he cast a young unknown English actor named Peter Sellers.

For Philip Loeb the Fifties represent an unremitting darkness. Early in 1952, Gertrude Berg, under great pressure to drop Loeb from *The Goldbergs*, now a popular television series, works out a settlement. Loeb, a militant union figure in Actors Equity and AFTRA (American Federation of Television and Radio Artists), has been a sitting duck. He is highly visible on TV screens across the country as Jake, the middle-class, hardly revolutionary husband to Molly Goldberg. *Red Channels* has gone after Loeb in its January issue, but Berg has expressed confidence in her performer's loyalty to his country. Berg fights to retain Loeb; she ultimately blames her sponsors for Loeb's dismissal. The sponsors say they are blameless. As Victor Navasky reports in *Naming Names*, General Foods urges Loeb's dismissal, Berg refuses, and CBS cancels the show. NBC is prepared to pick up the series, but no sponsor will touch it. Loeb is offered $85,000 to resign and is reported to have said, "I'm sorry, I have no price."

But Philip Loeb has a "schizophrenic" son who is institutionalized; Loeb's wife has died some years earlier and the son is his major concern. Treatment costs $12,000 per year. Loeb, whose salary on *The Goldbergs*, when the show was aired, was about $20,000 a year, finally agrees to resign. So there is a price. But the $85,000 has shrunk to about $40,000. And the price in human suffering accelerates. For the final three years of his life Loeb has little work and the payments to the institution have to be met periodically.

Sig Miller was close to Loeb for a time. "You had to be resourceful when the blacklist hit. I had to leave for Europe. I couldn't work here any more. If you weren't resourceful, you had to go into another business."

I ask, "You were blacklisted from radio?"

"Oh yes. They reached in everywhere. I went to Europe before they could subpoena me. I worked on a couple of pictures in England. The British didn't give a damn what my politics were. Those were the happiest years of my life, in London. Also, I don't remember Zero being so badly affected by the blacklist."

Sandy Friedman will tell me the same thing when I interview him about Rachel Productions.

Sig Miller has the sense that "Zero really loved Philip Loeb. Once Loeb was sick. Zero says, 'I'm going up to visit him.' So I went along. What does Zero do? He finds nine Jewish men and all ten of them stand over Philip Loeb who is sick in bed and they say some prayer over him. And Philip Loeb is marvelous. He just keeps on reading his newspaper in bed. He pays no attention to any of them, as if nothing is happening."

"Zero rounded up a *minyan*?"

"Yeah, he got a *minyan*, then Zero and I and the men left the apartment. That was all. That was his visit to Philip Loeb in bed."

Tales of an erratic visitor: "One time Zero gave me one of his paintings. I hadn't had a chance to hang it up yet. We were living on Thirty-second Street and hadn't organized the house yet. Zero comes to visit and he doesn't see his painting hanging anywhere. So he looks through the closet and there's the painting, and he's furious. So he grabs the painting out of my closet and runs out of the house with it."

"He took it out of your closet?"

"Out of my closet. I was planning to hang it up. I tell you, I hadn't been in touch with him during the final ten years of his life, though I maintained a warm relationship with Kate. You could say we sort of drifted apart. Somebody told him I had spoken against Philip Loeb—a total untruth. I assured him I would never dream of doing it, but he believed it. That cooled him off completely, plus the painting not hanging on the wall."

"You were the one that took him out of bar mitzvahs."

"Well . . . he was ungrateful. His whole career depended on what I did for him. I didn't do it because I wanted any kudos. I thought he was supertalented, too good to be wasted on bar mitzvahs. Anyway, I never said anything against Philip Loeb. Why would I?"

RACHEL PRODUCTIONS

Howard Da Silva and Arnold Perl present
The World of Sholom Aleichem
dramatized by Arnold Perl
directed by Howard Da Silva
music by Serge Hovey, Robert De Cormier
costumes by Aline Bernstein
lighting by Bernard Gersten

The *World of Sholom Aleichem* opens the weekend of May 2nd,1953, at the Barbizon Plaza Hotel on West Fifty-ninth Street in Manhattan. A few of the blacklisted are putting themselves to work.

Sholom Aleichem again. We have heard something about his world—it once was, it is now no more. But that world persists for many of us, for the *landsleit*, Tevye's countrymen, and for their descendants. We internalize those villages and cities teeming with Jews; memory wants not to elude us.

We find ourselves in a converted ballroom. Acting in his own production is Howard Da Silva—that very performer

Robert Taylor complained of because at SAG meetings Da Silva always had "something to say." Da Silva is trundling down the aisle. He is pushing a much-used baby carriage. It's spilling over with Yiddish books; the bindings are visibly battered. Da Silva sits on the apron of the stage and introduces himself. His name is Mendele the Bookseller. The allusion is to the grandfather of Yiddish literature, Mendele Mocher Sforim, a *nom de plume* literally meaning Mendele the seller of books. Mendele now draws our attention to the books in his carriage; from this trove, this little abundance of *Yiddishkeit*, he has chosen works by I.L. Peretz and Sholom Aleichem.[22]

But the first tale to be dramatized has no known author. The "Tale of Chelm" is folklore, from a time past accounting, from a place where fools not only predominate, they permeate the landscape. It hardly pays to make Chelm your dwelling place if you are not a fool of high calibre. The Barbizon offering tells of a transaction wherein a billy goat is purchased by a well-intentioned but gender-confused Chelmite eager to provide milk for his family. The shtetl of foolish souls once hired a night watchman to be on the lookout for the Messiah. He would stand on a rooftop all night and welcome the Messiah who might otherwise pass right by this tiny village. The watchman liked his new position well enough, agreed it was a considerable honor to watch for the Messiah night after night, but complained to the rabbi that he could hardly keep his family alive on the meagre salary provided. The rabbi agreed that "ten gulden a week is an inadequate salary. But one must take into account that this is a permanent job."

I.L. Peretz's "Bontche Schweig" tells of the meekest of men who has never had a day's comfort, for whom life has been exceedingly bitter, but who has remained modest and uncomplaining. In heaven the angels announce that the new arrival will be rewarded with whatever he chooses. After due thought, Bontche asks if it wouldn't be too much trouble to provide him "every morning for breakfast with a hot roll with fresh butter." Are we dealing with a saint or simpleton? In Peretz's original prose, the judge and the angels are shamefaced at "this unending meekness they have created on earth." But what is to satisfy a contemporary audience? Is Bontche to ask for retribution? A union for the oppressed? Where does justice lie? How do we conceive one's cup running over?

Sholom Aleichem's "The High School" concerns the attempt to enroll a Jewish boy in the mainstream *gymnasium* at a time when the Enlightenment had just begun to open the doors of such institutions to Jewish students by the merest crack. It's a story of disappointment and hope, a moment that Sholom Aleichem clearly saw as transitional, offering opportunity to an oppressed minority but also planting the seeds of disruption within a community whose cohesion depended in part on being denied access to mainstream culture. Again it takes us back to the disruption that secularism brought into play in the household of Yisroel and Tzina Mostel.

Morris Carnovsky and Sarah Cunningham play the browbeaten grocer and his ambitious wife who try to pry open the gates. They hire a tutor, bribe officials—anything to break through the quota system. Gilbert Green plays the intractable principal who won't allow one more Jew in. He doesn't budge; he wants to preserve the system. In 1948 Green had been indicted for violating the Smith Act—aimed primarily at the Communist Party; the act prohibited advocating the overthrow of the U.S. government.

Rachel Productions found it had something more than a modest success on its hands; *Sholom Aleichem* seemed to take on a life of its own. One of those who watched its extraordinary unfolding was Zero Mostel, and eventually Zero would perform in the TV production as well as the Broadway descendent of Mendele the Bookseller's treasure trove. Merle Debuskey, press agent for *Sholom Aleichem*, one of Zero's trusted colleagues in later years and one of the handful who saw Zero's only performance in Arnold Wesker's *The Merchant*, remembers *Sholom Aleichem's* modest beginnings.

"It was only supposed to play nineteen performances because that's all the money we could raise. We couldn't rent a theatre and so we rented this space in the Barbizon. It was an auditorium used for conventions, and when we got it we played a staggered performance schedule because it was also booked for lectures. When the show became successful, we couldn't continue there because of the other bookings, so we recapitalized the show and laid off for the summer so that we could reopen on an eight-performance-week schedule in the fall. As for Zee, he was much aggrieved at not being in the production. Morris Carnovsky was slated for the father in "The High School." Jack Gilford was perfect for Bontche, and all the other parts were small. Zero probably wouldn't have done the small parts."

"And the production took off."

"It was a beacon for the theatrical community. Here we were in the depths of the blacklist, and a group of blacklisted people, each of whom was respected in their area of work, had gotten together to do a piece of theatre which was described as a work of art and was eminently successful. These people couldn't work but they *were* working with considerable recognition. That piece was one of the more celebrated pieces of its day. Everybody in it was flying high. Prospective audiences were battling for tickets. It was phenomenal."

Concerning the effect of the blacklist on theatre, it was Debuskey's view that "By and large the theatre was happily removed from it, but one never knew for sure why an actor wasn't cast in a play. Equity passed an anti-blacklist clause in the basic contract, but you never knew."

In *Broadway*, his view of a half-century of theatre (Macmillan, 1970), Brooks Atkinson writes that *Sholom Aleichem* "became the focal point of McCarthyites all over the nation. They stigmatized the actors as traitors; they excoriated the critics who had praised the production. They tried to make a national scandal out of it."

Eventually there was the TV version of *Sholom Aleichem*. Merle Debuskey recalls, "Zero was anxious to work on it and he had some weight by then. Howard and Arnold, who controlled the property, felt that if the show were to get on TV, they needed people of the stature of Zero and Nancy Walker who at that time was a very well-known Broadway performer."

But in 1959, Ely Landau, chairman of National Telefilm Associates (NTA) which ran WNTA, Channel 13 in New York and New Jersey, and produced *Play of the Week*, was not immediately persuaded that Zero could even be employed. Don Richardson, Zero and Kate's old acting teacher, had suggested a *Sholom Aleichem* adaptation, which he himself would direct, to *Play of the Week* producers David Susskind and Henry Weinstein. Richardson also proposed the signing of a number of other blacklisted performers, and Landau, whose initial reaction was that he couldn't find a way to hire the blacklisted Mostel, began to appreciate the strategy of hiring blacklisted personnel en masse as a way of combating what all of them considered a scurrilous practice. The television production in some degree echoed the earlier historic action of Da Silva and Perl in organizing blacklisted performers. Coincidentally, Landau would be working again with Zero in the mid-Seventies, when his short-lived adventure in subscription movies, the American Film Theatre, produced the film adaptation of *Rhinoceros*.

The Zero who surfaced during *Sholom Aleichem* rehearsals, in which a number of blacklisted Jews like Jack Gilford, Lee Grant and Sam Levene were employed, demonstrated a double nature. One saw courtesy and hostility, generosity and greed. Zero, according to Jared Brown's *Zero Mostel*, made some effort to see that Nancy Walker, a Gentile in a Hebraic cluster, felt at home. Zero would lunch with Walker; throughout the meal he would carry on with a stream of Yiddish tales and an accent as thick as the celebrated wine Manischewitz assures us can be cut with the family knife. At some point during this series of Yiddish outpourings, it occurred to Walker that Zero was laboring double time in an attempt to provide this young comedian with a crash-course in *Yiddishkeit*.

But there is also the other Zero at work. Don Richardson found an ugliness in this other Zero, a man who was "constantly off in corners" letting his fellow actors know how much more capable this Mostel was and how, in the best of all possible worlds, the fruits of his considerable talent should have been properly recognized and all the leading roles should have been assigned to him. Richardson tells Brown about his own strenuous efforts to see that Zero was cast at all, only to find his student "whispering that this actor was no good and that one was no good. . . ."

But both the theatre and the TV *Sholom Aleichem* were well cast—Jacob Ben-Ami, one of the great artists of the Yiddish stage, eventually performed as Bontche in the Da Silva-Perl production—and both versions mitigated in some small manner against the onslaught of the self-appointed censors and the passivity of those who hadn't the courage to stand up against the tyranny of those years.

In 1956 some of the *Sholom Aleichem* theatre company in concert with writer-producer Sandy Friedman and producer Myron Weinberg were reunited. Banner Productions opened on September 16th at the Carnegie Hall Playhouse with *Tevya and His Daughters*. Again, Howard Da Silva directed and Arnold Perl wrote the play, based on translations of the Tevyeh stories.

June Prensky Gitlin, who was on the administrative staff for Rachel Productions, recalls some of the money-raising activities leading to *Tevya* in 1956. "My husband Harry Gitlin and I were residents of New Rochelle in those years. Through the temple, we got in touch with moneyed Jews in Westchester. Specifically, I remember making dinner for a bunch of potential backers, during which we had readings. They took place in my house and other houses in New Rochelle. One of the actors who came out to read was Zero."

Who never got cast as Tevya in Perl's dramatization, but became Tevye in *Fiddler* eight years later, on September 22nd 1964. Mike Kellin wins the role that Zero aspires to in '56, but Jerry Robbins is in the audience one night during the run and when it's time to make his own Tevye move, it becomes Zero's hour.

Banner Productions has a short-lived career. It produces *This Was Burlesque* with Ann Corio. It mounts a brief run of *Spring out of Season* by the blacklisted Ben Maddow. It designs a children's show, a few readings, and in a matter of months it ceases to exist. But there are still occasional checks issued to the Arnold

Perl estate. Perl, Da Silva, and Myron Weinberg are no longer among the living. Sandy Friedman, the surviving producer, receives some percentage of these occasional checks—he received one on the day we spoke—and he tells me that the money comes from an account connected to the original *Fiddler* company. Apparently some time after the opening of *Fiddler* on Broadway, Arnold Perl contacted Jerry Robbins, *Fiddler's* director, and reminded him that Robbins had seen Perl's *Tevya* at the Carnegie Hall Playhouse. Whatever the nature of their communication, and Robbins is the sole survivor of that meeting, the upshot of the encounter is that checks are still periodically issued to Perl's widow. It's likely that the *Fiddler* complex may simply have been fending off a nuisance suit, but it's conceivable that it may have been facing serious litigation.

In the summer of 1953 Kate is touring in *Three Men on a Horse*, Zero is performing in the Catskills, the boys are on Monhegan with their grandmother, Anna Harkin, and two more Jakes can be seen on *The Goldbergs*. After Philip Loeb's "settlement," Gertrude Berg offers the role to Robert H. Harris. He turns it down. Harold Stone appears as Jake for several weeks, Harris is again offered the role and this time he accepts. Harris will play Jake into the next year. Philip Loeb will occasionally visit *The Goldberg* set; he will come as a friend, a genial spirit.

In the autumn of 1954 Zero appears in a new play, *A Stone for Danny Fisher*, adapted by Leonard Kantor from the novel by Harold Robbins. The original director is fired and Luther Adler takes over rehearsals. The playbill will credit a Francis Kane as director, a pseudonym Adler used. The cast features Philip Pine as Danny Fisher, along with Sylvia Miles and Bert Freed. Viola Harris, the wife of Robert Harris, is hired as an understudy.

"I was into the technique of the actor," Viola Harris recalls. "I'd studied with Stella Adler and Benno Schneider and I had ideas about what acting should be. At rehearsals it was interesting to watch Zero. I felt he had no technique and was just improvising, and this went on not only in rehearsals but in performance. He was never in the same place twice on stage and when you worked with him you could never be absolutely sure just what was going to happen."

"Did he at least give you cues?"

"More or less. He seemed to me more like what you would expect a comic to be, not really an actor. At least that was my reaction at the time."

"I keep hearing that he wanted the stage and that your presence was almost immaterial, except as a foil."

"That happened more and more as he got more famous. At this point he was not such a big name. He kibbutzed around a lot. Being a very serious young actress, I felt it was a time-waster. He was always funny and clever and people enjoyed that, but I didn't feel he was a disciplined performer."

I ask if there were script discussions during the rehearsal period? "No, and that contributed to the problem. The director went out to the coast. Lots of friction. Harold Robbins was not happy, nor was the writer [Kantor]. They may have had financial problems; you just felt that things were not very secure. Because of that it afforded Zero the opportunity to take greater advantage than he might otherwise have if we'd have had a tougher director, someone who kept him in line. The show was about gangsters on the Lower East Side and I did not see Zero as being so right for the role of a hoodlum. I must say I wasn't as impressed with him as I'd been when I saw him as a comic at Cafe Society. I didn't feel he really listened, really reacted, did all the things I'd learned were the basic things an actor does."

The production has its lighter moments. "He was very amusing backstage," Harris recalls. "He had this big loud voice and it would just boom out. Luther Adler had taken over the direction and would come down on the subway with me and one day Luther brought me a bouquet. I think I reminded him of Sylvia Sidney—they'd just gotten divorced. Well everyone in the theatre began whispering about an affair. Except Zero, who never whispered "

"Would Zero have said something if he actually believed you and Luther were having an affair?"

"I can't tell you—probably not, I don't know. But he never whispered, and then there was the Sylvia Miles business."

The Sylvia Miles story, worthy of legendary status: "Every night Sylvia Miles would go into Zero's dressing room. Knowing Sylvia, how loud and aggressive she could be, one can understand how after a while she began to truly irritate Zero. But because he kidded around so much, it was not always easy for people to distinguish when he was serious and when he was kidding. So she must have assumed he was kidding when he would say, 'Get the hell out of my dressing room. I have to change. Don't come in. I don't want you,' in a very obvious way. But nothing seemed to help. She'd go in anyway. Finally he said to her, 'Listen, if you show up again I am really gonna let you have it. So watch out.'"

"So what was the 'it' he was going to let her have?"

"Well she came back. So what did he do? He pulled down his underpants and stark naked he started chasing her all around the backstage. She runs out screaming from his dressing room and he's chasing her without a stitch of clothing on. Needless to say, she never again went into his dressing room. I remember the scene vividly. At that moment he just became very dear to me. He threatened her and then he came through on the threat in his inimitable fashion. He had the chutzpah to do anything."

A Stone for Danny Fisher opened on October 21st, 1954, at the Downtown National Theatre, with Zero as chief mobster Maxie Fields. The *Morning Telegraph's* Whitney Bolton sees Zero as a "sort of connoisseur's Peter Lorre"—Bertolt Brecht had seen Zero as a possible substitute for Lorre in the late Forties. Bolton's Zero does "the eye and brow bit with becoming ease" and moves with a "strange shuffle." Walter Kerr in the *Herald Tribune* notes that Zero is "so far as I know the only living bald man with bangs" and that he has "a good bit of fun turning his Maxie Fields into a garish grotesque ('We can wait, can't we, Spit? One year, two years, three years . . .'). Mr. Mostel's baby-faced leer and drooping eyebrows do enliven the evening." Whether enlivening a gangster melodrama makes a good deal of sense or whether Zero's bangs ought to be engaging the spectators—well, critics do what they can.

Viola Harris recalls the blacklist vividly. Her husband Bob Harris who saw himself as an apolitical liberal discovered that he was on something called the "greylist." It seems there were actually three lists: black, grey and white.

"You're in trouble if you're not on the whitelist. Bob had already been investigated because of a Broadway play he'd done years before, called *Murder Incorporated*. There were a lot of Leftists working on that play, so it was presumed that Bob was on the Left just like the others. He was investigated and supposedly 'cleared.' He'd been getting a lot of work, at one point he was in four separate television shows a week, that included doing Jake and sometimes *Treasury Men in Action*. But Gertrude had asked him to replace Phil Loeb because she wanted somebody who would be squeaky clean."

"She thought Bob was clean?"

"Yes. So there he was doing Jake, and I would also appear occasionally. Then we were asked to be guests on Barry Gray's radio show. Gertrude urged Bob not to appear. She didn't want any more trouble. But we were so angry about *Red Channels* and all the various lists that we decided we were definitely going to be on the show. Barry Gray [a liberal commentator] asked us some innocuous questions and then he veered over to political issues. And Bob, who felt he owed some allegiance to Gertrude after the difficulty she'd had, the pressure she'd been under to fire Philip Loeb, steered clear of direct involvement in these political questions. He just avoided any direct response."

Nevertheless, Bob Harris found himself on the greylist.

"We had a friend, a TV director, who finally told Bob why he wasn't getting much work. There was a specific firm that wouldn't hire Bob, so we saw a lawyer, and we were going to sue. The attorney said, 'You cannot sue a shadow. The best thing to do is nothing.' The frustration was terrible. If this inability to get work was true for us who were complete innocents, you can imagine what it was like for those who were active in liberal circles. Someone like Phil was just ruined by this. And Zero was playing the borscht belt, taking little nightclub jobs, anything he could get to keep afloat, *because he could not get work.* It was horrible, horrible, just a terrible time. I remember I did this TV show and the director said to me, 'Viola, keep your mouth shut. Don't say anything about *anything,*' because the air was so thick with suspicion that you could not even be yourself. So we sat around the table, we had our pencils in our hands and were making notes, cuts in the script, and this performer who was witch-hunting lost his pencil. It fell to the floor and he bent to retrieve it at which point his costar said, 'Oh look, he's looking for Communists under the table.' She had the guts to say it because she was the star. Well, that was the atmosphere."

For Zero there are always light moments here and there, but these mid-Fifties are days and months of all but unrelieved gloom. Clara Baker believes that Zero's world "tottered" with the onslaught from *Red Channels* and HUAC. Nettie Crosley recalls a visit to the Hotel Goldman in New Jersey on an evening when Zero was performing. "My husband Eddie got upset because the tradition is that the hotel gives the entertainer dinner, and what they gave Sammy was leftover chicken, which was really not Sammy's bit. Then the owner says to Eddie, 'What do you want to be his friend for?' So later I had a fight with Eddie. I say, 'Why didn't you open your mouth?' After the show we sat down and Sammy took an eight ounce glass of booze and started drinking, which I had never seen him do. I was beside myself, it was embarrassing even to take the glass away. Then I found out what this was all about. He had taken a contract for so much money and by the time he'd finished performing they screwed him in terms of the small amount they had been prepared to pay him."

All reminiscent of *The Front*, where Zero as Heckie Brown is humiliated by the hotel management.

"He'd started to drink. Jewish boys didn't drink. Number one they didn't have *money* to drink."

If this was a terrible time for Zero, it became much worse when his mother died, on October 15th, 1954, during the run of *A Stone for Danny Fisher.*

"One night," Nettie Crosley recalls, "after a performance of *Danny Fisher*, Eddie and I go with Sammy to Moscowitz and Lupowitz," a celebrated Jewish restaurant on the Lower East Side, one of Zero's favorites. "Every time he'd see me he'd start crying. He did a lot of crying, the guy was crying for the past. And at that time his mother had just died and he'd gone to the funeral and his brothers tried to kill him, that's how he put it, because he'd married a *shiksah* and that's why momma died. And of course we scoffed at the whole thing. But you know they've now determined that enough stress will make you vulnerable to any goddamned thing that's cooking. Anyway, they were all big guys, even though Sammy himself was big, and he told us that they actually threatened him at the funeral. Maybe he was exaggerating, but her death and the guilt they were putting on him made him feel so bad. At the restaurant I kept saying, 'Why didn't you call me?' Because I was so used to protecting him."

In March of 1955 some of the blacklisted again join forces. *Once Over Lightly* was the brainchild of politically active theatre people and was produced at the Barbizon Plaza where the first blacklisted company, Rachel Productions, had mounted *The World of Sholom Aleichem*. The blacklisted Stanley Prager directed a blacklisted cast that included Sono Osato, Zero and Jack Gilford. Lyricist Yip Harburg suggested they call the show *The Banned Wagon*. Reviews were mixed, which meant either slow or sudden death at the box office. Zero was treated reasonably well, though some journalists opined that his antics—as Italian singer, diplomat, and precocious child—were wearing thin. According to Merle Debuskey, Zero was particularly offended by the *Times's* Brook Atkinson, who remarked on Zero's weight, decibel level, and sweaty attempts at humor.

Debuskey remembers that "At the next performance, Zero, using a cane, came down the aisle. When he got to the seat Atkinson had been sitting in, he proceeded to slam the seat with his cane and hurl curses in Yiddish, then went back into character."

During that time he and Herbie Kallem were busy painting

apartments. Bill and Jan McCartin recall the time Herbie and Zero came to paint their apartment on Bleecker Street in Greenwich Village.

"Herbie was the chief," Bill notes, and he consigned Zero to doing the inside of closets. "We wanted the place painted blue."

"Eggshell blue?"

"Midnight blue. As for Zero, he was lousy in closets. He'd come out sparring and sweating and say, 'Get me outta here, get me outta here.'"

"How many closets did you *have*?"

Bill describes it as "like a railroad flat. The hallway also had these narrow closets that you pulled out."

"Our landlord, Mr. Mattes, came to check things out," Jan remembers. "Herbie was on a ladder doing the ceiling and Zero was in the closet. And Mr. Mattes was questioning their 'technique.' 'Are you doing this, are you doing that?'"

Bill: "And *we* were *paying* for it."

Jan: "Then Herbie muttered something in Yiddish, some phrase, and Zero came lumbering out of the closet and said some derogatory thing in Yiddish."

Bill explains that "They both *knew* about the landlord, they *knew* he understood Yiddish. I don't know why the landlord had such a bad reputation, he was a kindly old man."

"But he was a landlord," Jan reminds her husband. "A very simple kind of guy. He used to go around and collect rents. We were the only ones who paid by check, and the other tenants would insult the hell out of him. He lived a long life, died at ninety-six. Anyway he didn't reply to Herbie and Zero's Yiddish, not a word to them. He was sort of astounded. He'd say to us, 'Where did you *find* these fellows?'"

Bill: "They obviously weren't his idea of painters, not the kind of painters *he* would get. They were neither professional nor the unprofessional kind he'd have hired."

Jan: "Zero could have made the most out of being a housepainter."

Bill: "He could take on any role. Zero could put on any kind of costume and the personality would begin to grow."

In June of 1955 the comedian Buddy Hackett took a brief vacation from Sidney Kingsley's play, *Lunatics and Lovers*, and Zero replaced him. Then Zero was hired for a West Coast tour which opened in Los Angeles at the Cathay Circle. On July 7th the long–awaited subpoena from the guardians of public virtue arrived in New York. HUAC notified Zero that he was to appear on August 19th, but then agreed to a postponement, rescheduling the hearing for October in Los Angeles. It was to be a fateful period in several ways. In the Mostels' ten-room apartment at the Belnord, two additional tenants had moved in. One was Kate's mother Anna, the other was the blacklisted Philip Loeb. Some time that summer Kate had an inkling that Philip Loeb was considering taking his life. In her book, *170 Years of Show Business*, she notes that she reprimanded him and apparently felt that this good talking-to had brought him back to his senses. The FBI was also snooping around, watching Zero when he was in town and keeping an eye on the apartment.

Viola Harris remembers seeing Philip Loeb those last two years. "Phil would come onto *The Goldbergs* set occasionally, and he was always flirtatious with me. And I liked Phil a lot. I didn't really know him. I was very young, very new in the business and I wasn't active in the unions yet . . . I knew Phil had a reputation for being very active in Equity, as was Sam Jaffe. The two were very good friends. And they were older men and I had great respect for them as a result. Phil could come onto the set, and I was amazed that he had such a delicious sense of humor. Looking at him you wouldn't suspect it. He'd be making passes in an offhand way. Then we met him one evening on Eighty-sixth Street "

It was Labor Day weekend. Zero was in California; Kate and the children were in Atlantic City. Philip Loeb apparently had the large apartment to himself, but he was planning to spend part of that weekend at the Hotel Taft.

"Bob and I just bumped into him on the street, and he looked vacant. He looked like he was off somewhere. And even when we talked to him we had the sense that he was not communicating. There definitely was something wrong and I remember saying to Bob, 'Do you think he's drunk?' and Bob said, 'No, but something is definitely wrong.' And the next thing we heard he was dead. I was overwhelmed by a sense of guilt, as if it was my fault, because I had not succeeded in getting him to come up to our apartment, and if I had done so, if he had talked to us, maybe we could have helped him. But I doubt it. I recall that he had no suitcase."

I comment to Viola, "He didn't need a suitcase for the Hotel Taft. All he needed was a little water."

The *New York World-Telegram and Sun* of Friday, September 2nd, 1955, reports that on Wednesday, Philip Loeb had registered at the Taft under the name of Fred Lang. "He hung a 'Do Not Disturb' sign on his door and never was seen alive again. . . . On a dresser stood a bottle containing fourteen sleeping pills. Nearby lay a doctor's prescription, dated Tuesday, for fifty sleeping tablets."

The late Murray Kempton, writing in the *New York Post* on September 13th, remarks that Loeb had told friends the name Fred Lang—in German the words means "long peace"—spoke to some deep longing in him. Apparently Loeb had brought up the subject of death any number of times in his final few weeks. Kempton theorizes that Loeb was simply worn out and longed to be free of all his worries. Loeb had had two major concerns. One involved his union activities. He would put in twelve-hour days, at no pay, working for Actors Equity and the Television Authority. His other concern was his son, diagnosed as schizophrenic. Loeb, a widower, had not only to maintain himself but pay for his son's inpatient keep at a private sanitarium. As mentioned earlier, the settlement with Gertrude Berg had guaranteed that, though Loeb himself would lose a steady income, there would be sufficient funds for his son for two years.

For the next three years Loeb took the little work he could find. During that time he was called to testify before a Senate committee looking into "Communist fronts." He denied belonging to the Party but certainly didn't please the committee when he told them he would never distance himself from anyone who fought for justice.

Loeb went on the road with *Time Out for Ginger*. Sam Jaffe viewed the producers of this tour as men who sensed that they can "get you a little cheaper." Then Loeb appeared for some weeks at the 4th Street Theatre Company as Tchevutykin in *The Three Sisters* at $87.50 per week. During this period, the money for his son's upkeep was exhausted; the boy was transferred to a state institution. Its principle function: to warehouse the mentally ill. Two months before he took his own life, Loeb received a letter from his son, pleading to be returned to the prior institution where a cure might be found—ironically, Loeb's son was under the delusion that communists were plotting to murder him. Loeb could do nothing for the boy, nothing for himself. His only resource: to find peace without paying out money he no longer possessed.

In his *New York Post* article Kempton quotes Sam Jaffe, "I cannot look back and think of anyone Philip ever harmed." Kempton comments that "his enemies did not even hate him. . . ." Loeb's sister, Sabina, weeping, tells the *Post*, "He's been hurt so terribly. . . . A person can just take so much."

Zero's stint in *Lunatics and Lovers* ends at the Alcazar Theatre in San Francisco. Enter a superior lunacy and a scene shift to Hollywood. Richard Gladstein, San Francisco attorney, is hired to represent Zero at the HUAC hearings. Zero has no money for counsel; his friend Seniel Otrow, an executive with Sealy Mattresses, pays for Gladstein's services.

From the Congressional Record:

INVESTIGATION OF COMMUNIST ACTIVITIES,
NEW YORK AREA—PART VIII (ENTERTAINMENT)

Friday, October 14, 1955
United States House of Representatives,
Subcommittee of the Committee on Un-American Activities,
Hollywood, Calif.

Committee members present: Representatives Clyde Doyle [acting chairman] and Donald L. Jackson.

Staff members present: Frank S. Tavenner, Jr., counsel; William A. Wheeler, investigator.

Early in the hearing Zero is asked about his affiliation with the young Communist League prior to his employment at Cafe Society.

> Mr. Mostel: I refuse to answer that question on the grounds of the fifth amendment.
>
> Mr. Tavenne: . . . did you become well acquainted with Ivan Black?
>
> Mr. Mostel: I would say I became acquainted to the extent that it was a business relationship. As a matter of fact, personally my attitude toward press agents is not one of the most complimentary kind, and I thought he was a necessity for a man who was in the entertainment field. He was not my great friend, although a friend.
>
> Mr. Tavenner: . . . did you acquire knowledge, personal knowledge, that Ivan Black was a member of the Communist Party?

Zero confers with his counsel.

> Mr. Mostel: Do you mind if I hesitate a moment? . . . It is a problem, it seems to me. That's why I am taking my time answering this question on these private opinions . . . I will be glad to answer any questions of that sort where I don't have to talk about other individuals.
>
> Mr. Tavenner: May I ask that the witness be directed to answer?
>
> Mr. Doyle: We are not satisfied with that answer, Witness, as being sufficient, and therefore I direct you to answer the question.

Zero again pleads the Fifth Amendment. Then Martin Berkeley's name materializes. Berkeley was an ex-Communist member who became notorious as a leading informer for HUAC. Tavenner reads Berkeley's testimony to Zero.

> Mr. Tavenner: "Zero Mostel, I met him in Hollywood, I will have to say around 1938, at the home of Lionel Stander. There was a meeting of the writers' fraction [sic] at which I was present, and he was among those who were there."

Mr. Mostel: I think Mr. Berkeley is in complete error. I was never here in 1938. I did not know Mr. Stander in 1938. I was a painter.

Tavenner won't give ground, neither will Zero.

Mr. Tavenner: Did you attend a meeting in the home of Mr. Stander at which Mr. Martin Berkeley was present?

Mr. Mostel: I have never been in the home of Mr. Stander in whatever city I may have run across him.

Mr. Tavenner: Did you attend a fraction [sic] meeting of the Communist Party in the home of Lionel Stander in 1942 or any other time?

Mr. Mostel: I have already answered that by saying I have never been at the home of Mr. Stander at any time.

Mr. Tavenner: Were you a member of the Communist Party in 1942?

This is pretty direct, and Zero won't answer. Tavenner asks if Zero has entertained at functions meant to assist either the Party or Communist-front organizations. Zero replies that he has performed at many types of meetings meant to battle cancer, heart disease, common colds "and a host of other favorites." There is much jockeying back and forth about Zero's willingness to discuss where he physically was and wasn't in 1938, and his refusal to discuss his political activities or allegiances anywhere during the same period. The Committee contends that since he addressed the question of his physical whereabouts, that testimony deprives him of legal grounds with which to invoke the Fifth Amendment concerning other questions related to that period. As Committee member Jackson puts it, "if Mr. Mostel says he was not here [Los Angeles] at that time it seems to me that would be a misuse of the constitutional amendment, because an answer to the question will not incriminate him." Zero notes during this interchange that he is not "a big legal brain."

Tavenner is armed with exhibits connecting Zero as entertainer to what HUAC contends are highly suspect organizations. One exhibit is from the Marxist publication *New Masses* announcing a rally sponsored by the Joint Anti-Fascist Refugee Committee, and one sponsored by the American Youth for Democracy which was planning a Youth Rally in support of the Maritime Workers. Zero peruses the names of other entertainers listed.

> Mr. Mostel: Incidently, there are some fine names on it. Durante and Milton Berle, Georgia Sothern.
>
> Mr Jackson: None of whom has been identified in open session as members of the Communist Party, however . . . . There is no question but what some very worthwhile performances were given by people who were entirely sincere in their motivation and who knew nothing of the Communist Party at all. I daresay if Mr. Durante and Mr. Berle were in your position today they would probably deny most vehemently that they had ever been members of the Communist Party.

Tavenner then produces an announcement from the April 30th, 1947, edition of *PM*, informing its readers that

> May Day has an added significance this year. Never before has the tide of reaction in America run so strong; never before was the threat of fascism, of the extinction of all civil liberties so great. . . .We in particular can live and work only as free men. Therefore, we join with labor in the great May Day demonstration for peace, security and freedom. We add our strength to the strength of the masses of people who cherish democracy.

Among the signatories are Walter Bernstein, a blacklisted writer who will eventually write the screenplay for *The Front*, Howard Fast, Will Geer, William Gropper, Chaim Gross, Uta Hagen, Langston Hughes, Rockwell Kent, Jack Levine, Eve Merriam, Zero Mostel, Paul Robeson, Moses Soyer, Louis Untermeyer, and Max Weber. Zero is asked by Tavenner whether his name appears as one of the sponsors, but Zero refuses to answer on previously-stated constitutional grounds. He responds affirmatively when Tavenner asks if he is a member of Actors Equity, but then Tavenner goes on:

> Mr. Tavenner: Have you been a member of the Communist Party at any time while you have been a member of Actors Equity Association?

Mr. Mostel: I decline to answer that question, on the same constitutional grounds.

Mr. Tavenner: Are you now a member of the Communist Party?

Mr. Mostel: I am not.

Mr. Tavenner: You are not?

Mr. Mostel: No, sir.

Mr. Tavenner: Were you a member of the Communist Party on July 7, 1955, when you were subpoenaed by this committee?

Mr. Mostel: I decline to answer that question, on the previously stated constitutional grounds.

Mr. Tavenner: Were you a member of the Communist Pary when you entered this hearing room?

Mr. Mostel: No.

Mr. Tavenner: When did you cease to be a member of the Communist Party?

Mr. Mostel: I decline to answer that question on my constitutional grounds.

Mr. Tavenner: Were you a member of the Communist Party yesterday?

Mr. Mostel: I decline to answer that question, on my same constitutional grounds.

Chairman Doyle takes over the questioning. He assures the witness that HUAC has a duty to investigate subversives but that Committee members do not "look forward with pleasure to this sort of thing. . ." and Zero assures him that "I sure don't, either." Doyle tells the witness that "I cannot help but feel, Witness, that there was a time when you were a member of the Communist Party," and Zero informs him, "That is a feeling, not knowledge." Gladstein, Zero's counsel, tells the chair that "You must be aware of Harvey Matusow and others like him, who admitted that they falsely charged membership." Apparently the discussion gets a little testy. Matusow comes to stand for the archetypal accuser of leftists, and Zero breaks into the confrontation between chair and counsel with his friendly plea, "Don't fight, boys." Doyle then assumes a fatherly tone toward the witness.

Mr. Doyle: You are in a great field of entertainment of the American public. From now on why don't you get far removed from groups that are known to be Communist dominated . . . that sort of thing? . . . Why don't you remove yourself far away from that atmosphere, sir? You can be a much better inspiration and joy to the American people if they know that there is not a drop, not an inkpoint, not a penpoint of a favorable attitude by you toward the Communist conspiracy.

Mr. Mostel: My dear friend, I believe in the antiquated idea that a man works in his profession according to his ability rather than his political beliefs. When I entertain, my political beliefs are not spouted. As a matter of fact, I am casual about my political beliefs, which I wouldn't tell anybody, unless you are my friend and you are in my house.

Mr. Doyle: I am not asking about—

Mr. Mostel: And I have bad instant coffee I make, I'll tell you that.

Mr. Doyle: I am not asking about your political beliefs.

Mr. Mostel: My dear friend, I believe in the idea that a human being should go on the stage and entertain to the best of his ability and whatever he wants to say, because we live, I hope, in an atmosphere of freedom in this country.

Mr. Doyle: That's right, and we will fight for your right to think as you please and be as you please, provided you do it within the four corners of the Constitution. Don't you think it is your duty as a great entertainer to at least find out hereafter where the money you help raise is going, whether or not it is going to some subversive cause against the constitutional form of government in out nation?

Mr. Jackson: Mr. Chairman, may I say that I can think of no greater way to parade one's political beliefs than to appear under the auspices of *Mainstream*, a Communist publication, on the same program, the same platform, as it is alleged here—you have refused to state whether or not you actually did so appear—with Dalton Trumbo, Hans [Hanns] Eisler, John Howard Lawson, W.E.B. DeBois, Dorothy Parker, Howard Fast, and Zero Mostel. That program to me speaks volumes as to why you are here. Communist propaganda cannot exist without the funds that are derived from programs of this kind . . .

Mr. Mostel: I do appreciate your opinion very much, but I do want to say that—I don't know, you know—I still stand on my grounds, and maybe it is unwise and unpolitic for me to say this: If I appeared there, what if I did an imitation of a butterfly at rest? Therefore, I was not—there is no crime in making anybody laugh. I don't care if you laugh at me.

Mr. Jackson: If your interpretation of a butterfly at rest brought any money into the coffers of the Communist Party, you contributed directly to the propaganda effort of the Communist Party. Now, there is where it is important.

Mr. Mostel: Suppose I had the urge to do the butterfly at rest somewhere?

Mr. Doyle: Yes; but please, when you have the urge, don't have such an urge to put the butterfly at rest by putting some money in the Communist Party coffers as a result of that urge to put the butterfly to rest. Put the bug to rest somewhere else next time.

The above represents some portion of the transcript as it appears in the Congressional Record. But there have been deletions by an anonymous editor. In a 1974 interview with Jerry Tallmer of the *New York Post*, Zero complains bitterly about Eric Bentley's use of the HUAC transcript in creating his drama, *Are You Now or Have You Ever Been*. Zero recalls some of his combative moments that were struck from the record. At one point he referred to a major studio as 18th Century-Fox, then moved it up a hundred years. At another point, he referred to a California House member as a "bleep." The "bleep" occurred during a tense exchange between witness and chairman. The witness, ruminating out loud, referred to the chairman as "a shmuck." The chair then requested a definition of the descriptive noun, its meaning not being readily to hand.

At this writing we're in the waning decade of a century of exiles, of wandering, of the displaced—even though history is almost by its nature the story of displacement, of tribes moving in on one another's territory, of colonizing ages, of revolutionary eras and nationalistic epochs rending and obliterating and reinventing the maps of the known world. In these waning days we are witnessing a particularly virulent example of forced or voluntary exile, of incessant wandering, of vast populations displaced and massacred not once but repeatedly, as if each displacement and massacre were nothing more than a dress rehearsal for the next.

Perhaps Camus was right, the murder of Louis the Sixteenth, of God's surrogate divinity, set something in motion that, almost two millennia later, we have not fully come to terms with. But on the other hand, what's one king more or less? We see rulers, heads of state, venerated on Monday and ground into dust by Wednesday. Presidents, prime ministers, emperors, queens, generalissimos, royal personages of one stamp or another come and go. Someone is always willing to bow the knee before them;

someone else always ready to riddle them with bullets. And the displaced come pouring across borders: when the potato crop fails two years running, when the nihilists cause the crown sleepless nights, when the police display too much ardor, when the revolutionary order unveils its weapons for reeducation, weapons such as the rope, the guillotine, the gas chamber.

The modern artist, a displaced being by definition, often doubly displaces self by a kind of willful disabling, an incapacity to accept whatever norms the culture elects. Thus Joyce flees a jingoistic, clergy-ridden Dublin; Brecht flees a Berlin drunk with Nazis; Ionesco and Beckett metaphorically flee stifling bourgeois comforts and the demented logic of Western Europe; and Virginia Woolf ultimately flees her grounded self. It takes men of a curious conservatism, of a misplaced traditionalism like T.S. Eliot and Henry James to attempt an almost ecstatic reversal, a drive at full throttle into the entrails of a prior age, and even they are arrested, fixated by what they perceive as the brazen, seductive face of contemporary values.

Is it an accident that in 1956 the blacklisted Zero Mostel's barely-noticed appearance should be in a drama by the only recently-noticed Bertolt Brecht who has wandered back toward the homeland and finally settled in Communist East Berlin? That in 1958 Mostel's first major role should be as the wandering Leopold Bloom in *Ulysses in Nighttown*, an adaptation of Joyce's epic novel of displacement? That in 1961 he should make his first starring appearance on Broadway in *Rhinoceros* by the displaced Eugene Ionesco and dredge forth what those who saw him do it regard as an electrifying portrayal of a human whose humanity is displaced by the bestial urgencies of a rhinoceros? That in that same year, 1961, he should appear on television as one of Sam Beckett's displaced tramps in *Waiting for Godot*? That in 1962 in *A Funny Thing Happened on the Way to the Forum*, he should act out that marginal being society mocks but cannot bear to liberate, the comic slave? That in 1964 he should at last take on the role of the displaced Tevye in *Fiddler on the Roof*? That in 1968 he should become another kind of outcast, one that homophobic society still cannot come to terms with, the screaming homosexual in Paddy Chayefsky's *The Latent Heterosexual*? And that in his final stage performance, that of Shylock in Arnold Wesker's *The Merchant*, in the latter days of 1977, he should be seen as another traditionally suspect being, supposedly outside the norms of the greater culture, mocked, despised and in countless other ways ill-used?

All this an accident? Most likely. But not entirely. Zero was not mad to take on all these roles; they were certainly not all beautifully written or conceived, but all seem to have addressed that alienated being within him. And in each case he brought with him a cunning, a daring, an inventiveness, and that boundless energy that sometimes enspirited, sometimes exhausted those around him.

To begin with—the early plays. Brecht, Joyce, Ionesco, the displaced writing of the displaced. If Zero Mostel did not always seek out these roles, then at the very least he tumbled into the well each artist constructs in the attempt to allay that terrible thirst that never leaves the exile.

In 1956 Bertolt Brecht is in East Berlin. In the decade following his testimony before HUAC, Brecht has reestablished himself with his own company, the Berliner Ensemble. The Brecht-Weill *Threepenny Opera*, born in the waning days of the Weimar Republic, has taken New York by storm in its somewhat sanitized but vigorous Marc Blitzstein adaptation at the Theatre de Lys where it has had two long runs. In June of '56 Eric Bentley, whose pioneering critical work, *The Playwright As Thinker*, has placed Brecht alongside other towering figures in modern drama, e.g. Pirandello and Federico Garcia Lorca, visits Berlin to confer with Brecht for what will be the last time. In his *Brecht Memoir*[23] Bentley tells us that he was eager to get "B.B.'s" reaction to the Twentieth Communist Party Congress in Moscow,

> at which Khruschev had recently "told all" about Stalin, but I did not force the issue, and he . . . wanted to talk theatre. . . . Brecht was saying, "Helli thinks Ethel Merman would be the best American Mother Courage. Could we get her?" "Alan Schneider has written us saying he wants to direct the play but with Helen Hayes in the part. Could she hack it?"

Alan Schneider once told me that he recalled Brecht considering Mae West for the role of Mother Courage.

"Tell me about *My Fair Lady*. Is it something we could put on with our Regine Lutz as Eliza?"

As for my own plans in New York, what had happened to the Leo Kerz production of *A Man's a Man*? He (Brecht) had wanted the play put on during the Korean War: it would have had a lesson in it for America. And Howard Da Silva's interest in *Chalk Circle*? Had that too come to nothing? I laid my current project out before BB: I wanted the rights to *The Good Woman of Setzuan* for Uta Hagen, Herbert Berghof, and myself. With these in hand, we would offer the play to his old and trusted producer, Hambleton [T. Edward Hambleton, coproducer of the Phoenix Theatre in New York]. Frau Hauptmann [Brecht's close adviser, editorial collaborator and in some sense alter ego] was listening hard. Brecht nodded and said, "*Gut, die Hauptmann* will put it in writing."

In August of '56 Bentley is in Truro, on Cape Cod. "Would Hambleton take the play?" he wonders. "And us three with it?" That is, Bentley, Hagen and Berghof?

With his partner Norris Houghton, he came to my summer place on Cape Cod to tell me yes. I was already writing the English lyrics at a small reed organ I'd purchased for the purpose in the Wellfleet antique shop. . . . The day was August 16. On that same day—melodrama à la Chaplin but flatly true—I received a cable from Johannes R. Becher, Minister of Culture in the German Democratic Republic, inviting me to a memorial meeting in East Berlin. Bertolt Brecht had died of heart failure.

Brecht had written his last, but the Brecht dramas, in their English incarnations, for which Bentley has been a principal adapter-translator, were just beginning to be visible. The Theatre Union had produced *The Mother* in New York in 1935, a production which Brecht considered *dreck*; the verbal and physical battles had resulted in Brecht's being barred from rehearsals. In June, 1942, Viennese director Berthold Viertel had directed scenes from *The Private Life of the Master Race*, in Brecht's original German at the Barbizon Plaza, and in June of 1945, Viertel replaced Erwin Piscator as director in an English-language version of the play. Brecht and Piscator, theatrical giants, refugees from Berlin where Piscator had been Brecht's mentor, had just had a nasty battle.

The production was mounted in the auditorium of the Twenty-third Street campus of City College before a handful of people. There were many fights during rehearsal; Brecht couldn't stand the work of the actress playing the Jewish Wife and "revised" her part by cutting out half her lines. Bentley writes that Brecht tried to prevent the play from opening, and when he couldn't negotiate that he tried to prevent the press from coming. In 1947 Charles Laughton starred in *Galileo*, in June at the Coronet Theatre in Beverly Hills, then in November on Broadway. New York critics were not particularly taken with Brecht's drama; they saved their praise for Barry Stavis's *Lamp at Midnight*, another dramatic study of the formidable but politic Galileo. There were some dim noises in the early Forties about a production of *Schweyk in the Second World War*, which Brecht was writing in Santa Monica. Visiting New York, Brecht hoped to persuade Kurt Weill to compose a score for *Schweyk* and use his influence to promote a Broadway production, but nothing came of it, nor was Laughton's influence of any avail in California. But *The Threepenny Opera* production at the DeLys meant a new beginning for Brecht, although raising capital for any Brecht undertaking in the United States remained difficult.

The Phoenix Theatre now committed itself to Bentley's project. Housed in the very space on Second Avenue and Twelfth Street where Maurice Schwartz's Yiddish Art Theatre first produced *Tevye the Dairyman*, the Phoenix penciled in *The Good Woman of Setzuan* as part of its 1956–57 subscription season.

Norris Houghton, whom I spoke with early in the winter of 1989, recalls that "T. Edward had known Brecht for some years. We wanted to do *The Good Woman*. Well, it was presented to us as a package. Eric persuaded us that we would have to deal with him and that he would want to direct. We knew nothing of Eric as a director, but T. Edward and I decided that we would go along with him."

But Eric Bentley tells me that "It was my thought that

Herbert Berghof would direct and I would write the adaptation, but Herbert didn't want to direct Uta. During rehearsals Herbert kept a low profile."

Rehearsals began that fall with Uta Hagen in the title role of Shen Te. Paul Dessau composed the incidental music and Wolfgang Roth designed a set which was based on Teo Otto's designs for the original Berliner Ensemble production. Zero was cast as Shu Fu, the boisterous but curiously innocent neighborhood barber. Shu Fu has matrimonial designs on young Shen Te; the woman has opened a small tobacco shop nearby and is already drowning in debt because of her instinctive generosity.

Like much of Brecht's work, *The Good Woman of Setzuan* is a cautionary tale in which the natural instincts of greed and corruption help sustain a corrupt sociopolitical order. Brecht believes that only through fallible man's vigilance, through his careful scrutiny of the societal structure he inhabits can a just order evolve. Given the belief that endemic corruption must first be acknowledged and then channeled toward some positive goal—who indeed is to make this judgment?—it would seem that no one system is preferable to any other, since through its cunning nature the corrupt being will adapt any system to its advantage and make itself at home within any mode of channeling. Thus, to envision Brecht as a Marxist at ease in the postwar communism of the Democratic German Republic is to be taken in by cold war rhetoric or the belief that isms are the ultimate arbiters of behavior.

Zero Mostel admired Brecht's approach to theatre. The two had met some time in 1942 in Hollywood, perhaps again in 1943 when Brecht, a comparative unknown refugee in the West, struggling to make a living in the film industry and attempting to gain a foothold in the Broadway theatre, was working out of his Santa Monica house on several plays, including *The Caucasian Chalk Circle* and the aforementioned *Schweyk*. It's likely that neither man knew much about the other at that time, but Eric Bentley reflects that "when B.B. was in Hollywood, he tried to know who was both talented and Red, and Zero was among those he found out about." Through Luise Rainer, then among the most acclaimed of Hollywood actresses and the estranged wife of Clifford Odets, Brecht was awarded a monthly stipend to finish the script of *Chalk Circle* as it was then called. Again there were thoughts about Broadway and Brecht expanded the role of Azdak, the corrupt and comic village judge, because he wanted to offer the part to his friend Oscar Homolka. But Brecht also intimated that the role might be performed by Zero Mostel.

Eric Bentley notes that Brecht had the unfortunate habit of playing one actor off against another. In the case of *Schweyk*, a draft of which Brecht completed in June of 1943, again Zero was approached, this time to consider the title role of the canny Czech trying to survive the Nazi occupation of Prague. Bentley believes that the approach to Zero was simply Brecht's way of prodding Peter Lorre to agree to perform as Schweyk before Mostel snapped up the part. Generally, Brecht's strategy was to involve an assortment of talents in work, to cast a wide net—it extended to writing collaborators[24]—in the hope that some combination of this widening group might help create favorable conditions for a production. But there was no foreseeable production of *Schweyk*, which was not produced until January of 1957, five months after Brecht's death in August of 1956, when it opened at the Polish Army theatre in Warsaw. By that time, Zero's only performance in a Brecht play had come and was rapidly fading from view.

During rehearsals at the Phoenix, Zero expressed his appreciation for Bentley's skills. Later events turned their relationship sour. Zero was incensed when Bentley served as the sole witness for Toby Cole in an arbitration proceeding between Zero and his one-time agent, and he had nothing positive to say about Bentley's use of him in the latter's *Are You Now Or Have You Ever Been*. Bentley, who is still raw from Zero's treatment of him in the Seventies, nevertheless dedicated his 1981 play, *Concord*, a take-off on Kleist's *Broken Jug*, "to the memory of Z.M."

In the Seventies Zero could recall little of value in regard to Bentley and *The Good Woman* production, and according to Kate's memoirs, which Zero helped to edit, saw Bentley as the man sitting with the typewriter, pounding out notes for the actors during rehearsals. Norris Houghton believes the typewriter may have taken on unhealthy proportions in Zero's head. "I suspect that Eric himself found that it was difficult to work with actors. At the first dress rehearsal I was aware that he was taking copious notes, but then he dismissed the actors rather than giving them any of his notes. Eric went home and stayed up half the night writing. It's my sense that he was turning these notes into critical essays which he brought to the theatre the next morning, and the first thing that happened was that the cast was assembled and Eric read to them these essays he had sat up all those hours creating."

During previews of *The Good Woman*, Zero responded to a note of Bentley's in which the director was taking his actor to task for "horsing around" during rehearsals. Bentley believes Zero misunderstood the criticism and took it to mean that he was not to improvise during the previews. Zero's response indicates obvious irritation but also pleasure at the chance to work with the first-time director.

"Dear Flak," Zero begins. "Until I got your note I didn't feel I was in the show. Now that I am feeling this I wonder what I am doing in the show. I knew Brecht fairly well and perhaps in an unguarded moment he expressed admiration for my work. I express gratitude to you for perhaps your unguarded and soft-spoken pat. I have had quite a lengthy career on the stage and I no longer look for approval. Sometimes I have the sneaky attitude that I might be really doing it for money. Then logically since this latter attitude is definitely at odds with my being in the show, I may even think I merely wanted to be in a Brecht play, despite the presence of others. You see I liked Brecht unguardedly.

"That the children or the kids (as you say) find it difficult to concentrate while I am on the stage is, I suspect, not so much to do with me. They might not be able to concentrate at all despite anyone's presence on the stage. Then it might be that their theatrical learning is remiss. Or my dear friend nothing will help them whatsoever. And if our star [Uta Hagen] is thrown I suggest you or Berghoff [sic] tell her to react to what is on the stage at the moment. You can't do anything on the stage twice the same way—that is a mania and a perfect pitch approach that belongs to electrical equipment. Sometimes I again have that vague feeling that there is not a Good Woman in her.

"About my changing attacks during preview, I feel I would be depriving my conscience of its honesty if I didn't try to find the truth of a role. Abe Lincoln and I were raised to tell the truth and with Abe gone I am almost obsessed with this idea. Besides I have had very little rehearsal and I believe I must rehearse somewhere or is that not the purpose of a preview?

"I have gotten on with every idiot who dared be nice to me or worked with me. I have almost made a petty career of that. But such balderdash as to disrupting companies belongs in some public school production by people or students who dislike their principal. Obviously I cannot change my personality—also I wouldn't—in any case I am stuck with it. . . . Brecht liked my personality and 1 am noncommittal about others who may have liked it.

"About my first entrance, I can either make people howl or hate me—whichever you want I will do. Remember I am also not alone on stage.

"I admit however it was a pleasure working with you.

"Your friend and colleague."

Signed with a cartoon face of a round, bald, mustached, moonlike fellow.

Throughout Zero's career, the issue of "relating to" other actors, of changing lines and stage business was gone over endlessly. In May of 1973, a decade after *Rhinoceros* and *Forum* and *Fiddler*, Zero is interviewed by Leonard Harris as part of a 92nd Street Y series called "Conversations in Theatre." Zero tells Harris, "My motivation to do a part is that every day I make a new creation. You make up this new creation with what you are that day. How can it [the role] be the same? The producer, the director and the chief usher, who don't have to play it every day, go for a vacation after you've broken your ass for many months to make it what it is. They come back very tan while you're very pale and they say, ' You changed the word!' But I never changed the word. I made it *real*. I made it live for that one night."

Well into *The Good Woman*, Brecht's barber Shu Fu takes the audience into his confidence. Shu Fu has in mind a delicate courtship of the gentle Shen Te, and strategy dictates an intimate supper. Does that elicit "vulgar thoughts" on the part of the spectator? Well nothing untoward will take place. There'll be "an exchange of ideas," the table decorated with white chrysanthemums, the communion of two souls, hopefully a moment of eye contact conspiring to elevate man and woman to a higher spiritual plane, and so on. A good moment for a Mostel soliloquy. Zero can move about the stage at will, take various stances night after night, but the *language*, Bentley's English adaptation, is very specific. "Dirty" or "sexy thoughts" won't do it. "Vulgar thoughts" has a schoolmarm delicacy edging towards a prissiness which deepens the irony before us, the sight of the ponderous Zero paying court in a semi-Victorian mode.

Like other directors, Bentley valued Zero's inventiveness and spontaneity. There is a moment in Scene Four where Shu Fu evaluates the attributes of Shen Te.

> Shu Fu: It surprises me how beautiful Miss Shen Te is looking today! I never gave her a passing thought before. But now I've been gazing upon her comely form for exactly three minutes. I begin to suspect I am in love with her.

In rehearsal one day, Zero took an exceptionally long pause between "exactly" and "three minutes," eyeing his watch intently. The orchestrated pause drew laughter from fellow performers watching. Zero decided to build the moment further. At the next rehearsal—two watches, one on each wrist. Larger pause, laughter more pronounced. Next rehearsal—three watches, Zero's eyes darting between watches. Bentley decided things were getting out of hand. "Next thing he'd be working with four watches. I had to put my foot down. Two watches were more than enough."

There is a moment when Shu Fu strikes the water-seller

with a curling iron. Zero's first strike resulted in laughs. Bentley conferred with his actor. Audiences had to believe the attack; it was important they be convinced that the hot iron was crippling Wong's arm. "He listened to me. He agreed about the seriousness of the moment, but when he attempted to turn the moment around—more laughs. There was nothing I could do, he was naturally funny."

But one recalls Zero's improvisation as the shopkeeper in the Malamud story, grieving over his dead child.

Did *The Good Woman of Setzuan* ever catch fire at the Phoenix? The company had scheduled a six-week run but audiences were small, considering the vastness of the house, and the run was brought to a close after the third week.

Reviews for *Good Woman* were mixed and ultimately of not much help to the producers. In the Sunday *Times* of December 30th, Brooks Atkinson announces that Bentley's production, lyrics and text adaptation are all flavorless. He does compliment the work of Uta Hagen, Zero, Gerald Hiken as the water-seller, Nancy Marchand as Shen Te's landlady, and Albert Salmi as the unemployed aviator who courts Shen Te for her money. But Atkinson finds the other performers lifeless and awkward. On the other hand, Thomas R. Dash, writing for *Women's Wear Daily* on December 19th, is quite taken with the production. He tells his readers that Bentley's English version "should provide a rewarding experience," and that the evening "should prove beguiling," though "rarely exalting or overwhelming." *Newsday* on December 28th, comes down in the middle; the evening is overly-long but intermittently "rewarding." *Theatre Arts* magazine, in its February, 1957 issue, compliments Bentley's "anti-naturalistic" staging as "very ingenious and lively," but counters this praise by noting that Bentley's adaptation delivers Brecht's message with "singular lack of thrust. . ." Without a single exhortation to "Run, you must see this before it closes," and with the press generally underwhelmed, the show was doomed.

In March of 1957, John Patrick's play *Good as Gold*, satirizing among other phenomena the FBI, bumbled into the Belasco on

Broadway after its tryout in Boston. For Zero, cast as a down-to-earth, street-smart philosopher whose wooden leg is the carrier for some choice eighty-proof whisky, Patrick's play seemed like a golden opportunity. The Broadway pay scale was rising, but the play itself never rose, and the run collapsed after four performances. The producers were apparently wary of its political satire and had induced Patrick to soften his bite; by opening night the play was moving rapidly toward a gumless senility.

In my meeting with Ring Lardner Jr. and Frances Chaney, the quick little disaster comes to mind. "What was that thing he took over the lead in?" Lardner wonders, and Frances Chaney replies, "Oh my God. I've forgotten the name of it—forget it, terrible little show, the flowers grew up onstage." But it is neither easily remembered nor forgotten. "*Good as Gold?*" Lardner suggests. And Chaney assents, muttering the title. Lardner persists. "He took over Buddy Hackett's role. Wasn't that it?" Chaney is impatient. "I don't know *what* he took over. Whatever it was, it wasn't much of a play. He may have taken over Buddy Hackett's role in a different play."

Zero had replaced Hackett in *Lunatics and Lovers*. As for *Good as Gold*, one's principal memory of it is that it came (on March 7) and it went (on March 9).

The authors Padraic and Mary Colum spent their last years on Morningside Heights, teaching at Columbia University, a far cry from the Dublin of their youth. The memory of their friend James Joyce was never far from them and one day Padraic Colum suggested to writer Marjorie Barkentin that she consider dramatizing what had become known as the "Nighttown" section of *Ulysses*. Barkentin, it seems, hardly needed urging, she had been dreaming of some adaptation of the novel ever since Judge John Woolsey's 1933 decision lifting the ban on what the U.S. government had contended was a pornographic work. Barkentin's script went begging for some two years, it could not find a producer, it seemed like such an odd, ephemeral piece of writing. Then, when Barry Hyams chose to produce Barkentin's script, a Leopold Bloom could not be found. Burgess Meredith was asked to play the role but Meredith wanted to direct; the task of finding a Bloom fell to Meredith.

For reasons which are hardly clear now, no one wanted the part. But No One, or No Man, if we go back to Homer's epic poem—Ulysses takes that name in eluding death at the hand of the terrible Cyclops—becomes both Everyman and Zero. Thus in a kind of *reductio ad absurdum*, the image of Zero flits into the mind of a somewhat exasperated Meredith. Perhaps No Man, this boisterous, panther-like Mostel, will undertake to move through Joyce's night. And so the blacklisted Meredith sits down with the blacklisted Mostel in Dinty Moore's restaurant and learns that Zero had been reading *Ulysses* back at City College "out loud in an alcove with other rebels" and that he knew "whole sections of it by heart." Years later Zero will tell the *Post's* Jerry Tallmer that "we'd take our bootleg copy and read it in the urinal."

Ulysses in Nighttown opened on June 5th, 1958, at what was called the Rooftop Theatre, the third and top floors of an historic building at the corner of Second Avenue and Houston Street. On street level stood the National Theatre, a landmark in the history of Yiddish theatre. It had been home to Boris Thomashevsky, to Jacob Adler, to playwright Jacob Gordin, to countless Yiddish stars, to Minsky's burlesque. Its name had been changed to the Roumania Opera House, and for a brief period to the Goldfaden Opera House. Avrom Goldfaden, "the father of Yiddish theatre," came to America in 1887 and announced that he would take over as director of the Roumania Opera and rename it after himself, a move which led to a bitter, month-long strike among the luminaries and supporting characters of the Yiddish theatre, and which featured not only wounded pride but some bruised bodies and a series of arrests by the local police.

The National, as it was renamed after the Goldfaden turmoil, would continue to enchant and infuriate Yiddish audiences and actors through the first half of the century, albeit with dwindling spectators in its final years, until 1959 when it and the rest of the building, which now included the Off-Broadway Rooftop Theatre, would be demolished to make way for the new Second

Avenue subway line, itself for the past three decades abandoned and boarded up, a casualty of budget constraints.

The writing credit for *Ulysses in Nighttown* indicates that Barkentin "dramatized and transposed" sections of the novel. In fact, though much of the drama hones in on the small hours of that celebrated night when the paths of Leopold Bloom and Stephen Daedalus finally converge, the play opens very much as the novel opens, with "stately plump" Buck Mulligan and Stephen living in the Martello Tower and moves late in the play to Molly Bloom's closing monologue. The image of the tower— Zero talks of having visited the actual Dublin site—"moves out of view" early in the drama to allow for the world of Leopold (Zero) and Molly (Pauline Flanagan) Bloom to take shape.

In his 1974 interview with Jerry Tallmer, during the Broadway revival of *Nighttown*, Zero notes that he went to Dublin after the original production in order to sense the town that Joyce physically exiled himself from but to which, psychically, he would always be bound. Zero announces that he visited the top of the Martello Tower, looked down and "there it was, 'the snot-green sea.' Joyce was such a precursor, as keen as Freud. Like all poets, he foresees things of years to come."

Tallmer asks Zero about Joyce's "ineluctable modality of the visible," and Zero roars:

> What's the big secret? . . . Klee very interestingly said: "The object is to make things that are not visible." Braque said: "A work is finished when you've completely obliterated the original conception." To me, works of art, by nature, are not definable. Why do you have to explain everything?

Zero tells Tallmer that he owns a pirated first edition, as well as sections published in Margaret Anderson's magazine, *The Little Review*. It's likely that this "pirated edition" Zero is speaking of is the edition published in New York by Samuel Roth, himself also a writer. The reader should be advised that this presumed pirate was the uncle of the author of this biography, and that contrary to the general impression in the literary world, encouraged first by Ezra Pound who acted as Joyce's agent, and supported much later by Joyce's biographer Richard Ellmann, Roth always claimed that he had paid Pound for the rights to the novel and that Pound had *probably* pocketed the money—no vast sum to begin with—and used the occasion to vent his anti-Semitic spleen on a Jewish author and publisher whose own notoriety on the literary scene made such venting appear quite reasonable. To complicate matters, Samuel Roth's eyesight wasn't a great deal better than James Joyce's and between these two gentlemen they managed to sustain several thousand typographical errors. Roth is also noted for having serialized sections of Joyce's *Work in Progress*, later named *Finnegans Wake*.[25]

Shortly after Zero's death, Burgess Meredith, who directed both the 1958 and 1974 *Nighttown* productions, reminisced for the September 18th, 1977, issue of the *Los Angeles Times*. He recalled that Zero's approach to other performers was that of a predatory beast both striking out and defending home turf. Meredith saw his behavior as "genetic," somewhat resembling "the hiss of a cat [or perhaps] the subsonic rumblings of a whale" and that this manner of being in the world, on- or off-stage, consumed most of Zero's "waking hours." Public dining with Zero tested one's equilibrium, Zero would enter a dining room as if he were "assaulting the Omaha Beaches." Other diners' "first instinct was to dive behind their tables like bunkers."

Commenting on Zero's performance, Meredith had the impression that the actor/comedian "seemed embattled and menaced," both by his fellow actors and by the spectators watching them. In the earlier Houston Street production, the old building "shook like the scaffolding at Cape Canaveral [and during these moments] we called it Zero Hour." Finally, Meredith remembers the night that the predatory, hissing, rumbling Mostel bit one of his colleagues. It was a moment of particularly high energy for Zero; the audience assumed that the victim's screams were simply part of the fun.

For the first production, dancer-choreographer Valerie Bettis was brought in to assist Meredith, who apparently felt that the play needed the formal logic of the dance, a risky assumption since dance movements veer toward a formality in which the humanity of the characters often tends to serve the form rather than the form serving the humanity. But fortunately we are dealing with Zero Mostel, who could outwit, out-talk, and generally subvert the best-laid plans of those guiding him through the minefields of art.

On opening night, the New York critics, many of whom had long since written Zero off as a tiresome clown on and off Broadway since his days at Cafe Society could not believe what they were seeing. Gilbert Seldes, covering the play for a recently-founded neighborhood weekly known as the *Village Voice*, told its handful of readers that "This *is* Bloom. . . . The utterly complete embodiment of Bloom into Mostel is a totally different thing from Mostel throwing himself into the part of Bloom—and it is a rare phenomenon in the theatre." The *Times's* venerable Brooks Atkinson, who had earlier detested Zero's work—recall his remarks about bulk, noise and sweat—now encountered what he deemed to be an extraordinary performance: Bloom "is played flawlessly by Zero Mostel . . . [this] outwardly respectable, inwardly epicene, secretive, cunning, cheap in self-esteem as well as infamy, haunted by a million vicious specters [character] is the core of the performance." The *Village Voice* theatre section, edited by Jerry Tallmer, had recently begun to bestow what it called Obies—as opposed to the Tonys which were exclusively for work on Broadway—and Zero Mostel was awarded one of the early ones, in 1959, for his performance as Bloom.

Pauline Flanagan, the original Molly Bloom, had just come to the United States from Ireland, and recalls the support Zero provided. "I was new to the country, and there was this gargantuan figure I was to play opposite. Zero really should have lived in Seventeenth-century France, he was ferocious and impossible in many ways. But he was a joy to work with and so kind to me. Under that enormous exterior, he was a sweet and wonderful man. During rehearsals at the National we would go out for lunch and Zero would go out of his way to introduce me to his old Jewish friends. And since we were on the Lower East Side he would take me to his favorite Yiddish restaurants."

Flanagan remembers "one wonderfully directed moment.

Zero would climb this stepladder and pray to God in Hebrew," perhaps a forerunner, and throwback, to Tevye's ongoing Yiddish and English dialogue with the Almighty. "But Zero would also have these outbursts," exclaiming various Mostelisms in one tongue or another, with his back to the audience.

"He was impossible in the elevator. It would he filled with *Mitteleuropean* figures working on other floors, none of whom took up the kind of space Zero did, and out of Zero would come these wonderfully outrageous exclamations."

Contrary to my own view of the effect of choreography, (and I never saw the production), Flanagan insists that Valerie Bettis's contribution was of enormous help. She also recalls that Burgess Meredith wrote a series of descriptive essays in which each scene of the play had its own visual design. Meredith, for example, saw one moment as a Kabuki performance, and one can envision the huge Rabelaisian Zero taking the Japanese ball and running it into the end zone.

Kate Mostel took over the role of Molly Bloom for two weeks. "I was getting married and going on a honeymoon and Kate stepped in. Of course I never saw her performance." Flanagan has an odd recollection of Kate: "In her book, Kate mentions that she took over the role for a time, but she never once mentions who it was that she was taking over from. I found that a bit curious."

The play opened at a time when most of the actors were unknown and no one had any money. But, as Flanagan notes, "some went on to become stars—people like Carroll O'Connor and Anne Meara." Zero probably had not seen the inside of a limousine since that fateful afternoon when Louis B. Mayer's limo took its fruitless cruise into the Garden of Allah, and now he was making his appointed rounds via the New York City subway system. "The bums would congregate near the Houston Street subway stop and Zero would make a point of giving every one of them a little money. But he would extract a promise every day. 'Promise me something,' he would insist. 'You must spend this money right away, and at the nearest pub.'"

Flanagan passed the National one day in 1959 "and they

were tearing it down. I watched this wrecking ball going to work on that marvelous old building," and that was the end of another landmark, of Minsky's burlesque, of the Roumania Opera House and the Goldfaden Opera House and finally of the National.

By 1974, Brooks Atkinson, long since retired, had been replaced by Stanley Kauffman, who himself, upon the demise of the *Herald-Tribune* had been replaced by Walter Kerr, whom the *Times* had coveted for some time in unrequited fashion. Here is Kerr on March 17th, performing his exegesis on Zero's latter-day Blooming.

> Reeling his way through the tumble of sour memory and dyspeptic imagination he has already done a number of quick, almost furtive, pantomime "turns," executing tiny ballet steps on tiptoe beneath a tableau of nymphs, putting hand on hip for a fast wiggle while his pursed lips waggle mutely, crossing his eyes at he twists derby sidewise on his head, acting out at silent-film speed how deeply flattered he is to receive an invitation he must decline .

> Just now, when the odd gesture comes, he is being crowned King Leopold I, ermine-edged red cape on his shoulders, horse-head scepter in his hand. After he has done one more minute vaudeville turn, letting the horse's head whisper him a message, he raises his hands to cup them fairly close to his face and then—in quivering rhythm—brings them nearer each other as though he were trying to compress an invisible ball of putty into the smallest possible shape.

Kerr's sense is that both Zero and his audience understand that a nightclub turn

> doesn't really belong here, isn't precisely James Joyce, whose layered and abrasive humors I would prefer to take neat; but if I don't do it, you may never laugh at all; in the circumstances, won't you help me to keep it separate and minimal?

Kerr's perception of Zero's undertaking is that the performer must bear a double weight on his shoulders,

> the weight of a serious evening in the theater that isn't asserting its seriousness in any cohesive way, and the weight of a reputa-

tion that demands he *do* something, if possible that he do something funny. Which way shall he turn, which master serve? Try an unmistakable solemnity, almost a *Strange Interlude* monotone, whenever he is thinking of the infant son who died after 11 days. Give the materials the respect they deserve. Then, when opportunity presents itself, push an invisible perambulator straight over the footlights at the audience, mime crushing two oldsters in a bear-hug. . . . Give the audience some relief from a relentlessly pursued myth—lost father, lost son, Telemachus and Ulysses, finding each other by dawn—that is nowhere defining itself. But try, try, *try* to keep camp and the Joycean canker in different pockets.

Kerr does here what he always does well; he isolates a physical detail and extrapolates a dominant chord which guides him in evaluating the production as a whole. This approach parallels to some extent that of the performer who shows us an action, an outerness, and from that outerness makes us privy to the innerness, to the character's intention and to that very being who intends. The critic's job is twofold: to appreciate the quality of the action, e.g., Zero's gestures, his shuffling and balletic shifts, his pantomimic turns, and from that to evaluate the insight and worth of the intention.

Joyce's Leopold Bloom is many things, to himself and to others: he is a Jew in a predominantly Catholic community; he is a lapsed Jew who has married outside the faith; the Gentile populace sees him as Jew, regardless of how he sees himself; he is a teetotaler in a city where pubs, liquor and alcoholics are major enterprises; he is obseqious, eager to please in a town where adult males are groomed to be proud, belligerent, or bellicosely chummy; finally Bloom is studiously involved in the cultures of the past and given to book-learning and introspection in a town where opinions normally drown out questions. Some of Bloom's qualities and conditions—the lapsed Jew given to book-learning and introspection who marries outside the faith—parallel elements in Zero's life. Joyce's intention was to sketch a modest, at times tediously ordinary, at times unsavory little fellow inhabiting the mythic dimensions of Homer's Odysseus. Both are trying to reach home; Odysseus is relentless and brave, Bloom relentless and cowardly. And yet both persist and are faithful to an ideal: survival, a return to the hearth, a return ultimately to faith. In this sense, if Zero is reduced to entertaining an audience that expects him to be working his shtick to full Mostel capacity, he is also employing the shtick tactics we associate with Didi and Gogo in Beckett's *Waiting for Godot*, trying to get through the day on his way to finding a way back to Molly Bloom and *past* Molly Bloom to his own true past, a past which he has already *passed* once on this day as he takes on the mode of Jesus-Elijah mounting to Heaven at the climax of the pub scene.

Barkentin's script intends to operate like a blueprint, to suggest high-quality stage directions, but it is full of language, of Martha Grahamesque suggestions, of surrealistic allusions to a character's innerness. It is simply too full of many things and not full enough of one thing. It is unhappily trying to make too much of "wonderful moments" from Joyce's prose, but Joyce did not write wonderful moments, Joyce wrote one, if quite complicated, enormously stratified moment. One moment, one day, one intention. In a sense Joyce wrote the whole modern Western world, but synthesized, cohesive, tight. Barkentin's script is scattered, loose, vague, poetically alluding to elements it hardly seems able to comprehend.

There is much in Joyce's Bloom that draws uncanny parallels to elements in the individual journey of Zero Mostel, and much that makes reference to key events in Jewish history. Ulysses-Odysseus cheats the murderous Polyphemus as Jacob cheats Esau, by cloaking himself in animal skin. Ulysses tells Polyphemus his name is No Man, Zero's name is zero, everything, nothing, Remo Feruggio, Samuel (the firstborn, given to God). Zero, like Bloom, marries an Irish-Catholic lass; at some point Kate Harkin Mostel takes over the role of Molly Bloom. There are of course the Israelites wandering forty years in the desert, as Ulysses wanders, as Bloom wanders, as Zero wanders. Bloom brings Molly the novels of Paul de Cock; Zero will soon coauthor a film script with Ian Hunter about a Monsieur LeCoq. Bloom cannot keep his eyes off other women; neither can Zero. Ulysses is tempted by other women; sometimes he gives in, sometimes not. Bloom is always tempted but can make nothing of his impulse past a self-involvement; Zero is tempted, and what does he make of temptation beyond an outrageous public stance? Ulysses faces enslavement by Circe the enchantress who turns men into swine; the Israelites are always in danger of succumbing to pagan rites, to false gods, to the Golden Calf; and Bloom's Nighttown fantasy–reality has him reduced to the role of humiliated slave under the heel of whore-mistress Bella Cohen, B.C., Before the Common Era.

Through the good offices of Toby Cole, who had pretty much taken on the function of Zero's agent, a European tour is set up. The blacklisted Sam Wanamaker, remembered for his role opposite Ingrid Bergman as the director in Maxwell Anderson's drama, *Joan of Lorraine*, is contacted in Liverpool, with the thought that his New Shakespeare Theatre might house the Meredith production. Through Wanamaker, the play is brought to London, under the auspices of the Arts Theatre. *Nighttown* opens on the 21st of May, 1959, then in July it moves to Paris as part of the Theatre des Nations. Zero is honored as Best Actor at the Festival, then the play moves to Amsterdam. Offers begin to pour in: to play Pa Ubu under Peter Brook's direction in Jarry's *Ubu Roi* at the Royal Court in London; to play Falstaff under Joan Littlewood's direction for the Royal Shakespeare at Stratford.

Toby Cole was anxious to have Zero accept the offer of Associated Rediffusion which was producing a televised adaptation of Harold Pinter's *The Birthday Party*. First produced onstage at the Arts Theatre in Cambridge in April of 1958, *The Birthday Party* was Pinter's first full-length play and was helping to establish his reputation as part of that growing and misnamed body of theatrical works known as the Theatre of the Absurd. Zero was asked to play Goldberg, the principal menace in a pair of menacing Jewish gangster-types—who turn up at a seaside resort, obviously out to do more than upset the community, and proceed to terrorize a weak, anxious boarder named Stanley.

Zero, who possibly has become a trifle hysterical at this new good fortune, this sudden surfeit of goodies, eventually turns down the chance to play Goldberg—not enough money, we're told. He also rejects the offers from Peter Brook and Joan Littlewood, negotiates for a part in a play, *The Gazebo*, and in a film, *The Private Eye*, and succeeds in turning these down as well. Toby Cole indicates that her British counterpart, the agent Adza Vincent, got into seemingly endless minutiae over Zero's contract for *The Gazebo*, apparently an indifferent play, on the understanding that Zero was seriously considering the drama, which he probably was not. As Jared Brown reports, when contractual details were settled, Zero would raise fresh demands. The producer at last threw up his hands. Brown notes that "It was neither the first nor the last time that Mostel would embroil his agent in fruitless negotiations rather than simply admit that he was not interested."

Two noteworthy offers did bear fruit, though the fruit of one has been buried these many years. Samuel Beckett had always taken inspiration from the great comics, more particularly the silent comedians like Chaplin and Keaton. In the early Sixties, Beckett, director Alan Schneider, and Barney Rossett, founder and then-publisher of Grove Press—the man responsible for publishing the works of Beckett, Genet, Ionesco, Pinter and Antonin Artaud in the United States—planned a feature film which would be composed of three avant-garde shorts. Only one of the three has ever been released, though two were actually completed and the third seems never to have materialized in any fashion. The first, entitled *Film*, was shot by Schneider with cinematographer Boris Kaufman in Lower Manhattan, in that no-man's-land between Soho and the Lower East Side, and it starred Buster Keaton. *Film* has no dialogue. It's a mime play about a friendless middle-aged man alone in his sparsely-furnished apartment. It was eventually released by itself in 1965, an idiosyncratic short running twenty-two minutes. For the second film, Beckett chose one of his two early mime plays, *Act Without Words I (Acte sans parole)* which, like many of his early plays and novels, he had originally written in French. The play had opened at the Royal Court in London in April of 1957.

For the film version, director Anthony Asquith, heeding Beckett's advice that only a clown of the stature of Charlie Chaplin or Zero Mostel could fill the bill, offered the role to the latter, who accepted. The completed work is called *Zero*. It has no dialogue and essentially one character, and its running time is under ten minutes. It has apparently never found a film distributor, though it was screened in 1960 at the Venice Film Festival. The play opens as follows:

Desert. Dazzling light.

The man is flung backwards on stage from right wing.

Whistle from right wing.

He reflects, goes out right.

Immediately flung back on stage he falls, gets up immediately, dusts himself, turns aside, reflects.

Whistle from left wing.

He reflects, goes toward left wing, hesitates, thinks better of it, halts, turns aside, reflects.

Zero's second offer had to do with a new play by Eugene Ionesco, to be called *Rhinoceros*, which was to have its initial production in Paris in January of 1960 and in London the following April. Like Beckett, whose *Godot* played in relative obscurity to audiences of ten or less in the city of Paris for months on end, Ionesco had begun in even deeper obscurity. At the third performance of his first play in Paris, *The Bald Soprano*, the audience at the Theatre des Noctambules consisted of the author, his wife, and a friend of one of the ushers. That was in May of 1950 and several weeks later the play closed. But by 1956 Ionesco had become one of the luminaries of the French theatre and of that avant garde which was shortly to sweep not only Western Europe but the New York theatre, primarily Off-Broadway.

If Beckett's *Godot*, in its Broadway premiere in the late Fifties, was something of a puzzlement and a titillation to New York audiences—and a disaster to mainstream critics like Walter Kerr, lest we forget—Ionesco's *Bald Soprano* and *Jack*, opening at the newly-built Sullivan Street Playhouse in 1958, took the city by storm. Within the next two or three years, the obligatory names among the supposed *au courant* of the New York theatre scene were Ionesco, Beckett, Edward Albee, Jack Richardson, Arthur Kopit, Fernando Arrabal, Harold Pinter, and Jean Genet. All at once, Ionesco could do no wrong, and the chance to originate an Ionesco role in English was not to be turned down lightly.

In London there was interest in Zero's performing as Berenger, the character who resists transformation into a rhinoceros. The play was to premiere at the Odeon in Paris on January 25th, 1960, under Jean-Louis Barrault's direction, with the London production to open at the Royal Court the following April, to be directed by Orson Welles. The Welles production would also star Sir Laurence Olivier in the role of Jean, the one who makes the monstrous transformation midway through the play. In mid-December of 1959, Zero is approached by David Merrick's office to appear in a new play on Broadway; Garson Kanin and his wife Ruth Gordon had made an adaptation of a French comedy by the Belgian playwright Felicien Marceau called *La Bonne Soupe. The Good Soup*, a gambling term, is to be directed by Kanin and features Ruth Gordon, Mildred Natwick, Zero's old buddy Sam Levene, and Diane Cilento who created something of a stir as Helen of Troy in the Broadway production of Giraudoux's *Tiger at the Gates* in the mid-Fifties. Zero is contracted to play the croupier in a Monte Carlo casino, with the understanding that he will relinquish the role in time to begin London rehearsals for *Rhinoceros* by early spring.

Rehearsals are underway in early January. Winter sets in—snow, freezing temperatures. Zero decides to take a cab home from rehearsals one night, but he never makes it home. The *World-Telegram and Sun* headline of January 14th reads:

ZERO HIT BY BUS AFTER FALL ON ICY STREET

The newspaper informs its readers that "Zero sustained multiple lacerations of the left leg when he slipped on an icy pavement near his West Side home [the Belnord on Broadway and 86th Street] last night and fell into the path of a bus." Jared Brown's research has the bus skidding onto the curb, knocking Zero down and actually crushing his leg. In either case Zero had just emerged from the taxi outside the Belnord when his left leg and the right rear wheel of the 86th Street crosstown bus collided.

An ambulance eventually speeds Zero to Roosevelt Hospital where his condition is listed as "good." Merle Debuskey, who was press representative for *The Good Soup*, first hears of the accident from a *New York Times* reporter.

"It was poker night for Kate and her women friends," Debuskey remembers. "Katie hadn't heard anything. I had to track down the hospital. By the time I got to Roosevelt, Kate and a few others were already there. The resident doctor came out to tell us he thought Zee would soon be on his feet. The producers, namely Merrick, Gar Kanin and Ruth Gordon, were awaiting word from me as to the next step concerning the play. Remember, it was the height of the blacklist and it was very important that Zero stay in that show. The intent of the producers was not to recast, if indeed it was possible for Zee to come out in time. He was transferred to the Hospital for Joint Diseases on Madison and 123rd Street and we were trying to get reports. I asked a friend of mine, Dr. Joseph Wilder, who was chief of surgery there, if he could take a look at Zero and find out what in hell was going on. Joe told me he couldn't get mixed up unless he were invited in by the attending physician. So Kate got the approval and Joe went in to look at Zero. Then he called me—he said he didn't know if Zero was going to be able to hold onto that leg. He said sure as shit Zero wasn't going to be out in time to get back into rehearsal."

Jules Munshin replaces Zero in *The Good Soup*, and Joseph Wilder, with remarkable determination, labors over a period of months to save and resuscitate the shattered limb. Zero, the incorrigible showman, gathers his own inner resources in his hospital bed. There are many visitors during these days that drag into weeks: the relatives, fellow entertainers, even Michael Hayes, the bus driver of the M-18. Frances Chaney, visiting with Kate on the day of the accident, remembers that "Poor Zero has to make it clear to Kate that it wasn't his fault. There's this poor sonofabitch with his leg mangled like meat on a butcher block and he just wanted Kate to know, just like a little boy, that he hadn't done anything wrong."

Aaron Mostel also visited. "He had this awful itch, and there was this new drug you could take, but it wasn't available at the hospital. I remember I phoned my brother Herman's nephew, Dr. Martin Keller, who was also my internist, and Martin called around until he located the stuff. My personal contribution was some booze to help kill the pain."

Merle Debuskey recalls: "Joe [Wilder] had been working on skin grafts. I had told Joe that Zero was blacklisted and that he and Kate really didn't have any money. Joe said, 'Don't worry about it,' that he would do what he could. And Zero and Joe became fast friends and Joe stayed on the project for the longest period of time. Whether Joe actually saved Zero's leg, I don't know, but he certainly was responsible for getting him to walk again, and eventually to dance."

Even in his hospital bed, Zero was onstage. When I spoke to Woody Allen's office concerning the period when Woody and Zero performed together in *The Front*, it was Woody's secretary who provided me with local color. Norma Lee Clark was in the next room to Zero's when the comedian was having his skin graft. "I was recovering from a knee operation and could hear Zero being boisterous. There were constant visitors, constant noise, a constant party. Zero heard there was a woman in bed in the next room—myself—and invited me over for a drink."

"What was he serving?"

"Scotch probably. Oh, everything. I could hear him yelling. A stream of visitors."

"So you visited him? You had your drink?"

"Sure. I had a swell time. I would ride over in my wheel-chair."

The rehabilitated leg would plague Zero for the remainder of his life; he would use a cane to help him navigate, but Wilder saw to it that he had a functioning limb. For five months Wilder performed a series of operations, and when Zero wasn't performing in and out of bed, he was instructing Wilder in the mysteries of visual art. Merle Debuskey notes that "out of that relationship, through Zero's influence, Joe became a successful painter."

When Zero left the Hospital for Joint Diseases, he invited Wilder to the Twenty-eighth Street studio. Wilder began to paint seriously. By 1981, he was in the National Portrait Gallery's "Champion of American Sports" exhibit; his portrait of Willis Reed has found its way alongside work by Andrew Wyeth, George Bellows, and Thomas Eakins.

As for the rehabilitated leg, it needed constant attention. It would swell if Zero exercised more than the leg could tolerate. During performances the leg's temperature would rise dangerously, and lack of circulation would cause Zero to lose all feeling in the leg. At times the pain was hardly bearable; Zero's dresser, Howard Rodney, would apply ointments backstage to bring the swelling down, to bring the temperature down, and to ease the pain. But onstage the cane would disappear. Zero would be moving freely, sometimes swiftly, sometimes dancing—the pain was a constant companion, but it was Zero's secret until he was offstage.

Zero's accident takes place on January 13th. On the 25th Barrault's production of *Rhinoceros* opens in Paris. Producer Oscar Lewenstein is getting mixed signals from New York; Toby Cole, probably walking a tightrope, can't fully reassure Lewenstein that Zero will be sufficiently recovered in time for London rehearsals. Lewenstein decides that Zero should play Jean, not Berenger; it's presumably a less strenuous role. These calculations come to nought; there is no way Zero can make it to London. Instead of a speedy recovery, an additional operation is scheduled.

On April 28th, the Orson Welles production, with Welles himself nowhere in sight, opens at the Royal Court.[26] Duncan Macrae plays Jean opposite Olivier's Berenger. But by April, New York producer Leo Kerz has already optioned *Rhinoceros* for Broadway. According to a news item in the *New York Herald-Tribune* of May 2nd, Kerz and his cast are "tackling some production problems such as how to produce aurally and visually the central phenomenon of the play—the terrifying transformation of human beings into rhinoceroses in full view of the audience." Kerz has his hands full over many issues. He announced the signing of Eli Wallach to play Berringer—note that Berenger, with one r in Paris and London, has acquired an additional r crossing the Atlantic, with the second e changed to an i—and then announces that Ray Bolger has been engaged for the same role. Eli Wallach threatens to sue and Kerz somehow manages to dispose of Bolger. Zero is asked to play Jean, or rather as he is now to be known, John. Bobby Lewis, one of the veterans of the Group Theatre, is engaged to direct. There is a production meeting in Zero's hospital room, but it is Joseph Anthony who will finally mount the production the following January. (The interim months will allow Zero to appear in the TV version of Beckett's *Waiting for Godot*.)

The *Tribune*, reporting Kerz's concern about rhino transformations, tells its readers that the producer "has put to work the sound effects department of MGM, which is now taping sound tracks from Africa and Asia for possible use as background effects in the play," and that composer Eli Siegmeister is creating background music to accompany these effects. "The visual transformation" of human into rhinoceros "has been entrusted to [puppeteers] Bil and Cora Baird."

But theatre history records that Zero dispensed with all outer-human support, that he simply reached down to the inner Mostel where there was more than sufficient rhinocerariness to discomfit if not panic the most disinterested spectator. The *Tribune's* Walter Kerr reports after the opening at the Longacre that the remarkable image of the Mostel transformation leads us to understand that "evolution has reversed itself before your horrified, but nevertheless, delighted eyes."

In Lausanne in 1954, Ionesco ruminates on the qualities that precipitate the making of drama.[27] He speaks of "two fundamental states of consciousness," designating one as a nothingness, a deep lightness, and its opposite, an infinite weight of blackness. He asks us to recall those moments in our lives when it seems that "the substance of the world is dreamlike" and it is as if we are then able to peer right into the center of this substance which is composed of total and absolute light. And this absolute light carries within it the narrative of all events that have ever transpired. These events come to be seen as "useless, senseless . . . impossible." Recall Kenneth Patchen's volume of poetry, titled *Sleepers Awake at the Precipice*. Ionesco's precipice is "a world unknown," and one's waking to this precipice brings on a sense of "anguish [and] giddiness." Often this giddiness will transform itself, and when that occurs the anguish dissolves, giving way to a sense of release. In this new state the only significant understanding is of quiet astonishment, of "wonder," and we see the world and all human endeavor as "absolute futility," and all endeavor and "language appear to lose their articulation" and they "disintegrate and collapse." In the face of this nothingness, of this absurdity, we are left with nothing but the impulse to a kind of laughter which is unending.

Ionesco then considers that too often this joyous consciousness of the insubstantiality and lightness of the universe cannot maintain itself and gives way to its opposite.

> . . . what is light grows heavy, the transparent becomes dense, the world oppresses, the universe is crushing me.

Matter takes on an unendurable density. The universe is unremittingly packed with matter; the weight of this matter is infinite and annihilating. We are now imprisoned by remorseless substance.

> Language breaks down in a different way and words drop like stones or dead bodies; I feel I am invaded by heavy forces, against which I can only fight a losing battle.

Seen in this light, *Rhinoceros* becomes a play of liberation, but a liberation which perversely sits within an incalculable prison. As the play unfolds, normal bourgeois Parisians develop unreasonable, insatiable longings; they yearn for and cry out for transformation into essence of rhinoceros. Some are able to resist for a time, but the siren song of other rhinoceri proves more than humankind can bear. Berringer, an amiable, half-conscious alcoholic, rises to whatever heroic proportions the bourgeois culture can muster—he resists the transformation even when rhino seduction seems to have entered his marrow. Early on Berringer is badgered by his comrade John, as played by Zero, to mend his ways, to refrain from nightly festivities, to put his nose to the grindstone, to cultivate his mind. Zero's John is prissy, self satisfied; he manages to instill in Berringer, as played by Eli Wallach, a sense of guilt if hardly a sense of consequence.

When Zero's character succumbs, it is to an almost impossible need for liberation. Liberation cannot happen too rapidly— his room is instantly too hot; his walls are behaving in the time-honored fashion of supports threatening to asphyxiate; his garments are utterly constricting; his visceral bulk and the innerness it houses cry out to be released. But released from and to what? Civilization as an ongoing state is an absurdity; it is too deeply without purpose; it weighs and presses with a numbing artifice. Furniture is absurd, ditto walls and pajamas. But when furniture is smashed, when walls and floorboards splinter, when pajamas are hastily ripped from bodies, the liberation is to—a running, snorting rhinoceros, running and snorting towards the nearest damp, dark, dank, unrelieved swamp. We're confronted with a new heaviness, a new denseness running into another heaviness, another denseness. Absurdity leads nowhere but to its sibling, the next absurdity becomes the new convention, the new stifling mechanism. We are veering precariously toward a universe where mirrors transform into mirrors.

Leo Kerz paid for Ionesco's trip to New York so that the Rumanian-French playwright might watch rehearsals as well as embark on a lecture tour. But there was bad blood between producer and playwright. According to Ionesco's friend Tom Bishop of New York University's French Department, Kerz and Ionesco were battling over the latter's lecture fees. And then there were the Mostel hijinks. As Zero told it, "There was a little reception for the playwright at the French Consul's house in New York. Ionesco spoke no English. He got up and I said, '*Il n'est pas le vrai Ionesco!* He's not the real Ionesco! I am the real Ionesco. He is a liar.' And we had a big fight. He said that was the best speech of the evening. He said it was very Ionesco-ish.

I'm crazy about him. He can write for me anytime he wishes."

Bishop remembers the evening differently, but perhaps it wasn't the same evening. "Kerz gave a 'coming out' party at the home of a plastic surgeon. It was in a penthouse on West Fifty-seventh Street, near Carnegie Hall. The place was full of intellectuals, of members of *Who's Who*. Ionesco knew no English and he didn't know a soul. He turned to me for help. Into the room comes Zero and Kerz introduces the two of them. And Zero begins playing with Ionesco. 'I like your play,' he tells him, 'maybe I'll do your play.' Then, 'No, I won't do your play.' He's vacillating or seemingly vacillating, and I'm interpreting all this. So finally Zero tells him, 'You're nice so I'll do the play. But then again I won't do your play,' and so on." And the critic Rosette Lamont, another of Ionesco's colleagues, witnessed Zero actually lifting Ionesco in his arms and carrying him about during one of these gatherings. From Paris to Zero.

Rhinoceros opens on January 9th, 1961. Joseph Anthony's cast, in addition to Zero and Eli Wallach, includes a number of accomplished performers: Anne Jackson (Mrs. Wallach), Morris Carnovsky, Mike Kellin, Jean Stapleton and Dolph Sweet. The press, by and large, is ecstatic. Richard Watts Jr., in the *New York Post*, no early admirer of Zero's work, now declares that no other performer could have managed the human-to-rhino transformation in full view of an audience, and without makeup. There are dissenting views; George Oppenheimer in *Newsday* has mixed feelings.

> Mostel is so brimming with humor that . . . a certain menace and meaning are dissipated. This in no way detracts from his performance. . . . by the very quality of his buffoonery, he seems to infect the other players and affect the ending. Although he is not even on stage at the end, his presence is felt and what might have been (and was in the London production) a scene of terror never quite achieves the required eeriness. The audience, conditioned to Mr. Mostel's antics, has come to regard the rhinoceros as a figure of fun.

Walter Kerr is extravagant in his praise and at the top of his verbal form. He describes the play as an entertainment in which an extremely talented rhinoceros plays Zero Mostel. At first sight you think it *is* Mr. Mostel, sitting there at a sidewalk cafe, pronouncing "as usual" as though it were spelled "azh zhushuyewel" and occasionally patting those few fine strands of hair that swirl across his glistening pate as though they'd been painted there by Aubrey Beardsley.

And then this weighty, though delicately balanced object gets to its feet in anger, when it becomes quite apoplectic enough to create its own steam bath, you're still not ready to swear that it isn't the actor you've seen before, with his Equity dues paid up. Then comes a moment . . . in the second act, when the whole of playwright Eugene Ionesco's world is rapidly abandoning whatever was human about it and violently returning to the jungle.

Now the rhinoceros beneath the skin begins to bulge a little at the eyes, the Kaiser Wilhelm mustache . . . loses its spiky endpoints, droops, disintegrates into a tangle that makes it second cousin to a walrus. The voice starts to change. "I hate people—and I'll r-r-run them down!" comes out of a larynx that has stiffened, gone hollow as a 1915 gramophone record, and is ready to produce a trumpet-sound that would empty all of Africa. The shoulders lift, the head juts forward, one foot begins to beat the earth with such native majesty that dust—real dust—begins to rise like the afterveil that seems to accompany a safari.

And so on, arching along from one hyperbole to the next, breathlessly attempting a visceral exegesis.

Leo Kerz had an idea, admirable on the face of it but ultimately disastrous if you are going to keep anything running on Broadway. Producers are notorious for lifting phrases from negative reviews which then blaze out in advertisements as glowing reports from the front. Kerz decided that he would quote no one. Since so many of the reviews were positive, the actors were alarmed; they had assumed they had a hit on their hands and didn't expect to depend on word-of-mouth to keep the show running. Two camps quickly polarized; each issued public statements. On Wednesday the 11th, the cast and its producer held a heated debate. The cast threatened to picket the producer's home. Kerz, adhering to his original intent, nevertheless had his office compile a brochure in which the complete notices were printed and then distributed to passersby before the matinee on

Wednesday, January 18th. Press agent Harvey Sabinson notes that day: "The play's two stars, Eli Wallach and Zero Mostel, will join Kerz in a tentative peace move and help distribute the brochures in front of the Longacre."

The first Longacre run lost money—Jared Brown's impression is that Kerz sunk his own personal fortune into the Ionesco play—but then *Rhinoceros* went on the road, playing the Edgeware Beach Playhouse in Chicago in August and early September, with Ralph Meeker temporarily replacing Zero, returning to the Longacre in mid-September from the 11th through the 22nd and then beginning a Theatre Guild subscription tour. The performance of September 14th was designated a benefit for CORE, with Kerz referring to the Congress of Racial Equality as "America's Freedom Riders." The production then went to California, to the Alcazar Theatre in San Francisco, opening on October 2nd, and to the Huntington Hartford in Los Angeles for a three-week run beginning October 23rd. For Zero, *Rhinoceros* appeared to be a personal triumph.

But not to the author. Bishop believes that Ionesco admired Zero's performance and his mode of species conversion, though he was used to Jean-Louis Barrault's method. As Berenger, Barrault did not attempt a physical transformation without exterior supports. Ionesco was somewhat put off by Zero's flamboyance, but Nelly Vivas, who worked for Ionesco's agent, Nina Karlweis, tells me that Ionesco was more than put off by the Broadway production, that he simply detested it. Her recollection also is that Ionesco's original ending had two rhinoceri onstage at an outdoor cafe, perhaps refreshing themselves with a little alcohol, and one of them remarking, "I thought I just saw a man go by." Bishop doesn't know where this original ending, if indeed it is the original, exists, since neither the Paris nor London productions concluded with such cafe customers. But Ionesco's own remarks after the New York opening confirm Nelly Vivas's sense that Joseph Anthony's production brought much discomfort to the playwright.

In *Notes and Counter Notes*, Ionesco admits that though *Rhinoceros*'s popular success delighted him, the production baffled him. He finds directors of his work either infected with a timidity that doesn't allow them to mine the "full potentialities" inherent in the text, or they burden the work by loading on "cheap embellishment," turning a serious lady into a prancing whore. Ionesco is also pained by the consensus among U.S. critics that he has written a comedy in *Rhinoceros*. He sees his play as a picture of a darkening, menacing world; he is fighting nothing less than totalitarianism and the manner in which a fascistic state turns its people against whomever it designates as the enemy.

It may be that Zero's own triumph in the play, his tour de force, was of such magnitude that, as George Oppenheimer puts it, "a certain menace and meaning are dissipated." Oppenheimer seems muddled as to what this meaning may consist of, but he is certain that it consists of *something* that simply isn't onstage. What *is* onstage, what remains in place of "meaning" is something we have come to call performance, or acting. But can we be in the hands of performance or acting if the event or performance of acting is such that it wipes out meaning or else blocks one meaning and substitutes another? One that is not intended by the writer? What then does the event we call *Rhinoceros* mean? Eli Wallach, late in 1988, reflected in a phone conversation we had that Zero's overpowering performance wrenched Ionesco's meaning so that audiences, instead of being alerted to problems, found themselves reassured by the course of events.

The general acclaim for Zero was of such intensity that he began receiving "plays about snakes, water buffalo, camels, newts—every whacked-up animal under the sun. I suffer from idiots," he told Norman Wilner in *Esquire* magazine, "who send me bad plays to read."

The *New York Times* ran a curious science article on Sunday, May 22nd 1988. You will recall Moodus, Connecticut, and the farm to which Yisroel Mostel brought his wife and children many years ago. From science reporter Walter Sullivan we learn that almost two hundred earthquakes have been recorded near Moodus the previous fall. They seem unaccountable. The first known quake was felt in 1568. Native Americans believe their ancestors experienced such quakes centuries before. The Native Americans translate Moodus as "place of noises."

My own conceit: can it be that Zero, under the earth of Moodus, is rehearsing his rhino-resurrection?

In June of 1988, Ionesco again visits New York, this time for the First New York International Festival of the Arts. Ionesco tells the *New York Times's* Mervyn Rothstein:

> Theater doesn't exist at the moment. It's bad everywhere. Between 1950 and 1960 it was good. Beckett, Genet, Adamov, *moi*. It was theater where you posed a problem, the most important problem of all: the problem of the existential condition of man— his despair, the tragedy of his destiny, the absurdity of his destiny. Another interesting problem is the existence of a God, a divinity, as Beckett writes about in *Waiting for Godot*. Man without God, without the metaphysical, without transcendence is lost.

Our modern theatre in the United States has long spoken of its success in what it purveys as realism. But Ionesco's view is that

> Realism does not exist. Everything is invention. Even realism is invented. Reality is not realistic. It's another school of theater, a style.

Ionesco had come to speak at Columbia University. Rothstein inquires about the topic, "Who Needs Theater Anymore?" Ionesco's response:

> People have needed the theater for thousands of years. There's no reason for this to change.

Rothstein asks: "Why do they need theater?"

> For nothing. The theater is useless, but its uselessness is indispensable. Why do people need football? What purpose is there?

Ionesco tells Rothstein that despite the lack of good theatre now, "It will come necessarily. Because it must. Because theater is a pure necessity of man." Rothstein then asks, "Isn't it useless?"

> In appearance it seems unnecessary. But uselessness and superfluousness are things that are necessary.

The claims of uselessness, the sense that art is good for nothing—but what kind of nothing? And what is the real anyway?

And what would Zero, the man who mimicked a liberation from a certain causality, say to Ionesco today? "Your words are gold? Your words are *merde*? Are we lost? Found? Why don't you shut up? I need to paint. Why don't you talk to me? Why don't you let me alone?" But who is it, Zero, that is letting you alone?

Zero as performer: not unlike Rabelais, not unlike Gombrowicz? The literary critic John Bayley recalls the art of the Polish novelist and playwright Wittold Gombrowicz: "Yet he still felt like Rabelais, who had no idea or intention of producing 'pure art,' or 'articulating his epoch' but who 'wrote the way a child pees under a bush in order to relieve himself.'"

So—Zero as *enfant terrible*, natural genius, American style? And does this chap articulate his epoch? One wants to believe so. But perhaps the testament of his life is closer to the epoch than the testament of his art.

Zero as exile: the blacklist appears to be waning; its grip to be lessening. Why should this be so? Perhaps even witch-hunters lose their zest for combat. These patriotic seizures inflate and eventually flatten out. In June, 1995, a Republican Congress was busying itself attempting to amend our Constitution so that flag-desecraters, whatever that species might be, could be ware-housed among the criminal brotherhood. Wasn't George Bush pledging allegiance at every possible instant during his success-ful and frantic run for the presidency?

Prior to work on *Rhinoceros*, Zero makes a television appearance as Estragon (Gogo) in Beckett's *Waiting for Godot*. As with *The World of Sholom Aleichem*, the forum is *Play of the Week*. The producer at this point is J. Worthington Miner. Tony Miner was one of the pioneers of TV drama, most noted for producing CBS-TV's live one-hour drama series, *Studio One*. *Godot*'s director is Alan Schneider; until his accidental death in London in the mid-Eighties, Schneider always had first call on new works by Samuel Beckett, and he staged the first *Godot* in the United States at the Coconut Grove Playhouse in Florida with a rather bewildered Bert Lahr as Estragon. On *Play of the Week*, Burgess Meredith is cast as Vladimir (Didi), and Kurt Kasznar and Alvin Epstein repeat their Broadway roles as Pozzo and Lucky. It turns out that Zero is anything but delighted with Alan Schneider's direction. On the telephone with Toby Cole, he expresses the wish to be re-blacklisted. This carping at the work of his colleagues (directors, performers) seems to become endemic with Zero as his own public stature grows. Judging from the finished product, neither Mostel nor Schneider acquit themselves as one might hope.

Godot—Beckett's play has taken hold of the modern consciousness. Today the way of *Godot* has become the West's traditional perception. In fact, the revolutionary drama has become a cliché. The truth within the cliché begins to lose its hold on us, even as we believe we are more tightly in its grip. Zero, the pooh-pooher of angst, is no stranger to angst. Existential despair courts him, and he responds. He appreciates the attempt at seduction.

Zero as exile. Are Vladimir and Estragon in a wasteland *past* that wasteland we recognize as the modern world? Probably not. But Zero in company, onstage or off, disallows the sound of angst unless bellowing is a surrogate for it. Zero in company is the congenial, bad-bellowing-boy. The exile is the one who goes off to his study without Herbie Kallem, who seeks out nightly privacy to open one of his fifty-thousand books. That Zero, in exile, that worn-out Zero of angst is in pain quietly.

But isn't *Godot* a comedy? Since when aren't comedies narratives of pain?

The *Godot* version we're addressing has problems. To begin with, any recorded *Godot* (film, TV) immediately sabotages one of Beckett's principles. *Godot* is an event in which a prime performer is uncertainty. The questions: Does an immanent force reside outside the sterile workings within these few isolated beings? Does anyone see Didi and Gogo? *Is* there anyone to see anyone? These questions need to maintain their integrity as questions, not degenerate into answers. But the very use of an outside eye, the camera that dollies and pans, the editor who cuts to close-ups—all these undermine the question. The play is deprived of its radical uncertainty; an agent moves in with state-of-the-art control.

Zero's performance: In one sense Zero fills the bill as a vaudevillian who leaps from one activity—fearing, sighing, starving, insulting, dancing—to another in order to get through one interminable day after another. But there needs to be an internalized Gogo supporting this figure and he is simply absent in this production. What confronts the spectator is another clown figure nesting within the first; the continuity of enigmatic being is nowhere to be found. Actors with none of Zero's resources, his ingenuity and understanding, can manage this continuity. It's a matter of training; it has nothing to do with inspiration or genius. Unfortunately, Zero has to scamper to get to the next moment. To find the threshold of that new moment, he must constantly reinvent the character. But isn't this the very existential problem Beckett is wrestling with? Yes, it's one of them, but the uncertainty that supports the vaudevillian, that supports this gross, tenuous clown must be an *essential* uncertainty, not of technique but an uncertainty of substance cohering within the nature of the character.

With the work of Beckett and Ionesco, Zero had come to the proverbial crossroads. Even though Olivier was to veto the idea of Zero as costar in a revived *Rhinoceros* in London, on the assumption that Mostel wasn't a sufficient drawing card in

Britain, it was becoming evident that Zero, banned by Louis B. Mayer, battered by HUAC and its sycophants, was taking on the aura of a celebrated international commodity. And that gave him leverage. Two paths seemed open, and though he might have mediated, even zigzagged, between "art" and "commerce," the bulk that has become familiar to us was listing toward the latter. I'm obviously using imprecise terms. "Art" runs the gamut from the classic repertoire—Sophocles, Shakespeare, Molière, Ibsen—to the contemporary theatre of politics and the avant-garde. And "commerce" implies, at its best, the brilliance of Broadway, the blockbuster musical, the engaging comedies of Neil Simon and various dramatists from London, and the world of theatrical hype.

Even these relative terms are to be questioned. One man's avant-garde is another's conservatism. By the early Sixties, many of us working in what was generally alluded to as the experimental theatre considered the work of Beckett, Genet, and Ionesco part of the old guard. Major avant-garde forces for us included the Living Theatre, the Open Theatre, the Bread & Puppets, the Firehouse Theatre in Minneapolis, the San Francisco Mime Troupe and El Teatro Campesino, an offshoot of Chavez's Farm Workers Union. If you considered the avant-garde in any serious fashion, you had to have some understanding of Antonin Artaud's "Theatre of Cruelty" in Paris in the Thirties and Forties and hopefully of Meyerhold shortly after the October revolution in what became the USSR and of Piscator and Brecht in Berlin. Almost none of us in the West knew anything as yet of the work of Jerzy Grotowski, though by the mid-Sixties word began filtering back about his extraordinary Polish Laboratory Theatre in Wroclaw. Peter Brook's *Marat/Sade* production, which hit Broadway in 1965, was probably the first glimmer the traditional theatre-going public had of what we might call "the new avant-garde," and that event had to take place above Fourteenth Street. And for some of us working "below Fourteenth Street" in the experimental theatre, Brook's "Theatre of Cruelty" production of Peter Weiss's play already smacked of a glossy paraphrasing of work we had been doing in the relative obscurity of Off-Off-Broadway.

Toby Cole tried to encourage Zero to align himself with the burgeoning theatre of writers like Pinter and Beckett, and to take advantage of opportunities to perform in the classic repertory—on several occasions the Royal Shakespeare Company tried to interest Zero in undertaking Falstaff—but there were always contingencies. Finally, it was not to be. In my talks with Tony Cole, she is adamant in charging Zero not only with a betrayal of herself—more on this a little later—but with betraying the theatre. Cole believes that Zero could have affected the development of the new theatre in the Sixties if he hadn't opted for Broadway and the smash musicals.

Albeit with the benefit of hindsight, such hope seems to me to have been unduly optimistic. A number of Pinter's dramas did come to Broadway, generally with British casts in excellent productions, including *The Caretaker, The Homecoming,* and *Old Times.* They were acclaimed, they had respectable runs and have all become part of our Western heritage. Assuming Zero had performed as Max, the loathsome father of equally loathsome sons in *The Homecoming,* I can't see how Zero's presence would have changed the fate of a play which is arguably a modern classic. Zero might have helped move Beckett to Broadway. After the Broadway run of *Godot,* all Beckett plays premiered Off-Broadway.

Alan Schneider directed *Endgame, Happy Days, Play* and *Krapp's Last Tape,* as well as Pinter's *The Lover* and *The Collection* at small houses like the Provincetown Playhouse, the Cherry Lane, and the Gate Theatre. Schneider once confessed to me that his talents did not extend to the energizing needed to put together a producing package; perhaps with Zero's support he might have had the leverage to bring the Beckett works to Broadway, but ultimately to what purpose? Given the unlikelihood that a Broadway producer, faced with ever-mounting costs, would have risked the investment, would droves of people from the outer boroughs and suburbia have rushed in night after night to see the wonderful Mostel bellowing from the inside of a garbage can in a work that, for all its inner richness, is outwardly static and densely cerebral in the tradition of

Racine? Granted the wonders that Mostel in a garbage can might perpetrate and granted the equal wonders of Beckett as purveyor of the lunatic vaudeville turn, there is unhappily an obstinate Cartesian dryness to *Endgame* and *Happy Days* under the canopy of which the happy-go-lucky theatregoer, looking to exit chortling over the jokes or humming the tunes, begins to sink into spectacular numbness. Zero might pull them in fast, but Beckett might drive them out faster. In an intimate Off-Broadway house, the Beckett play has a chance to find an audience congenial to its nature and to develop its potential, but in a Broadway venue the work would most likely rattle around like the dry bones seeking an hospitable habitat in the endless expanse of the Negev.

Even when possible scripts failed to send Zero into raptures, even when he kvetched about the money and grumbled that money would not sway him, eventually he opted for the money. And money could only mean Broadway, and pleasing the nightly crowd, sometimes with lowbrow entertainment, sometimes with kitsch, that concoction of the middlebrow posturing as "high art." Broadway meant constant catering to an audience that invested in seats, carfare, dinner and baby-sitters, an audience that by and large wanted to indulge its wish not to do what Bertolt Brecht always wanted it to do—to think.

But nothing in art is simple. Brecht always wanted to play to "the workers," "the people," even if the people never wanted to play back. Brecht would have been delighted, he probably believed, to work with Zero or Chaplin or Keaton or Raimu or Mae West. Brecht had in mind not boring his audience; he believed entertainment was imperative, but Brecht's entertainment for "the people" who never showed up at his theatres—the Berliner Ensemble in East Berlin has never been a "workers'" theatre; it's been a theatre for the bourgeoisie—has always included a series of rude awakenings, jolting the audience back into the understanding that it was not watching life but artifice, fake life. And that it was watching fakery in order to be recalled to the more brutal fakery of the world outside the theatre.

It may be that Zero understood that need to jolt an audience, the imperative that demanded the spectator be jolted back into thought. But if he understood this jolting, what did he understand that the audience was then to think *about*? To be wakened is hopefully to be wakened *to* something. Is it sufficient to be wakened by Zero Mostel to Zero Mostel, the messenger conveying himself, his pain, his buffoonery? And is that conveyance richly insightful, as nourishing let's say as a Hershey bar?

But Zero believed in entertainment, and knew that the masses, "the people," even "the workers" intuitively sensed what he was up to—if they could afford the price of the ticket. And they grew to love the jolting he was offering; the more Zero threw away the script, to the dismay of everyone else in the production, the more they loved it. And Zero came to throw away the script more and more. Would that flamboyance, that insouciant dispensing with text have served Beckett or Pinter or Ionesco or Brecht or Genet?

Zero opted for Broadway, for the masses, for the money. And for more money. He'd been starving—well, not quite eating out of garbage pails—but financially life had been grim for Zero and Kate. Zero claimed that Kate was driving him to make money, that he hated this drive. But a little money is a dangerous thing; after a while you can't seem to get enough of it.

A Funny Thing Happened on the Way to the Forum had a funny thing happen to it before it ever got started. People wanted out who then wanted back in, and people wanted in who then wanted out. Jerome Robbins was first offered the chance to direct. He accepted, then changed his mind. Then George Abbott took over. Then Robbins came back in when *Forum* was floundering in previews. The writers favored Phil Silvers for the leading role of Pseudolus, but TV's Sergeant Bilko saw the script as so much "shtick." When the film was produced, Silvers wanted in and took a supporting role. Milton Berle was approached after Silvers, said yes, then asked that much of the script that Abbott had edited out be edited back in. Perhaps he loved the shtick that Silvers hated. But Berle and the producers came to a parting of the ways. And then Zero was approached.

Zero wasn't enchanted with what is termed, in musical-comedy parlance, the *book*. At Stephen Sondheim's house he listens to the score. It's Sondheim's first shot at composing a musical. The score pleases Zero, but the script, hardly the work of Beckett or Joyce, won't go away. Kate badgers him: don't be such a snob, your chance for the Really Big Time, grab it. Zero doesn't grab with equanimity.

Ring Lardner Jr. remembers that "At that time our friend Waldo Salt [blacklisted Hollywood writer] had rented a loft above Zero's on West Twenty-eighth Street. Waldo liked to paint, but basically it was a place to write. Waldo went off for a time, maybe Hollywood [with the blacklist waning], and sublet to Ian Hunter, and Ian and I used it as a place to work on these television series." And to write a musical called *Foxy*, based on Ben Jonson's play, *Volpone*. "We'd usually have lunch with Zee at the vegetarian deli, and it was at the deli that Zero asked me to read the script of *Forum*. I don't think either Ian or myself thought much of it." Lardner believes the script went through numerous revisions but the version he read seemed to him "pretty strained. And I think that I thought that Zero shouldn't do it, and he was very hesitant about it."

Frances Chaney's eyebrows lift. She wants to be certain she's heard her husband correctly. "You urged him not to do it?" Lardner nods and Chaney announces, with the sad wisdom of many years, "Oh Ring, your record's complete." But the record is not complete, not publicly, and now Lardner completes it: "I advised David Selznick not to buy *Gone with the Wind*." And Chaney can only add softly, "Ah!"

Lardner's urging eventually falls before that of Kate Mostel. Toby Cole remembers that even in the taxi, on their way to George Abbott's office to sign the contract, Zero is grumbling, "I don't want to do this play." But after a time he begins to see, or convinces himself that he is beginning to see, hidden virtues in the boisterous, street-smart, pun-driven, multiplotted work that Silvers and Berle turned away from for markedly different reasons. One virtue: the role of Pseudolos reunites Zero with George Abbott who directed *Beggars' Holiday* back in the early post-War days of 1946. For another, Zero is able to help his buddy Jack Gilford audition for and win a featured role in the musical.

Zero respected Abbott; when the irrepressible one began acting up at rehearsals, the director would quickly reprimand him: "Stop acting like a child." It would quiet Zero for the moment. The script had also quieted down, or had come to seem bowdlerized as a consequence of Abbott's heavy editing, but again only for a moment. Much of the shtick, the byplay, the Byzantine sub-sub-plots found themselves restored as rehearsals moved along in the late hot spring of 1962. And Zero found his way into the work. There were the songs—and the girls, the full-breasted, willowy beauties who became the object of what we might call the double-jointed Mostel eye—and there was the general pizazz of slapstick, innuendo, and brass.

But the show, despite the frantic energy of performers like Jack Gilford and David Burns and John Carradine and Zero Mostel, was clearly in trouble. In its New Haven and Washington tryouts, notices were poor and audiences listless, or so one is now told. What did *Forum* lack? Drive, structure, clarity, humanity? No one seemed to know. And then Hal Prince conferred with Zero and advised him that the musical equivalent of the play doctor needed to be called in to save the show. And this play doctor was none other than that same Jerry Robbins who had named names before HUAC. And one of the names that Robbins had mentioned was that of Madeline Lee Gilford, Kate's closest friend and the wife of Jack Gilford. But, as previously mentioned, Zero said, "Listen, Hal, I'm a professional and Jerry's a professional, and if he can help the show, get him. Besides, we of the Left do not blacklist."

Jack Gilford wasn't as sanguine as Zero a few moments later when they conferred about the entry of Robbins. Gilford's response was to telephone his wife Madeline in New York and tell her that he was quitting the show. And Madeline convinced him to stay, not to "blacklist" himself.

Frances Chaney notes that "Zero was pretty rough with Jerry Robbins, beginning with those Washington days." And

Ring Lardner adds that "Zero did maintain this thing, starting with *Forum*, that he'd never talk to Jerry about anything but work, that he'd never have any social conversation." Chaney remembers that "Zero was a devil. He could be absolutely horrible. You hear all sorts of things of how he could be to actors."

Lardner recalls a difficult situation of his own. "Ian and I faced a similar problem with Jerry. We were already doing out-of-town tryouts with *Foxy* [performers included Bert Lahr, Robert H. Harris and Gerald Hiken] and Jerry was asked to take over. Ian and I were facing up to what we would do in the event Robbins actually agreed. Well, he came to see a version of *Foxy* in Cleveland. Then finally he telephoned and said, 'Listen, I'm not gonna do it. I know that *Foxy* is gonna be the big hit of the year, but I feel an obligation to do this kinda ethnic thing called *Tevya's Daughters.*"

Chaney quips, "Pay my respects to my Jewishness."

"Yeah. He was gonna do *that* show instead, although he knew that *Foxy* was gonna be the big hit and *Tevya* [later renamed *Fiddle on the Roof*] was not."

"Tragedy tomorrow . . . comedy tonight." And Kate remembers how Zero, registering a mock Socrates with hemlock cup nobly positioned at the ready, would whisper *sotto voce* to Jack Gilford under audience laughter, with no change of expression: "Who got you this job?"

Gilford remembers that anything was possible, indeed permissible, in Zero's eyes once the curtain went up. Zero's simple gaze had one actor, onstage as a Roman soldier, convulsed, trying to keep a straight face until he could safely retreat into the wings. But since he was doubling as a monk, the actor was forced to reappear several moments later. One night Zero was relentless. Hooded by his monk's cowl, the actor assumed he was safe, but Zero's gaze began to bear down on him. The monk lowered himself to avoid the assault. Zero followed suit, lowering himself in order to maintain his lunatic countenance at proper zapping level. The monk descended lower and still lower toward the floor of the stage, and Zero as Pseudolus the slave stayed in pursuit until his own head rested against the stage floor. Then, peering full blast into the poor monk's face, the pushy, remorseless slave demanded to know, "Don't you have a brother in the army?"

George Abbott remembers that if Zero could be generous, he could also be competitive in the most offensive way, that he began to perform one of Jack Gilford's pieces of business onstage before Gilford could ever get to it. And even physically, Zero began to roughhouse with Gilford in a manner that recalls his ferocious handshake with Herbie Kallem, a manner that was so uncalled for and so brutal that Gilford stopped speaking to him for months. And Ruth Kobart, incensed at Zero's stealing scenes, upstaging his colleagues, breaking other actors' concentration, orchestrated a mild protest one night by refusing to take her curtain call with the others. Zero, who was constitutionally incapable of apologizing to anyone, banned her from his dressing room until such time as she might offer an apology for her unprofessional behavior. But the audience loved the ad-libs, the energetic spontaneity, the moment one night when Zero as the Roman slave announced that Sonny Liston had just taken the heavyweight title away from Floyd Patterson.

Forum becomes one of those enormous hits that producers fantasize about, along with purring Mercedes and wonderfully-appointed mansions in the Hamptons, and Zero is even further confirmed as a major presence in mass entertainment. Some time after the opening of *Forum*, Gordon Rogoff and Andre Gregory—both identified over the years with the avant-garde, Rogoff as drama critic and director, Gregory as director and actor (e.g., the film *My Dinner With Andre*)—approach Peter Brook and propose a Broadway production of Brecht's *The Caucasian Chalk Circle*. (Recall that in 1942–43, Brecht had hoped for such an uptown run with Luise Rainer and Oscar Homolka.) Brook's initial response is to wonder why he should bother. He informs Rogoff and Gregory that he has already seen "the perfect production," referring to Brecht's own Berliner Ensemble in East Berlin.

But theatre people always get the itch to do a show *their* way, and the three men begin to discuss a possible cast. Rogoff and Gregory consider recruiting Judy Garland to play Grusha, the kitchen maid who saves the life of the governor's abandoned child, and Peter O'Toole is mentioned as the upright young soldier. But what most intrigues Brook is the possibility of Zero Mostel as Azdak, the village scribe who becomes the agreeably bribeable judge. As noted earlier, Brecht had fattened up the role for Oscar Homolka, even as he appeared to be offering Azdak to Zero. Recall that Azdak becomes the major figure in the latter scenes. It's he who must pass judgment on whether the child is to remain with Grusha or be returned to its biological, scatterbrained mother. But Brook is also interested in directing Zero as Pa Ubu in Jarry's *Ubu Roi*, the second occasion Brook makes this overture. He foresees a package deal that would include the two plays. Toby Cole eventually presents a note from Zero indicating his interest in both Azdak and Ubu, but what kills the project is the Brecht estate's terms. The estate, most likely represented by Brecht's son Stefan, requests ten thousand dollars to secure the rights, a sum which seems modest in today's market but strikes Rogoff and Gregory in the early Sixties as out of line with what they consider manageable. The project dies, though over the ensuing years Zero's hunger to perform both Azdak and Ubu will occasionally surface in public statements.

During the run of *Forum*, Eric Bentley visited Zero backstage to make an intriguing proposal. There were two versions of Brecht's *Man Is Man* about to open in New York. The Living Theatre, working from a translation by Gerhard Nellhaus, was in rehearsal at their own theatre on Fourteenth Street. On Forty-second Street, John Hancock, who had staged the drama at Harvard, was rehearsing the Bentley translation under the title *A Man's a Man*. Bentley was sufficiently uneasy with Hancock's work to seek out Zero. In the latter's dressing room, Bentley asked if Zero would sit in on a rehearsal with an eye to taking over direction. As Bentley saw it, the production needed to bring out certain humorous elements and Hancock wasn't fully in touch with the comedy of the play.

Zero did come to a rehearsal and he sat in the back of the

hall. Bentley feels that Hancock must have understood why the comedian was visiting. At any rate, Bentley and Mostel met after the rehearsal and Zero spun out a batch of intriguing directorial ideas. According to Bentley, who was wavering between replacing and retaining Hancock, "they were so radical that none of them could be instituted without replacing the director." Zero did not replace Hancock and Bentley contends that "John finally pulled the production together." Both *A Man's a Man* and *Man Is Man* opened and both ran for about one hundred and fifty performances. And Zero never directed Brecht.

The story Toby Cole relates concerning Zero's betrayal of her is a nasty one. It portrays Zero as a child who, though he doesn't appear to want to hurt anyone, nevertheless manages to inflict wounds. In addition Zero refuses to take responsibility for his actions. Cole was simply edged out as Zero's agent without the actor's ever having the guts to tell her that she was being dumped. The third party in this minidrama is Zero's attorney Sidney Cohn, a veteran who knew how to lock horns with HUAC, and before whose canniness Toby Cole, having no reason to mistrust her client, was like a sitting duck about to be shot out of the water.

Early in 1963, Cole was attempting to interest Zero in a comedy by the novelist Saul Bellow who was trying out his theatre wings. *Bummidge* concerns a top-flight comic who undergoes a painful psychoanalysis at the height of his career. Bellow, now one of our Nobel-Prize writers, later changed his title to *The Last Analysis*; the comedy eventually starred Sam Levene and it had a brief life on Broadway. It's a slight, charming work about Bummidge's fixation on a woman he hasn't laid eyes on for half a century, and most particularly it focuses on a certain well-remembered mole on the lady's thigh. To Toby Cole's chagrin, Zero elicited no particular interest in the Bellow play, but in his perverse fashion he also seemed not altogether uninterested. It had become part of Zero's pattern not to burn all his bridges, to keep authors, directors, and producers "slowly dangling in the wind."

Late in 1962, the "ethnic thing" that Jerry Robbins had phoned the *Foxy* company about made itself known to Zero when Joseph Stein dropped off a copy of his script, *Tevya and His Daughters*. Tevyeh again! Yisroel had delighted the Mostel children by reading to them from the tales of Sholom Aleichem in Yiddish. And here was an opportunity actually to perform as the beloved Milky One.

But Zero didn't like the script. Stein, he felt, hadn't done justice to Sholom Aleichem. Cole, pushing *Bummidge*, advised Zero to tell the *Tevya* people he wasn't interested. But Zero wasn't prepared to relinquish either *Bummidge* or *Tevya*. Better to keep everybody dangling awhile and see what might develop.

The original *Tevya* producer was to have been Fred Coe, and again we are speaking of one of the pioneers of television drama. Coe was producer of NBC's Philco-Goodyear Theatre; his writers included Paddy Chayefsky, Robert Alan Aurthur, Tad Mosel, and the later blacklisted Walter Bernstein who would write *The Front*; his directors included Arthur Penn and the later blacklisted Martin Ritt who would direct *The Front*. Out of Philco-Goodyear came Chayevsky's *Marty* and *The Middle of the Night*, as well as literally hundreds of live dramas from what is generally viewed now as "the golden age of television." From TV, Coe branched out into theatre and film, producing plays like William Gibson's *Two for the Seesaw* and *The Miracle Worker*, both directed by Arthur Penn. Coe had an approach to the blacklist which is instructive and not particularly edifying. "Before he died in 1972," Victor Navasky reports in *Naming Names*, "the writer Robert Aurthur recalled complaining about the blacklisting of an actor to producer Fred Coe and asking him to do something about it.

> And Coe told him what they could do: "'Right on this phone we will call the newspapers and summon a press conference for tomorrow. I will let you use this office, and you can tell the reporters exactly what's going on. At the end of the conference I will roll a carpet from here to the elevator and I will have photographers lining both sides taking your picture as you leave.' Coe looked me right in the eye. 'You will then get into the eleva-

tor,' he said. 'The door will close and you'll never come back.' A pause, and then he said, 'But you'll be a big hero.'"

If Zero had any inkling of Coe's relationship to the blacklist, it made little impact. When Coe forwarded a revised *Tevya* to him, Zero kept stalling, but Zero was stalling everyone, and in October of 1963 he took a two-week hiatus from *Forum* in order to work with director Burgess Meredith on a TV pilot to be produced by Screen Gems. *The Zero Mostel Show* was to be a true-to-life sitcom about and performed by the four nuclear-family Mostels: Zero, Kate, Josh and Toby. It was to be a weekly, half-hour series, depicting the actor-painter-husband-father, his spouse, and his brood in various, somewhat true-to-life situations.

Toby Cole was appalled for two reasons. It seemed incomprehensible to her that her client who heaped scorn on the medium in general would ally himself with what he had deemed its most despicable aspect. But if true, what could have prompted this conversion? She suspected the prompter. Two years earlier Zero's lawyer, Sidney Cohn, had advised his client that the theatre held no future for him, that he should give it up (along with his agent, Ms. Cole), and that he should concentrate on TV within whose foundations gold was to be mined. The second factor for Cole was that she, Mostel's agent, knew nothing of the Screen Gems development until she read about it in the paper.

If Zero taped the pilot in October, gossip about the proposed sitcom was already in the *New York Times* the previous May 23rd, when critic Val Adams ran a story about how the Mostel family saga would be edifying viewers in the fall of 1964. A.J. Russell, who had written for Jackie Gleason and Art Carney, confided in Adams that he, as newly-appointed Boswell to the Mostels, would be alert to opportunities whereby Zero might, in his comic fashion, utter a little Shakespeare, and Russell would toss it into the show. On July 28th, Adams ran a follow-up story to the effect that Mostel's Twenty-eighth Street studio was also to play a featured role in the life and times of.

Whenever Cole first learned of the enterprise, she put through a call to Sidney Cohn who informed her bluntly that "You have nothing to do with it." Cohn envisioned several years of TV, following which the star could retire, presumably to Twenty-eighth Street, Monhegan, his own living room, or wherever he chose, and "live off the residuals for the rest of his life."

But in the end something in Zero—his good angel?—intimated that there were more productive ways to spend the rest of one's life. Zero dropped the sitcom. He also finally dropped *Bummidge* or *The Last Analysis*, and by January of 1964, without granting her the courtesy of so informing her, Zero dropped Toby Cole. She had been busy negotiating the *Tevya* project that had resurfaced for Zero. *Forum* producer Hal Prince had supplanted Fred Coe. Zero had been up against performers like Danny Thomas, Walter Matthau, and even the inimitable Danny Kaye, all of whom had been under consideration, when Sidney Cohn telephoned Cole to advise her that she no longer represented Zero Mostel, and that Hal Prince's choice for Tevye, as it was now to be spelled, would be handled by another agent—himself, Sidney Cohn.

The subsequent phone conversation between Cole and Zero was awkward and painful for both parties. Was Cohn telling the truth? *Had* she, Toby Cole, been dropped? Without even being so informed by her own client? Zero refused to say yes or no. Cole persisted; Zero was evasive. At last, in response to her acknowledgment that she was hurt by *whatever* was going on— for surely somebody was being lied to—Zero is reported to have said, quietly, like a child, "What's the matter? Didn't Sidney say it nicely?"

21

The actress Bettye Jaffe lives alone on a quiet residential street in Beverly Hills. When I visited her in the late spring of 1988, the memory of her husband Sam Jaffe's death several years earlier was still vivid. Bettye Jaffe was not so much grieving as she was delicately fingering the texture of loss. As we spoke, she recalled happier events some thirty years earlier.

"I was doing *Tartuffe* at the 92nd Street Y in New York. It was part of the Y's poetry series. We had lost our original Tartuffe and someone said, 'Let's get the best Tartuffe anyone's ever seen.'" The performance, postponed once, was rescheduled for January 9th, 1956.[28] The Tartuffe they had in mind was Sam Jaffe. "So the director and I went to see Sam at his apartment on Waverly Place. Sam later said to me that I was used as bait. When we arrived, Sam was packing to move because he was broke; he'd already been blacklisted for seven years. He was blacklisted when he got an Academy Award nomination—Ward Bond did his best to tell film people not to vote for Sam. Sam had on white gloves while he was moving his books—he'd gotten chapped hands from the hard winter. Well, he was moving around the corner from the Y, a terrible little apartment. The moment we looked at each other, it was like the French say: blinded by lightning—we just stood and stared. Four years before that I'd seen *Gunga Din* and it went through my head that I would marry Sam."

Zero was invited to the opening night party, and Bettye, sitting between the two actors, mentioned that her birthday was on February 28th. We are a people heavily influenced by symbols, and as Bettye describes it, "Zero and Sam just stopped dead still and stared. Sam's wife Lillian had died on the 28th. I knocked the breath out of them." I wonder, but don't ask, whether Zero mentioned his own birth date, supposedly February 28th but actually the 29th. Zero later said to Sam Jaffe, "She's in love with you. You should marry her." Sam was sixty-four at the time, more than twice Bettye's age.

The wedding took place at the office of the justice of the peace in Moodus, Connecticut. "Zero cried the whole time, but loud. He was so sweet. Afterwards we went out and had hot fudge sundaes. At least Sam and I had them. Zero thought hot fudge sundaes were disgusting."

The blacklist was unrelenting. For Sam, the door to producers' offices was shut. Hard-pressed for money, both Sam and Zero took to investing. "Once they invested in some 'dental phenomenon' invented by some New York dentist. They were fleeced. They never got a cent back. At one point this investing led Zero to being totally broke. Not all because of this dentist, but the dentist didn't help—he simply finished Zero off."

But there was also a lawyer who was perfectly willing to finish off both men. "Sam was down to four thousand dollars and this lawyer said to Sam—mind you, this is *another* fleece—'You got any money to invest? I got a terrific investment for you.' So Sam thought, 'What I'll do is I'll invest my four thousand, I'll make some money, and then I'll give Zero four thousand dollars.'"

"From my profits," I suggest helpfully.

"So Sam gives all his money to this lawyer. Then Sam tells this news to his friend Herbert Rabinowitz, who is also a lawyer and received his doctorate under Justice Frankfurter. Herbert says, 'Sam! Go to that guy's office, you and Zero, and sit there until you get your money back! You're never gonna get a cent otherwise. Anything that sounds as good as what this lawyer is telling you can't be any good.' So Zero and Sam take sandwiches and go to this guy's office. The secretary says he's out. They say, 'It's okay, we'll wait.' So they sit there and they talk for a while and then they take out their sandwiches and coffee—"

"They had a thermos?"

"Yes, a thermos. And they are in the waiting room four or five hours, and finally the lawyer comes out of his office and gives Sam a check. Two days later the lawyer declares bankruptcy. Sam said that when they got the check he and Zero ran to the Amalgamated Bank because the people in the bank knew them so well they would push the check right through."

Bettye remembers other financial woes, not the least among them the issue of alimony. As she tries to piece it together, Kate was threatened with prison until the Mostels could come up with money for Clara. I, who have spent time with Clara, find this threat hardly credible. As Jaffe reconstructs the situation, the actor Karl Malden came to the rescue by making a generous loan to Zero, or perhaps it was an outright gift.

As for the two Sams, Jaffe and Mostel, there was surely a symbiotic tie between them. Whenever Sam Jaffe flew, he would take out insurance for Zero. The action speaks to one of the gentle if boisterous love affairs in contemporary theatre.

If times were difficult, the time for comedy persisted. The eternal adolescents pursued the harebrained action, on the town and within enclosed areas. Bettye recounts a Hollywood party "before Zero was so famous he would have been recognized." The guest list included a preponderance of physicians and Zero decided that he would present himself as the eminent Doctor So-and-so. "All night he was this doctor. When the doctors found out what he was doing they were absolutely furious, he was so darned good at it. Another thing—Zero and Sam could make up skits where they would speak all different languages— Japanese, Chinese, whatever."

"Pidgin?"

"Mostly."

In 1961, despite the fact that Sam Jaffe had no desire to live in Los Angeles, there was the possibility of work in Hollywood. Sam had been offered a featured role in the TV series, *Ben Casey*. The Jaffes relocated to "La-La Land" and found the blacklist still a potent force in the industry.

"Matthew Rapf, one of the *Ben Casey* producers, finds a copy of this awful book, *Red Star Over Hollywood*, on his desk. Sam's name is circled. Matthew shows it to me."

"Shows it as a gesture of support for Sam?"

"His brother Maurice, a Hollywood writer, had been black-listed. He wanted to show me that somebody was working to get Sam fired. All you had to do was make a phone call and say somebody was a Red."

"And this was happening as late as 1961."

"Yes. In 1962 we bought a home, so we were settling in. We would fly back to New York for Zero's openings, and sometimes we would fly back the next day.

"Sam and I flew in for the [*Fiddler*] opening. Zero had gotten us tickets and he knew where we were sitting and he played to Sam a lot of the time. We were bathed in tears."

I ask if Bettye had the sense that *Fiddler* was going to take off.

"Oh it was thrilling. Even as you asked me that, a chill went through me. It was one of the most exciting things I've ever seen, and you knew that it was going to be the biggest hit of all."

Shades of Mendele Mocher Sforim inhabit the Imperial Theater on the night of September 22nd, 1964, as Zero slowly propels, not the book-laden baby carriage Howard Da Silva dragged along in the first moments of *The World of Sholom Aleichem*, but a wheelbarrow stacked with clanking milk cans.

The garments of a time-honored heritage burden this God-fearing Tevye—the traditional *kippock* (yarmulka) and the *zitzit*, the tassels of the *tallit* (prayer shawl), sit like silent acts of homage, the head-covering in memory of the Sinai Desert's baking sun, and both the yarmulka and prayer shawl in homage to the omniscient God of Scriptures. The bearded, weary, gently ironic Jew has come onto the Imperial Theater's stage for this recurring journey into a lost time. And he announces to those watching:

> As the good book says, Heal us O Lord, and we shall be healed. In other words, send us the cure, we've got the sickness already. . . . I'm not really complaining—after all, with your help, I'm starving to death.

Newsweek reports on October 19th that ticket orders for *Fiddler on the Roof* are pouring in to the Imperial from numerous regions of the globe: from the North country (e.g., Anchorage, Alaska), from the tropics (e.g., Honolulu), and from the intermittent war zones of the Middle East. Even in the midst of a bitter newspaper strike in Detroit, word of mouth had helped to pack the orchestra and balcony of the Fisher Theater.

Which is not to say that Zero and Jerry Robbins hadn't been having their differences. About Zero kissing the *mezuzah*, the tiny metal scroll of Scriptural passages nailed to the doorpost: Zero insisted that it was a *mitzvoh* (a commandment) for Orthodox Jews to kiss the *mezuzah* on entering the threshold, and Robbins insisted that the action looked ridiculous, that hardly anyone in the audience would understand what Zero was intending. Zero played his entrance again, but when he substituted the sign of the cross, Robbins saw the handwriting as well as the *mezuzah* on the wall and gave in.

At another point, the costume designer produced *zitzit* in what Kate Mostel called "the prettiest pastel colors you've ever seen: pink, blue, yellow, pale green." More *shtum und drang* from Zero. He insisted that the *zitzit*, had to be white or "We'll be laughed off the stage." Originally one single blue-colored thread was the primary consideration by which Jews were to recall the commandments of the Lord, and the other tassles were and remain traditionally white. Again Zero scored, and so it went through rehearsals.

> Tevye: *(To God.)* I realize, of course, that it's no shame to be poor, but it's no great honor either. So what would have been so terrible if I had a small fortune? *(Sings.)* If I were a rich man/Daidle, deedle daidle/Digguh digguh deedle daidle dum/All day long I'd biddy biddy bum/If I were a wealthy man.

Songwriters Jerry Bock and Sheldon Harnick had a rich heritage to draw from in designing this poor man's kvetch, the kvetch that stopped the show. Precursors: the scat singing of

Louis Armstrong, Bing Crosby, and other jazz figures; the impro-
visations of the Yiddish theatre's Aaron Lebedev and his
"Rumania"—"Ay digguh digguh dum/Digguh digguh dum
dum"; Danny Kaye's "Dinah" in the Forties; and Cab Calloway's
"Minne the Moocher" back in the Thirties. And there is
Gershwin's *Porgy and Bess* seducer, Sportin' Life, segueing into
scat in the middle of "It Ain't Necessarily So." Where it all
started, how scat got into Dixieland, into black jazz, white jazz,
and Yiddish comedies we must leave to the musicologists. For all
we know, Joseph, overseeing the granaries, or making himself
scarce from the enticements of Potiphar's wife, was scatting in
the middle of the Fertile Crescent.

This poor kvetching Mostel had an odd effect on the company of *Fiddler*. Said Jerry Bock, "Before we cast the show, Zero
haunted us. We had an image at first of Tevye as a thin, gaunt
man, but Zero in a strange way can be thin and gaunt. . . ."

In New York, on opening night, the Broadway critics were
ecstatic. *Newsweek* records that from Zero "there radiates so sup-
ple, luminous and wide a light as to transform the stage into a
scene of high, compelling art." There is obviously something
that transforms this furious Mostel when the lights come up;
Newsweek puts it baldly, informing its readers that Zero moves
into "an art which transcends musical comedy values and the
ethnic framework. . . . it transcends and revolutionizes the uses
of comedy for our time."

Not all critics loved the show and Zero went on the attack in
a *New Yorker* interview that ran on January 2nd, 1965:

> A few self-elected Sholom Aleichem experts want to give
> you this little twist of the arm, so they say the show is "too
> Broadway." What does that mean? Nothing. Off-Broadway,
> things are the same, except the shows make less money and
> the actors are exploited. Or the guardians of culture describe
> some little thing I do as "a Broadway gesture." What the hell is a
> Broadway gesture? I goggle my eyes, they say. I've been in the
> business for twenty-two years, and for twenty-two years I've
> goggled my eyes, but now it's described as a Broadway gesture.

In the December 4th, 1964 issue of *Life*, Zero specifically takes Robert Brustein, writing for the *New Republic*, to task. Brustein has questioned the authenticity of *Fiddler's* Sholom Aleichem. Zero, moderately beside himself, notes that

> I've known Sholom Aleichem since I was a kid, and I'm the only one who reads Yiddish in the whole company. The dialogues with God that are in the show—I got those put in. I got in the line that's the whole essence of Sholom Aleichem—when Tevye says to God, "With your help, I'm starving to death." He's the only great writer who ever wrote about people making a living…can they make a piece of bread to eat!

The Mostel scythe is cutting a wide swathe. In the *New Yorker* interview Zero attacks other Tevyes he has seen.

> You should see what they did to Tevye in the Russian theatre. Junk! Or go to the Polish theatre. . . . They made a big propaganda play out of it. Or the Yiddish Theatre. I saw Maurice Schwartz do Tevye, and I can tell you that it was sentimental and maudlin . . . Our show is an honest piece of work.

In the summer of '88 I spent several hours with Paul Lipson who had been Zero's first understudy for Tevye and had graduated from Avram the villager to Lazar Wolf the butcher and finally to Tevye himself, a role he was still playing on June 17th, 1972, when then-Mayor John Lindsay congratulated the company on its three thousandth, two hundred and twenty-fifth performance. With that performance, *Fiddler*, that "little ethnic thing," broke the Broadway record for longest-running show, held since 1947 by the Lindsay-Crouse comedy, *Life With Father*.

"The original script," Paul Lipson notes,[29] "did not have the character of the fiddler in it at all. I think that a number of people were involved in developing the fiddler concept, including Jerry Bock, Sheldon Harnick, and Joe Stein, but perhaps Jerry Robbins more than the others. The fiddler concept eventually became the backbone of the whole play. It was amazing how many things it meant to different people, but it seemed obvious to me that the fiddler pretty much represented the spirit of the Jewish people in the shtetl. Regardless of what would happen to the characters, you would play the music and that certain spirit was always with them. In several of the scenes the fiddler dances around unseen by the players. The fiddler is at the wedding; no one sees him, but he's obviously central to the event. When Tevye breaks down after Chava and the Gentile boy run off together, and there's this sad ballet behind him as he's sitting there singing this little song of lamentation, the fiddler follows sadly after the young couple in the ballet. Then at the very end, when the whole family is leaving to go to America, and they're all packed, and at the very last moment Tevye says to the wife and children, 'Come Golde, let's go,' and he starts pulling the wagon around in a circle into the horizon, out comes the fiddler behind them. At that moment Tevye actually looks at him and acknowledges him, as if to say: Hey, everything's gonna be all right."

Lipson remarks on the confusion between Tevye and the fiddler. "For years people who hadn't seen the play would say to me, 'Oh you must be the fiddler.'"

Lipson recalls his experience as Zero's understudy: "Do you want to know something? I went on as Tevye before I'd ever had a rehearsal in the part. I was originally signed to be Zero's understudy and to play the small part of Avram, with the understanding the producers would sign somebody with a name to stand by for Zero. This name understudy business happens when it's a great big hit and they've got a great big star. When we get to Washington during the tryout tour, at one matinee Zero becomes ill after doing the first number. He'd come down with food poisoning. I was standing in the wings, ready to go on in my little part which followed shortly, and Ruth Mitchell, who was production stage manager at that time, said to me, 'Do you want to do it? You can carry the book if you want to.' And I said, 'I've watched carefully and I think I know it well enough, except I've never rehearsed the dances and I may paraphrase a lot of the words, but yeah!' So out I went and I did it." And did it again. "Zero was out for six performances during the two weeks we were in Washington. Not consecutively. He got better, then he got worse, and I kept going on, and by this time

I'd learned the part very well. And then the publicity came out—not so much making me a star, but it said, 'Hey, this show in Washington that's already got such great word-of-mouth is not a one-man-show. Other people can do it!' I don't think Zero liked that particularly but he never said anything."

I ask, "Did you in some way have to block out Zero's performance in order to find yours?"

"No. Right from the beginning there's not a Tevye who ever went on who did not give part of Zero's performance. Because in creating the role there were so many things that were particularly Zero's that became frozen in the part, so that anyone doing Tevye could not do it without some semblance of Zero unless he gave a very, very dull performance. Eventually I got to *play* Tevye and got to rehearse Tevye—and that happened several times after we opened on Broadway because Zero was out quite a few times—then it had to be my performance. You have to bring something of yourself to that role, whatever your creative parts are—and yet Tevye is always going to have the aura of Zero around it."

We discuss the staging. I tell Paul Lipson that "blocking to me is a dirty word, it always implies an artificial way of staging. It's imposing movement on the actors. But since it seems to be the language of the commercial theatre, let's use the term *blocking* without prejudice."

Lipson remembers that Jerry Robbins gave Zero great leeway, certainly during rehearsals. "But once the show is set, actors don't change their blocking, not in a Robbins show."

I mention that I've been hearing differently about Zero's performance.

"Oh no. Within his *own* thing, when Zero was on his own [without other performers depending on him] he would do some wonderfully creative things, and sometimes he would do outlandish things, when he got bored. But the major blocking was always the same. Zero knew that. He had that kind of discipline."

Was he responsible to the others? Was he aware of the qualities of other characters onstage with him?

"Yes. Again he was an artist and realized that if he didn't respond truthfully his performance would be lessened. Every so *often* it would be *A Night With Zero*, and we'd say, 'Oh, here he goes again!' But even then it was within the framework of the show. He couldn't cut loose completely from it."

Merle Debuskey's memory is that "Occasionally Zero would get bored and be a bad boy, but he was too smart a performer not to know the play depended on a cohesion. I saw virtually everything he did, and in the early stages of *Forum* and *Fiddler* he was disciplined. Remember that at the time of *Forum*, Jerry Robbins couldn't have been too unhappy—he was probably delighted that there was some connection with people Jerry thought he could never work with again. But *Fiddler* was the second time around for him with Zero, so by then Jerry may have had a different view, he might not have been so tolerant of Zero's improvs."

Paul Lipson speaks of a scene in the first act. Tevye and Lazar Wolf are negotiating the marriage contract of Lazar and Tevye's daughter Tzeitel.

> Lazar: Look, Tevye, why do we have to try to impress each other? Let's shake hands and call it a match. . . .
> Tevye: *(To audience.)* I never liked him!. . . You can have a fine conversation with him if you talk about kidneys and livers. . . . On the other hand, not everybody has to be a scholar?. . . And with a butcher, my daughter will surely never know hunger. . . . He is a good man. He likes her, he will try to make her happy.

"The Cossacks," Lipson describes the moment, "come into the inn to have a drink and they begin to dance. Zero and Lazar Wolf acknowledge that the marriage is all set and they get up and start to dance." And sing *L'chaim*, to life.

"And the Jews in the inn start to dance to celebrate the marriage agreement. The Jews are lined up on the proscenium holding hands and dancing across the stage and all of a sudden the Russians are dancing between their legs. And at one point, one of the Russians bumps into Zero, into Tevye, and Tevye looks up in horror at the Cossack and sort of bows and apologizes and asks him to dance with him. It's a charming moment. Well, one night, as the story goes, Zero had some friends sitting in the house seats which were way down front, and as Zero is bending over for some reason or other the Cossack bumps into him and hits his rear end. And Zero exclaims, '*Oy, shir tsibruchen em tuches,*' ('I almost broke my ass'). Well, this naturally got a laugh from Zero's friends. But Zero being Zero, pretty soon it became a full-blown line—he used to say it every night! And by this time the producer and the authors became furious and, as I understand it—I don't know how true it is—they threatened him with a lawsuit if he didn't cut that line, because it was not that kind of show."

Lipson recalls another incident. "He did something else one night which was perfectly charming. The house onstage used to move—it had wings which opened and closed and also it would move back on the turntable. One night at the end of a scene, the house didn't close properly. So Zero went over and pulled the wing closed and said to the audience, 'Wow, that's what happens, I didn't pay the rent.'" And at this point I share with Paul Lipson the story of the night the lights went out in Zero and Clara's apartment because Zero had forgotten to pay the electric bill.

The question of Zero's not being cast in the film version of *Fiddler* surfaces, an issue that won't go away. In this meeting with Paul Lipson, I'm the one who asks about it, and Lipson remembers that "we used to try to figure out why Zero didn't get that part. Maybe Norman Jewison, who directed the movie, wanted an actor he could control better." The role eventually went to the Israeli actor, Topol.

"Were Zero and Jerry Robbins at odds?"

"Sometimes Zero would resent direction. Every so often there'd be a flareup. Nothing besides that. Considering the history of the HUAC hearings, it was a miracle that the two of them ever got together for *Forum* in the first place."

Lipson recalls the struggle to finalize the show: "We rehearsed for six weeks in the terrible heat that summer of 1964.

We were on West Fifty-seventh Street, in some big loft over Henry Bendel's, The show wasn't frozen until two or three nights before we actually opened. During the several weeks we were in Detroit and the two weeks in Washington there were constant rehearsals *every day* for changes, additions, deletions. So many changes, radical changes.

"There's a number that Jerry worked on all the way into the end of the Washington run; it was a big production number for the second act. Up till then, all the big production numbers were in the first act and Jerry wanted another big one in Act Two. And so we went on and on with this production number in various forms and finally it just never came in. Instead we substituted a very simple, very beautiful ballet behind Tevye singing this plaintive little song about how his daughter, 'Little bird, little Chavaleh,' had gone off to marry the Gentile Fyedka. And for this there'd be countless hours of backbreaking rehearsal, working on different forms of this ballet."

There's another song that never made it to New York. "I got to sing this one in Washington before we ever came to Broadway. It was supposed to be Zero's second act show-stopper, like his first-act 'If I Were a Rich Man.' [It] was called 'When Messiah Comes.' and it was a lovely song. [But] it just got mild applause because it was too late for that kind of quiet song "

"Do you remember any of it?"

"The constable comes to the villagers and tells them they have three days to sell their houses and their household goods. Tevye asks why."

> Constable: *(Irritated.)* I don't know why. There's trouble in the world, trouble-makers.
> Tevye: *(Ironically.)* Like us!
> Constable: You aren't the only ones. Your people must leave all the villages —Zolodin, Rabalevka. The whole district must be emptied. . . .
> First Man: And what if we refuse to go?
> Constable: You will be forced out.
> Lazar: We will defend ourselves. . . .

Constable: Against our army? I wouldn't advise it!

Tevye: I have some advice for you. Get off my land! (*The villagers crowd toward the Constable and his men.*) This is still
my home, my land. Get off my land! (The Constable
and his men start to go. The Constable turns.)

Constable: You have three days! *(Exits.)*

First Man: After a lifetime, a piece of paper and get thee out.

"The villagers are standing crestfallen in the street, it's winter, and somebody says, ' How do you like that? Three days and
get thee out.' 'Get Thee Out' was the name of the song. When
the villagers left the stage they'd sing, 'Get thee out, get thee
hence, get thee out from whence we came.' Sounded like the
Yacht Club Boys [a comic choir, of sorts, from Thirties movies,
somewhat like the Ritz Brothers]. Well that song went the way
of other songs. The final version finds the villagers standing
around desolate, and somebody says, 'Rabbi, you're always
talking about the Messiah. Wouldn't this be a good time for him
to come?' And the rabbi answers, 'We'll have to wait for him
someplace else. Meanwhile, let's start packing.' And they sing
the song 'Anatevka.'"

All: What do we leave?
Nothing much.
Only Anatevka. . . .
Underfed, overworked Anatevka. . . .
Intimate, obstinate Anatevka. . . .

"But in the original, all the way through Washington before
they took it out, they say, 'Tevye, you're always talking about
the Messiah. Wouldn't this be a good time for him to come?'
They ask Tevye, not the rabbi. And Tevye sings:

When Messiah comes, he will say to us
I apologize that I took so long.
But I had a little trouble finding you
Over there a few and over here a few.
You were hard to reunite, but—
Everything's going to be all right.

Max Waldman's photo of the four Mostels, Kate, Zero, Josh and Toby, in one their quieter moments. 1962.

Herbie Kallem and Zero ensconced on one of the ubiquitous delivery trucks on Monhegan Island with the Island Inn in background. Circa 1960. Courtesy: Gillis Kallem.

Jackie Mogel in the Lupi Gallery, Monhegan Islan Circa 1983. Photo: Arthu Sainer.

Doug and Harry Odom in their living room, Monhegan Island. Circa 1983. Photo: Arthur Sainer.

Zero at bat on Monhegan's ball field. Circa 1970. Courtesy: Michael Nelson.

Jan and Frances Kornbluth in France Monhegan cottage. Circa 1983. Phot Arthur Sainer.

As Pseudolus in *A Funny Thing Happened on the Way to the Forum.*
Photo: Van Williams.

As Leopold Bloom in *Ulysses in Nighttown.*

As Jean in *Rhinoceros*.

As Tevye in *Fiddler on the Roof.*

Zero and Marian Seldes at the first rehearsal for Arnold Wesker's
The Merchant. 1977.

Zero as Shylock in his only performance
of *The Merchant.* 1977.

A lovely song but it came too late in the show. Oh there were lots of songs that came into and went out of the show, songs that were revised and then they went, they disappeared."

Lipson recalls the big second-act production number: "They worked on it in Detroit. In it, Tevye goes across the marketplace, with the entire stage full of pushcarts and vendors and all that, to a little house downstage right, where incidentally Charles Durning, who was the priest until the priest got written out of the show, is sitting, and the priest has already performed the ceremony, wedding Chava to the Gentile, Fyedka And then Tevye comes out of the priest's little house... [T]he scene was tentatively called 'Tevye's Nightmare' because the news he hears is something he just can't take, and Tevye goes around the stage and he's so completely bewildered, and you hear these voices: 'Tevye Tevye, Tevye Tevye,' and the whole stage starts to spin because Tevye's mind is spinning. 'Tevye Tevye, Tevye Tevye' spinning and spinning. *Wellllll*, the pushcarts fell into the orchestra! I can't tell you what happened. There were two turntables, one going one way, and inside of the big one a smaller one going the other way. And this was the big production number and it *went*. It just got tossed out. All that scenery *went*—and what evolved instead was this little scene where Tevye's complaining about his old horse who's complaining about his aching leg and Golde his wife appears and tells him she's been to the priest and the priest informed her that Chava and Fyedka were married by him. And Tevye pushes her away.

> Tevye: Go home, Golde. We have other children at home. . . .
> Chava is dead to us! We will forget her. Go home.

And Tevye goes and sits down on his cart and sings.

> Tevye: Little bird, little Chavaleh,
> I don't understand what's happening today.

In the background, one by one, we see the three daughters dancing off, the oldest daughter Tzeitel with Motel the tailor, that was a happy arrangement. The next daughter Hodel dancing off with Perchik [the revolutionary], that was an arrangement Tevye eventually approved of. And then suddenly out comes Chava and Fyedka and she has this pulling movement, towards her family, towards Fyedka, and finally they dance off together. And the fiddler dances off sadly behind them as Tevye finishes the song. Such a simple ballet, such a genius thing that Robbins did there. *That* replaced that whole big mishmash and told the same story so simply and beautifully."

I remark that one tends to get caught up in machinery. And Paul Lipson announces that "Today all you *see* is machinery. Spectacle, spectacle!"

Lipson notes Zero's contribution to the staging: "Zero would come out, he'd say, 'Let's try this, let's try that.' And Jerry Robbins appreciated it. Robbins is the last man in the world to say no. He respects and loves that kind of creative thinking. He's also the toughest man in the world when it comes to cutting if he doesn't like something in the show. He has this remarkable ability to let people try things. Zero came up with some wonderful ideas."

"I notice there's no Yiddish in the play."

"That's right. And they were very careful to keep it exactly that way. There were only two Hebrew phrases in the entire play: *l'chaim* and *mazel tov*. And no accents. That's what made the show universal. They were all Jews—there were intonations, naturally. So many of Sholom Aleichem's lines were translated literally, you had to give these lines a sort of inflection."

I ask Paul Lipson, "Did you ever have a sense of hostility, a night when the audience just didn't want to hear about Jews?"

"Not at that time. Don't forget, we went through the Six-Day War, in 1967. At one point we were in Vegas and Theodore Bikel was playing Tevye and the audience broke into applause at one of the curtain lines. I think you would have to say the show was an affirmation of family life, of religion, of poor people struggling and prevailing. It was not simply Jewish in that sense."

Lipson remembers one particular night in Zero's dressing room: "I was still the understudy. I was probably playing Lazar by that time, a bigger part, so I felt more comfortable about approaching Zero. I said, 'I love the way you play Tevye, but you know I'm more qualified than you to play the part.' Immediately he jumps—whoa!—and the eyes are bulging. And I pull out this bottle cap and hold it out and I say, 'This was my father.'" And Lipson holds out an old milk-bottle cap to me, and I read, "Lipson's Milk Pasteurized. Pittsfield, Mass."

"He got such a kick out of it."

And there is the telephone number. "Phone 22618..."

"I said to Zero, 'As a child I was carrying milk cans and bottles way before you ever thought about it.'"

And there is a Kate Mostel story that Paul Lipson shares with me at the end of this hot summer afternoon.

"We're returning from Luther Adler's funeral. [Luther Adler had also played Tevye.] I had delivered the eulogy and I'm riding with Kate and Luther's widow and one of Luther's sisters. And we're all reminiscing, remember this about Luther, this about Zero—for Zero was also gone by this time. And I start to say, 'Remember the night . . .' And I'm stuck. 'Oh gosh, I can't think of this guy's name.' And Kate says to me, 'That's all right, Paul, at our age it takes three people to do a name.'"

Paul Lipson himself died on January 3rd, 1996. He was eighty-two and had played Tevye over two thousand times.

WOODY AND ZERO
a short play of sorts

Scene: Central Park, a nice day. If someone were to pass by, they might notice two personages in quiet deliberation.

Woody. Anti-Semitism.

Zero. Yes?

Woody. Needs to go.

Zero. Agreed. Filthy habit. Where should it go? *(They're quiet, deep in thought.)* Am I crowding you?

Woody. No no, I strike you as crowded? I appear crowded?

Zero. You ask me about appearances? Tell me, Woodrow, I don't oppress you?

Woody. *(Considering.)* Well . . . since you've raised the issue—

Zero. There's no issue! If anything, I impress, never oppress. Nothing oppressive about me.

(They're deep in thought again.)

Woody. I was thinking . . .

Zero. Yes? *(Nothing. More thought.)*

Woody. We're both intelligent individuals, right?

Zero. Ah! Who would doubt it? *Just let them try! Lemme at'em!*

Woody. I mean here's what I have in mind.

Zero. My heart has skipped a beat.

Woody. You want to hear this? *(More deep-in-thoughtness.)* Now what I'm getting at is—

Zero. Get at it, get at it! *(Quietly.)* Proceed, carry on, forge ahead, forward march, and so forth.

Woody (Warming to his subject.) Intelligent Jewish guys, you agree? Now stop me if I'm overstepping the bounds of reason. *(No interruptions.)* I myself am the quiet noisy type Jewish chap, no doubt you've witnessed this type. Seemingly aggressive, but in fact two-steps-forward-one-step-back kinda guy, forever pondering this and that, that and this.

Zero. I do believe my watch is giving up the ghost. But this watch *has* no ghost.

Woody. Whereas you—*you*, to emphasize the personal pronoun—are the *noisy* noisy Jewish type.

Zero. Ah, you hardly understand me.

Woody. Barely. I understand you barely.

Zero. Let me get this straight. You see me, Alyosha, as a china-shop bovine, as an intruder into the unseemly?

Woody. You mean as a kind of bloated mammal Neanderthal size fifteen shoe forty-five waist washed up onto the lawn of a Southampton estate during happy hour, so to speak?

Zero. Breathless idiomatic phrasing. But let us pursue this issue forthright without invective.

Woody. I just wish to bring in a small point about our personae.

Zero. Let me aid you, because if the truth be known I'm picking up your drift. You, Woodrow, embark on a stratagem in which your character employs a fade-into-the-woodwork mechanism. You suggest and imply that your character is on this earth as an archetypal ridiculous mistake. Your character *appears* to be a self-effacing Upper West Side nervous, scholarly type who would be quiet if only the environment would leave you in peace. Now what *I* understand—see if you can stay with me on this—is that environment is *bullshit*, that each of us is *really* out there with his, her or its hidden agenda or subtext, and that *nobody* in this city, this urban center of medium chaos, is ever going to leave anybody else in peace. *(Zero is getting warmed up.)* Now I, as sensitive as the next mammal, I with my acute nose for any shmuck coming down the pike, am onto their game, I understand that *nobody* is capable of leaving *anybody else* in peace! And so my act is to can the pretense, my act is to lay it all out, my act is to pull out my total Zeroness at full capacity, at full throttle if you'll permit an archaic automotive metaphor.

(Woody is all attention as Zero goes into higher gear.)

Zero. I understand, mind you, that this laying it all out is bound to offend timorous souls who want to believe that they are inhabiting a little county a trifle southwest of Eden and that things would be terrific if only we noisy Yids would pull up our camels, wives and Torah scrolls and move out of the development. And also that these closet Jew-haters absolutely quiver and kvel with inner satisfaction, as opposed to outer satisfaction, when they witness this seemingly noisy, pushy Mostel effecting his noisy, pushy routine. *You,* Woody, are to them a noisy, ill-mannered Jew who is simply *repressing* the full extent to which he can be noisy and ill-mannered, whereas I, these troglodytes believe, don't even have the *intelligence,* the *wit,* to comprehend that I *ought to be* repressing anything. They believe I believe I'm satisfied to be noisy and pushy, these uninformed, maladjusted, overly-socialized Yahoos.

(Zero's outburst leaves both men agog. Silent stares at each other.)

Woody. We're getting a trifle overheated, agreed? And absolute hunger is rounding the corner.

Zero. Absolute hunger? Cornering I and thou?

Woody. Howsabout a nosh down the block?

Zero. A small, discreet repast!

Woody. The Stage Deli?

Zero. (Ecstasy rapidly setting in.) Pastrami, pickles, cole slaw, paper napkins!

Woody. Doctor Pepper.

Zero. Be still, my heart. A day to be alive.

Woody. Movies later?

Zero. Seen 'em all.

Woody. All? You seen *everything?*

Zero. All, and before there was even an all. All, all, *all.* Most of it child's play, fool's gelt.

Woody. A soft shoe under an elm on our way to the feeding venue?

Zero. Elm? Do elms still thrive, Alyosha, in this Olmsteadian habitat?

Woody. You want it straight? I'm a city boy, urban type, I wouldn't know an elm from a block of chismwood.

Zero. (As they rise.) My first will be on rye, then I'll switch to seeded roll, then a subtle segue or cross-fade to garlic bagel or perhaps a quaint touch of bialy.

Woody. I thought you'd be partial to the Reubens, layers of turkey, roast beef and Russian.

Zero. (Impatient.) I'm already with my chin into the cabbage borscht.

Woody. (As they exit toward Seventh Avenue, no longer visible.) Which chin would that be, Zee, upper, lower or mid? Careful there of my big toe, Zee. I bruise without forewarning.

For seven months Zero is Tevye *Der Milkhiger*. As Hal Prince recounts it, confirming a conversation I've had with Prince's press representative, Mary Bryant, Zero's contract had come up for renewal "and I balked at a number of his demands." One point at issue: an increase in salary. Prince's offer and Zero's expectations were far apart. But according to Prince, "The capper was the daily limousine." (Lear: "O, reason not the need!") "Times have changed; today that sort of perk appears in most star contracts. I *still* don't approve."

So Zero was not to be chauffeured, but the break from the theatre was deeper than he could have imagined at the time. From 1965 until his all-too-brief appearance in *The Merchant* in 1977, the last play he was ever to do, Zero's involvement in theatre was not only minimal, it was superficial. It hardly challenged the best in him. There was Paddy Chayefsky's *The Latent Heterosexual* in 1968; there was the *Ulysses in Nighttown* revival in '74; and a seemingly endless string of Tevye revivals. One would like to believe, and it may well be true, that Zero hungered for new theatre work, perhaps new Becketts, new

Pinters and Ionescos, certainly he and Chayefsky and Burgess Meredith spoke of forming a company that would produce serious theatre. But it is to be mostly film, with an occasional television stint, that will occupy him, and most of the film work, despite flashes of brilliance, will be too pedestrian, too perfunctory, hardly invoking the need to stretch his abilities or to explore other facets of himself or the medium.

In August of 1965 Zero is off to Spain for the filming of *Forum*. Shooting takes place in Madrid and in suburban Las Matas. For Zero it's a reunion with Jack Gilford and an opportunity to visit the Prado and pay his respects at the grave of Goya. Generalissimo Franco is still in office; it's three decades since the Loyalists were beaten by "the four insurgent [fascist] generals," but it's also a time for "Comedy Tonight."

Richard Lester has been chosen to direct Zero's film comeback, the actor's first feature since the 1951 potboilers. And Lester, coming off successful projects, in particular the Beatles' *A Hard Day's Night*, proves to be a major blunder. "It's no one's fault but my own," Zero is to reflect to the *Los Angeles Herald Examiner* in 1968. "I asked for him—and he's a very nice guy. I liked what he did with the Beatles. . . . But *Forum* was so funny on the stage, I don't think it was the vehicle for experimental movie-making."

Lester focused on rapid cutting, blatantly odd camera angles, gratuitously employing film in the manner of some underground filmmakers (e.g., Stan Brakhage) and of the early Jean-Luc Godard. In effect, Lester's cool, nervous camera came not to support but to compete with the hot burlesque aura of Zero, Jack Gilford, Phil Silvers and Buster Keaton. Lester spoke of aiming for an "anti-epic," of creating "bad Roman taste of the 1st A.D." At the Samuel Bronston Studios, the company retrieved leftover props from *The Fall of the Roman Empire* and Lester pushed for hideously-colored interiors, "awful purple" sets, all of which give the final print a kind of pranksterish dayglow kitsch to complement its plethora of puns, slapstick, and double entendre.

In looking at a print of *Forum* today, there is the unsettling impression that while the principal comics work vigorously to assure us that they are having one terrific time, a palpable sense of strain becomes unbearably evident as the movie thrashes from one reel to the next. The quality of improvisation, rather than suggesting a happy liberation, reinforces the impression that the world before our senses is strangely off-kilter. The final print demonstrates a filmmaking project in which the actors are more than a little hysterical and become too burdensome; ultimately they are enormous nuisances. The picture frame by its very nature, despite the alarming intimation that the image of Zero in it is never going to cease "performing," represents an enclosure that constricts the dynamism that is Zero "live." To view Zero prancing, undulating, ogling, goosing and doing his thousand-and-one Zeroisms is to understand that breadth is needed, old-fashioned breadth such as an old-fashioned proscenium stage provides, and that without this breadth, without the pressure of the now-traditional stage frame, Zero's work is reduced to a series of antics, of forced signals. It is as if upon looking through a telescope, our expectations of viewing an exotic, pristine Jupiter are shattered by the frontal invasion of a too-present, jowly, smiling earthling who is all too familiar and not particularly welcome.

Keaton has it even worse. Keaton doesn't even appear to be having any fun. Philip Scheur, reporting on September 29th, 1965, in the *Los Angeles Times*, tells us that the seventy-year-old Buster Keaton, once a nimble seven-year old whose father Joe Keaton could easily fling him into the wings of numerous vaudeville houses across the United States, was now forced to tear around the hills of "Rome" seven times, not withstanding the chariot wheels thundering in front of and to the rear of him. At one point, Keaton's world-renowned flat hat comes in violent contact with one of the numerous trees in the Casa de Campo Park, and the hat's occupant is unceremoniously dumped onto the ground, regardless of what the shooting script called for.

Keaton, who had shortly before this been working in Rome as General Erwin Rommel, Hitler's desert fox, in *War—Italian*

Style, seems all but absent in *Forum*, perhaps anaesthetized. Keaton possibly is somewhere, but too far from the forum. When he is energetic, the effect strikes one as an aberration; the character is never located.

Zero, we are told, is having a ball. The *New York Times's* Bernard Weinraub sketches for us a suspiciously idyllic moment. An elderly Spanish woman is combing Zero's curls over his forehead. All at once, as if recalling the eruptive hijinks of Banjo in *The Man Who Came to Dinner*, Zero grabs at the woman, initiates a rapid tickling, and barks out protestations of love, romantically assaulting this startled, Continental version of Nurse Prim.

Both on and off the set, Zero is inventive, impatient, observant, the snarling connoisseur, the comic fooling around or the fool comically covering up the sense that the film is getting out of hand. The terms that producer Hal Prince balked at on Broadway are now duly met—each morning a chauffeur arrives in a black Cadillac to whisk Zero from the Castellano Hilton to the film studio.

During the shooting, Zero ruminates about the possibility of *Fiddler* as movie: its performers would include the urbane Jack Lemmon as Tevye, the passionate, full-blooded Anna Magnani as the Jewish wife, the bloodless Alec Guinness as the Jewish butcher, and none other than Cardinal Spellman as the pious rabbi.

Finally, after much exertion in and around Madrid, a tiresome *Forum* is launched. The world takes little note of it and Zero moves on to the next project.

During 1966 Zero and Kate make a trip to France to confer with Marcel Pagnol. The French novelist and filmmaker has had a legendary career, creating stories of the Provence countryside. His films include the extraordinary simple and lucid *Baker's Wife*, with Raimu's masterful portrayal as the baker, as well as the Fanny trilogy, *The Well-Digger's Daughter* with Raimu and Fernandel, *Topaze* with Louis Jouvet, and the three-narrative, comic epic *Letters From My Windmill*. Over the years Zero has cherished Raimu's characterization of the baker, how the sturdy Provencal peasant was brought to life without employing tricks or a particular acting technique.

During the conference with Pagnol, it is Zero's impression that the film director would look favorably on a remake of *The Baker's Wife*. Another option would have Zero serving as producer of a musical adaptation of the film with himself in the Raimu part. Pagnol recalls to Zero that Raimu hadn't any idea how he managed anything on screen, and Zero begins to wonder how he himself can possibly perform the baker after watching Raimu. In the end the conference leads to no project.

LeCoq—Yes, maybe, and finally no.

In 1967 Zero and Ian Hunter begin writing a feature film to be called *Monsieur LeCoq*. Zero's attorney Sidney Cohn, together with Carl Foreman, in Hunter's words "cooked up this deal." Foreman, a pioneer unfriendly witness, had returned from self-imposed exile in England. Sidney Cohn had forged an arrangement with HUAC Chairman Francis Walter whereby repentant former Communists would meet Walter in executive session, denounce only themselves, and thus be "cleared" by the Committee. Foreman had been able to work in England but wanted to come home. The private meeting with Walter, arranged by Cohn, allowed Foreman to renew his career at Columbia Pictures, although the filmmaker was now suspected of naming names and Walter suspected by the Right of having been paid off so that Foreman wouldn't be burdened with the onus of actually naming anyone.

All the principals in this bizarre arrangement seemed to get what each longed for most, but this clearing formula, which would remove ex-unfriendly witnesses from the blacklist, apparently functioned for no one but Foreman. Victor Navasky notes that it was Cohn's position that he would not act as counsel for informers, but the formula of denouncing oneself and only in executive session was never again employed. Foreman, rehabilitated in Walter's eyes, resumed writing and producing for Columbia, and by the early Sixties had established an independent producing unit within the Columbia Pictures complex. It was this unit, in alliance with Cohn, who also acted as Zero's counsel, that was to produce *Monsieur LeCoq*.

The creators seemed to have had nothing but the title, but it was all they needed. Zero and Ian Hunter were living across the courtyard from one another at the Belnord; the apartments were enormous, mirroring one another, and each day Zero would amble over to Ian's apartment. "He would come over about ten in the morning and we'd discuss the day's work. Then I would rough out a scene on the typewriter while Zero busied himself with the *Times* crossword puzzle. Then Zero would read my scene; at the same time he'd be acting out all the parts, ad-libbing, using gestures which to him were like thoughts. These gestures helped me understand what we were doing. Zero had put the thing on its feet—an instant production. Then we'd go to lunch. Then I'd rewrite based on what Zero had done in the morning."

The producers are taken by it. "Carl and Sid loved it. Finally Zero goes to London to work in the movie *Great Catherine* and eventually I join him to put the finishing touches to our script. We had a wild, funny piece of work. Zero's notion was that the camera could do anything, but that 'anything' could get rather costly. I tried to keep the film less expensive, but Zee wanted all these special effects. Anyway, there we were in London, making final arrangements for shooting. For thirty days we ate in the Savoy Grill. We discovered that pressed duck was the best thing. A. Alvarez, who wrote the Sylvia Plath biography [Hunter is referring to *The Savage God: A Study of Suicide*, which, though it centers on Plath's suicide, is not a biography of her.] heard from us about the pressed duck—word was getting around about this duck—and he started coming around and we'd treat him to duck."

Trouble.

"They hired this director. Something about him worried me, but I couldn't put my finger on it. Then one day I went into this fish house in Chelsea and I found my director there. He was so stone drunk he didn't recognize me."

And more trouble.

"Off they went to shoot the film in the French countryside." Shooting took place at Arles, twenty miles south of Avignon; at Nimes, with its Roman ruins; and at a historic Louis XIII chateau at Montfrin. The production company is called Highroad-Open Road, the producer is Adrian Scott of the original Hollywood ten, and the director is Seth Holt. Performers include Julie Newmar, Akim Tamiroff, and Ronnie Corbett; and they are shooting ostensibly from September 18th on. But on November 8th, 1968, *Variety* runs a story from *LeCoq's* producers. Shooting is to be suspended as of November 15th due to the liklihood of inclement weather and will resume the following spring."

"I'm waiting in London," Hunter recalls, "and all at once Zero is back from the French countryside. He tells me the director keeps falling asleep during takes. There doesn't seem to be anybody in charge. Foreman is in Hollywood; he knows nothing about the problem. When he finds out about the mess we have on our hands, it's too late."

If any of the *LeCoq* footage still exists, no one I've spoken to knows where it's stored. *Playboy* ran some stills in its September 1969 issue, showing Julie Newmar in a bubble bath; the nubile Newmar is beckoning to Zero who obliges by climbing into the tub and commencing a vigorous scrubbing of areas of the lady's anatomy.

During my November '88 visit to Toby Mostel, I inquire about the now-legendary *Monseur LeCoq* and Toby dredges up a nicely-typed carbon of the shooting script. I am staying overnight at Toby's house in Eastport, on the Maine coast, and I take *LeCoq* to bed with me. At length I settle back in this wonderfully quiet room with its self-portrait of Zero hanging at the right side of this more than ample double bed and begin to read.

The script is a brilliant, overwrought mess, bespeaking a highly sophisticated sense of the camera, a fine instinct for slapstick, an overindulgence in the life of the senses and of the aesthetics of intrigue. The narrative: Max LeCoq's lady friend gives birth to a little man whose name is Monsieur. At birth Monsieur is not only all but fully developed—both Max and Monsieur are played by Zero—he is something of a genius. Poppa Max is engaged full time in petty thievery, and since we are told that the acorn never falls far from the tree, it's not surprising that Monsieur's genius first manifests itself through the time-honored discipline of pickpocketing. In due time Monsieur is corrupted—that is, seduced into going straight—and this alarming development brings about his parents' downfall. What has led Monsieur astray, into the straight and narrow? A prim; remorseless creature in his elementary school class. Lisette, soon to blossom in gorgeous fashion, is, when we first encounter her, a slim bastion of unremitting virtue who demands nothing less of the enamored Monsieur but that he conform to her idea of the just life. Monsieur, overcome with love, degenerates into virtue personified and in due time exposes Poppa Max to the eyes of the gendarme. Max topples from a roof attempting to escape justice in the midst of an ordinary criminal act and falls to his death. Efficiency being what it is in such well-planned stories, Max manages to take his spouse into the next world with him by judiciously landing on top of her. The orphaned Monsieur becomes a brilliant detective named Inspector LeCoq. Lisette's physical attributes accelerate alarmingly. She and LeCoq engage in an on-again, off-again relationship which features among other divertisements a penchant on LeCoq's part for falling into Lisette's bath water while the maiden is freshening up. Lisette and an assortment of other beauties are viewed periodically in garments intended to enhance their natural attributes. The narrative is hot with intrigue and complicated double-dealings. LeCoq is consistently brilliant and somewhat overheated, and so it goes through its several hundred pages.

The humor of *LeCoq* is excessively macabre and its general nature, given moments of "healthy" nonpathological humor, seems to me needlessly if predictably dark. Its vision: that the darkness of life is to be relieved only through a forced tunneling into sexual gratification. Or perhaps not even gratification but odd titillations, half-charges rather than discharges. Structurally, the script is dense and yet too often predictable: LeCoq will triumph, LeCoq will erect, so that the spectator's sense of discovery is diminished early and the developing tale becomes wearisome. The script cries out for a no-nonsense hand, for an eye to distinguish between the wonders of playfulness and the strained artificiality of the frivolous. There is too much willfully generated excitement for one modest feature. A skilled editor might have cut and structured the completed footage into a cohesive and sharp narrative. But much of the film was never shot.

But another film was shot in 1967 and it became one of Zero's best-loved vehicles. Mel Brooks had been a writer for Sid Caesar, and Zero and Brooks may have met through their mutual friend, the writer Speed Vogel. Brooks had written several short films, including the Ernie Pintoff cartoon, *The Critic*, and had worked on TV commercials for Fritos. Now he felt he was ready to write and direct his first feature, which he intended to name *Springtime for Hitler*. When the movie opened in West Germany, it bore that title, but box office proved weak in Frankfurt and *Variety* reported that "In another try, the.distributors are bringing it out with a new title, *Die Macher, The Leaders*." In Italy the title translates as *Please Don't Kill the Old Bags*. And in the States, Brooks called it, simply, *The Producers*.

Much of the shooting took place in Manhattan, at Himan Brown's Production Center in Chelsea. Brooks finished shooting two days under schedule, but the star-director relationship was not without its moments of exquisite pain. It is Brooks's sense, given Zero's constant request to leave early because of the state of his leg—a request Brooks felt he couldn't honor because of the cost of a day's shooting—that things went reasonably well. The two men were at odds over a number of Zero's moments. Brooks believed that though Zero might see the trees (e.g., his own performance) with much clarity, he failed to understand that Brooks had mapped out an entire forest.

Jared Brown reports that when Brooks talked to Zero in terms of a mosaic, the painter in him could appreciate what the director was envisioning. Even so, Brooks submitted occasionally to what he perceived to be Zero's better judgments. This picture of delicate harmony isn't in keeping with Gene Wilder's recollection. Wilder's impression is that after awhile Zero was reduced to muttering, that in Zero's eyes no one on the set, with the single exception of the veteran Mostel, had the foggiest idea what they were doing. During the shooting, Wilder recalls, conditions reached a state where Zero would pretend there was no such thing as a director and Brooks would ask his crew whether the "fat pig" was ready for the next shot.

The Producers is the saga of genial, down-at-the-heels Max Bialystok, once "king of Broadway." Bialystok's backers have been elderly ladies whom Max has charmed through soft words and occasional nuzzles. Leo Bloom, a neurotic accountant, chances into Bialystok's office, the two hit upon a scheme— Bialystok eagerly, Bloom with much trepidation—to make their fortune by selling twenty-five-thousand percent of a sure flop to Max's elderly backers. Each backer will lose a small investment but Bialystok-and Bloom will find themselves on what a more innocent age used to call Easy Street. The supposed sure flop they eventually uncover is a sophomoric drama written by an unregenerate Nazi fanatic in the West Village who has devoted the years since World War Two to the cherished memory of his beloved Fuhrer. The action accelerates as rehearsals begin; Zero as Max sees an army of greenbacks marching earnestly toward him. He is already enjoying his profits, but he is also constantly propping up the fainthearted Leo Bloom (Gene Wilder), steeling him to the rectitude of solid thievery.

This cautionary comedy of anxious swindlers has taken on the status of a classic; its admirers have become a minor cult, but its first reviews were mixed. The *New Yorker's* Pauline Kael particularly detested *The Producers*. She was incensed at what she saw as the extraordinary crudeness of both Brooks and Zero and notes that the film assumes that all manner of shtick are showstoppers. Kael is also unsympathetic to what might be called the George Jessel-Henny Youngman-Milton Berle brand of humor—Jewish, in short. "Screenwriters" in the earlier years of motion pictures, she advises her readers, and probably she is excluding the years of the silents, "used to take the Jewish out," but with the advent of television and the plethora of Jewish comedians who "exploit themselves as stereotypes, screenwriters are putting the Jewish in. . ." I suppose that in *The Producers* Zero does push the ethnic-stereotype button, but it's almost as if Kael is offended *for* me, an offense *I* don't particularly feel, and her sympathies put me out of sorts. She has a serious concern with Brooks's direction, contending that the man doesn't know where to put the camera, and it's true that the shots seem arbitrary and at times intrusive. Ultimately Kael's opinion can't be dismissed: the film is hysterical, often tasteless, and Brooks's camera angles speak to little of relevance inside the frame. And yet something else is at work.

At the time of its theatrical release, *The Producers* seemed to me gross, pushy, and strained. Seeing it years later on a small TV screen, I found Brooks's rookie romp remarkably comic. What has happened? Either my judgment has come unhinged or the radical reduction in image has revealed some previously obscured virtue. It seems to me that Zero in small, if that isn't an oxymoron, ceases to be overbearing. Pounding against the frames as its nature seems to demand, the Zero image pounds less against the observer. If the image still threatens a breakthrough, it would occur against the miniature frame and not the full-sized you or I. In some way we seem to be spectators at a kind of Punch and Judy performance, with Zero as a Punch who is simultaneously ferocious and benign. The manageable distance between us and the TV screen also releases the comic inventiveness, the goofiness, the wonderfully subtle vocal asides in a way that the traditional movie screen, emphasizing bombast in stereo or whatever technological breakthroughs were breaking through, never released. The demure hysteria, the gross choreography of the slapstick seems oddly transformed into an event of social criticism. We never *learn* much, but our age-old prejudices are warmly reinforced.

Kael complains that the joke that makes up the plot—the sure flop predicted for *Springtime for Hitler* never materializes, instead a smash hit is driving Bialystok to financial ruin—is an old joke. All jokes are old jokes. *Tartuffe* is an old joke; so is

Macbeth, and *Hamlet*, and *Lear*. Balzac knew *Lear* very well when he wrote *Père Goriot*. Crazy fathers disinheriting themselves for their daughters who prove to be ingrates—that isn't a good joke, and pretty old? New stories, new jokes? There are only different cultural insights, variations on venerable fables, a sense of the movement of history. *Hamlet* with all its poisonous intrigue and eavesdropping becomes a French farce in other hands, and *Macbeth*, with ambition and the need to murder for security run amok, is a kind of *Sorcerer's Apprentice* refashioned. If *The Producers* did nothing but repeat its one joke, the film would be in trouble; instead the joke is played out, and even as we suspect what's coming, we like to see events played out

Bettye Jaffe recalls: "One afternoon Sam and I went to see *The Producers*. It had just come out, word hadn't gotten out yet about what fun it was. There were only two other couples in the entire theatre. The six of us were just screaming. Then we called Zero when we got back to the house and we were raving about the movie. And Zero said, 'I *hated* it. I looked like a beached whale.'"

What is one to say about *Great Catherine*, released in the United States in January of 1969? Bernard Shaw's Russian empress is the tantalizing Jeanne Moreau, beloved of the French New Wave cinema, Peter O'Toole coproduces and stars with Moreau, and Zero, adviser to the empress, is called upon to manage some monumental (routine in Mostel terms) gorging: of bagels, sturgeon, roast wild boar stuffed with kasha. Producer Jules Buck has a problem: a 650-year-old British law, proclaimed by Edward II, designates all sturgeon in Britain the property of the Crown. The fears prove needless; Buckingham Palace grants a dispensation and Zero is permitted to wolf down a sizable helping of British property. Jack Hawkins and the wonderful Akim Tamiroff are also on hand for—one thing or another.

The belly is full but the films are thin and there will be less substance ahead.

In the late Sixties Paddy Chayefsky's playwriting career seemed to have run into a midlife crisis. Like others whose early work was deliriously praised—Odets, Saroyan, Tennessee Williams, Edward Albee—Chayefsky was having a difficult time in the marketplace. *Marty, The Middle of the Night,* and the Kim Stanley film vehicle *The Goddess* were all critical if not financial successes, but Chayefsky's Lenin-Stalin play, *The Passion of Josef D.,* which opened in 1964 at the Ethel Barrymore Theatre, was generally dismissed as an interesting failure, though I found it to be one of Chayefsky's more vital works and I valued his courageous move away from realism. As for Zero, he was a busy but churlish fellow; nothing seemed quite right. The word was out that he was hungry to do serious theatre, as if he had never been encouraged by Toby Cole, whom he had cast aside, to work with some of the best new writing talent.

In the early winter of '66, Burgess Meredith, Zero, and Paddy Chayefsky unveil their plan to start a new theatre. Perhaps their model was Hambleton and Houghton's Phoenix Theatre. Unlike the Lincoln Center repertory company at the Vivian Beaumont or the Tyrone Guthrie in Minneapolis, this new operation would not have a permanent group of performers but would open-cast for the several plays they would produce each season. Under consideration: Chayefsky's new play, *The Latent Heterosexual,* a musical adaptation of Sean O'Casey's *Juno and the Paycock,* as well as revivals of the Barkentin *Ulysses in Nighttown,* Beckett's *Godot,* and the Brecht-Weill *Threepenny Opera.* Zero is also considering a Molière, possibly one of the comedies he performed at the Brattle, and lurking at the back of his mind there is the thought of tackling Hamlet, the pudgy Dane, as well as the lean and prideful Lear. And of course the amply round Falstaff. These are not the best-laid plans, but they come to nought nevertheless.

In 1967 *Esquire* publishes the text of *The Latent Heterosexual* and in March of '68 the only production this company was ever to do opens at the Kalita Humphrey Theater (designed by Frank Lloyd Wright) in the Dallas Theater Center. Chayefsky wants "just to be left alone to do my work as a writer," to experiment with his new comedy far from the Great White Way, but the press, which can certainly ignore you when you desperately crave attention, can also plague you with its presence when you want to be left to your own devices.

I'm not certain why Clive Barnes, then chief drama critic for the *New York Times*, who flew to Dallas to review Chayefsky's experiment, simply couldn't have been barred from the theatre— he is hardly unrecognizable—but apparently the producers' plea that it was premature to be descended upon by New York critics was to no avail. (I should note that no amount of coverage or lack of it, no ecstatic or dismissive critique could stop The Living Theatre from doing exactly what it wanted to do, certainly not when it was running its own space.)

Burgess Meredith admits, beyond the fact that mixed reviews didn't encourage a New York opening, that neither he, nor Zero, nor Chayefsky had the organizational skills or the obsessive, constant drive to make that company idea come to fruition. The late Paddy Chayefsky's brother Wyn tells me there's no truth to the story that one reason *Heterosexual* never came to New York and the idea of the company foundered was that Paddy, having written a leading role for Zero, found that he simply couldn't work with him. Jared Brown notes that Paddy and Zero had some ugly scenes over the casting of the female role. There certainly were enough reasons not to work together, but weren't there other, stronger reasons to try to make a go of it? There is always a nervy, lunatic kid-genius lurking some- where with a will to raising dollars and someone else with ter- rific organizational skills to be found; you have only to want it all badly enough and to be somewhat of a lunatic yourself. *Heterosexual* will make it to Los Angeles's Huntington Hartford Theatre with a May 2nd opening, but that will be its final run, and the end of the dream of a new company.

As for the play itself, Chayefsky told friends that he had modeled the character of John Morley, a gay poet of drag-queen propensities, after Zero's talents. Chayefsky's conceit is that the bitch-queen-poet, having written a sensational best-seller, is try- ing to fend off the Internal Revenue agents who plan to cut the federal government in on a generous helping of Morley's pie. A genius tax lawyer, Irving Spaatz, dreams up a dodge whereby

Morley, in the words of *Newsweek* which also descends on the opening, "spawns corporate identities like an ameba [sic] burping copies of itself," and finally, in a scheme calculated to send the IRS off empty-handed, will take to wife a high-priced and particularly gorgeous call girl. Morley is horrified: "I don't want a big-breasted bawd sitting in the kitchen all day reading the *Daily News*!" But financial interest prevails and the ensuing marriage provides emotional complications for another hour or so. Zero, who appears with Jules Munshin, is praised for his work, but Chayefsky's writing is received with more naysaying than the author cares to hear about.

And time for another blockbuster, mass-market film. In the latter part of 1968, with tumultuous events unfolding almost day by day—the assassinations of Martin Luther King and Bobby Kennedy, the growing resistance to the war in Vietnam, the burning of draft cards and the pouring of blood on draft records, revolutionary upheavals in Paris, the riots in Chicago's Lincoln Park while the Democratic convention is taking place blocks away, the exorcism of the Pentagon, the growth of the Weather Underground and the Black Panther movement—while the New Left is split between nonviolent civil disobedience and a growing violence that includes "bringing the war home to the middle-class"—while this turbulence is all around us, Zero is shooting an amusing charmer called *The Great Bank Robbery*. Location shooting is in northern and southern California, with the feature scheduled to open in 1969. Zero had company he particularly liked: Akim Tamiroff in a typical bandito role, and his beloved Sam Jaffe as fellow buff in the exquisite art of blowing open bank vaults.

For Bettye Jaffe, "It's the old joke. Sam and Zero had too much fun making it. Every night was a party. Everybody loved everybody. We had a grand time—and you know with that attitude the film isn't going to be a big success."

Paramount originally held the option to Frank O'Rourke's novel, and in 1967 the formerly-blacklisted Jules Dassin had been announced as director, with Melina Mercouri to take on the role of the female shill. By the time the cameras were rolling, Mercouri had given way to Kim Novak, Hy Averback was the director, and distribution had switched from Paramount to Warner Brothers-Seven Arts.

There is a party element to this strange comedy, much of it shot on location in the rugged cow-country terrain of Sonoma and at the Disney "Golden Oak" Ranch in Placeritta Canyon. *Bank Robbery* is a slight, rather lovely and ridiculous tale of courtship. The sought-after one is that universally-acclaimed mistress, sometimes known as gold or silver or more often referred to as Money. We first meet Money aboard a train laconically chugging through frontier territory. Bank robbers quickly lighten the train's load. The loot inadvertently winds up in a safe in the only bank in the town of Friendly, and everyone west of New Jersey seems apprised of just where Money is now residing. The bank is controlled by the town banker who doubles as mayor, and he assures associates that the safe is impregnable, for his bank was designed by professional robbers.

Well, a number of individuals are greedy enough to want to relieve the bank of its stolen pile. Some of these individuals have as their mentor a certain Reverend Pious Blue, pastor of the Church of the Cosmic Heart. Blue (Zero) and his second in command, zaftig celebrant named Lyda Kabanov (Kim Novak), first wend their way through Friendly armed with tambourines and heavenly voices, inspiring townspeople with interminable choruses of "Bring in the sheep." Others with a particular interest in the interior of the bank vault include a handful of Chinese, imported to do a little tunneling from the laundry next door, and some Native Americans who seem taken with the maxim that honesty is the best policy, for they simply storm the bank repeatedly, head-on, in broad daylight, with horses, six-shooters, and battering rams. A particularly engaging moment features Sam Jaffe as Brother Lilac; a Cosmic Heart colleague of the Reverend Pious Blue, Brother Lilac loves to make oil paintings, and we discover him inside the bank, painstakingly rendering an exact reproduction of the exterior of the bank vault so that Blue and his spiritual sisters and brothers can blow up the exterior with more precision.

Somewhere well into this multilayered farce, Zero delivers an obvious, good-humored sermon to his Friendly flock, retelling the episode in Numbers whereby Balaam is busy smiting his ass. Never mind that the account in Scriptures is more substantive than Zero's tongue-in-cheek allusion, its comedy takes us back to the Berle-Benny-Gleason-Caesar-Ed Wynn radio, TV and vaudeville modes. The final sequence involves another nice touch, more visual than the Balaam double entendres; we witness a sensational if ultimately inept try at escape by balloon, featuring Pious Blue and assorted gonifs who want to light out of the territory fast. Two teams of seamstresses, *Bank Robbery's* press agents tell us, were kept busy in a hangar in Sioux Falls, South Dakota, fashioning dual versions of the largest passenger-carrying hot-air balloon on earth; each balloon needed one quarter of a million cubic feet of hot air. The film was to have been set in 1875, five years after the massacre of Custer and his troops, but events were moved ahead nine years when researchers discovered that gas works never got West before 1884.

Much effort was expended on this slight, ponderous feature which is little remembered almost three decades after its opening. Again the nagging question, to which the answer is all-too-obvious: was this compelling work for the man whom MGM in 1942 envisioned as the next Charlie Chaplin?

In its August 21st, 1968 issue, *Variety* reports that Zero will be featured in a musical version of Bertolt Brecht's play, *The Exception and the Rule*. Leonard Bernstein is to compose the score, with lyrics by Stephen Sondheim, book by John Guare, and direction and choreography by Jerome Robbins. The opening is scheduled for February 18th, 1969, at the Broadhurst Theatre. But the musical never opens. John Guare tells me that not only did the work never open, it was never rehearsed. Almost twenty years later in 1987, Josh Mostel is cast in the same musical and this time there is an actual if private run-through at the Beaumont-Newhouse complex in Lincoln Center. I ask Josh, "Is this the same musical Zero was scheduled to appear in in '69?" He tells me, "I never *heard* of a '69 production. Once I ran across an actor who told me he got *fired* from some such production." "Why didn't the '87 production ever open?" "Bernstein decided not to go ahead. He felt his own music was from too many periods."

While Zero was busying himself in the late '60's with plans for serious theatrical events that failed to materialize and insubstantial movies that seemed to materialize with numbing regularity, the outside world was busy with what it knows how to do very well—that is: guard the fruits of the earth from the have-nots, assassinate political leaders who had developed some degree of enlightenment, and repress movements for independence. Soviet tanks rolled into Prague in August of 1968, effectively choking off what had come to be known as the Prague Spring. A number of Czech writers and filmmakers, among them Janos Kadar, Milan Kundera, and Milos Forman, managed, some prior to the invasion, to find their way out of what had effectively become a grim, Sovietized Czechoslovakia and reach Western Europe and the United States.

Kadar was initially known to Western audiences as director of *The Shop on Main Street,* a film that also brought the Warsaw-based Ida Kaminska, a member of the legendary Yiddish theatre company founded by her mother Ester Kaminska, to the attention of the West. In New York in the late winter of 1968, Janos Kadar teams up with Harry Belafonte to produce a film adaptation of Bernard Malamud's short story "Angel Levine." Belafonte was interested in creating a venture for which members of minority groups might serve as filmmaking apprentices. The Ford Foundation awarded Belafonte a grant of twenty-five-thousand dollars, and performers Eli Wallach and Anne Jackson requested cameo roles as a way of contributing to the project. There had been talk of a film adaptation as early as March of 1962, with Jack Gilford as the tailor and Ossie Davis as the black angel. Nothing had come of it. Now Belafonte was lining up actors. His early choice for the tailor was Edward G. Robinson, but by February of '69 *Variety* was reporting that Zero Mostel had been hired.

Writers William Gunn and Ronald Ribman changed the tailor Manischevitz's name to Morris Mishkin, and Zero and Ida Kaminska were finally cast as Morris and Fanny Mishkin, an elderly Jewish couple suffering from physical ailments and a serious lack of money. Belafonte himself performed as the black angel.

Malamud's original story speaks of Manischevitz, the tailor from the Bronx who

> in his fifty-first year, suffered from many reverses and indignities. . . . his establishment caught fire, after a metal container of cleaning fluid exploded, and burned to the ground . . . damage suits . . . deprived him of every penny he had saved. . . . his son, of much promise, was killed in the war, and his daughter . . . married a lout and disappeared with him as off the face of the earth. . . . His Fanny, a good wife and mother, who had taken in washing and sewing, began before his eyes to waste away.

One day an angel appears to this Job of contemporary misfortune. The angel is black—large, heavy head topped by derby hat, attired in an "ill-fitting suit" with discouraged cuffs. He has been sent to help alleviate the poor tailor's misery. Zero appears to have made a permanent nest in the mansion of suffering. Once again he inhabits a role in which offspring disappear or are lost to him in some essential way (Bloom's son Rudy in *Ulysses in Nighttown*, Tevye's daughter Chava in *Fiddler*) and he himself is saved, after earthly buffers are lost to him, only through an act of faith.

Shooting for *The Angel Levine* began on February 17th, 1969, with most of the interiors shot at Filmways Studios on East 137th Street in Harlem. In May, the *Los Angeles Times's* William Wol treats readers to Zero's reflections on the timelessness of great films. It's not clear how Zero is evaluating *The Angel Levine*—is his Mishkin sufficiently suffering? What is Zero's position on angels? Zero's general utterances convey a degree of wistfulness; he knows full well the dispensable nature of commercial films, churned out like so many feet of sausage. Zero tells William Wol that the bulk of the Hollywood product is forgettable within days, sometimes within hours. But it's also clear that he has much respect for the work of Janos Kadar.

The reviews in the summer of 1970 are equivocal. Nothing in them suggests an enthusiasm sufficient to send movie fans storming the box office. Some of the coverage is positive, respectful of Kadar and his actors, and some of it is steeped in disappointment. *Cosmopolitan* tells its readers that though Bernard Malamud "is famous for writing bitter, dark, complicated ghetto tales, [the reviewer] isn't sure this fragile film . . . is what the author had in mind when he wrote about a black Jewish angel trying to redeem himself by helping a despairing Jewish tailor." The reviewer is of the opinion that "quite a bit of basic Malamud comes through," though the film generates "some confusion." And Zero? He "weights the film with more humor" than the tragic denouement is able to digest. As for Ida Kaminska, she is "so elegant and handsome on her deathbed, it's hard to believe she needs help."

Richard Cohen, writing in *Women's Wear Daily*, is quite taken with much of the footage; at times the work is absolutely "glowing." But in the long run Kadar lets him down. "I cannot tell you what makes Mishkin curse [God], except that it is necessary to achieve the director's . . . pessimistic view of life. The scene is incomprehensible, and the movie, which had been fine up to [the moment of Mishkin's curse], collapses." Nevertheless Cohen credits Kadar with infusing the film with "as many moral and ethical concerns" as the venerated Ingmar Bergman. As for Zero and Harry Belafonte, they layer *Angel Levine* with "grace and vitality," and Kaminska's "old Jewish-lady testiness [no mention here of death-bed elegance] keeps it all far away from sentimentality and pathos . . ." But Cohen insists the fatal curse subsumes all the grace and vitality, the moral and ethical structures Kadar has built up. "Nothing prepares us for Mishkin's rejection of God and Levine, and the whole thing becomes meaningless." As for *Time's* correspondent, Mark Goodman, he finds himself plagued by a "persistent background wail" that evokes a sense of the Tower of London in earlier, grisly centuries. What Ann Malamud, the late Bernard Malamud's wife, remembers best about the film is that "Bern and I walked out. It was so poor we couldn't bear to sit through the whole thing."

Kadar planned a second English-language feature. In *The Lies My Father Told Me*, Kadar wanted to cast Zero as a Canadian junk dealer, someone with the Tevye-like soul of a poet whose son is blinded by the vision of the almighty dollar. The junk dealer turns to his grandson and touches the child's heart with wondrous tales.

Zero never played the part, never knew a grandson—but there *is* a Zero of wild and lovely imaginative powers. And we also know the aggressive Zero who kept pushing changes on writer Ted Allan and kept holding out for more money. The writer finally told Zero that the story was about *Allan's* childhood, not Mostel's. As for the money, Zero believed the producers would finally succumb to his demands, only to learn that Kadar actually started the picture without him, and in fact replaced him on the first day of shooting in Canada, an action that brought from the discarded star an outraged cry of disloyalty. It was the breaking point in Zero's relationship with the Czech emigré.

The press would be reporting other projects that never materialized. It was said that Zero would star and collaborate on the screenplay for *The Studio*. Writer-director Robert Siegler informs the *New York Times* that he and Zero plan to produce several features. *The Studio* is to tell the story of a misunderstood painter who isn't recognized because his work isn't in fashion with the trend-makers. Siegler sees this work primarily as a comedy but with a 10-percent level of what he calls poignance. But this 10 percent, echoing the life of the misunderstood Vincent Van Gogh, suggests a poignant subtext, a Mostel wish fulfillment. But the onstage Zero, the incorrigible, comic Zero, was never able to find within him that level of discipline that Ian Hunter always hoped his painter-friend would nourish. Ultimately going against contemporary trends won't do it for you. To be seriously misunderstood and neglected requires the ability to be truly alone with the Muse—no matter what the cost.

But nevertheless Zero is surely that remarkable throwback, that anachronism we fondly refer to as the Renaissance Man. On

October 27th, within a few days of the Los Angeles booking of *The Latent Heterosexual* and of conferences for a new film to be shot in Japan, Zero tries his hand at another discipline The occasion: the fourth anniversary of the founding of the Symphony of the New World, a racially-integrated orchestra. Participants at New York's Philharmonic Hall, later renovated and renamed Avery Fisher Hall, include singer Marian Anderson and conductors Benjamin Steinberg and Zero Mostel, offering works by Mozart, Shostakovich, Moussorgsky, Franck and Rossini. Donald Henahan witnesses the event for the *New York Times* and reports that Zero surely knew Rossini's *Semiramide* overture by heart, though it was anybody's guess as to whether he was conducting it forwards or backwards. Zero, always comfortable with his body, as director Elia Kazan has attested to, used that ample frame to wiggle cues to the orchestra, his conducting hand often behind his back, and indulged in inaudible lip-synch in a note-for-note competition with the seasoned soloists. Whether he added an audible World Series score or tornado report during the Rossini has not been recorded.

And what of Mostel the Oriental? The Far East beckons in the person of a fictional private eye, one Hoku Fat. While *The Latent Heterosexual* is bemusing audiences in Los Angeles in May of 1968, its star is conferring with the film division of the American Broadcasting Company. ABC Pictures wants to fly our Renaissance Man to Japan to shoot a feature they are going to call *Mastermind*. In July of 1969 there are preliminary production meetings at ABC, with Tokyo planned as the principal site for filming, but the feature is finally shot in Kyoto, commencing in October of 1969.

The name and the persona of Hoku Fat tickle Zero. The private eye is coming from a career as Kamikaze pilot and there is some current intrigue with a pair of Israeli spies whose names are Hammacher and Schlemmer. The screenplay is supposedly the work of William Peter Blatty, who wrote *The Great Bank Robbery* and would soon write *The Exorcist*, and the producer is *Bank Robbery's* Malcolm Stuart. It is Zero's belief that the boxoffice failure of *Bank Robbery* will surely be matched, and perhaps surpassed, by this Asian enterprise.

But to imply that *Mastermind* proved unsuccessful suggests that the completed film actually opened—somewhere. To the best of anyone's knowledge, the film never opened. Perhaps William Peter Blatty actually wrote the screenplay, but the writing credits on file at the Motion Picture Academy, and on the actual print of the film, lists a screenplay by Terence Clyne and Samuel B. West, from a story by Terence Clyne.

The *1982 TV Feature Film Source Book* lists *Mastermind* as having to do with a detective "conducting an investigation in Japan [who] gets involved in a Samurai battle, the Japanese baths, a raid on the Dragon Club," while *Newsweek* in its November 3rd, 1969, issue quotes the studio's description as "a humorous mishmash of events," in which Hoku Fat, like the dreaming nightclub attendant of MGM's lamentable *DuBarry Was a Lady*, "daydreams of himself as an old-time Samurai swordsman when he isn't solving mysteries or engaging in telephonic chess matches with Abba Eban and J. Edgar Hoover." There is a report that between location shooting, Zero is conducting a foreign-exchange program with the film crew. Our man is learning a bit of Japanese in return for inducting the crew into the mysteries of Yiddish.

But if *Mastermind* seems never to have opened theatrically, it eventually found its way onto television, at which point, some two decades after the film was shot and edited, I was able to see what none of the fuss was about.[30] *Mastermind* is one huge, casual mess, a piece of slapstick that seems to operate on no adult level that I could discern. But at least the credits are somewhat visible. The film was directed by Alex March and edited by John C. Howard, with Gerald Hirschfeld listed as director of photography. The cast features a number of Asians and Americans, the latter including Bradford Dillman who had made a name for himself in *Compulsion*, as well as veterans Jules Munshin and Sorrell Booke. Frankie Sakai is listed, along with Zero, in a starring role, as Captain Yamada.

In its weekly issue of May 30th, 1973, *Variety* notes that "Production commenced in October '69, with a May '70 release date skedded. So far as can be determined, pic has never even had a test engagement here or overseas " The *Daily Variety* of May 31st, in a story by Lee Beaupre, reports that "Three ABC Pictures never returned any theatrical income to the company. *Diamonds for Breakfast*, a Marcello Mastroianni-Rita Tushingham starrer for producer Carlo Ponti, opened in London in 1968 but was never dated in the U.S." As for *Mastermind*, Beaupre repeats the previous day's wisdom about its not even having a test engagement. The article reports that thirty of ABC's thirty-six films, as of 1970, showed the company in the red some forty-seven million dollars. *Mastermind* cost ABC $2,900,000 and ABC's loss on the film was exactly $2,900,000. Was a good time had by all? A few souls learned a little Yiddish and Japanese.

Reenter *Der Milkhiger*, that Tevye who refuses to live life without a Mostel to warm his bones. By 1971 the film version of *Fiddler*, with the Israeli actor Topol in the lead, was in direct competition with the stage musical. "It was a great tragedy," Bettye Jaffe reflects, "that Zero didn't do the film. He was always feuding with Hal Prince during the time he was playing Tevye. The men had a lot of problems together. As for the movie, I couldn't stand it. Naturally I was prejudiced. Instead of a village, it looked like they'd created a city. The whole thing was out of whack. It wasn't wonderful the way the play was. I'll tell you, when Zero didn't get the part, it almost killed him. He called Sam every day and they talked for an hour, an hour and a half, and Sam had a way of soothing people that he loved, a way of advising them, and the two of them kind of worked it through together."

Hal Prince assures me that there is nothing to the rumor I've picked up from Barney Josephson regarding Prince's contractual stipulation that under no circumstances was Zero to be cast in the film. "It's the first I've heard of that. I assume Topol was cast because, being younger, it was felt he had more universal, even romantic, potential."

A romantic Tevye?

The photographer Mal Washburn, a close friend of Zero's, recalls that when the movie of *Fiddler* was released, Zero wanted to see it but found it difficult simply to walk into a movie theatre filled with people who would undoubtedly recognize him. "He was very sensitive about the situation, about not getting the part, and he was trying to figure out how he might sneak in somewhere without being noticed." Washburn solved the problem. He had a contact at *Fiddler's* distributor and was able to arrange a private screening. "It was just the two of us in this small screening room. Zero and I are seated side by side and the movie begins. Zero doesn't say a lot. It's clear he's not having a terrific time, because every few minutes he raises his arm and slams me in *my* arm. Well, by the time the movie is half over, I get up and move to the other side of the screening room. I can't sit with him. My arm is already black and blue!"

Zero had an opportunity to play Tevye again on the stage, and he wanted no part of it. And his agent, now Sam Cohn, informed producer Lee Guber that Zero had no interest in a new *Fiddler* at Long Island's Westbury Music Fair. But Zero and Sam Cohn had Kate Mostel to deal with. Over and over I have heard that for Kate there simply never was enough money. Kate was brought up "money poor," then found her husband blacklisted—poor again. Kate went on the road to bring in money. After Guber's offer is refused, Kate begins working on Zero. She understands, she tells her grumbling spouse, that he has no interest in performing Tevye once again, even for thirty thousand dollars for a run of three weeks, but how could it hurt if they just went out to look at the Westbury space? Zero tells her he doesn't need to go on playing Tevye forever, but then, perhaps to placate her, he agrees to take a little peek at Westbury, to see if a production in the round might not offer something new.

As Kate tells it, Zero was hooked the minute he walked into the Westbury theatre and he began blocking the play in his head. The three-week run happens, and Kate tells us that the production set new box-office records—for Westbury? For *Fiddler?* It turns out that Westbury isn't the last curtain. In one venue or another, for the remainder of his life, Zero will be wedded to *Der Milkhiger*. There is a final *Fiddler* tour in 1977; it plays Los Angeles, Denver, St. Louis, Washington, D.C., New Orleans,

Detroit, Miami, and finally closes in June in New York. Kate reports in her book that the plan was to do this "farewell tour," then bid Tevye adieu and donate the Tevye costume to the Museum of the City of New York. Toby Mostel joins the 1977 tour as assistant stage manager. He is on very bad terms with his father; at one point they've even ceased to speak, but Toby has a premonition that Zero isn't too long for this world and he wants to be "near the old man."

Clara Sverd Mostel, now Clara Baker, also had some interest, years after their separation, in wanting to be "near the old man" but recalls that "it must have been perhaps thirty-five years ago," which would take us back to the early Sixties. Clara recalls that Zero was performing in a music tent which used to be known as the Oakdale Musical Theatre, in Wallingford, Connecticut. Clara can't dredge up the title of the musical, but is sure it was neither *Forum* nor *Fiddler*.

"I felt funny about going backstage, but my friend Shirley says, 'You're too provincial.' Backstage Zero's clowning around, obviously nervous, uncomfortable." Zero tells his childhood sweetheart that he's scheduled to have a show mounted at the Whitney Museum in New York. "I said, 'Oh Sammy, that's wonderful. You always wanted that, didn't you?' He says, 'Since when did *you* ever care about my art?' I say, 'Sammy, are you still fighting with me after all these years?' And I stretched my hand out very dramatically, and I said, 'With that I will leave you.' And I shook his hand and he squeezed my hand oh so gently. And that was the way we said goodbye. I never saw him again."

By 1972 the studio system was a thing of the past, film employees were presumably freed from serfdom. We find Zero a supporting player—what happened to the star of *Fiddler*?—in an independent production, *The Hot Rock*, released through 20th-Century Fox. The film is a souped-up, inordinately complicated thriller-comedy with Robert Redford, George Segal, Ron Leibman, Paul Sand, Moses Gunn and Zero. There's a propelling jazz soundtrack which features Gerry Mulligan on baritone sax, trumpeter Clark Terry and a handful of other jazzmen underscoring a wild narrative about the theft of a precious stone immured within a glass case of formidable tonnage and guarded by a supposedly tamper-proof lock, a nervous alarm system and innumerable, appropriately suspicious guards, all within the confines of the Brooklyn Museum. Redford and conspirators, each of whom has one or more specialties—lockpicking, engineering, ordinance, traffic control, aeronautics, guerilla raids on impenetrable fortresses, stunt-flying and test-crashing of automotive vehicles—plan the theft of the stone in a manner which makes the Israeli rescue of Jewish hostages at Entebbe seem like a simple excursion to the dry cleaner's.

Within this labyrinthine story, Zero appears as a sweet, sinister, chiseling parent of one of the conspirators. He resonates with the impulses of ambulance-chaser; unlike the youth-in-bloomness that emanates from Redford and coconspirators, Zero is already grey, beefy, stooped, and like the nasty image of Jews throughout Gentile-written history, an overlay of obviously false humility makes him an untrustworthy alien. In effect, he is the least trustworthy, most unsavory specimen in the film.

The white, straight-limbed heroes, young Christians and Jews alike, want both money and kicks; the sinister Dr. Amusa, representing a developing world nation at the United Nations, in an urbane performance by Moses Gunn, has as his agenda, when he hires these whites to steal his own country's precious gem, an admirable political motive. But Zero, as sleazy Abe Greenberg, has neither a redeeming political agenda nor the love of exercising a gorgeous young body. Dishonest Abe is out for nothing but tawdry money, lucre, *gelt*—that is, money becomes tawdry in *his* hands—and this Abe will see the earth damned in the process. In performance, Zero holds back nothing; he makes Greenberg (ironically, green mountain) a swine, an unredeemed swindler.

Shooting began on February 17th, 1971, at the Nassau County Jail in East Meadow, Long Island. Director Peter Yates also shot in the Brooklyn Museum's Hall of African primitive arts, in the recently-vacated Charles Street police station in the West Village, adjacent to which photographer Diane Arbus once lived, and in Manhattan banks, local highways and the Rockland County Reservoir where Redford's character tests an explosive device. Zero appears intermittently, obsequious and vaguely threatening, muttering to himself, thinking dark thoughts. Whereas Redford's Dortmunder, George Segal's Kelp and Ron Leibman's Murch are shitting fear, joy and occasional panic, Zero's Abe Greenberg ultimately shits nothing but subversion. A fitting apprenticeship for Shylock.

The film opened in January of 1972 to mixed reviews There's an interesting retrospective by critic Steve Blackburn in the 1983 film publication, *Cinema Texas*:

> The crime is carefully contrived so that it's really okay for these guys to steal this diamond—nobody's going to get hurt, and the victim's just a museum. . . . Audiences *want* to worry about the characters. There's really nothing to worry about in this film except for a briefly engaging moment when it seems that the gang has turned on one of its members . . .

and threatens to push both Zero and Paul Sand, playing Zero's son, down an elevator shaft. Blackburn sees violence as a tactic for seduction.

> Either you worry that the character you identify with will get killed, or you feel righteously gratified when the proper people get blown up or drilled between the eyes. To paraphrase Dirty Harry, we don't mind shooting, as long as the right people get shot.

And on a note that speaks to the time of the Kent and Jackson State shootings, to Vietnam, Watergate, to the Black Panthers and the Weathermen, *The Hot Rock's* worst offense in 1972 may have been its failure to take some moral position. For Zero it is three years away from the political issues permeating *The Front* and two more before the anti-Semitic concerns dealt with in *The Merchant*.

In the spring of 1972 Zero works on a low-budget feature shot in Mexico, and almost immediately after he is off to the Japanese island of Oshima and to Tokyo's Toho film studio. In Mexico, location shooting is in the village of Atotonilco, a short drive from San Miguel de Allende but, according to the *Los Angeles Times*, "centuries removed in terms of telephone lines." The role in *Once Upon a Scoundrel* is that of Carlos del Refugio, a pompous, insufferably likeable rogue. In Japan, Zero plays Kublai Khan to Desi Arnaz's title role of *Marco Polo*.

The latter film seems to have mercifully come and gone without much fuss; its major claim to fame is its having been the first U.S. production to film a surgical procedure employing acupuncture. The producers also recreated sections of the Great

Wall of China after fruitless negotiations with Beijing concerning location shooting at the actual site. Zero's diet at the hotel housing the cast was principally "pickles and rice three times a day and old seaweed." *Marco Polo* limped into view late in December and the *Hollywood Reporter* told its readers that "Mostel screams, shouts and repeats every comic shtick he's famous for, just as if he were playing to the last row of a Broadway theatre." Or to passengers on a ferryboat going up the Hudson more than thirty long years ago?

The Mexico shoot seems to have been a happier one, though events that ensued after filming were a puzzlement for director George Schaefer. Perhaps best known for his frequent direction of the TV series *The Hallmark Hall of Fame*, Schaefer was chairing the Department of Theater, Film and Television at UCLA when I saw him in the spring of 1988.

"James Elliott, who was a young film producer, brought me this script of *Once Upon a Scoundrel*, and I was charmed by the story," Schaefer tells me. "It was the kind of simple idea that needed some wonderful performer like Chaplin, or like Laurel and Hardy, comedians who could take off on it. I told Elliott if he could come up with either Zero Mostel or Peter Ustinov, I'd direct it."

The day after *Scoundrel's* screening at the Second Thessaloniki International Film Festival on October 30th, 1973, *Variety* reports that this official U.S. entry is "pure entertainment for the family...." *Scoundrel* is set in a small Mexican village ruled over by a ruthless baron who is in love with the young Alicia (or Alica in the credits), played by Priscilla Garcia. "To eliminate Alicia's fiancé Luis, Refugio accuses him of stealing a duck. According to the law Luis is imprisoned until Refugio will forgive him." Thus far we are being treated to a slice of *Measure for Measure* and now a portion of Molière turns up on our plate. The villagers convince Refugio he is about to die and that it's time to forgive Luis. It doesn't work. Another villager, Aunt Delfina, played by Katy Jurado, concocts a different plan. Refugio is drugged and then buried. Recovering and climbing out of his grave, Refugio discovers that all the townspeople behave as if he were not present; they convince him that he's a ghost, a wandering soul who must make amends before he can rest in peace.

Schaefer's lawyer considered the low-budget film a shaky enterprise in the hands of producers who might be running a fly-by-night operation, but Zero's participation and the chance to work in Mexico proved too attractive for Schaefer.

"And I trusted Elliott, but I had yet to encounter these *other* people. Elliott died rather young. He was only about thirty-five when he came to me, and he died within a short time. Anyway, the shooting was not easy. I was involved in choosing the location and we found this lovely village of Atotonilco. Well, Mexico proved to be very hot and dusty. And the tempo! Everybody takes long siestas, and these long siestas increase your budget. You just have to learn to relax. Nobody's in a hurry. Lunch is not an hour or ninety minutes but two-and-a-half hours. That's lunch."

I suggest that Zero liked a lot of lunch.

"I don't think Zee minded the lunch one bit. He was very happy. He had the dogs with him—"

"The dogs?"

"He had the dogs," Schaefer reiterates, "and Katie had accompanied him. They took a little house in the vicinity. The cast adored Zee, and he and I got on famously, so that part was working out fine."

"What did the two of you talk about? The scripts? Life?"

"We discussed the next moment of the film, why a certain thing would be happening, how much the audience had to believe. And about the wonderful bits Zee planned—for example, his collapsing from the potion, the manner of his collapse—these bits were all his inspiration."

Schaefer relates the opening sequence as they planned it, and how Zero enriches that opening. Below is the sequence that Schaefer and Zero worked from.

1. EXT. RANCHO REFUGIO—DAY
The Rancho Refugio is an attractive, rambling rancho obviously owned by a man of position and wealth. As we watch

we see a flag being run up on a flagpole. It bears the Refugio crest. There is the sound of a BUGLE. SERVANTS scramble about converging on the front door of the house. The BUGLE continues to create an atmosphere of excitement and suspense.

2. MED. SHOT: CARLOS REFUGIO
The front door of the house. The SERVANTS form into two lines facing each other and creating a path from the doorway. PANCHO and SANTOS move to the door and come to attention. PANCHO is cadaverously thin; SANTOS enormously fat. The two men reach for the double door and open it. SENOR CARLOS REFUGIO is seen with the BUGLE. He blows his final blast—puts a CIGAR in his mouth and comes out of the house to the roll of a drum played by one of the SERVANTS. He is large, clumsy, and middle-aged. His unshaven, moustached face falls into a thick-lipped petulance, a drooling scowl, or a toothy grin depending upon the rapidity with which he gets his way. Whatever fat there has been on the land has found its way to his middle. PULL BACK as he moves toward us. The SERVANTS bow, SANTOS and PANCHO follow him like an honor guard.

CARLOS REFUGIO goes to a beautiful white stallion called SANTIAGO. SANTOS offers his hands for REFUGIO's boot. REFUGIO hands his cigar to PANCHO and mounts, not without difficulty. PANCHO returns the cigar and he and SANTOS stand at attention as this 19th-century feudal lord rides off. We watch him disappear in a cloud of dust as the CREDITS end.

"As we filmed it, Zee is going through this line of servants in front of the mansion. He's slapping this one, pushing the next one's head back, knocking another one about, straightening up the next one, and then finally he reaches this beautiful white horse and starts feeding this horse carrots. It's all happening fast. It was really a wonderful opening shot, and that shot has been destroyed by this stupid bastard of a coproducer—who'll be nameless, Carlyle is a pseudonym—and this idiot producer yanked our opening and replaced it with some dumb cartoon."

Schaefer is getting wonderfully worked up remembering this nameless producer. "He turned out to be one of the monsters of the world—a mental case. After we finished shooting he kept delaying the film. He wouldn't even send it up from Mexico so we could complete work on it. He kept puttering with it himself, and he kept not releasing even *his* version. In the cassette version that's out now you see parts of what we were able to do, and it will give you an idea of how good that film might have been. As for Zee, he came up with wonderful touches. There's a little doll he loves that he takes to bed with him at night. At the end, when he's forced to give away his fortune, the only thing he can't seem to give away is this doll. And at last he gives the doll to a small child. We had a wonderful Mexican child for that moment."

Schaefer continues, "I did the film so I could work with somebody like Zee. I gave him tremendous leeway to come up with these special pieces, the way I understand that people like Buster Keaton made up pieces in the early days of film. I never imagined the picture would make a lot of money, but I thought it would be a nice family picture, particularly on TV. We had a wonderful cinematographer, Gabriel Figueroa, some fine performers, and Alex North wrote a beautiful score. Unfortunately this idiot producer tried the film out in Westwood [near West Los Angeles and Santa Monica] for the college crowd, but it's not geared for a college crowd. It's not hip or anything. On the basis of that tryout he made *more* changes."

"He was actually editing?"

"Yes. He was changing everything. I wanted nothing more to do with it, and I took legal action. I wouldn't let them release the film with my name on it. He finally released it, then he sold it."

Scoundrel seems to have been sold a number of times. At one point the film was the property of a company called Diablo Productions, a subsidiary of another company called Pacific Basin Financial Group. Schaefer insists "the film was never decently released. I did see the film in a cassette store one day so I spent another sixty-nine dollars on top of everything else I'd lost just to have a copy of it. I do have a black-and-white dupe of what we shot. There's no sound track on it. I just made it for legal purposes. Ron Bishop came to me once—he'd made up a press kit for a Florida release—and we talked about restoring some of the cut scenes. I volunteered to re-edit the whole thing, just to have a proper film, but nothing came of it."

"At one time," I inform Schaefer, "they were thinking of calling the film *Wandering Soul*."

"I never heard that," he tells me. "I heard they were thinking of calling it *The Dead Duck*."

"I never heard that," I say.

In its edition of April 12th, 1980, the *Hollywood Reporter* notes that Los Angeles Mayor Tom Bradley has proclaimed a Zero Mostel Week and that *Scoundrel* is being held over at the Fairfax Theatre.

Schaefer says: "I never heard about that."

I ask Schaefer about the screenplay credit. The name Rip van Ronkle sounded suspiciously like a tongue-in-cheek Mostelism, but according to the *Los Angeles Times* the late Rip Van Ronkle wrote the screenplay more than twenty years before James Elliott brought it to Schaefer.

Schaefer says: "I had no reason to question the name."

An event occurs in November of 1972 which is particularly unpleasant for Zero and those close to him. The past reappears, and it reappears courtesy of Eric Bentley, Zero's director in *The Good Woman of Setzuan*. Bentley, who has earlier edited a volume bearing on the right-wing assault of liberal forces, a work entitled *Thirty Years of Treason*, now creates a documentary-style play which has its debut at the Yale Drama School. *Are You Now or Have You Ever Been* is Bentley's edited, condensed rendering of the HUAC hearings. In its first production there are eighteen witnesses, including Ring Lardner Jr., Larry Parks, Jerome Robbins, Arthur Miller, Paul Robeson, Lionel Stander, and Zero. At some point the eighteen are reduced to seventeen, and the one deleted is Zero Mostel. Zero appears in the first published version, a Harper & Row paperback, but in a subsequent volume of three plays, published by The New Republic Book Company, under the umbrella title *Rallying Cries*, the Mostel character has disappeared from the script. What happened?

Zero hated the play. He hated having a role in it, and according to Eric Bentley, Zero made trouble.

Ring Lardner Jr. remembers that "The four of us, Zero and Kate, Frances and myself, went up to Yale. Zero at that time had mixed feelings about anyone calling attention to the fact that he had been blacklisted. He was emerging from the blacklist, had emerged successfully, and he'd just as soon everybody'd forget about it. So in a sense he thought this use of him as a public figure was not helpful. In addition, he felt that the script didn't do justice to what was going on at the time of the hearings "

During my meeting in '88 with Lardner and Frances Chaney, Ring seems at best bemused by the Bentley play. The atmosphere is harsher in 1973, when Vicki Richman interviews Lardner and Mostel for *Changes* magazine.[31] Richman has gone to Zero's loft and reports that the two men have nothing but bitter feelings toward Bentley. He quotes Lardner: "I felt no drama, and I felt no history." And Zero: "A man of no talent like Eric Bentley always chooses the wrong material." Lardner: "The Theatre of Fact is no theater at all. There's material for a good play in the hearings. But with fiction you can tell a lot more of the truth than you can with a documentary." Zero tells Richman:

> The blacklist had tragedy, even humor. It had none of the meaningless terror suggested in the play. Ring went to jail, and he wrote a marvelous novel. A lot of artists thrive on poverty and suppression. The blacklist helped me. As a film actor I probably would have wound up very rich playing the fellow who never got the girl. I never would have done things like *Rhinocerous* [sic] and *Ulysses in a Nightgown*. [sic]. Actually it was my wife and my children who suffered most because we had no money. But she had great strength.

Richman tells us that Zero became enraged at one point. "Bentley never once called me, and I was one of the witnesses."

Richman speaks up for Bentley's importance as a drama critic. "When drama in America meant Doris Day and *My Fair Lady*, Eric championed the dialectical and revolutionary drama of Shaw, Brecht, and Pirandello." Zero and Ring Lardner Jr., according to Richman, "represent the type of theater that Eric has scorned, and they know it. In self-defense Zero speaks of his work Off-Broadway and of his own relationship with Brecht. 'Bentley ruined Brecht for American audiences,' he says, trying to reject Eric on the terms that he feels rejected by him." Richman understands that Zero is proud of his demeanor before HUAC, "proud that he refused to testify . . . that he was black-listed" and "would like a play that can capture that pride." Lardner says: "The play suggests no feeling of what went on before or after the hearing. You don't get the feeling of the blacklist, which lasted for fifteen years."

In 1988 Frances Chaney, still irritated, recalls "an irritation that I felt profoundly and I knew Zero felt it too. Here's this guy who gets material which is in the public domain, government transcripts, and for Christ's sake *does nothing to it* to encapsulate it into a play or put it in a play form or anything, *he simply puts it on*. However, the other irritation is that there were some very stupid things done. *I think* it was in this production, they had mixed casting, blacks and whites, blacks as part of the committee doing the investigation. It was peculiar slanting. It was cockeyed."

I ask, "So in fact the Committee becomes as blameless as the unfriendly witnesses?"

"Right. Here's this material and here are these poor shmucks and there it is, and you watch it."

Lardner's feeling is that "It didn't give you any sense of history. You didn't know what had gone on before or subsequently to the people involved, and in its form of just one person after another testifying it didn't have any dramatic structure." Lardner reflects that "Zero may have been affected by the fact that Lionel Stander came out much funnier than he did. He felt more strongly about it than I did."

Chaney: "And he was vociferous about it."

"During the performance?" I ask hopefully.

Chaney: "No, in the lobby. He *was certainly saying what he thought*. But he was still being funny. Well, he thought, I paid my dues, leave me alone. At the same time it's important to remember that Zero never for one moment changed his attitude and he called people shits who were shits."

As for Bentley's work, it seems to me very much in line with the Brechtian aesthetic that informs the plays of the German dramatist Peter Weiss, *Marat/Sade*, and more particularly in his documentaries—in *The Investigation*, about Nazis on trial for crimes against humanity, and in the terrorizing, matter-of-factness that illuminates his *Discourse on the Progress of the Prolonged War of Liberation in Viet Nam and the Events Leading Up to It as Illustration of the Necessity for Armed Resistance Against Oppression and on the Attempts of the United States of America to Destroy the Foundations of Revolution*.

Here is a moment from Bentley's *Are You Now or Have You Ever Been*.

Mr. [Lionel] Stander: After the major studios blacklisted me, I worked for independent producers . . . until Larry Parks said he didn't know me as a Communist.

Investigator: Let me—

Mr. Stander: That appeared in the paper. Just to have my name appear in association with this Committee! It's like the Spanish Inquisition.

Investigator: Let me remind you—

Mr. Stander: You may not be burned but you can't help coming away a little singed. . . . Does the Committee charge me with being a Communist?

The Chairman: Mr. Stander, will you let me tell you? Will you be quiet while I tell you what you are here for?

• • •

Mr. Stander: I have *knowledge* of subversive action! I know of a group of fanatics who are trying to undermine the Constitution of the United States by depriving artists of life, liberty, and pursuit of happiness without due process of law! I can cite instances! I can tell names. I

am one of the first victims, if you are interested. A
group of ex-Bundists, America Firsters, and anti-
Semites, people who hate everybody, Negroes. minority groups, and most likely themselves—
The Chairman: Now, Mr. Stander, unless you begin to
answer these questions and act like a witness in a reasonable, dignified manner, under the rules of the
Committee, I will be forced to have you removed from
this room! *(Pause)*
Mr. Stander: I am deeply shocked, Mr. Chairman! . . . I want
to cooperate with your attempt to unearth subversive
activities.

Here is a moment from Peter Weiss's *Discourse on . . . Viet Nam . . .*
Each actor, Weiss tells us, "represents a number of figures [identi-
fied only by numbers] whose statements and behaviour as a
whole typify a particular historical development."

FROM PART TWO, PHASE VI:
6. The President
   of the Republic of Viet Nam
   has arrived in New York
   on a state visit. *(10 [Eisenhower] goes to Diem and embraces him.)*
6. President Eisenhower's embrace
   demonstrates the close friendship
   existing between the United States
   and the Republic of Viet Nam
10. You have accomplished great things
    forging a progressive
    and steadfast country
    out of chaos

    • • •

14. [Cardinal Spellman to Diem]
    The whole world sees in you
    the God-fearing anti-Communist
    and saviour of Viet Nam

And a moment from Brecht's *Saint Joan of the Stockyards.*
> *The Workers:*
>> We are seventy thousand workers in Lennox's
>>> plant and we
>> Cannot live a day longer on such low wages.
>> Yesterday our pay was slashed again
>> And today the notice is up once more:
>> ANYONE NOT SATISFIED
>> WITH OUR WAGES CAN GO,

The Brechtian aesthetic demands that the playwright maintain an emotional neutrality, that he not prod the audience, that the spectator not get caught up in the easy lure of victim psychology but maintain enough objectivity to understand the manner in which sociopolitical forces work in particular cultures. It isn't that the victims of the blacklist and of genocide and the ravaging of a Vietnamese society don't cry out to us, but the Brechtian theatre asks not for sympathy but demands our clarity. Brecht—and we must not forget Brecht's mentor, Erwin Piscator—do not ask: Isn't it awful? Instead they ask: What steps will you now take? What actions are you prepared to initiate to confront and transform the social order? We may disagree about the nature of that order; we may even believe that Brecht himself had a muddled picture of the dynamics that propel communities, but it's important to understand what writers like Brecht, Bentley, and Weiss, and directors like Piscator and Meyerhold were trying to effect.

To accuse Bentley of using the lives of the blacklisted for his own purposes is only to say that Bentley does what writers have been doing since Homer, Aeschylus, Shakespeare, Dante, Henry James, and Lorraine Hansberry. You may find the documentary approach tedious, not as delightfully creative as the work of the masters, and you might accuse Bentley of elitism, for there is obviously that aspect of Bentley that finds the world of Broadway insufferable, that considers smash hits and celebrities not only an irrelevance but a waste of people and resources. But Bentley's work is not without purpose; it has a place in the contemporary world of thought.

We are in the first days of March, 1973. Tom O'Horgan, protégé of Ellen Stewart who founded the Off-Off-Broadway Cafe La Mama, then renamed La Mama E.T.C.—O'Horgan who directed Paul Foster's play *Tom Paine* and the Ragni-Rado-MacDermot rock musical *Hair*, O'Horgan the scholarly composer, the self-effacing musician, the theatre director who found himself in the forefront of a noisy flower-children upheaval in the late sixties, who went from Ellen Stewart's La Mama to Joseph Papp's Public Theatre and back again—this busy, quiet Tom is tabbed by producer Ely Landau of the short-lived American Film Theatre[32] to direct one of the noisiest dramas extant.

In this film version of Ionesco's *Rhinoceros*, Gene Wilder is playing Berringer, now known as Stanley, and Zero is again that archetypal rhino pretending to be a simple, well-attired humanoid named John. In Stanley's apartment, O'Horgan is meticulously choreographing Wilder and Mostel through one of the heavier moments in comic devastation, with Wilder playing a kind of Thomas Merton to Zero's Caliban.

Wayne Warga of the *Los Angeles Times* has been sitting in on rehearsals, and on March 4th he reports on O'Horgan's dry run at physical mayhem. Zero is accelerating into convulsive mode, scratching, tearing, kicking, gasping, while Wilder frantically tries to uncover a comfort zone in the midst of a human tornado. At one point there is confusion: Zero is to smash one of several seemingly-identical statuettes; he insists on grabbing the one prepared by the prop department for smashing, but then insists on *not* smashing it until the scene is actually shot. He tells Tom O'Horgan he's averse to smashing anything. Warga notes that Zero will eventually smash the furnishings and the staircase. One might add that the sidewalk as well as various fire hydrants, baby carriages, and oak trees will be spared.

The gargantuan one is predictably awesome, and yet the outcome is another major mistake. Wilder and Zero again play off one another, as they did so effectively in *The Producers*, but the film is aesthetically out of control. Perhaps the medium is wrong once again, as in *Godot*, as in *Forum*. The theatre, for all its immediacy, for all the violations of the proscenium that many of us encouraged in the Sixties, following Meyerhold's revolutionary aesthetics in Soviet Russia and Artaud's truncated, nightmare visions in an otherwise bourgeois Paris, the theatre is a conservative medium. For all the nudity and personal threats and fierce slogans and exhortations to smash the theatres, to move out into the streets and start the revolution within the hour, the nature of theatre seems not so much to resist as almost to embrace any and all action, any and all behavior, in a fashion not unlike Mother Earth which has not infinite but much patience with us as we lay waste and devour her resources. Theatre seems to allow all and encourage nothing. Theatre is simply present, quietly, modestly, conservatively, for us. But film is another matter. The frame is something else. One has to understand as Eisenstein, Vigo, Keaton, Bergman, Kurosawa, Werner Herzog, and Orson Welles understood the nature of the frame, the nature of the shot, the nature of camera movement in relation to crowds and solitary characters, to violence and quiet, to light and to dark. In a sense, film is nothing but light in motion; it is hardly an arbitrary substance. And Lester in *Forum*, Schneider in *Godot*, Brooks in *The Producers*, and O'Horgan in *Rhinoceros*, in one fashion or another, find themselves lost or dependent on arbitrary movement within the shot, or arbitrary rapid editing or montage: changing the camera angle or the size of the foreground image or goosing the sound track in a way that impedes comprehension of the event.

It isn't that these directors are without vision, but too often they're out of sync with the author's vision—even if, as with Brooks, the director is also the author—or they fail to understand that the presence of live performers in a sequence of light in motion and the presence of certain narrative material needs to be addressed on their own terms, and that one's agenda, however interesting, may be inappropriate. For me, Brooks's *Producers* conveys magic on a small screen, and O'Horgan's *Rhinoceros* has its occasional moments of magic, but much of the time it is simply trying to catch our attention. It is simply having a tantrum in the guise of a diversion.

The year 1973 proves to be a busy one for Zero the movie actor. There is—*Foreplay*. *Foreplay*? The sought-after and supposed liberation of cinema from the dead hand of censorship via the introduction of the rating system brought with it an acceleration of porn: soft, hard, and whatever lay in-between—let's call it intermediate porn. But porn's progress from sleaze parlor to mainstream family theatre soon brought with it a jaded response to the erotic tale and the sexual pun. The prurient seemed not so much accepted as condescended to by moviegoers who appeared to be saying: Okay, you've given us *that*, *that* was okay for *last* night, but what'll it be tonight? The ante constantly had to be upped, but how to do that and to what purpose?

Foreplay, also *Four Play*, also *The President's Women*, is composed of several segments. It features Zero, Estelle Parsons, Rip Torn, Paul Paulsen and other luminaries, and is designed to exploit the funky, stag-party explicitness or male-convention mirth that, for good or ill, is claimed as part of the American birthright. Several writers, including Jack Richardson—recall his fine *Gallows Humor* Off-Broadway in the late Fifties—took inspiration from Nixon's resignation, Tricia Nixon's much publicized wedding, and the notorious Patty Hearst kidnapping to concoct this stew. Terry Southern was to have written a segment but perhaps mercifully it slipped his mind.

In *Foreplay*, Zero plays a U.S. president who resigns his office and is compelled to have sex with his First Lady on prime-time TV in order to free his kidnapped daughter. All this hilarity is supervised by director John Avildsen who conceived the project, and who confides, ruefully, to *Playboy* that Zero was demonstrating vintage Mostel during the shooting with his "proclivity to grab all the women who came within a ten-yard radius of him." We're also treated to the information that Zero went through several cases of an aftershave lotion named "Sea Breeze" which the makeup girl would pour onto him after each take.

The entire project—its conception, development and exploitation—suggests a response to some adolescent hunger for a pathological holiday, at a time when the country, coming down from Vietnam, Watergate, and the Kent and Jackson State killings, was trying to discover something about itself that it had forgotten. One has to hope that that forgotten something isn't encapsulated in this dismal orgy of sexual gymnastics after dark.

On the heels of hijinks in the Oval Office, Zero takes on, or reverts to, the type of roles he effected two decades earlier. He is cast as a devious Arab, spying on clean white Westerners like Sam Waterston, in a rehashing of the Eric Ambler story, *Journey into Fear*. In the hands of Orson Welles, an earlier *Journey into Fear* (1942) had its spellbinding moments. Welles's film opens cold on a killer dressing to go out. There is an old 78 rpm phonograph record which gets stuck. The killer packs his gun into the top of his trousers. The needle stays stuck on the record and the first scene ends before one is even given the title of the film. Today the device of delaying credits is commonplace, but in the Forties it was revolutionary.

In the 1973 *Journey*, some thirty-one years after Welles, Daniel Mann takes a company of actors for location shooting in Istanbul, Athens, and Genoa, and then for a final six weeks of interiors in a West Vancouver studio. The cast is a strong one; besides Waterston, it includes Joseph Wiseman, Shelley Winters, Yvette Mimieux, Donald Pleasance and Vincent Price. The narrative treats us to vague, muddled rumblings about the CIA and oil interests, and in Zero's eyes there is little that appears memorable outside of Genoa salami. The film had limited theatrical exposure in the fall of 1975 and then made its Home Box Office debut on January 9th, 1976.

As previously noted, on May 20th, 1973, Zero visits his old haunt at the 92nd Street Y. The occasion, called "Conversations in Theatre," takes place in the Kaufman Concert Hall and Zero carries on a dialogue with moderator Leonard Harris before what we presume to be an attentive audience hungry for insights. Here are fragments of Zero expounding in the venerable hall, under the legendary names of Moses, Socrates, Maimonides, and other ancestral giants:

"I always come to the theatre early and take a nap. That's my way of dealing with my nervousness. The interesting thing about a character is to find the mysteries. I hate explanations. I wanted to do just a few parts. I sorta fell into the parts. I do them my little natural way. There's always some kind of unconscious art which guides us. That's the secret of all art. Braque said that a picture is finished when the original conception is completely eradicated. Whatever part I did, whatever conception I had went out of my mind and became the life force, and the life force has so many interesting and wild and imaginative things [within it]. No one can explain why Beethoven in the First Symphony uses what became a revolutionary chord and altered music for all time "

On his work in *Rhinoceros*: "Morris Carnovsky watched me develop the role and he would say, 'He's a freak.' I don't know why I was a freak. I trusted the work. When you're faced with a great work you trust it. Once you plot, think up what you're going to do, you're not an artist. It has to well up from inside you. I told Bobby Lewis I didn't want to use makeup [for *Rhinoceros*]." Lewis appeared not to understand, or so Zero believes. On Tom O'Horgan's filming of *Rhinoceros*: "I found he hadn't trusted the script [sufficiently]. All that busy stuff is not my cup of tea. Very often today directors drown works with ideas."

And now various disciplines are hungry to be embraced by our Renaissance Man. In the summer of 1973 Zero holes up on Monhegan to devote countless hours to his singing, for the world of opera has finally sought him out, some four decades after Mrs. Perlmutter's positive assessment in the Catskill Mountains.

BBC producer Patricia Foy recalls:

> This absolutely enormous, delightful man got off the plane at Heathrow. The cast were waiting in the rehearsal rooms, wondering what kind of a man was coming into their opera. He went away to Maine, where he couldn't be found at the end of a telephone, but he used to walk down to the general store while he was rehearsing the part and phone me in London. He sang *Schicchi* over the phone, surrounded by sides of bacon and cans of beans and soon the whole village was singing *Schicchi*, all the way from the window cleaner to the postmaster.

Some corrections to Patricia Foy's narrative, as reported by the British journalist James Thomas: Nice conceit, Ms. Foy; however, Monhegan is hardly one of those quaint, fairy-tale villages out of Victor Herbert or Franz Lehar where everyone will burst into the same song; also Monhegan has never had anything resembling a window cleaner and its postmaster is actually a postmistress—for years until she retired it was Winnie Burton and now its Karen Wincapaw. But Zero was certainly on Monhegan, certainly training for his opera debut, and Doug and Harry Odom's general store did carry sides of bacon and cans of beans.

Gianni Schicci, with Robin Stapleton conducting the Royal Opera House Covent Garden Orchestra, was a joint venture of the BBC and CBS; it was taped for viewing in the United Kingdom and for CBS's *Festival of Lively Arts for Young People*. It aired in the States in the autumn of '73. Reuters describes Zero at rehearsals.

> He hulked in for his first cue like Frankenstein's monster, grabbed a coatrack and played it like a cello. He then lifted it

over his head, simulating violent rage and made as if to harpoon his producer. Mouth open, tongue lolling and eyes bulging, he did a 10-second imitation of the Hunchback of Notre Dame—all before reaching the stage.

When the singing began, Mr. Mostel and a more experienced opera singer tripped over one another vocally. The conductor ruled that Mr. Mostel had been right.

"Hah," Mr. Mostel boomed, his face wreathed in a smile of evil triumph.

In the waning November days of 1973, the ACA Galleries on Manhattan's East Seventy-third Street mounts a one-man show of Zero's paintings. But the artist, hardly one to shy away from notoriety when it's a question of show business, has a different view of publicity when his paintings are at stake. Gallery owner Sidney Bergen has agreed to open his two floors to an ABC-TV camera crew; Zero's show, with all the fuss, all the hoopla of a celebrity's art opening, is to be videotaped. But the ever-unpredictable Zero raises the roof, can't anyone understand that art is serious business? He doesn't want channel surfers and undiscriminating celebrity hounds ogling the oils and collages he's grappled with for months in the privacy of his studio. It's a tasteless way to present an artist's work. And besides, TV color is lousy! And he's being asked to price his work—how can one put a price on a work of art?

Zero's plaint to a *New Yorker* correspondent is that the very idea of the show is a mistake, he can see that now. He wants to reclaim his paintings and take them back to his studio. The *New Yorker* assures its readers that the actor/painter's tone is a bit self-deprecating. But Zero seems genuinely tired. He is also making television appearances on *Sesame Street*, is involved in a publication entitled *The Sesame Street Book of Opposites*, for which he poses in top hat, scarf and the kind of underwear some of us remember as union suits, and, as noted earlier, he is appearing in several feature films of indifferent calibre. Genuinely tired, and quite likely driven.

On March 10th, 1974, the indomitable Burgess Meredith unveils his remounted *Ulysses in Nighttown* with Zero again in the role of Bloom, at the Winter Garden, the very house that once saw Al Jolson striding down the runway into the orchestra. I gather that this reworked *Nighttown* lacked some of the inspired moments audiences recall from the original version in the homely, intimate setting of lower Second Avenue. Toby Mostel believes that comparisons of this nature speak to a snobbery that insists that "uptown" can't hold a candle to productions in lofts, barns, or damp cellars. But I've heard from others that the comparatively elaborate set at the Winter Garden, contrasted with the poverty and simplicity of the original, tended to transform an ephemeral event into too much of a concreteness.

And at last, *The Front* (at one time it was to be called *The Front Man*). Shooting began in New York City on September 15th, 1975. Its director, Martin Ritt, and its writer, Walter Bernstein, had both been blacklisted, and for several years had attempted to raise money to produce a feature film which would candidly explore TV's role during the ugly days of the blacklist. Bernstein reports that the major studios had no desire to air what had been a dark chapter in their own lives. When David Begelman, who had been Ritt's agent, took over as president of Columbia Pictures, he authorized the production budget for what came to be known as *The Front*.

Walter Bernstein remembers the dark, yet curiously comic days of his own blacklisting, as printed in the press packet accompanying the release of the film. "My name appeared in a booklet called *Red Channels* and I could no longer work. It was as simple as that." Bernstein had written for many of the leading live television dramas, including *Studio One*, *Philco-Goodyear Playhouse* and *Robert Montgomery Presents*.

> I had supported a comittee for Soviet-American friendship; I had supported Russian War Relief; I once had written an article for *The New Masses*. But that was it. If your name was in *Red Channels* and unless you cleared yourself, you were blacklisted.
>
> I did a few scripts using pseudonyms, but the networks became wise to that so you had to produce a front. So, I spent the next eight years writing "under the table." In finding a front, you had

to get someone who legitimately could be accepted as a writer, who could participate in a story conference, etc. Most people wanted money for it, so you paid them 10 percent, or 15 percent of your writer's fee. . . .

One front returned a script to me claiming it wasn't good enough. Another front stopped working for me because his analyst wouldn't let him. There was another case involving a man who's a rather well-known writer-producer today. He offered to let me use his name, and for a couple of times it worked all right. Then one night we both had a show on the air, one of which was his, the other mine, both under his name. Mine got good reviews, his was panned, and that was the end of that.

The final irony was that I became fairly well known in New York for writing under different names. Once the story editor of a prestigious program asked me to write a show for him. At the time I had no front and said I'd have to find somebody before I could do it. But I couldn't find anybody, and the story editor called me and said the producer thought I was stalling. I said, "But I can't find a front." And the editor replied, "The producer *knows* you have a front because he was at MCA the other day and there was someone doing assignments for them who said he was Walter Bernstein's front." I said, "That's not true, I don't know anything about it." But it was that *crazy*. I never found out who the person was. Obviously, somebody was getting work by saying he was fronting for me.

Bernstein tells of a writing assignment from an agent at the William Morris office which needed a TV pilot script for one of its ad agencies.

So I wrote the script, sent it in under a pseudonym, was paid for it and forgot about it. Some time later, the agent called back and told me I had to go see the producer from the ad agency because he wanted some changes made in the script. I told him I couldn't go using the pseudonym because people at the agency knew me. A few hours later he called back and said, "I fixed it up, I told the producer I was taking the writer off the script because he was uncooperative and I was getting you to do the changes." So I went to the agency, as myself, and had to listen to the producer excoriate the other writer for not being cooperative. Then he told me about the revisions he wanted, which were very ordinary. I did them, I brought them back to the office, they were satisfactory and the producer said, "Why didn't they get you in the first place? You're a much better writer than the other guy." And so I got paid twice for writing the same script!

I remember writing an hour show for a producer who had a mistress who wanted to be a writer, so we put her name on the script. During rehearsals, I got a call asking me to come to the studio because there were some problems. . . . they hid me in a corner, and I watched this woman accepting compliments for the script. I think she really *believed* she had written it. . . .

The most infuriating thing was that nobody would admit there was a blacklist. Producers told writers their scripts weren't acceptable. They told actors they weren't right for the part. . . . Most of the people I met at the TV networks were perfectly nice liberal people doing these terrible things. They said, "It's not personal. I don't like it and I wish it weren't happening"—but at the same time they were literally destroying people's lives.

Martin Ritt was a veteran of the Group Theatre. He had performed in Odets's *Golden Boy*, had worked with Bernstein in the early days of television, and had acted in and directed over a hundred TV dramas. The blacklist struck him in 1951 and he was hardpressed to support his family: he taught an acting class at the Actor's Studio, with students who included Paul Newman, Joanne Woodward, Lee Remick, Rod Steiger and Maureen Stapleton. His direction of an evening of three one-act plays— Arthur Miller's *A Memory of Two Mondays* and *A View From the Bridge* were two of the works—led to Broadway offers. He performed as the eldest son in Odets's comedy-drama about Noah called *The Flowering Peach*. By 1956 he began to receive offers to direct films again, and little by little, with the blacklist beginning to lose its iron grip, he moved back into the mainstream.

But even with a budget assured for *The Front*, Ritt had problems. Seeking an authentic visual representation of the early days of live TV drama, he tried to rent one of the early television studios, which were owned by CBS and NBC, but both networks turned him down. "With just cause I think," Ritt notes. "The film does take a shot at television itself, which was totally venal in that period. The networks *knew* that fronts were 'writing' but they bought these scripts, which meant they had no objection to the content of the material," and could pay an unknown "writer" five hundred dollars as opposed to some seven thousand if Bernstein's name were on the script.

In October of '76, a month after shooting of *The Front* was completed, Bernstein told *Cue* magazine that "The networks are still scared. When the script . . . was sent around to get reactions as to whether anything in it might cause problems for eventual TV showing, CBS replied that there were no difficulties since the film was 'comfortably historical.'" Zero, in another Columbia Pictures press release, speaks of the blacklist period as "a time of terrible foolishness. . . . the actor, what can he do, give acting secrets to Russian actors?" And further: "What kind of society is that, when the informer becomes a hero? That's sickening." He warns that audiences expecting a slapstick comedy because of the presence of Woody Allen and Zero Mostel are in for a surprise.

The surprised ones included the producers at Columbia who had presumably read Bernstein's script. Andrea Marcovicci who plays associate producer Florence Barrett, the love interest, recalls that "Suddenly there are these two guys and we expect them to be funny funny. I heard a rumor that after the movie was screened for the head of Columbia Pictures the guy was absolutely quiet and then he said, 'I thought this was a comedy,' and Marty Ritt said to him, 'Didn't you read the script?'"

The Front brought together a number of the blacklisted. In addition to Ritt and Bernstein, they included performers Zero Mostel, Herschel Bernardi (who had also played Tevye), Joshua Shelley, John Randolph and Lloyd Gough.[33] Neither Michael Murphy as the blacklisted writer nor Woody Allen as his nonwriting buddy who agrees to become his front had been touched by the blacklist. "Murphy," Andrea Marcovicci recalls, "was pretty young during the blacklist. He had a number of questions during our two weeks of rehearsal." Woody Allen was apparently responsible and low-keyed. Zero told *Newsweek* that Woody was "short but reachable. He knew his stuff, showed up on time and didn't have any tantrums."

I met with Andrea Marcovicci in the late hot summer of '88 in a groundfloor West Eighty-sixth Street apartment which her mother was about to vacate after many years. Books and packing cases littered the floor as we spoke. West Eighty-sixth Street, a curious center for many of us. Josh Mostel lives two blocks west, on Riverside Drive. I lived on West Eighty-seventh, half a block from Josh. David Margulies who plays a blacklisted writer in the film lived at this time down the block from the Marcoviccis. Michael Posnick who directed the first Bentley version of *Are You Now* also lives down the block, as did Ian Hunter, as did Zero and Kate when Zero was hit by the 86th Street crosstown bus, and as did Philip Loeb until he left the Mostel apartment one Labor Day weekend to end his life further downtown.

Loeb's suicide is one of the seminal moments in *The Front*. Hecky Brown is a composite of Mostel and Loeb—a nightclub celebrity to whom many doors are now shut, who works the Catskill resorts during the blacklist only to see his performance fees chiseled down by opportunistic borscht belt impresarios, an actor who loses his bread-and-butter role on a television series and takes an overdose of sleeping pills, or, as in the film, jumps out the window of a downtown hotel.

Andrea Marcovicci remembers the strange make-believe-reality suffusing *The Front*. "I was on the set when they shot that hotel scene." It's a moment when the bellhop appears at Hecky Brown's room with a cocktail, and Zero as Hecky, with ironic, courtly bravado, overtips, bows the bellhop out the door, makes a silent toast perhaps to the world of survivors, takes a swig and—then is seen no more. The camera focuses on a partially opened window and the curtains are blowing through a deserted hotel room.

"I also watched him working in the scene where they told him he was being fired. I had nothing to do but stand there and listen to him, and I started to cry. He would do it over and over and play it completely to the hilt, whether the camera was on me [as associate producer] or him."

I ask about the atmosphere on the set during the shooting. "It was celebratory, there was a sense of vindication, everybody was fired up. I felt very jealous because I was so young. When I was cast I had to do my research. I read all the HUAC transcripts. I read Eric Bentley's *Thirty Years of Treason*. It took me two months of research to feel I deserved the part. But there was no way I could actually be inside this experience. There was a sense of togetherness between Marty Ritt and Walter Bernstein and Zero and Herschel that I didn't think Woody and I even penetrated."

"Do you know why you were chosen for the part?"

"Oh yes, I know why. I was very lucky to simply be what they had in their mind's eye for that girl Florence Barrett. I was so young, so self-involved—I wish I could go back to that set with the eyes and heart that I have now. I was a very troubled kid, and I think I had that right combination of fervor, neuroticism, and dedication to my work that Florence had to hers. I think I simply *was* that girl to them."

Andrea speaks about performing Ophelia opposite Sam Waterston's Hamlet at the Delacorte Theatre in Central Park at the time of her audition. "I was also singing at a nightclub. One night I finished at the club and stayed up recording until five in the morning, and I slept an hour and a half and woke up and read the script and went to the audition, not knowing at all that it was Woody, not knowing anything about the situation, and shaking like a leaf from lack of sleep. I'd turned down a lot of movies because I wanted my first to be something I could really be proud of. When you are really that tired, often you can give one of your best performances, you can be totally honest.

"I read a scene with Woody. That was difficult because he wouldn't look at you. He was very neurotic about auditions and I don't blame him. He had suffered so much being on the other side of auditioning. He kind of had his back to me, but as we read I could see that he was beginning to take me in, and Marty was taking me in, and I thought I'd done very well. And they said, 'Would you go outside and look at this other scene?' I was in Marian Doherty's office, she was still a casting director then, and there was this old wooden door and I could hear everything in the other room. Somebody said, 'My God, she's perfect, she really looks perfect,' and somebody else said, 'Yeah, but can she be funny?' And I came back in and switched a button in my head which allows me to lighten my delivery—I was so *serious* about everything then—I let it go a little and I got some laughs. There's a hair's breadth of difference between a dramatic and a comic scene. It's a feeling. I couldn't teach it in a million years. I could tell they were happy. Then I got what I thought was a call-back, this time in a room at the Sherry Netherland, and I walked in and it was a meeting and Marty said, 'Welcome to the cast.' I was just thrilled. I went outside to the plaza at the Plaza Hotel and threw my hat in the air, just like Mary Tyler Moore."

Andrea remembers, "Playing Ophelia made me so upset every night. I used *The Front* as a way of leaving *Hamlet*, which was moving from the Delacorte to Lincoln Center. I should have done both shows, it would have made me a better Ophelia. I'd lost my father and every night I went to my father Polonius's funeral. I couldn't go through my father's death one more time. And here *you* are, twenty years to the day my father died. We moved when my father died and now my mother and I are moving again."

Marcovicci enjoyed working with Zero. "He was very sweet and generous. It was my first movie and he was teaching me the ropes a bit. When I'd be standing next to him and they were about to roll, he always would say to me, 'Hold your head up just a little bit, because you're so pretty and it's a little better camera angle for you.'"

"Was he right?"

"Yes. My mother says it to me to this day. Zero was really sweet and very proprietary. He was constantly making me laugh and making the crew laugh. People expected Woody to make them laugh, and Zero was compulsively funny. I think Woody didn't have the energy it would have taken to get in there and be funnier than Zero. Woody wasn't interested in that kind of contest and Zero was overwhelming at times with his compulsion to get a laugh.

"I believe all of us felt we were making a film that would vindicate people. You know, since *The Front* I've had thirteen years of coming of age as a political being. I was brought up as a Catholic and I remember going up the steps of the Marymount School on Eighty-fourth Street and seeing a huge poster that said: Better Dead Than Red with a big red skull on a black background. I remember hearing that Charlie Chaplin was a Communist. You want to hear something crazy? I wanted the Communists to take over so I could be a martyr. It was my only chance for sainthood—the Communists would take over and I would refuse to renounce my faith."

I ask Andrea about political discussions during rehearsals.

"Discussions? Everyone *knew*."

"They talked shorthand?"

"Absolutely. For them it was shorthand, for Woody and me it was how to play the scenes. They didn't sit around and talk about the blacklist. They considered me very removed from them. I was this twenty-five year-old girl who wasn't even alive during the blacklist as far as they were concerned. If I'd had the wisdom I have now I would have sat down with them. I would have insisted on going to lunch with them. I would have asked them to include me more. We rehearsed for two weeks at Columbia. During that time we did *some* talking about the blacklist. Michael Murphy did most of the talking, he had a lot of questions."

On Woody and Zero: "I remember Woody being incredibly funny, but only with me. He'd whisper things in my ear. I really adored him, he tickled me so. I think he got more withdrawn as the film went on. As for Zero, he was a real joker but not when you were actually doing a scene. We had jerry-built dressing rooms adjoining each other, you could hear everything in the adjoining cubicle, and one day I'm talking to somebody and Zero calls out, 'Quiet out there, I'm farting!' His jokes were so bathroom-oriented."

On rumors about Zero and Kate: "I heard that Zero and Kate were having a terrible fight at home. And she said, 'Okay, it's now over, *over*! I want you to leave, pack your bags!' And she sat down in the living room and he went into the bedroom and she heard packing. And then he came out absolutely naked except for his shoes and a bowtie on his tutu and he was carrying suitcases, and he said, 'Aren't you even gonna say goodbye?' And Kate turned around and took one look at this incredible sight, and they never got that far into a fight again."

The Front was hardly a box-office hit. In October of 1976, *Variety* reported that "Two victims of the post-war blacklist contend that many of the negative reviews . . . are the results of unjustified bias by the critics," Gale Sondergaard, widow of Herbert Biberman of the Hollywood Ten, felt that *The Front* showed real people living real lives; and Lester Cole, also of the Ten, thought that "some critics were offended because the accused Communists were shown to be 'simple, dignified, ordinary people.'"

Two films were released after Zero's death. *Watership Down* opened in New York on Novembr 3rd, 1978. Zero was not seen but only heard. The film, based on the novel by Richard Adams, is a feature-length animated cartoon in which Zero supplies the voice for Keehar the seagull. The story is an allegorical journey of rabbits across the English countryside; they represent paratroopers battling Hitler across the face of Western Europe. David Denby in *New York* magazine's December 4th issue writes that Zero is "doing his wonderful pidgin-Russian routine. Noticing that the male rabbits are trying to set up a new community without women, the sarcastic bird inquires, 'Vehr isz mates?'" And *New West's* Stephen Farber informs his readers that "The most delightful conceit is the character of a loudmouth seagull, brilliantly brought to life by the voice of the late Zero Mostel. . . . Alas, one gull does not a movie make."

Best Boy is a feature-length documentary, during which Zero is visited backstage after a *Fiddler* performance by the mentally retarded Philly Wohl. Philly has become a reclamation project undertaken by his cousin, the filmmaker Ira Wohl. In one of the film's opening moments Ira Wohl explains, "I began to wonder what would happen to Philly [at that time in his early fifties] after his parents were gone." Philly has been retarded from birth, the parents have always protected him, he has always lived with his mother Pearl and his father Max, but now the parents are elderly, the father ill, and Wohl understands that Phllly must learn some degree of independence before Max and Pearl both die. Through Wohl's efforts, Philly begins to go to a learning center for the retarded, he is sent on shopping errands alone, he has his first taste of a moderate independence and is thrilled by it. One of Philly's supports is Ira Wohl and his production crew, for these moments of independence are being filmed by the cousin he trusts. The crew follows him to school, to the store, eventually to the theatre and into Zero's dressing room where Philly and Zero collaborate on a rendition of "If I Were a Rich Man." We then see Philly striding proudly along in the dark street, the strains of the song filling his soul.

The press is ecstatic over *Best Boy*. Laurie Stone, writing in the *Village Voice* on October 15th, 1979, describes the film as "the absorbing record of the changes the filmmaker initiated and carried through." She notes that Wohl "tells an affecting story about family life, growth and separation." In the *Wall Street Journal* of February 29th, 1980, Joy Gould Boyum announces that the film, which has won an Academy Award nomination and the New York Film Critics award for best documentary feature, "is extraordinary," that Pearl's responses to Wohl's attempt to wean Philly away from his parents "are complex and telling. She [Pearl] is deeply concerned (will the occupational center Wohl has found for his cousin look after him carefully enough?). She is possessive and even jealous (when Philly, after an outing at the zoo, tells her excitedly of his experiences, she responds with 'so now you won't want to go shopping with Mommy anymore')."

In the *New York Times* on March 16th, 1980, Anette Insdorf speaks of the film's warmth, its compassion, its sadness and beauty. And Ira Wohl remembers how Philly, attending the New York Film Festival's showing on October 5th, 1979, bounced around the theatre, signing autographs. *Best Boy* is indeed a memorable film and Zero is memorable for that moment in which he allows the ecstatic Philly to share top billing with him.

27

Zero Mostel and I had a nodding acquaintance during many
summers on Monhegan Island. We talked about nothing in particular; he knew I wrote for the *Village Voice* and would kibbitz
me on occasion, at the dock, on the path. Eleven years after
Zero's death, I went to Monhegan to ask of others what I could
no longer ask of him: about theatre, film, Jews, the blacklist,
painting, all of it. By the summer of 1988, not only was Zero gone
but so was Kate, and Herbie Kallem, who died in 1994, had fallen
victim to Alzheimer's disease and was vegetating in a home in
South Burlington, Vermont. But the survivors who loved, hated,
had been amused or offended by or indifferent to Zero were all
over Monhegan. Zero had left his mark on the island, even as the
island leaves its mark on whoever comes to its shores.
Monhegan is an embracing island even as it obstinately leaves
you alone. You bring your life with you to Monhegan. You take
from the island what you can. It receives from you what you,
willingly or not, leave with it. Zero left a good deal, and though
the island is larger than Zero or any of us, in the summer of '88 I
looked for the Zero that was still with us. And here in '98, even as
I write these words, that search goes on.

Harry Odom remembers that Zero was "always acting. In the store he'd just apt to start dusting the shelves or something like that."

Doug Odom recalls: "He'd come into the store sometimes and fall down flat on his face. People would think something happened."

Harry says: "He was very much interested in the wines we stocked. He used to tell us some of the ones that I really should have on hand, the real good ones. Once he brought back this big magnum of really good stuff. He got it from his friend at Sherry Lehman."

I ask whether they considered Zero a drinker, and Doug assures me that "He'd *take* a drink but it was nothing out of the ordinary."

"Were you both part of the poker game?"

Harry shakes his head "Not us. We were in the store sixteen hours a day."

Perhaps Zero painted the brothers?

"Never," is what Doug remembers. "He came in the store once that last summer and he said, 'I oughta give you one of my paintings. Next year I'll have one for you.' But of course he died. He hadn't been away from here but a very short time. Everybody figures what done him in was that diet."

Harry says: "Doc Rothstein said once, 'I don't believe in that nonsense.'"

Dan Rothstein, transplanted from New York City, had been Monhegan's general practitioner for a number of years, until he moved to Florida around 1980.

Doug says: "When he was on that diet, he'd come in to telephone. Our meat counter was right back there, just before the phone, and Harry'd take a piece of salami and hold it out and Zero would begin cursing him."

The brothers are warming to all these memories. "We showed a bunch of his movies one summer," Harry tells me. "Andy Wyeth got them from Joe Levine [film producer Joseph Levine], and Jamie Wyeth probably got them from his father."

Doug recalls: "We used to keep the cans of film back of the store."

Harry adds: "Sure, all laid out in back of the store. You know, I asked him once, 'How come you didn't do the movie of *Fiddler*?' He said they wouldn't pay him enough money. He was sad, he was very good in that show." Harry laughs. "He was over the store one day and I said, 'I got your record of *Fiddler*. You want to hear it?' And he said, 'Are you outta your mind? *I* would want to hear that? You know the number of times I sang that? It would drive me crazy!'"

Doug tells me that "He used to give Harry these Jewish swear words. He'd tell Harry, 'When this guy comes up, you call him this or that.'"

"Oh yeah," Harry says, "I had to cut *that* business."

I ask, "Did you do it?"

"Well . . . I did it *carefully*. I said something, I think it was to Herbie one time. And Herbie said, 'Who taught you *that*? Don't tell me,' he says, "I know.'"

Bettye Jaffe also purveyed Yiddishisms courtesy of Zero and her husband Sam. "The ones that I picked up—when I used them, they were *terrible!* This expression"—she won't favor me with it during our meeting—"just popped out once at a dinner party. After everybody recovered, I said I learned that from Zero and Sam."

I reassure her. "Those are the first words people learn."

"Of course, they're said with such passion."

Harry notes "It was always something. Once they had a birthday party for one of their little dogs. Zero says to me, 'You bring that dog a present, and I'll tell you what he wants—he wants one of them aprons you got on.' So I bring Zero's dog one of my large aprons." One size presumably fits all.

Doug tells me: "Zero was always doing things for us. He got us tickets to see him in *Fiddler* out at the Westbury Music Fair. We're sitting there watching the show and he's ad-libbing something about me and Harry. He'd *do* that."

Could the Odom brothers be spotted in the audience?

Harry: "Oh yeah, he'd got the seats for us.. He had us picked up at the hotel and then drove out there and then had us driven back." Which helps to remind Doug of the impressive appointments at Westbury. "He had this terrific dressing room. Back in New York, *Jesus*, the dressing room was a cubbyhole. Out there it was like an *apartment*. I mean he had a big double bed where he could rest. And then he had this old hoofer [Howard Rodney, his dresser] who was sort of his valet—somebody said he knew him back in the Depression—and he would take care of him."

Rodney nursed Zero's reconstituted leg. He was one of the people who watched over Zero, and he was picking up broiled fish and chicken soup at Rose's restaurant in Philadelphia when Zero collapsed at the hospital.

Until the plethora of telephones, Monhegan's contact with the outside world was rather primitive, several short-wave units to alert the Coast Guard station on neighboring Manana Island in the event of emergencies and a handful of public phones for moments of ordinary stress. The rudimentary conditions put Harry in mind of another vintage Mostel anecdote. "Before everybody had all these new telephones, I had this call from Hollywood. The connection was poor, the party wanted Zero, I could make out that much. I asked, 'Now who is it he is to call?' And it sounded like—"

Doug interposes helpfully. "Shit Fields."

"Shit Fields. So I went out the door and here's Zero coming by the church with this little dog. I says, 'You wouldn't believe it but I got a call and as near as I can make out his name is Shit Fields and he wants you to call.' So Zero says, 'Don't you know who that is? Shep Fields diddely diddely diddely doo? He's an agent now.'" Doug translates the diddeliness. "Rippling music, wasn't it?"

"So Zero gets on the phone and calls him and he says, '*Shit? Is this Shit Fields?*' Zero was never quiet about these things. You could hear it through the whole store."

Sue Rosenthal was a fellow painter from New York; her small Monhegan cottage stands adjacent to Herbie Kallem's more substantial one. But in the summer of 1997, the cottage is without her sweet and fretting presence. A truck managed to run her down early in 1997 and finished off all five feet of this eighty-plus, blue-jeaned creature. Sue was a friend of this writer's; she loved to feed me day-old doughnuts from the Trailing Yew. She had the heart of a benign scavenger—several winters ago she stopped in the gutter in Greenwich Village's Sheridan Square to reclaim a bit of string someone had dropped or discarded, and I remember exclaiming, "Sue, maybe it would be a good idea to get out of the gutter, there's all kinds of traffic coming at us." She was a kind of old-world gossip. She knew all the old-timers, she knew Monhegan history, summer style, and she loved to share stories with me. Her sense of Zero—the Mostel complex was three houses from hers—reflects that of other Monhegan women. "He was the most unfriendly person I knew, he would never greet me on the road. I guess he saw that I made no attempt to greet him either."

But Sue and Kate conversed over many summers. "Kate talked a lot about her asthma, it plagued her all her life." Sue was aware of "a toughness about Kate. I don't believe anybody could touch her." The vulnerable Kate was a private soul, she turned to Zero in moments of physical distress and he was not always sympathetic. The tough Kate was the public Kate, garrulous, frontal and seemingly implacable. Sue remembers that "after Zero died Kate joined the Breathers." Charlotte Selvers was a colleague of psychologist Fritz Perls; now widowed and carrying on without husband Charles Brooks, Selvers has been conducting "sensory-awareness" workshops every summer in the Monhegan schoolhouse. The workshop students have come to be known locally as the Breathers. For Sue, who saw herself as a realist of the old political Left, Kate's reaching out to the Breathers suggested a kind of debilitating mysticism as an outcome of prolonged grieving.

Sue herself was alert to the habits of fellow natives. She brought a wonderfully wry perspective to her observations. Like other neighbors she watched the rise of the Mostel house as it reached skyward several hundred feet from her own dwelling. "The plans were drawn up by Jerry Tam [painter and wife of the now-deceased artist Reuben Tam]. At first nothing faced the sea but a fireplace—*no window*. I'm sure they have a window now. Well Zero wanted privacy and he had trees planted between his house and Henry Kallem's. This got Henry very upset; he cried, 'When the trees grow up I'll never be able to see the ocean.'" Sue paused, preparing me for the full import of subsequent events. "So guess what? The trees grew up, and neither Henry nor Zero are around to see the ocean." Nor is Herbie Kallem.

Frances and Buddy Kornbluth, their children and now their grandchildren have been Monhegan summer people for many years. Frances is a member of Monhegan's artists' association, which means she posts studio visiting hours. Zero, unlike the Kornbluths, the McCartins and Charley Martin, never joined the association and never encouraged tourists to drop in. The Kornbluths' house is near the Mostels'; the children grew up together during summers in the Fifties and Sixties, and both Frances and Buddy have many stories to tell.

Buddy Kornbluth recalls that Zero once asked him to buy a fishing pole and a reel. "I said, 'What size do you want?' He says, 'I dunno, just get me a fishing pole.' So I bought him a pole and a reel and he hung it on top of his mantelpiece and he didn't use it once. So I said to myself, 'All right, maybe he'd like to go out fishing and he's afraid to ask me.' So Zero and Kate and Frances and myself go out on my boat. We're about half a mile away from the island and Zero says to me, 'Let me run the boat.' I say, 'All right, you want to steer?' He says, 'What do you do?' I say, 'It's like driving a car. You want to go left, turn the wheel left.' So we're driving along and he's having a ball. And he says 'Kate, we gotta *get* one of these things!' Suddenly, as happens on Monhegan, the fog rolls in—and we can't even see the island. I knew from my compass course where I was. I knew I reverse my reciprocal and I could come back to the island. Zero's curious, he says, 'How do you find where you're going?' I say, 'I took a power squadron course. You read the charts and you have your compass.' He turns around to Kate and says, 'Kate, cancel the order!'"

Buddy remembers the Mostel bathtub. "When Zero built his house, he ordered this bathtub. It was six feet along."

Custom-made?

"I don't even know. I never saw a bathtub this big in my life, and I was so envious. I said, 'Jeez, I wish I had one like that.' But Zero tells me 'they're no good, you could drown.'"

Frances notes that "he had this genius quality, he could immediately get into any situation. Zero's playing Tevye at the Falmouth tent theatre on Cape Cod, he's praying to God and it suddenly starts to rain outside. Well, there's this hole in the tent. Zero looks up at the rain coming through this hole and of course he says, 'Thanks, God.'

"As a painter he was very private, he never talked about his art. As for the other artists here, he wanted to relate to all of them, he bought their work. I was the only artist whose work he never bought."

Buddy speculates, "Frances, maybe he didn't like Jews." But there were other "only artists" whose work Zero never bought. Sue Rosenthal, for one, perhaps Reuben Tam, and John Hultberg, and Bill and Jan McCartin. But our conversation is now focused on Jews. "I'll tell you something about Jews," Frances says. "Zero's Orthodox parents would never acknowledge Kate. They never saw or acknowledged the two boys. Zero was very bitter about that. And yet Kate was a very fierce fighter for the Jews. We were at a big dinner party at Herbie's one night and Andrew Wyeth's work came up and why his paintings were so popular. I said, 'Somehow or other he communicates the human condition.' Well, Kate went absolutely nuts. 'Human condition? What does Wyeth know about the human condition?' In retrospect I could see that she felt Wyeth's work was illustrative and sentimental. . . . I'll tell you, Kate was working all those years Zero was blacklisted. She'd be on the road, on tour, while he was up here with the kids. She supported that family. He was here with a maid and two little kids, and they had to eat."

Even lapsed Jews, I reflect, get hungry, and Gentile wives do battle for them.

Zero hired several models during the Monhegan summers, and they included Jan Kornbluth, Jackie Bogel and Ann Dolan Court.

Jackie Bogel and her husband Billie Boynton, now year-round Monheganites, run the Lupine art gallery and framing shop, and it was there during a lunch break that Jackie spoke to me. Her appearance is that of a classic heartbreaker; she is a stunning, soft-spoken, modest, and elegant beauty. She tells me that Zero and Herbie had a weekly arrangement. "I modeled just for the two of them, one afternoon a week, from one to four. It was probably August of '71 and some of '72. I was nineteen. It was very professional. They didn't talk to me particularly except to tell me when to change positions. They were very loose about what I did. Zero might suggest I move one arm a little, but they were pretty open to how I posed. Zero had a platform in the middle of the studio for the model. He always had an opera or symphony going on the tape recorder. He and Herbie were both larger-than-life figures to me and I was a shy person. Zero wouldn't talk to me much, but he did anything he could to make me feel comfortable. At the end of the three hours he'd give me a little lecture on what we'd been listening to, a little bit of music appreciation, maybe he'd throw in a joke. I really was afraid to converse with him, unless he asked me a question."

I ask if Jackie could observe what was being painted.

"Not much. Once he caught me sort of looking at the canvas and he asked me what I thought of what he was painting. And I said something that indicated my unsureness of just why *I* was there. Since the thing was so abstract I couldn't see how he was painting *me*. And he said, 'Oh you want *realism*? You want *realism*? Anyone can paint like *this*!' And he whipped off a quick little realistic sketch of me on a sheet of drawing paper and said, 'That's *nothing*! That's where you *start*!'—And he sort of put me in my place."

Jackie recollects the atmosphere in the studio. "There was a very calm sense when Zero and Herbie were working. You really knew they were close and that they were enjoying immensely sitting there painting together, and I felt very comfortable in their presence. I don't remember breaks, although I must have taken a ten-minute break in the middle. The first summer I had been about fifteen pounds over my normal weight and I lost that weight over the winter, and when I went back again Zero remarked on being quite disappointed that I didn't have a classical body anymore. My body just wasn't as interesting."

I ask who found who for the modeling. Jackie: "I can't recall. There's always a group of young people around the island doing housekeeping and odd jobs. I had never posed before. It was just one of those things—somebody needed a model and it was five dollars an hour."

"Did you have any sense of Kate's presence while you worked?"

"No, she never came into the studio. It was really just Zero and Herbie's time."

Jan Kornbluth, daughter-in-law to Frances and Buddy, was visiting the morning I spoke to the elder Kornbluths. She remembers modeling for Zero the year she got out of college. "Probably 1969. I was young, very shy. Bruce [Kornbluth, now her husband] came up to me and said, 'Zero wants you to pose.' Bruce and I were very good friends with Toby, actually with both Toby and Josh. I said, '*What?*' I was just terrified, I'd never done anything like that. But I said I would do it. It sounded exciting and interesting. I was flattered."

Frances: "Smith girl goes out into the world."

"The day I went in there I was scared to death. I barely knew him. What I remember is he couldn't have been kinder, he put me at my ease, I didn't feel at all strange. They put on all sorts of wonderful music. What I remember is they put on the score of *The Most Happy Fella*. My session was twenty minutes, then we'd break for ten. There were four of them, Zero and Herbie and Charlie Martin and Mike Loew, but sometimes it was just Zero and Herbie. At that time I posed alone, and then they wanted to have a couple of us so they asked Ann Dolan. We each posed two mornings a week."

Ann Dolan, a Minnesota girl, had been active, along with Billie Boynton, in Eugene McCarthy's 1968 presidential campaign. While on Monhegan during the summer of '68, Ann learned that her mother had died in an automobile accident.

What Kate Mostel saw in Ann Dolan was, as Frances Kornbluth puts it, "a poor Irish girl whom she symbolically adopted." Ann became a spiritual daughter to Kate, who saw in Ann something of her earlier, younger self, and when Monhegan lobsterman Rusty Court, an open-faced young man with flaming red hair and a smiling countenance, asked for Ann's hand in marriage, it was Kate who made the wedding. The ceremony took place in front of Rusty Court's house, near Lobster Cove.

"It was around '73 or '74," Frances notes, "Kate got all the cold cuts sent up either from Katz's Delicatessen or Zabar's. She also made a beautiful shower for Ann. Kate loved Ann. Ann cleaned for Kate and Zero, she did all sorts of things around the house. Ann was like an adopted daughter." Not one of Tevye's daughters but the daughter Zero and Kate never had. I mention to Frances that I interviewed Clara Baker the previous summer, and she is curious to know if Clara lived "a normal life." My only response is "Who lives a normal life?" And Frances quickly points out that "With a man like Zero you have to make yourself a doormat. You have no identity."

Jan Kornbluth remembers that "Zero and Kate had this classic relationship. Zero would go partying on the island, get a little drunk and then be afraid to come home because Kate would tell him he was acting like a fisherman." Frances sees Kate as overly-conscious about status, "certainly as far as Zero and his career were concerned. And at the same time she reveled in the idea of democracy." So that Kate's ideal image of Zero was of an egalitarian celebrity, removed from the crowd by virtue of his notoriety and yet standing with the masses in some paradisiacal stance of brotherhood. And Kate's image of herself on the tiny island of Monhegan was that of a social leader. "She'd get ticked off," Frances notes, "when Phyllis Wyeth, Jamie's wife, with whom she vied for social leadership, wouldn't invite her to the Wyeth parties"—parties that might include Teddy Kennedy and other stars in the mainland firmament.

But the Mostels, whose taste ran to frequent celebratory bursts, were not to be outdone as festive organizers. Jan also remembers "the parties for the dogs! It was Max's or Ookie's birthday and they'd make these huge cocktail parties. Ookie had a terrific birthday party one year."

From partying, our conversation gravitates with an almost icy inevitability to the many broken marriages suffered both among the summer people and the lobster-fishing families. The Court marriage ended in divorce; Ann Court left Monhegan, and Rusty Court also left, in company with Cathy Payne, the young wife of Billy Payne. As noted earlier, the fine-featured Billy Payne wed himself to the Island Spa which he began operating when Lorimer (Zimmy) Brackett suffered a disabling stroke. Zimmy, that gaunt, taciturn New Englander, passed on to the next world several years ago. What was the Spa has moved to what was Richard Semple's Carina House where the art of the bargello was taught. Carina House has been renamed Carina. Billy Payne runs it with his poet-wife Jan Bailey and they stock serious contemporary literature and what smacks of being organic produce and fine baked goods, all of which is giving the Monhegan Store, sold and resold several times since the legendary days of Doug and Harry Odom, a run for its money. So the exigencies of nature and the restlessness and curiosity of men and women leave their mark.

Frances Kornbluth recalls: "Kate used to go into Zimmy's, she believed in keeping up the economy of Monhegan. You buy things at Zimmy's even if you don't need them."

As we talk, the past is welling up. I am seeing Zero and Kate ambling along the principal dirt road with Max and Ookie; Zimmy behind the counter of the Spa, barely civil to women customers whom he considered, I suspect, to be some alien, unpredictable breed; Doug and Harry Odom, genially reopening the store after supper, perhaps a little flushed from a celebratory encounter with a Bourdeaux of some wonderful vintage year; painter Ted Davis, short, balding, ever ready to contradict, if quietly, anything under the sun that you might bring up, and in the early evening stolidly fixed at the checkout counter, passing the time with Doug and Harry; Herbie with his grizzly whiskers and blue cap smashed down on his head, picking up supplies and climbing with some effort the steep hill from the dock.

Herbie Kallem had to recover from two broken marriages; Sally Kallem divorced him in the Sixties when their only daughter Gillis was still a child, and Herbie's third wife, theatrical producer Claire Nichtern, was loath to spend her summers on Monhegan, so that much of Herbie's emotional support came from the neighboring Mostels. Frances Kornbluth remembers that "Kate, who loved Herbie, would have him to dinner all the time, and Herbie was so *loyal* to her, and they'd *fight*—they were like a married couple. Anyway Kate was not the most stable person in the world—with the way she had the asthma, you *know* there's a big emotional base to it. For example when she played cards *she'd go nuts*. She'd start screaming and yelling if somebody else was winning."

We talk about Zero's diet that last summer. "Radishes, perhaps cucumbers. And he drank Perrier and took this protein liquid. Billie Boynton and Jackie Bogel were getting married that summer of '77 and Josh was coming to the wedding. My son Bruce calls and asks is it okay if Josh sleeps a few nights in my new studio. 'What's the matter?' I ask. Well, Kate doesn't want Josh cooking in the house because the smells might bother Zero. Kate was really upset that Zero was on this diet."

Frances remembers her one evening in Zero's studio. "Zero never invited anyone to the studio except the boys he'd paint with. Us women used to play poker different places, and Zero and Herbie would play with us at the beginning. One night we were to play at Kate's. So Buddy and I went over and the house is locked, it's dark. We knock at the studio and Zero comes out and says, 'She's sick, she's not gonna play, game's off.' Remember we didn't have phones in those days. So Zero says, 'Come on in.' He was going to be in *The Merchant* and he starts showing us around. He's getting into the feeling of the play by doing all these illustrative, imaginative ink drawings of all the characters. And he's showing Buddy and me this stuff and we can tell he's proud of the range of the work. This was like two or three months before he died. And it was the only time he ever shared any of his work with us. He was very humble about it."

Buddy Kornbluth adds, "And proud, he was proud."

My first view of Gillis Kallem was from the window of the upper studio I rented for so many summers at the Trailing Yew. Through that window I would constantly see Herbie, either working at his metal sculpture or at one time adding a small sun porch to the second story of his house. Later he could be seen building his studio to the rear of the house. And on the Kallem deck during my first summers in the Sixties I could sometimes spot Sally Kallem and her infant daughter Gillis. In the summer of 1988, with Herbie an invalid in the South Burlington home and so many of the others dispersed or dead, I meet with Gillis Kallem in the living room of the Kallem house. In '88 Gillis is living in San Francisco, teaching elementary school—she has since moved east—and she is here to sell Herbie's house in order to pay for her father's upkeep. Gillis is an upright, open, and sensitive young woman, and she talks to me about the past.

"My father hated to paint the insides of closets, so during the blacklist, when he hired Zero to help paint houses, he had his once-in-a-lifetime chance to have power over his buddy. The two were always struggling for power, so my father made Zero paint the closets and had great joy in telling this story and laughing about it. From the best I know, Zero survived in that period by painting the insides of closets."

Gillis recalls Zero's last summer. "He was out here practicing lines for *The Merchant*, and I was housecleaning for them every day. I felt I was there that whole summer so he could have somebody to speak his words to. I was cleaning and he was practicing the lines out loud. It was also the year he was on that diet, where he drank the powder three times a day. Strawberry, chocolate and vanilla were the flavors. He had one in the morning, one at lunch and one at dinner. And he could have a certain amount of food, like three or four ounces of lobster meat for special occasions. So he's on this horrible diet, and he hated it, but he did it. And that fall he died. Ranting and raving *The Merchant* lines at me all around the house, and then eating his drinks."

"Did he expect some kind of response from you?"

"Well *I* felt too inhibited."

"Were you cueing him?"

"No no, he would look at me and he would sort of do his lines. I felt really awkward. And then I would say something back to him and he would talk in this very loud voice. He'd say 'You must *enunciate!*' And then he'd make me say it three times over, whatever it was I was saying. I was doing dishes, beds, feeding the dogs, whatever. They always employed a housekeeper. I cleaned up in the studio also, though it wasn't my primary responsibility. But I was never allowed in there when there was a model. It made me suspicious. I could never understand—why can't *I* see a woman naked? *I'm* a woman."

I ask if Gillis had a sense that Zero was going around in character or was he just memorizing lines?

"At times he was definitely in character. But I didn't feel that he took the character beyond the lines of the play. But maybe he did. There were times when it felt like he was entirely possessed by this play, and by this character."

"And you were what, about twelve?"

"Yeah, twelve, thirteen. You were just *always* aware of his presence. He was loud, forceful. At times it was scary. That summer they were out for all of July. They'd usually come out for a whole month."

What turned Zero on?

"My father was convinced, and I've witnessed it enough times, that with five or more people on the porch or anywhere in his presence, Zero went into character—bang. And if my father was around, because of their relationship, Zero would play off my father either in a *nice* way or a negative way, like he would put my father down. There was a funny dynamic between the two of them."

"How would Herbie respond? Would he respond?"

"Oh he might say, 'Oh you're a shmuck, shut up.' Or he just might ignore it, or he'd banter back, depending on what the insult was, it wasn't consistent. But the two were very close buddies. I think they'd met during the WPA. My mother's side has roots to fishermen on this island, several generations back. My father came out after the war with all the other artists. For some reason people from New York knew about this place, it was beautiful and cheap. This house was built in the Fifties. My father borrowed money from Zero to buy the property. And Herbie's mother said to my father, 'Give something to Henry.' So both brothers built houses before Zero's was built. My parents met out here, then they separated and ran into each other on the street one day. My father was married before. When he came back after the war his wife Esther divorced him."

Gillis recalls Herbie's Monhegan day: "My father would be driven every day to get up, do stuff, then go right over to Zero's. Then they'd just hang out all day, it was like time had to be spent together. They had a very obsessive relationship, my mother didn't care for it. By no means was it why my mother divorced my father, but it certainly didn't help. And they'd end up having lofts above each other when Zero bought that building on Twenty-eighth Street."

The poker players: "Every Thursday night—poker—rain or shine. Here, or over at Zero's, though Kate oftentimes had the ladies' poker over there, and the men's poker would be over here. And then poker all the time in Zero's studio on Twenty-eighth Street.

"I ended up not actually liking Zero very much because of the way he treated my father. As a kid all I wanted was a little record player, so my father buys me a record player and I'm perfectly happy with it and he shows it to Zero and Zero says, 'You cheap sonofabitch, why couldn't you buy your daughter a goddamned nice stereo, cheap sonofabitch,' and constantly bantering like that. My father would take it and I would feel inside: I don't *like* you, you're a mean person. A lot of people have high regard for Zero and I'm one that doesn't, and I think rightly so. I think he was a good person and a genius of a performer, but I saw a very unpleasant side of him, the way he related to my father who was his best buddy. Of course my father would play into it just as much as Zero."

The Mostel handshake: "My father wore this big ring that I think Zero gave him, and Zero would shake his hand so tight that my father would go, 'Ooh woo woo, let go!' It was the right finger on his right hand. Zero would squeeze till the ring was digging into him, and I'm a little kid, six years old, and I'm thinking, why are you hurting my father? So I would get mad at him. Of course I didn't express it, Zero was too scary."

"Was he aware of you? Did he talk to you as to a child one was interested in?"

"Maybe at times, but not often as I think back on it. I'd ask questions and talk with him, but I felt like mostly I was a listener."

"Josh said to me, 'My father was like a child.'"

"Yes he was, he needed constant attention. One thing about Josh and Toby, my father gave them lots of love. I don't know if they would admit to it or whether they think it's true, but I've been led to believe that my father was like a second father to them and they didn't get much love from their parents. I believe Zero and Kate just didn't know how to love their kids, they were very critical and didn't ever do things like hug them. My father would just hug and kiss them and maybe smother them, maybe he gave them too much love. As for Kate, she was a very critical person. I was her little daughter for years until I became everybody's teenager. Then there was no place for me in her life and I became just a good-for-nothing, thankless child."

"In her book Kate says she has a list, who's okay and who's not."

Gillis replies: "I don't know if I made that list. Any time I had an argument with my father, she would side with him. She could be very . . . like venom would come out of her mouth. And she could be *very mean*. I remember one time she gave me a watch and it broke, and she goes, 'You can't take care of *anything.*' She had a very negative outlook."

I ask if Zero and Herbie spoke Yiddish together.

"All the time. It was like code words. Let me tell you about *Fiddler*. My father played the record here and everywhere. Growing up I heard *Fiddler* and Zero's voice all the time. I saw the show a couple of times in the round on Long Island. Some of it is *so sad*. There's a sad moment in the latter part, and I looked over at my father and there were tears in his eyes and he said to me, 'Just look down there.' I never forgot that day. I thought, 'Oh, they really love each other.' Then there'd be a race to get backstage."

Gillis recalls Zero's ad-libbing: "He was notorious for not sticking to his lines. His line might be: 'I'm on my way to see so-and-so,' and if Herbie was in the audience, oh, he'd look right at him and say 'I'm on my way to see Herb.' A lot of people wouldn't catch it, but the performers might think, 'What has he done now? God, what line are we up to?'"

Zero's hair: "He had these wisps he'd brush forward that he used to let me braid and comb. I did different styles, I was obsessed with playing with hair. There'd be long sessions sitting on the porch and drinking whatever and combing his little wisps this way and that way. I always thought how funny he looked, one year the hair dyed red, one year brown, for the plays."

Kate's book: "She was struggling, she'd go up to this room and lock herself in to write and she'd show it to Zero and he would edit. This was a nice loving time between them. She'd say, 'This is all shit, trash.' So he would read it and tell her it was all marvelous."

At the close of our interview Gillis remarks, "I'm trying to imagine the process of this book you're writing. You're taking down all these stories, it's like you're almost going to write a fable. Or you're patching together a legend."

A legend out of patches. The fabled, patched-together Sam Mostel.

I track down Brian Hitchcock, photographer, carpenter, silent cracker-barrel philosopher, descendent of the makers of the fabled Hitchcock chair. Brian settled on Monhegan in 1969, worked on the renovation of Jamie Wyeth's house and then helped in the construction of Zero's house and studio.

"Zero tried to intimidate everybody. He used to scare the bejeesus out of the poor working girls at the Periwinkle"— a fabled luncheonette, originally run by Josephine Day's husband Dinty. "He would tease these girls unmercifully. I was unteasable. I'd just say, 'See you later, fat man.' I always called him The Cypher. But I dunno, we could talk. I used to watch him paint a lot. He tried to make fun of everybody. I don't know how malicious it was, but he'd work on you if you'd let him. Herbie and I were very good friends, but for Herbie the sun rose and went down on Zero. As I say, I was close to Herbie, but I did a ton of work on that house for Zero and Kate."

Brian recalls Zero's special touch as umpire of Sunday-afternoon softball games in the Monhegan ball field: "Zero would ump and Herbie and I would sometimes play with the Monhegan kids. Also we went into shore to play against the prison team in Thomaston, and Zero would ump that game as well. They loved Zero in that Thomaston prison and of course on Monhegan. Zero's umpiring calls were sometimes appropriate to the occasion if not exactly accurate to the game. One was either safe or out depending on whether Zero thought the game needed to be closer."

"Did Zero have much to do with the poodles?"

"They had Yorkies. Well I guess they had poodles too. They made birthday parties for them." Every day was a kind of party. "Zero and Herbie would talk all the time, about baseball, about women. The year he had that opera voice-coach, people would kid him. They'd ask him, 'Is the fat lady dead yet?' He had half the island insane with his singing. They'd say, 'Knock it off already.'"

Again, the last summer.

"I had a boat so I'd ferry Zero around. I'd take him to Port Clyde and bring him back again. The year that he died, he had to go into Penn Bay Hospital in Rockport every week for blood tests. I had an old Volkswagen van parked at the dock in Port Clyde and Zero would push it to jump-start it. Herbie would go in with us and it bugged me that Herbie wouldn't steer because the only thing I didn't want to miss was taking a picture of Zero trying to jump-start my van."

"You never did get the picture?"

"I never did. Well, Zero would go to the hospital and then we'd all go shopping. My Lord, what that van carried. It carried Kate's desk that she wrote the book on. Zero went to an antique store in Camden one afternoon, he just walked in and he said, 'I think I'll buy a few things,' and came out with five thousand dollars worth of antiques. We stuffed 'em all in the van and lugged everything back to the island. He was always terribly afraid nobody knew who he was. He'd walk into a store and ask, 'You of course know who I am?' And they'd say no and he'd be mortified. He'd go into this great act. Well, on this particular trip he sent me and Herbie up the street to see if they had any Perrier, and of course Herbie liked to pull Zero's chain. Zero was down the street getting the antiques taken care of and Herbie told the guy in the store, 'Listen, we got this guy, he's right out of the funny farm and he thinks he's Zero Mostel, and he does have some money. We're sort of the family keepers, so when he comes in here to pick up this Perrier and he tries to tell you he's Zero Mostel, for God's sake go along with him or he'll be insufferable.' Herbie and I laugh like hell, then Zero comes in and says, 'Well my good man, now that we've made our purchases, of course you know who I am.' The guy says, 'Oh yeah, you're Zero Mostel.' Zero was flabbergasted. He had nothing to say. Totally disarmed, he looks at Herbie and me and he says, 'You bastards, you did that to me, didn't you?'"

Brian recalls: "Zero insisted on helping Herbie with his sculpture. We'd go out to an old junkyard and pick up iron. Everything Herbie picked up he'd have to run by Zero, and Zero'd say, 'No no, you don't want that piece, you want *this* piece over here.' It'd be something like the bull wheel from some monstrous piece of machinery. The poor van would groan and struggle. Every week, all summer long, we went on those trips."

"Was he under a doctor's care for that diet?"

"He was supposed to be. He had blood tests, they were particularly interested in his potassium level, something like that. He wasn't concerned about the diet, he thought he had it all under control. Kate was a little worried, she thought he might be losing weight too fast. But he died of an aneurysm, a blowout. It would have happened anyway, it's a weak part in the artery, just like an inner tube. They just thought he had some lung problem is what Kate told me. I talked to her only an hour and a half before Zero died. I was supposed to go to Philadelphia to make some posters for *The Merchant*, either there or in Washington. Kate said he'd been out that day and was just going to spend the night in the hospital for a final checkup and he'd be out the next day and she'd check with him and find out when he wanted me down there. I woke up the next morning and heard the news on the radio."

28

*S*hylock is one of the great pariahs of Western literature. Shakespeare knew how to fashion unredeemed villains; Iago, a world-class hater, was arguably his blackest creature. Shakespeare saw to it that Macbeth and Claudius, corrupt, devious, exemplars of paranoia, nevertheless attempt to claw toward some manner of spiritual sustenance; in fact, these unredeemed souls, each in his perverse way, hunger for nothing less than redemption. But alas the deeds of Macbeth and Claudius have forged these intricate, poisonous structures, these webbings of poison from which they can't extricate themselves; they can't pray, they can't locate an effective channel to remorse, and in due time Shakespeare finishes them off with the sword, a clean way to effect the end of evil Christians. (Never mind that Macbeth is pre-Christian; for all purposes he's a sinning believer.)

But if Iago, stubborn to the last, and Macbeth and Claudius, stubborn but contrite, are unredeemed, they are also not without a kind of sleazy, grim nobility; one doesn't wish to humiliate such grand gentlemen. But old Jewish Shylock, contrite as he is, is exposed to humiliations you wouldn't wish to heap on a stray atheist. Shylock's life is spared so that he may be led to the true path, a path of course structured by the Church—even after Henry the Eighth has told the Pope where His Holiness can take his solemn rituals and monasteries. But if the chagrined Shylock turns Christian, how does it avail him? Shylock is cut off from the only livelihood he knows, that time-honored usury Ezra Pound rails against when he is bedded down with Mussolini, that usury every credit-card company in the West knows how to fashion. Not only is Shylock deprived of his business enterprise, his only daughter Jessica is living what we used to call the life of Riley with a Christian playboy, an upper class loafer and sponger fully anticipating an intensified life of ease, courtesy of the despised father-in-law's career in usury. Thus Shakespeare, mining the Shylock vein, leaves us with a potentially lapsed Jew transformed into a sniveling, about-to-be baptized Christian who has nothing further to tell us about the sacredness of studying Torah, a crushed Jew who all but pays obeisance to that insufferably righteous dispenser of justice, the moralizing Portia.

This disconsolate, unredeemed Shylock has left many of us with a bitter taste. In the wake of Shakespeare's *Merchant of Venice*, a lot of rationalizing and revisionist thinking has come into play. The English dramatist Arnold Wesker set out some years back to transform Shylock's character and his fate, and formulated his Shylock as one faithful to Torah and to *Halacha* (the Law). This freshly-construed Shylock spoke to a Zero Mostel who had or hadn't, depending on one's point of view, himself grappled with questions of Torah and *Halacha*. And thus we come to Zero's final public performance.[34]

Publicist Merle Debuskey speculates: "I don't know if Wesker wrote the part for Zero, but since his Shylock and Shylock's close friend Antonio are men who love learning, who love literature, art, philosophy, and the world of ideas, Zero felt the play expressed something of his own soul. From time to time Zero had looked down his nose at acting, but with *The Merchant* he had a different attitude. I saw Zero's only performance at the Forrest Theatre in Philadelphia, and it was marvelous. The play was very interesting, but unfortunately it was not well produced."

Was Merle Debuskey referring to the director?

"It had to be [John] Dexter. He was the dominant force. The actual producers [the Shuberts, co-producers with Roger Stevens for the Kennedy Center in Washington] had very little say about it. Had Zero been able to perform the show all the way through, he would have opposed Dexter in certain ways and the play would have been better when it got to New York. And Zero's performance would have been something everyone would have wanted to see."

Debuskey recalls a moment when Zero "transcended himself." The scene has Antonio visiting Shylock's home. "Shylock invites him to stay over. The ghetto gates have been closed for the night. Jews aren't allowed out of the ghetto and no one's allowed in through the night. The Christian authorities in Venice have destroyed every Jewish book of learning they could get their hands on. If you were caught with one you were in terrible trouble. Well, Shylock has gathered a whole slew of these books and hidden them, and on this night he opens a trap door and begins pulling out Jewish books as a treat for Antonio. In this moment Zero's own love for the written word emerges with marvelous clarity. I've never seen a moment like this before or since."

In the spring of 1988 I begin a correspondence with Arnold Wesker who had kept a "New York Journal . . . During Rehearsals of 'The Merchant' 31 July–18 November 1977." I am also in touch with Marian Seldes, who performed the role of Rivka in Wesker's play. What follows are excerpts from Wesker's journal and fragments from Seldes's autobiographical work, *The Bright Lights: A Theatre Life*, interspersed with comments by Merle Debuskey and Aaron Mostel.[35]

Arnold Wesker:
Sunday 31st July

. . . Spoke on the phone to Zero . . . who announced he'd lost 49 pounds. "I've no clothes to wear!" He'll lose another 10 pounds, he says. . . . He sounds very fit, says he feels in top form and that he now knows the play "and I still find it marvelous!"

Kate (his wife) is in hospital and will be there for a long while and one of the side effects is that it produces a thin skin. He's going to collect a skin surgeon at the airport today who's coming to see her. . . .

Monday 1st August, 6 a.m.

. . . Drove to Zero's flat for a coffee, on Central Park. A huge continental-type flat full of cases filled with "objects d'art" and walls covered with original paintings and prints, many of which he'd painted. I thought I'd hate his paintings, but they're not without some power. He's got no voice of his own, though. Bits and pieces of other paintings float through his canvases. He showed me a folio of small sketches he'd done while studying the play. Some were quite impressive; many were nonsensical. Together they produced an atmosphere, albeit nothing that I recognized as belonging to my play—but Cervantes would no doubt have said that of Picasso's illustrations to Don Quixote. Zero has lost so much weight! He still looks like a big man but I'm glad I suggested it. On his walls are framed notes from people like Ira Gershwin—it's like stepping into a kind of fairyland.

. . . By 7:30 I was in [my] flat, very stoned, with nowhere to go, no energy to pick up a phone or attempt work. Tried watching TV. Dozed on couch. Zero rang about a line in the play.

"What does it mean, 'all law is diseased in parts'?"

I began to explain but he interrupted to say: "John told me you'd changed it."

I said, not that I could remember. He said never mind, he understood what the line meant. What a strange call. He must be alone in the flat and feeling in need of contact with someone from the production. And so we were all alone in our flats: Roberta [Maxwell], Julie [Garfield], Marian [Seldes], [Sir] John Clements [who played Antonio] . . . all waiting for today. John D. said in one of his moments of high exuberance: "I've been waiting and preparing for this moment for six months; Arnold's been waiting for over a year!"

Later. After the read-through

. . . It is most odd to have had such a thrilling day and find myself alone in this flat, eating a fish salad, when I—we—should all be together. It has been no ordinary day and yet I'm here, by myself, being ordinary. ZERO HAD LEARNED ALL HIS LINES! But the beginning.

I finally walked out this morning . . . first to the tiny post office on 10th, bought stamps, posted my cards, walked a couple of blocks, dithered in a stationery shop, bought more cards, a pen, a notebook, panicked and took a cab to Minskoff's rehearsal studio on 1515 Broadway. Got into the lift with Zero.

Actors, people milling around. Equity procedures to be attended to. Said hello to the cast. Discovered that our first choice for Nerissa had declined because, being black, she didn't want to play a "hand-maiden"—Sam Levine [sic] (Tubal) complained, half-jokingly, about his part being cut. Zero made jokes about: "My God! The writer's here! Awful man. Can't write. No heart."

He made, so Roberta Maxwell (Portia) told me, funny faces at me when I turned my back. The Schubert management came in looking like the Mafia, strolled among the players. When they left John D. said to them very pointedly: "See you in five weeks time!"

. . . . "I block in four days [said John Dexter] and, don't worry, I have a runthrough so that we can all see the length and breadth of the play, and I can see where my moves aren't working and how the flow is going and so on. Some people say it's a bad way to work but it's the only way I know . . ." Then he invited everyone to sit down to a champagne lunch which had been laid out by Sardi's.

By 2:15 everyone was sitting around, desperately anxious to begin. I watched Roberta, who was opposite me, she was sitting in a tight, wound-up state, her sharp eyes, birdlike, waiting to be let fly. It seemed to me I could see her heart beating hard. . . .

And we were off.

John had told them to give the reading what they could, something, more than a mere recitation, but no one was prepared for what followed. It was not simply that Zero had learned his lines for that very first day, but that everyone made such sense of the play. It is a dense play, full of ideas, but it flows, is a story, has vivid characters AND IS FUNNY.

John had seated people in special relationship—Jessica and Lorenzo next to each other, Antonio and Shylock at either end of the long table, Portia next to Shylock. . . . Everyone knew they were locked into a special experience. . . . It was a private, personal and intoxicating atmosphere. Time and again actors hit the right note, the correct meaning. Zero was of course emotional but with the great distance of his humour to offset it. Clements played it with sober, straightforward intelligence—the contrast causing its own electricity. I simply sat and forced myself not to exclaim my pleasure. Once I turned to look at John D.—it was like the first night of *Roots* [an early Wesker drama]—his eyes were shining at what he'd put together and was hearing for the first time. (As I'm writing this Zero has just phoned, a bit lonely but also excited, and informed me that at one point John had tears in his eyes)....

In the break everyone relaxed a little. It took one hour 57 minutes to run the first act. (Two hours 56 for the whole play. Surprised. Thought it would be 3 and a half hours long.) Lots of jokes.

"Anyone want to relieve themselves before we begin again, do so now," said John.

"I've just relieved myself," said Zero, "and missed! Can we do it again?"

. . . the second act went a little slower, the air gone from the puffed up, excited balloon. . . . The reading ended leaving us all drained but elated. Pray we're not deluding ourselves.

Marian Seldes:

. . . He had the compulsion to play games, tell jokes like a school-boy. It was necessary to be in a receptive mood for high jinks and most of us were most of the time. His good friend Sam Levene was playing Tubal and was a dour sidekick for him. Howard Rodney, his dresser, was constantly near him, ready to do any errand and to be the butt of all his jokes.

At the first reading it was clear that the jokes were simply time-fillers. Zero . . . was prepared to draw on his own life's learning for the complicated part Arnold had written. Zero loved Jewish history, his family, painting and architecture. . . .

Several of the actors read sonnets before rehearsals. Zero made outrageous comments about them. Sir John critiqued them. There was a good deal of joshing about American versus British acting, but underneath it Zero was firm in his belief that sound and speech were secondary to true acting impulses.

Dexter told the company to go to the Metropolitan Museum and look at the Titians. "Find yourself there; choose something from a painting that you can choose in the play. Remember the broadness of the clothes when you move. . . .

The weeks in New York included private times with Arnold discussing our parts, costume fittings, a dinner party in a restaurant that Zero gave the company and a party in the Village that Arnold's wife, Dusty, arranged for us. In the restaurant we overate. All but Zero. Our host drank seltzer. He had lost fifty pounds on a special liquid protein diet and he did not cheat.

As rehearsals progressed John's notes urged us to control and drive the play. . . . "Remember the sounds are of 1563, not 1977." Then John stressed his major theme: "I know the story; tell me the ideas."

John's face became alive with his passion for perfection. "Oh, love the words, for Christ's sake, love them! This is a play of ideas and words. In the last twenty years we have had the theatre of behavior—your Tennessee Williams is an exception, a poet, yes—in this play there is such variety! They are all articulate, brilliant people. They know what they want to say..."

Arnold Wesker:
Fourth day

. . . Zero arrives. Embraces me with oversized and much too loud kisses. Poor Kate is in hospital and he complains; "Sick people are terrible. 'Bring me this, bring me that, do this, do that.' I'm tired."

I love the way he talks Yiddish. Makes me regret even more that I understand so little. He goes to his room performing a false trip on the way and then pretends he's blind and can't find the door handle. . . .

We come to the Renaissance speech. John D.'s big moment. He's worked out some extraordinary blocking, it involves pushing the tables around to indicate the movements of power leading up to the formation of the Italian city states. Halfway through there's an announcement that a bomb has been put in the building. Bombs placed by Puerto Rican protesters have been found throughout the day and one has gone off on 42nd Street killing one person. We talk about it. Sir John wants to stay. . . . Most of the actors also. . . . Zero continues rehearsing it with great fun, milking the bomb scare and becoming hilarious as John gives him the tables to move illustrating the growth of the Renaissance.

"Not only do I have to learn the fucking lines but I have to move the fucking furniture as well! . . . Now, where the hell am I? Who am I? Where was I? I don't know where I am any more, pushing these tables around here, there!"

. . . when the rest of the company are sent off he begins to go through it alone. His powers of concentration are tremendous.

Marian Seldes:

In four days we would be on our way to Philadelphia. There was to be a runthrough for the producers—members of the Schubert organization. The only other guest would be Zero's wife, Kate. It was at this particular rehearsal that we saw what Zero was going to do with the part. It had a kind of innocence and thrilling inventiveness that completely justified the risk of casting such an eccentric actor in a classically-oriented play.

. . . John had cautioned us: "There is no reality in this play—only *truth*. The set isn't real, you are not 'real' people. You are actors playing parts."

. . . Zero in rehearsal: He always wore a hat, a dark blue beret with a toy bird pinned askew on one side.[36] His trousers were too large for him . . . He moved lightly, with agility. The ghastly accident that crippled him when he was hit by a bus in 1960 did not seem to have affected his mobility. . . . He watched every scene. Made suggestions, laughed, did imitations in the wings. Younger actors sat exhausted, read newspapers, drank coffee. Zero observed.

. . . In a scene that was eventually cut, Zero had to rage against the complacency of a young Venetian. In rehearsal he grabbed a goblet and threw it on the floor. Tiny shards of broken glass bounced into the air near our faces. John warned him not to do it as there was no way to clean the stage between scenes in performance. At the next rehearsal Zero, carried away, broke the glass again. The scene took possession of him.

He worked on his part obsessively; watchful, wary, guarding his acting moments as an animal guards its young.

. . . A limousine took him everywhere. In Philadelphia, on September 2, after what my notes remind me was "an amazingly smooth first preview after a grueling afternoon full of mistakes," Zero called to Julie Garfield and me to get in the car and took us back to the hotel. Julie and I were going to have coffee and discuss her feelings about playing Jessica. "Bring me some seltzer—" I thought he was joking. Howard Rodney kept seltzer, celery tonic, available for him everywhere. I was surprised there was none in the car.

At one in the morning on September 3 an unfamiliar voice on the hotel telephone:

"Where is my seltzer?"

"Zero?"

"What are you doing?"

I was half-asleep. We had a matinee the next day and a note session before then. My bones were aching. "I've gone to bed."

"Why don't you come up here?"

"Oh, no, Zero"

"I'm in twenty-one nineteen"

"Zero, it's too late."

"Ah . . . just for a little while."

I got out of it. He hung up. Had I been rude? Was he lonely? Was he going to call Julie, too? I could not believe he wanted to see me. He wanted—an audience.

Merle Debuskey: "After the first preview I went backstage to Zero's dressing room. He was intent on discovering whether I was being nice or I meant what I said about his performance. He was really shoving me around verbally. He was sitting with his leg propped up, it was hurting him. It took him a little while to realize I meant what I said. He was very happy. *He really was happy.* I said, 'You don't need me, I'm going home.' And Katie was coming down the next day, maybe with Sidney Cohn. He hadn't wanted Katie at the first preview, he was too nervous. Anyway I had a summer place on the beach at Westhampton. I was supposed to stay over in Philadelphia but Gerald Schoenfeld, one of the producers, was driving back that night so I thought, 'Terrific, I'll go back and the next morning I can go to the beach,' because I thought they were well on their way, [and] it was just a question of sharpening the production. Zero had stopped bullying me because he was too tired, and he was up and pleased with his work, and I said goodnight. And the next morning I was down at the beach, perhaps it was noon, and I got a phone call from the manager of the show telling me that Zero had had an attack of some sort and they'd have to cancel the performance and I should do whatever I had to do. So I kept on top of the story. They weren't sure if it was a heart attack or what. And they withdrew the performance and continued to rehearse, waiting day by day."

Aaron Mostel: "I visited him in Philadelphia. I says, 'What happened to you?' He says, 'I lost sixty pounds.' I says, 'You know, I lost forty pounds, but I do it under supervision.' Sammy was living on some flavored soda, some powder, and he wanted to give me a box. He shows me a pair of his pants, he says, 'I gotta buy a new wardrobe.' So I says to him, 'Sammy, you're gonna kill yourself.' He tells me, 'I'm going to the biggest dietitian.' I says, 'Kate?' I don't give a goddamn, the guy is sixty years old, he's been eating good food all his life."

Marian Seldes:

The first preview had to be treated like a rehearsal with an audience We were all drained of energy at the brief note session on the following day. We sat in a circle below the stage of the Forrest, sweltering in the September heat. Zero had his wig on, combed carefully around the yarmulke that now replaced the beret above his huge, smiling face. Partly costumed, we gathered around John. He thanked us for last night's work, gave a few typically incisive, usable notes and dismissed us.

. . . Arnold suggested we have some kind of a cast party after the evening performance. "We need to be together; we're a family." I said I would help him arrange it. Zero went to his dressing room, followed by Howard, to have a celery tonic. He gave me a wink.

The steady, low roar of the matinee audience on the intercom was interrupted by [the stage manager] Brent's voice, but it did not say the familiar words. . . "We are terribly sorry, but due to Mr. Mostel's illness this afternoon's performance has been canceled." The audience fell silent.

Brent hurried backstage to explain that Zero was on his way to Jefferson Hospital. He had suddenly felt faint and terribly sick. A doctor was with him. We were asked to come back to the theatre for a rehearsal in place of the evening performance.

Arnold Wesker:

. . . he developed pains in his chest and was taken to hospital diagnosed as suffering from a virus. He needed rest. For a week he was resting. On the following Wednesday, I spoke to him on the phone in his room in the hospital, complaining that they wouldn't let me come to see him because they kept saying he needed to rest. "Rest! Rest! I'm so rested I'm like a plum pudding!" He was due out the next day, Thursday.

Marian Seldes:

For four days John rehearsed the company with Zero's understudy, Joseph Leon, reading the part. He expected Zero back for rehearsal on September 9. Encouraging reports were issued from his hospital room. The company sent notes and flowers. Sam Levene went to see him every day.

My friendship with Sam deepened in the following week. He talked to me about Zero, about his own career, about mine. . . .

On the day before Zero expected to be released, Sam took him some art books.

We were rehearsing, were dismissed for dinner, came back and took our places for the courtroom scene.

Arnold Wesker:

Thursday 8th September

At 7:30 this evening as I was sitting in the stalls watching John D. rehearse the court scene, Marvin Krauss the general manager walked down the aisle to tell John that Zero's heart had stopped at 6 o'clock and had been stopped for an hour. He's surrounded by doctors, Marvin told us, but they can't get the pacemaker to resuscitate it.

At 7:00 I had been in the wings watching the actors go on and off and generally wisecracking with them, enjoying backstage atmosphere. John had seen me and called me down.

"Zero's been unconscious since six," he whispered with his arm around me, "it's his heart. Marvin's over there with him now."

I sat in the stalls behind Andy Phillips (lighting designer) and in a numbed state watched John continue shaping the court scene with dramatic beauty. . . . It was while he was improving the court scene that Marvin came in.

I knelt in the aisle by John, we held each other's arms.

"This can't continue," he said, referring to the actors acting on stage. "What do I tell *them*?"

"That Zero's had a heart attack," said Marvin, "and we'll call them together tomorrow at one and let them know what's happening."

John braced himself, took a cigarette, went onstage, told everyone to sit and very swiftly announced what had happened, Marian and Julie (Rivka and Jessica) at once dropped their faces into their hands. The others just sat stunned. John sent Marian into Rosies (the Kosher bar and restaurant across the alley where we all frequently drank and ate, and from where Zero had his meals sent) in order to look after Sam Levine [sic] who'd been with Zero when it happened and was now at the bar drinking.

Marian Seldes:

Sam was in the alley outside the stage door. We embraced. Sam had been in the room with Zero when he died. We stood in the alley, and Sam, wet-eyed but in control, told me what had happened.

Arnold Wesker:

One by one the actors left the stage, except Sir John who seemed very sad and shattered. John D. was near to tears, drawn, numb. We floated around looking at each other and not knowing what to do or say. John was concerned for me and the play, I was anxious for him. In fact the air of helplessness was made of many things. (They couldn't find Kate!) I felt helpless about poor Zero, one couldn't go to him or be by him or even in the corridor of the hospital; I felt helpless about John who'd put eighteen months work and a whole lot of genius into this production; and about the company who must be shattered and . . . in need of what I couldn't give them; about my play, my plays which I now feel are jinksed [sic]. I remembered an unprecedented heat-wave hitting London when *Roots* moved from the Royal Court to the West End; my father dying on the first night of *The Kitchen*;

Kennedy being assassinated while *Chips with Everything* was on Broadway; the fate of *The Journalists* contracted but never performed by the Royal Shakespeare Company, and my subsequent lawsuit against them; my mother dying on the first night of *The Merchant* in Stockholm almost a year ago on the same date, the eighth, but of the next month, October.

Sir John invited John D. to sit with him in his hotel for a drink. He declined. I was about to go out, John D. called me back—he wanted to assure me we'd get the play on somehow . . . two phone calls. One from a distant cousin . . . both to inform me that it had been flashed through on TV that Zero was dead. . . .

My play had killed him. He dieted for it and was under pressure for it and silly bugger! he overdid it! Oh Zero, Zero, Zero! Now I'm crying for you. You were so rested, you were like a plum pudding!

And what ironies there are.

Last night I found a copy of William Fishman's book *East-End Radicals* and bought it for him. It was to be for him coming out of hospital today. My inscription, aiming at his brand of humour, was: "Where this story ends my family's story begins. Thank you for coming out alive!"

. . . As I left the theatre I saw Brent in tears. . . . I bought two bottles of white wine to drink through the night. Someone from the cast rang to find out if I was all right or needed company. . . .

What of the rest of the cast? Should I . . . call them together here in my room? To do what? To say what?

Marian rang down to tell me that people had gathered in Sir John's room and that I must come to them. . . .

Friday, the next day

The papers carry the headlines. Our story pieces together.

It seems that Sam Levine [sic] who had been with Zero had brought him some books to read. Zero has said he couldn't cope with those so Sam asked would he like him to go out and buy a *Hustler*—the girlie magazine. Zero said: "I don't need a *Hustler*, I think I need a nurse." He was feeling dizzy. He fell, Sam tried to steer his fall away from a table, but it made no difference, Zero was unconscious. Doctors rushed in and tried to massage the heart. Then they opened him up attempting to put a pacemaker there. Nothing worked. Within an hour he was considered dead.

In Sir John's room we talked, slowly at first, then relaxing into humour. Roger Stephens [sic] (one of the producers) telephoned. I told him we had to go on.

Marian Seldes:

The questions that cannot be answered were asked. The empty, helpless, inadequate efforts to explain to oneself, to each other, what this loss meant—to Zero's family, to all those who loved him, and to this play. It was repeated that Zero would have wanted the play to continue. . . .

In Sir John Clements' suite at the Barclay a group of us stayed together drinking wine and making telephone calls. . . . Arnold called his wife. Julie Garfield called her mother. Repeating and repeating the unbelievable, the unacceptable truth.

At midnight the group broke up. Arnold, shattered, talked of Kate Mostel. All his plans were fragmented. We finished the wine and went to the elevators. "Well, Marian—we had our party." . . .

The following day we met at the Forrest and John told the company we would go ahead with the production. Sam was going to leave; it was not possible for him to stay in Philadelphia any longer. . . .

John and I walked up and down Walnut Street discussing possible recasting. What hurt John almost more than losing Zero as Shylock was the dissolution of their future plans. They had discussed Falstaff and Galileo and other major roles. John . . . wanted to create a theatre in which the actor could express himself through great playwriting. For a while we walked in silence, neither of us wanting to go back to the empty, sad Forrest.

Early on an August morning in 1989 Sue Rosenthal tells me that one of the physicians attending Zero when he died is staying on Monhegan. As if someone had fabricated this bit of irony, the man is renting Herbie Kallem's house. Later that same morning I'm sitting on the deck of Herbie's old house with David Scott, a practitioner in pulmonary diseases. Scott was in residence at

Jefferson Hospital in Philadelphia and remembers that Zero was on the thirteenth floor, in the area assigned to VIPs, and that the patient was at the nursing station, about to be discharged, when he was stricken. (In her book, Kate has Zero in his room when he collapses.) One of the difficulties the staff immediately had to contend with was the considerable distance separating the VIP area from the intensive care unit. There was no time to move the patient; emergency procedures had to be instituted at once. Ultimately it made no difference. And Zero's diet? Scott believes the diet played no role in the events of that day.

"He had developed what we call an aortic aneurysm. The rupturing of the aorta could have occurred at any time. There are tests that are able to spot such potential danger, but in Zero's case there was nothing to indicate such tests were necessary." Scott along with other staff members worked on the patient for a considerable period. "But our efforts were essentially futile. Zero had no blood pressure, no pulse. There just wasn't anything to resuscitate."

The Merchant went back into rehearsal in September, with the former understudy Joseph Leon now playing Shylock. Wesker recalls John Dexter's first words to the cast:

> "No one can follow Zero and no one is going to try. Zero interpreted the role in an inimitable way but all great roles have more than one way of being delivered . . . there will be no two-minute silence or two-minute anything . . . in ten minutes we will start to rehearse the play again . . . I always thought the hardest thing was to lose an old friend, but to lose a new friend is painful as you'll know when I tell you all of the plans I had to use Zero as Falstaff, Galileo . . . those plans are gone. . . ."

After a tryout engagement at the Kennedy Center in Washington, *The Merchant* opened in New York at the Plymouth Theatre on November 16th. Wesker reports in his journal that he is in a state of shock. "The reviews were negative. It was a brilliant first night, but the reviews have murdered the play's life. None of us can believe it. . . . The bastards have done it again." The principle assassin is Richard Eder who had recently taken over as chief drama critic for the *New York Times,* replacing Clive Barnes. As Wesker notes, and as I, a drama critic for the *Village Voice* for more years than I care to remember, know too well, an evenhanded review can be deadly given where and how the negative and positive elements are placed.

Arnold Wesker:

[quoting Eder] "Its dramatic structure is weak and its dramatic impact fitful and uncertain..." What did that mean? The audience had been on the edge of its seat. The impact was not only certain but constant, the evening had been held up by applause after applause as it had been every preview night and every night in five weeks of a pre-run in Washington.

On the other hand the review was not unintelligent. In London it would command audiences. But the headline "Intelligent but weak," and the last line, "the evening is stimulating but only sometimes successful," were killers. And what sense did they make? If the evening was stimulating, why didn't that imply achievement? "Only sometimes successful." Successful in what? There's no carefulness here. . . . Why couldn't he say, "The evening is stimulating and, though not always successful—for what is always successful—yet it should be seen." Would that have been dishonesty? "It should be seen" would have made, in four words, a total change in the lives and fortunes of many artists. . . .

The Merchant closed after eight previews and four performances. Wesker notes that a longer and "revised version . . . was produced in Birmingham on 12 October 1978 to very enthusiastic reviews from the daily press and tepid ones from the Sunday press. . . . To date there are no plans for a Broadway production."

Ten years later, on June 10th, 1988, Wesker writes to me from the family cottage in Wales. "One thing you need to know. I've changed the title from *The Merchant* to *Shylock.* I should have done that from the start, its fortunes may have fared better— though it would not [have] prevented the unpredictable Almighty from calling Zero off to a new location for a new movie. My German translator long ago suggested I call the play by that title. That's the title it goes under in Germany. The play is, I can see, going to become my obsession. There is great resistance to performing it in London despite that the Birmingham production received excellent reviews. I think it's because Jews are not too popular just now. [The Israeli–Palestinian conflict, with Hamas, the Party of God and Holy War replacing Arafat as principal antagonists, goes on as I write this.] I also think they like their Shylock as he is. So a lot of my energy is spent trying to secure commercial sponsorship . . . like the Ancient Mariner, I stop whoever I can to tell them the story and seduce their interest. I feel it's a very important play not simply in the theatre canon but for the Jewish community. And I'm fighting for it. Who knows, perhaps someone will read your book and say it's time New York had another chance to see this play."

But the ghost of Zero, for good or ill, will forever haunt any future production of *Shylock*.

Merle Debuskey recalls: "I got the awful telephone call. I had to take care of the obituary. And that was that. There was no funeral. That was his wish."

I ask, "How would you know that?"

Merle: "Kate said so."

Doug Odom: "Max Rosenthal called the store. There were barely any phones on the island then."

Brian Hitchcock: "I woke up the next morning and heard the news on the radio. I was pretty stunned. I ran down to Billie and Dougie Boynton at their place. They couldn't believe it."

Bettye Jaffe: "Sam picked up the phone. It was Toby Mostel. And Sam began to scream."

Earl Wilson's column, *New York Post*, September 10th, 1977: "[Kate] insisted that his wishes to be cremated 'like Einstein' be followed."

Clara Baker: "Jews do not accept cremation, but he was so angry with his family sitting *shivah* when he married out of his faith that he never forgave them for it and cremation was almost a slap in the face to them."

Aaron Mostel: "I was up in Liberty, New York, in a motel, and the owner says to me, 'Aaron, sit down.' 'What's the matter?' I ask. He says, 'Do you know that Zero died?' I says, 'When?' He says, 'In Philadelphia.' So I get on the phone, then I start driving to New York. But they had already cremated him."

I say to Aaron, "I read in the obits he wanted to be cremated like Einstein."

Aaron: "I got copies of all that crap. Once we were sitting in a funeral car going to the cemetery where my older sister Celia was buried. Sammy felt the service went on too long. Well, you know a rabbi, instead of two minutes he talks twenty. But I say, 'Sammy, she was a great lady, people want to laud her.' Then I tell him, 'Sammy, we're all buried in one place in New Jersey, we'll save a hole for you too.'"

"He didn't expect to die."

"He didn't expect to die, he was sixty-two years old. Kate made the decision—no service, no nothing. We wanted to pick up the body, we have a family organization and we have a cemetery in Ridgewood, New Jersey. Everybody has a plot."

"Kate made the decision with the boys?"

"The boys didn't know from nothing. I drove to New York and I phoned. I got Toby. He says, 'They did it already.'"

Merle Debuskey: "There used to be an annual New Year's party. It rotated between Zero's, Ian Hunter's and Ring Lardner's. At Christmastime, after Zero was gone, my wife and I took a vacation and wound up in Morocco. So we missed the party. At the end of our stay I pick up the *International Herald Tribune*. I read that Sy Peck [Seymour Peck, former editor, Arts and Leisure Section, *New York Times*] has been killed in an auto accident on his way home after the New Year's Eve party at Kate's. He was a good friend. He wasn't well but he didn't want to miss the party. That was my last connection with Katie and Zero."

Mildred Loew: "Kate was moody. After Zero died she felt bereft because widows of celebrities aren't bowed down to any more. She missed the adulation."

I ask Mildred, "Did she confide in you?"

"There was nothing to confide. She'd say what she had to say, that he was a killer. Now Herbie was Zero's closest friend. Herbie was his lackey. He had their house built when they were in Europe. Herbie did everything for them—Zero never left him a dime, everything went to Kate. And he wasn't so screwy when it came to money. Neither was she. She could be very generous, take me to the theatre, to lunch. Then she'd say, 'Gee, I have a coat I don't want, do you want to buy it?' I'd say no. So she'd sell the coat to Sarah Shulman [wife of painter Moe Schulman] for twenty-five dollars. She needed the twenty-five dollars? How could you do that, take twenty-five dollars from a poor artist's wife for a coat you don't want anymore?"

Arlene Simon: "She didn't want to come back to Monhegan. 'I don't paint,' she'd say, 'I like to watch television. I love to shop, there's no shopping on Monhegan, the boys are grown. Without Zero, why come here?'"

I note that she did come back.

"For a while. There were things she loved besides shopping. She played the piano, that was special, and she loved to eat out. We used to invite them both and Zero would say, 'Please, I'll come over later, have Kate for dinner.' As I told you, she loved the old Fred Astaire movies, she rented a whole bunch one day and we had a marathon viewing at her house. I tell you, neither one was cautious about their bodies. Kate had started sculpting, she was sanding marble, this woman with asthma, and Reuben Tam and I came over one day and said, 'Kate, you gotta stop that.' She was sculpting the poodle's head. The last time I saw her was less than a month before she died. She was 'hosting' Michael Loew's wake. She was in great spirits. The next thing we know we get a phone call from Toby. He says, 'Kate's dead.'"

Frances Kornbluth: "Kate and Zero loved Monhegan. On this island you're without defenses. Kate and I once sat quietly on their porch looking out at the water, she told me it was better here than on the Queen Elizabeth coming back from England—

Zero'd done a TV show with the Muppets. But people on a success track, a career track, have to give up everything else in terms of society's demands, and they have to just move with their careers. Zero always wanted to paint—he made so much money with *Fiddler* he could have retired, *he did not need more money.* But Kate had a style—when they built the house here she had a decorator, everything had to be this affluent 'style.' Look, she would probably be alive today if she didn't have the San Remo apartment painted and stayed in there with her terrible asthma. The woman was always sniffing when we played poker. She had the apartment painted *and she stayed in it*—even a normal person would have had problems. Here on Monhegan she had Ann Court come over every day when Ann first arrived. The house had to be neat and clean. She was compulsive about it, and yet she would stay in all that dust. After the funeral service for Mike Loew, we walked into the apartment and you could smell the paint fumes."

Jan Kornbluth: "I don't think Kate cared about much anymore."

Frances: "She was depressed. She taped the Muppets going to the Met Museum for our grandson Ian. When we visited her in the city she was so sad, she was sitting alone in that gorgeous apartment, not feeling well, wheezing, and she told us she was so happy—she was buying this place in Amagansett. She also bought this secondhand blue Mercedes, she'd always wanted a Mercedes. But there wasn't real joy, how could there be?"

Gillis Kallem: "After Zero died, if you got Herb and Kate together, you got 'Life is no good. Just everything is shit.' I'm not surprised she died when she did, she really wanted to go. Life got hard for her, the asthma, the loneliness. And her skin would split from all the cortisone and she would bump into a corner and need stitches. That was an ongoing thing—Kate cuts her leg open, they race her into shore."

I say, "I remember some of the Breathers hanging out at the Mostels one summer after Zero died. Perhaps Kate had joined the sensory-awareness groups."

Gillis: "I'd forgotten about that summer with the Breathers. You know, that was probably a good year for her. She had them all over for cocktails. So she was into new things and she gave some old things up. You know, I think she might have modeled for Zero and Herbie at one point, but then once my father said, 'Maybe Kate would model for us,' and Kate goes, '*No way*, I don't do that anymore.'"

Bettye Jaffe and I talk about the death of loved ones. She remarks, "It's difficult to let some people go, isn't it?"

"Yes, but they're not ours to hang onto. My wife is helping me to understand that."

Jaffe says, "Sam [Jaffe] taught himself Hebrew. He was very knowledgeable about the Bible and the Talmud. Zero and Sam's favorite book was Job, they often discussed the Book of Job. It was thrilling to be around them. Life is just not as much fun now."

"Job didn't have much fun, but it seems he had understanding. What it is he understood I've never been sure."

I remark to Brian Hitchcock, "It's now eleven years since Zero's death. Is there still a sense of loss on this island?"

"The island has never been the same. Zero was enormous. There was a sense of immortality about him. I could see the change in Herbie, he couldn't believe Zero wasn't around."

"Herbie seemed to age a lot."

"He was going through the first stages of Parkinson's [Alzheimer's?] at the time. He was just . . . getting old, like the rest of them. Kate tried to stay awfully busy—but you take a Zero out of anybody's life . . . Kate used to cry a lot on bad days. All in all, Kate could be tough, and she could also be very generous."

My first meeting with Josh Mostel took place in his apartment on Riverside Drive, at most a two-minute walk from my own apartment. He offered me coffee and wanted to know why I wanted to write a book about his father. I made some remarks which now strike me as inane, about the charismatic quality of his father, about the special contribution Zero brought to theatre. These considerations are valid but the uttering of them to an offspring attempting to get the psychic weight of his father off his back doesn't seem helpful. If I'd been straight with Josh, I would have said that I thought a book about Zero would help support my habit: writing novels and plays. After our initial meeting, Josh and I would run into one another in the street, on the subway, or I would phone him or leave notes with the doorman. Communication grew more difficult. I felt we could discuss anything on earth (the arms race, the ozone layer), anything but Josh's father.

I invited Josh to lunch and spent days planning the menu. I even discussed strategy with Aaron Mostel. The menu had to be non-threatening; it had to suggest that I wasn't pumping him about Zero. On the appointed day I had lunch without Josh. An hour and a half after he was due, he telephoned. Was this the day? Oh! Well, he'd forgotten. Did I still want him over? Well, he'd be right there.

Josh appeared eventually. I reheated his lunch. While I worked at the stove, he asked me where we were going to do it. What *it*? Was I going to perform surgery, or had I been transformed into a psychotherapist? I said we were going to do it in the living room and I transported his reheated lunch to the living-room table. But at some point we were facing each other on the couch. I felt I had to have a game plan. I had to establish my position, otherwise the lunch would degenerate into a dispiriting encounter that was nothing but a lunch. I said, point blank, "I'm going to write this book about your father regardless of what you and I do in the next hour. You can help me or not. You don't *have* to be here. We don't have to do anything about Zero. *Anything*. But I am going to write this book nevertheless, so why don't you get off this couch and go eat your lunch?"

And he did. He has a good appetite. And he's far too heavy. I suppose in some way he's eating his father. I've seen him in one play, *The Boys Next Door*, about a halfway house for the emotionally disturbed who are living communally, and in the John Sayles film, *Matawan*, about a labor crisis in a mining town, and Josh strikes me as an accomplished actor. Not a performer in the mode that Zero laid claim to, though there's an element of showmanship in Josh, but more of a focused player, one with acting tools who isn't compelled to take stage center.

The lunch. A toss-up as to which of us was more nervous, but I was truly grateful when Josh got up and went home. I was too uneasy to employ the journalist's companion, the tape recorder; it would not have helped put Josh at his ease. *His ease?* There wasn't a mote or a speck of ease in that room during lunch.

In short order, after a rapid transfer of lunch from plate to recipient, Josh had once more found sanctuary, such as it was, on the couch. *Stretched out.* He answered every question, volunteered nothing, between responses and questions, dead silence waited with us.

We've seen each other since, in the street, buying our Sunday papers at the same vendor's, on the subway, occasionally on Monhegan. Josh couldn't be nicer. I've never again invited him to the house and he's never invited me to anything. Here are some points he made during the epic lunch:

"The only grandmother I knew was Anna Harkin, she lived with us for a time. I was maybe in the tenth grade when my grandmother died. I had no contact ever with Zero's parents. Did Zero talk Yiddish? In delis, in wherever he felt like breaking into it. Claimed he could speak many languages, but he made most of them up as he went along, including Esperanto which was unique to him. Kate said he had the guts of a burglar. Once on the Kennedy Center roof some Japanese were touring and the famous Zero Mostel was pointed out to them, at which point the famous Zero Mostel took a bow and broke into Mostel-brand Japanese.

"There were a lot of childish things about Zero. One of them was the way he'd conspire with me and Toby, when we were kids, so that we would all be afraid of Kate, make the boys afraid of their mother, as he supposedly was. Well he was just great when I was a kid, but then *he* was a kid. When I got older Zero got competitive. I tell you, getting famous made him crazy! Crazy! And he was surrounded by sycophants those years, people to flatter him, to live off him in some way. Well I didn't flatter him, I never hesitated to give him shit. We had a sort of game in which we'd do a lot of shouting—in the guise of humor we'd tell each other off.

"I think Zero really wanted me to fail, or else succeed partly through his efforts." In an article Josh wrote for *Esquire,* he notes that the family's nickname for him was Schmuck. "In school Zero would slip me fifty bucks. But then he never gave me a dime after that. When I was out of school it was Kate who helped me fix up my place, who gave me money, who saw to my needs. Zero would never do any of that. He was humiliating, this father of mine. What it was about Zero was this self-centeredness. He would do terrible things, terrible things, just so self-centered. But then I also think he could be wonderful, and he was just marvelously creative."

Josh discusses Zero in the theatre: "I remember him going offstage one night during *Fiddler.* He was upset at his own performance and he pounded against the flat right in the middle of Motel's speech."

I reflect, "That wasn't such a good thing to do."

"Why the hell not?"

"I can't believe it improved Motel's performance."

"How the hell would *you* know what would improve Motel's performance? Do you think Zero was an idiot? My dad was an artist."

"You were just telling me what kind of a child he could be."

"Well, he could be both ways. Maybe it was a mistake to pound on the flat, but maybe not."

We move on.

"He put me on a Monsanto TV Special. I was a first-year acting student at the time. I was humiliated! I said, 'Fuck it, I don't have to work with him!' He always had a part for me in something or other and I always turned him down."

A Columbia Pictures' press kit indicates that Marty Ritt offered Josh a role in *The Front* and that Josh initially turned it down. Ritt thought that Josh was apprehensive about appearing in the same scene with his father, but Josh, according to the press

release, felt the part was too small. "After a father-son talk . . .
Josh dutifully arrived on the set for his one-scene part."

Josh: "He always professed to have a great love for art and
to have no use for theatre. He thought the great people were
painters and the great fools were actors. When we moved to the
Belnord he set up a studio so he could paint at home, but he
couldn't stand it, it was *home* and Kate was around. He just left
it. I never heard of Kate going down to Twenty-eighth Street."

I ask, "Did you have any sense of your father's Orthodoxy?"

"His Jewishness? Well, he didn't like lobster. My grandmother Anna Harkin, when she lived with us, would serve
creamed beef on toast. Zero couldn't stand it, he was highly
insulted by this creamed beef on toast and he hated my grandmother from then on."

"Did he paint you and Toby?"

"He painted, he drew, he did lots of pictures of me and Toby
as kids. When we grew up, when we stopped being kids, he
pretty much stopped painting and drawing us."

For over a year people kept advising me to see Toby. I kept saying, 'No no, if Josh is difficult, Toby must be impossible.' I was
convinced that Toby was more than I could deal with. But
Elaine Wechsler, whose talents have included curating art
shows, managing galleries and mapping strategies for the continued career of our mutual friend, the painter John Hultberg,
persisted, she acted as a go-between, and at her urging I finally
set out to meet with the younger Mostel.

By the autumn of 1988, Toby and his wife Aileen had settled
into Eastport, Maine, relocating from Amagansett, Long Island,
and from Portland, Maine. Eastport is far north, in Machaies
County, and gives off the sense of a depressed area. But it is the
kind of depressed area that reminds one of certain other beautiful
territories in the Northeast: Vermont villages and towns like
North Bennington and Vergennes and Ripton. Eastport looks
toward the Bay of Funday and to another country, Eastern
Canada, specifically to Nova Scotia.

Eastport has a kind of stricken beauty. Its houses are primarily white; the village has been in disrepair. In 1988 one sees storefronts being renovated along the eastern side of Water Street. At this time industry has all but vanished and yet men drive their pickups and vans through the all-but-deserted town. Toby walks easily through the town on his way to one errand or another or to no errands, and there are two diners sitting at either end of Water Street where the homefries nest alongside the morning eggs. Eastport suggests that precarious balance of old hard-hat, rural America into which the counterculture attempts to sink roots, very much like Vermont in the Sixties. Its terrain and the first frosts of autumn—I arrive on Election Day—and its enduring isolation from big-city tremors quicken the heart; a muted sadness and a perverse joy mingle within you in this far outpost of mainland America.

I arrive well after dark, having taken a wrong turn in a rented car out of the Bangor Airport, which added some ninety minutes to my trip. I ask directions from a long-limbed young woman in delightfully brief shorts who points me to "that humungus house down the road, you cain't miss it." It's a deep, wonderful, clapboard house. Its deepest recesses comprise not one but several studios connected through a kind of breezeway. Aileen and Toby have planted a garden along the south side of the house and the exterior walk that parallels it is primarily fashioned of that red brick one spots frequently in Vermont. The interior is filled with Zero's art, painted or collected, and on the floors and tables of one room after another are thousands of volumes of books and periodicals Toby has inherited, and which Toby and Aileen are in the process of cataloguing and transferring to the bookshelves being constructed to house them. In one of several front rooms are the two pianos that once graced the elder Mostels' living room, and as I kept losing and refinding my way in this massive house, the two pianos were as landmarks with which to get my bearings.

There is a third occupant on the premises, the Mostel parrot with its bright, intermittent echo of earlier, overheard remarks. I learn that Toby's asthma, another inheritance, makes the presence of more traditional pets too precarious.

There are two major events taking place on the night of my arrival. Republican George Bush is about to win the '88 Presidential election over the Democrats' Michael Dukakis. It is also the fiftieth anniversary of Kristallnacht, the night when Hitler's thugs rampaged through Berlin, smashing the windows of Jewish shops, setting fire to synagogues, and beating as many of Berlin's Jews as they could conveniently get their hands on.

I have been with Toby for some three minutes and it requires every ounce of discipline I can muster to keep from walking out the front door and driving several hours' south back to the unthinking neutrality of the Bangor Airport. For a reason that seems unaccountable to me now, I have just asked, after mumbling an apology for my late arrival, whether there isn't a local synagogue nearby. I explain that this is the fiftieth anniversary of the night of the broken glass, as it came to be known, and of the burning of the synagogues in Berlin. Without batting an eye, Toby asks me if I plan to burn down a synagogue tonight. "Do you want to burn one down?" is how he puts it. If this response to my idiotic question—why in the world would I *expect* Eastport, Maine, to have any kind of shul?—is meant as some kind of low-key humor to help put me at ease, it doesn't do the job. As the evening wears on, I will learn that Toby has a wonderful capacity for hostility, no doubt honed through years of exposure to the elder Mostels.

Toby and Aileen feed me supper, then he and I settle in for several hours of talk. Most of our dialogue takes place that first evening, but we walk the next afternoon, have tea in a local bakery and then walk further about the town. We also have several energetic quarrels. I go to bed early that second night and leave very early on the third morning, heading back to Bangor. What follows are remarks, primarily from our first evening together.

"Ian Hunter said about the blacklist that in some crazy way all of you had a terrific time, even as it was terribly painful."

Toby: "Zero may have had a crazy time with Ian and the boys, but Kate was terrified. There were no jobs. She had to work in department stores. Zero had to do whatever he could. He had to borrow money. Zero's attitude about money is that it would come sooner or later, and it didn't much matter where it came from. And Kate's attitude was that there was never enough of it. She hated the blacklist. She hated the thought of us being in poverty. And Zero may well have gone out drinking everyday with the boys, I don't know, I don't remember. The boys had a certain camaraderie, they shared political ideas, that whole circle was politically involved and knowledgeable, and they lived long enough to find their positions validated—Nixon thrown out, Chambers reviled as a fool. That strength of feeling, of having been right when everybody was persecuting them, enabled them to survive. But they had friends who died, for Christ's sake—Philip Loeb most notably—people who were hounded to death and careers ruined."

"Did you have conversations about what was going on during the actual time of the blacklist, or did they try to keep you kids safe from it?"

"They never tried to keep us kids safe from *anything*. They weren't good at editing their thoughts or their conversations. There was one time that the FBI was nosing around, trying to serve a subpoena. Zero and Kate were home and they had me answer the door while they hid under the bed. I was about four years old. It was 1952 and they had me do their dirty work."

"What did you *think*?"

"I was terrified, I had nightmares. That a four-year-old should take the brunt of the FBI against a couple of so-called adults does not strike me as responsible behavior by adults. They did a lot of things to children that they had no business doing. They were wonderful friends in their professional fields but they were rotten parents."

"How did you envision them if they weren't older people you could look up to?"

"My feeling about growing up is that I grew up alone. My brother shares that with me. Our nightmares were of abandonment. Those two people we lived with abandoned us again and again. I don't have much of a picture of my father at all from the time I was young till I was about thirteen. I have no memories of those years, they don't exist. And my brother said he didn't have many family memories before twelve or thirteen. All of Kate and Zero's friends recognized that they weren't meant to have children because they were too self-centered or too involved with other people. They weren't involved with their children and they made us crazy. To her dying day my mother said, 'I was a good mother to you.' I think she was *terrible*, she thought she was wonderful. I remember the first time I went to Tim Bly's house. He was a classmate starting in seventh grade, and his house was very quiet, and you could hear a clock ticking and it made me anxious. *My* house was always noisy, there was always a fight going on or music blaring or people screaming. I was about twelve. I have all kinds of memories of my *friends*, going back to two or three. I don't have any memories of my parents at all.

"The way Zero dealt with kids and a wife was no sooner was he home than he left—went into his room and shut the door. Zero used his studio on Twenty-eighth Street as a way to get away from Kate, and as a result she hated all of his artist friends, she hated paintings, she hated museums, she hated art because she saw it as something that took him away from her. And it was true. But you had to accept the fact that when Kate was around you couldn't do any work. Kate didn't understand what work was, so that anybody who had to do a job where you had to sit there, if Kate was there you couldn't do it."

"She must have understood in terms of her own acting—"

"She didn't understand anything. My mother was not an introspective person."

I ask Toby whether Zero saw Kate as a buffer between himself and the world he didn't want to face. Toby compares the Mostel family to the series of small buffer states before World War One, self-centered states that used the war as an excuse to turn on one another.

"And that's what our family was like. Sometimes it was me and Kate against Josh and Zero, sometimes Kate and Josh and Toby against Zero, etc. It was shifting alliances, a battlefield, trench warfare, and very crazy. Whenever we got home from school we didn't know whether it was going to be World War

One or what. Kate was not a buffer, sometimes she was an ally, sometimes the enemy."

I share with Toby Josh's memory of Zero cutting off what Josh calls the fifty-dollar shmears during his undergraduate days at Brandeis and how it was Kate who provided Josh with some material support.

Toby: "At a certain period Zero was mad at both of us and wanted to cut off funds completely. Apparently that had happened to *him* and he was a firm believer in what happened to me shall happen to *you*, some kind of Old Testament vindictiveness that he brought to family life."

Apparently Toby experienced his father as an angry elder of Biblical proportions and it's not inconceivable that, consciously or not, Zero saw himself in that primitive, Yahwistic role.

Toby: "This [vengeful father] would appear through the sieve of the nineteenth-century heavy stage-father type, along the lines of the elder Germont in *La Traviata*. [Germont the father applies the time-honored guilt trip to pry his son Alfred away from Violetta, Alfred's mistress, by informing the woman that she is ruining his middle-class son's chance for respectability.] What happened to me along the same lines is that neither Kate nor Zero wanted to give me money when I went away to the Rhode Island School of Design around 1966, so I went to Zero's brother Milton the accountant and said, 'Look, this is crazy. They have to give me something.'"

"There was no rationale for their withholding?"

"They were not rational people. Zero would have an idea: 'You will do *this*,' and then you say, 'But that's crazy. Why should we do *that*?' And he would say, 'I have spoken!' You couldn't reason with the guy, he lived in another universe. You ask what family life was like—when we weren't battling and everybody was in the same room, which was usually at the supper table, I guess it wasn't so bad. Zero was very smart."

"Who cooked?"

"Kate cooked. She burned the fuckin' fishsticks every Thursday night."

I say, "Come to our house. We'll give you a good meal."

Toby: "Oh I'm a good cook now. Kate was a horrible cook. She hated cooking."

"Zero, I'm told, was a good cook."

"Zero was the worst cook in history. He thought he was a great cook and went around bragging he was a great cook. Every so often he would cook and stink up the whole house, and neighbors would call and complain, 'What is that smell? Your kitchen is on fire!' And he would serve up something inedible."

"But he was trying to provide *something*."

"He was completely deluded. His cooking and acting methods were perhaps the same. In acting he took from everywhere, a pinch of this and that, a shovelful of this, and it looks fine on stage. But you can't do that in cooking, you cannot use *every spice* and then expect it to have a taste other than tasting like grey matter. Kate at least admitted she was a terrible cook. Zero was more honest onstage but at home my considered opinion is that he was totally and completely dishonest as a father and probably as a husband, though my expertise only involves Zero as a father, a real pig, a Nazi. I called him Adolph Hitler once in the middle of a fight and that led to much hysteria and chasing me down the street with a knife. He was a dictator, a totalitarian, a fascist; we were slaves to be ordered around and if we dared to raise our voices to get rid of the shackles, chains, and cannonballs that he tied around our feet every night, he wanted to kill us. There was no middle ground."

"Could he perceive you or were you simply an audience for him?"

"I don't think he ever saw me. And I think my mother had an inkling about who I was about three weeks before she died, *and that killed her*. That's what I think. I think I killed my mother at that level."

"You both shared an asthma problem."

"So what?"

We discuss Toby as a teenager trying to paint in Zero's studio. "Zero's idea of making a comment was, 'Do it this way. This is the right way to do it.' Well, maybe so. And then I might do it that way or not. He had a way of talking to me which was always humiliating, always very sexual, always domineering."

"Sexual?'

"Sexually humiliating. Always made me feel completely diminished, as if I were nothing, a speck, a blot. As you grow older, if you live that long, you have a sense of who you are and what your worth is, and if this other guy keeps on telling you you are not worth anything at all on any level, then you begin to say, 'Well fuck you, Fatso,' which is what I said to him and that is what led to ten years of intense fighting. I left the house. I was in analysis. I was trying to bring my life together because Zero and Kate spent their whole life trying to demolish me and they fuckin' near succeeded."

"Did you move out?"

"Sure. Basically I left when I was seventeen. I returned home a few times when I was sick or in-between places. I couldn't live there. Fuckin' Zero couldn't live there either. He had to go to a studio. Josh couldn't live there. Kate stayed home and bothered the maid. Kate bothered people. My wife Aileen is a person that Kate loved. We would go out to Kate's house in Amagansett and set it up for her and paint it and drag the furniture around, and Aileen would usually have jobs [layout artist for various publications] and every five minutes during a job Kate would come in and say to her, 'You want a Coke? Want some Cheerios? Want to go down to the beach for a few minutes? Want to do this or that?'"

I comment that it's a kind of nervousness.

"Well it's an inability to recognize that someone else is working. And Kate hadn't the vaguest idea what work was. She didn't have any idea that anybody could have an inner life—I have a rich inner life, so does my wife, so does Josh, so did Zero—where you can sit still and concentrate on something. Kate did not know what sitting still and concentrating was. Consequently she would bother you until you couldn't stay there. I am sure that drove Zero crazy. When Kate was in a room you had to entertain her and be respectful at the same time. She was great at parties, always the center of attention. She gave Zero a run for his money, and as Speed Vogel said, she buried him. You're talking about a strong lady."

I remark, "She didn't bury him, she burned him up."

"Well . . . he went first."

Toby talks about Kate's move to Amagansett to be near her friend Cora Zelinka, a teacher whose husband Sidney was a screenwriter, and how Cora, an intermediate bridgeplayer, took Kate, a beginner, to a group of games.

"Kate sat with the zlubs [the rookies, to put it kindly], but within three minutes there was hysteria at Kate's table. They were having a good time, and at Cora's intermediate table they were working, they were just playing bridge. And Cora says she felt jealous all night because every three or four minutes that whole zlub table would burst into hysterical laughter because Kate was there and she was great under such circumstances."

Toby comments on his father's abilities as an actor:

"He was the greatest *I've* ever seen, with the exception of John Barrymore in certain of his movies. You have to go back to the nineteenth century to get comparable strength and versatility. My mother compared him to Brando. Zero was tremendous onstage. In *Fiddler* there's a scene where Hodel who married Perchik sings this song, 'Far From the Home I Love,' and Zero had to sit there by the railroad tracks while she sang, and *he disappeared*—sitting in the center of the stage. Which means when he wanted to he could absolutely do what the script or the director said to do. And he wasn't a pig about acting, he let other actors have their due. *Fiddler* was three hours long and Zero was onstage for two hours and forty-five minutes, and if other actors complained that he was the center of attention, well, it's in the script. Actors complain about others who make more money and have bigger roles. They think the universe is askew. Nobody went to *Fiddler* to see the rabbi's son, they went to see Zero and he gave them the worth of their seat. They felt they got a good buy when they spent twenty-five dollars for an orchestra seat. They also felt Zero was performing for them only. Jolson's audiences felt that he was singing to them directly and Zero had that quality too. And they felt they were friends of Zero and could come up and talk to him as if they were friends of long-standing after seeing him in the theatre. This is extraordinary. This is a force of nature, something else altogether."

I ask about the issue of Zero's not playing Tevye in the film version.

"I had always heard that Zero wanted too much money and wanted a say in how the picture was directed, and that was something Norman Jewison couldn't deal with. I have never seen the film, I saw some previews, the barn is five stories high—Zero says, 'This is a Jewish milkman, he doesn't have a barn, he has a lean-to.'"

"And he never saw the movie?"

"I don't think he was interested. He didn't get the part? 'Fuck 'em' was his attitude. He wanted the last word on how the picture was shot without actually being listed as director."

"Do you think he could have directed?"

"Sure. He knew the movie business from the ground up. He knew what cameras and lights were for. He was a painter, he knew how to create images, he knew how to move people."

I'm interested to know if Zero might have developed the way Keaton did.

"He could have been marvelous. Zero basically directed the John Avildsen movie, *Foreplay*. I was there helping. Zero and Joel Silver, the assistant director, ran that movie, with Zero setting up the shots that Avildsen had not figured out for some reason. Of course in Zero's version of the world nobody ever knew anything and he was always right, and in everybody else's version they gave him the idea. You hear it about W.C. Fields, about Beethoven, about Frank Lloyd Wright."

"You worked as an assistant stage manager on some of Zero's shows. Why would you even go near those projects?"

"The pay was good."

I persist. "Why would Zero even want you there? Why didn't he just get another assistant stage manager?"

"It would have tarnished his image as parent."

"Was the experience valuable for you?"

"I worked on *Foreplay*. I was Zero's go-between. The people whose house we were staying at on Long Island wanted to talk to him all the time and he needed to rest. So my job was to keep people away from him, which I did very well because I'm very hostile."

Toby talks about Edwin Booth's deciding to go on the last tour his father Junius was making because of a premonition it might be his father's final tour. "And being a romantic, I sort of had the same idea. I wanted to do a tour with Zero and be there and help if I could."

"You had a premonition?"

"It doesn't take much sensitivity to see that a man who's been overweight for thirty years, who drinks and smokes like a maniac is not going to live forever. I wouldn't call it a premonition, it's a question of statistics. I thought I should be there in case anything went wrong—and nothing went wrong. Although he died five months later. He was not on that diet during the tour [of *Fiddler* early in 1997]. I was the second assistant manager on the tour, and then the first assistant in New York, and I rose up through the ranks. I ended up calling the show [cueing lights, etc.] in New York. It was a tedious, horribly boring job. The money was great. I had been a housepainter in New York, it's hard work—this stage-managing pays a lot better."

"Did the two of you spend time together?"

"Nah. At the beginning, in Los Angeles, we spent a little bit of time together, and he got tireder and tireder, and slept more and more. In New York we had a fight and didn't speak for—five months. But that was par for the course in our family. We had the fight because I threw a turntable cue half a beat early, and no one was hurt—those dancers are eminently aware of the whereabouts of the floor. Zero's interpretation of it is that I was trying to kill him, though he was in no danger, and he came backstage and smacked me one in the mouth with his fat fist, screaming and yelling the whole time. And it was a major father-son confrontation. This was his line, he always thought Josh and I were trying to kill him when in fact it was the opposite. And I had to apologize to him—it was his fault—he was such a stupid fat slob—and then I quit and then the production stage manager said, 'Why don't you take a few days off, cool down, we'll try to work this thing through,' and I was as mad at Zero then as I'd ever been at anybody."

"The union could have helped."

"Who cares about the union? This was elemental. It was Niagara Falls versus Victoria Falls. Anyhow I calmed down and was very cool and professional to Zero for the rest of the run. I felt he had overstepped his bounds to me as another human being. He was never known to apologize to anyone, he was going to pretend that nothing had happened. By the time he died we were on speaking terms again, and he offered for me to come down to Philadelphia to do that thing [work on *The Merchant*], but I said I didn't want to. I'm just as glad I never saw him when he was dead."

I mention the diet and Wesker's belief that he had suggested such a diet to Zero.

Toby: "Zero was fat starting from when he was about twenty-seven. By the time he was forty he was at least one hundred and fifty pounds overweight. That plus drinking plus smoking causes high blood pressure."

"Drinking—you've mentioned that several times. Did he drink a lot?"

"Zero was an alcoholic."

"That's the first I've heard of it."

"Well . . . write it down. He drank, smoked. He was a high-stress kinda guy, and high blood pressure can kill you. After thirty-five years of eating like a maniac, and smoking and drinking his head off—"

"Was AA ever a factor?"

"Never. I don't see how anybody could be surprised at Zero's dying at sixty-two, considering how he had spent the forty years prior to that. He went on that diet because his heart doctor said, 'You have to go on a diet or you're gonna die,' so he went on a diet and he died anyhow. He was under weekly supervision, it was absolutely monitored the whole time. And the fact is he was living on borrowed time. You don't get a ruptured aorta from a diet, you get it from forty years of overeating and drinking and smoking."

Toby doubts that Zero was bar mitzvahed but it's speculation on his part. "Zero would have us believe that he had stopped being a practicing, religious Jew by the time he was two. So give it ten years. Let's say he was twelve. Josh and I didn't have any formal religious training. I consider myself a Jew, not in a formal but in a cultural sense. I'm not religious, have no desire to go to a synagogue or a church."

"You think of yourself as a spiritual being?"

"I *am* a spiritual being and I will not move aside one inch for any of these religious maniacs that are so popular in America these days." I neglect to ask which religious maniacs he's thinking about. "I dare say if they understood God, I do too. So does my parrot."

"Flaubert would say so." The reference, and we both understand it, is to Loulou, Felicite's beloved parrot in *A Simple Heart*.

It's Toby's view that Zero and his siblings were not close, regardless of what members of the family now convey, and that in thirty years he remembers attending one family Bar Mitzvah and one Seder. "Julian, Milton's older son, lived with Zero and Kate for a year—there was a spare room in the back. One day in a bar Julian was heard to mutter, 'Imagine, I lived with them for a year and they never even call to say hello.' And Zero in another bar on the same day was muttering, 'Imagine, he lived here for a year and never even called to say hello.' They are Mostels, that's the problem, they're always waiting for the other guy to make the gesture. And my mother brought the same attitude to the marriage, she was not gonna ever call anybody, they were gonna fuckin' call *her* if they wanted to talk to her. So she would sit there by the phone waiting for it to ring, and somebody would call her up and then she'd be disturbed and she'd say, 'Hello', like that. And they'd say, 'Am I interrupting you?' And she'd say, 'I'm watching TV.' And it was always that person's fault, and yet if that person didn't call she was insulted because nobody was calling her. She was as crazy as he was. It just came out of a different culture, the poor Irish white trash from Philadelphia."

Toby recalls his maternal grandmother:

"Her name was Anna McCafferey Harkin. She took care of me and Josh. She used to scuff out to the kitchen in the morning and make tea and toast. At least she made it for me. Josh lived next to the kitchen, I lived down the other end. We lived in the Belnord till '66, then I lived with them a little while at the Majestic. The Belnord's a great apartment, six thousand feet, it's as big as this house in Eastport. You would think that four people would be able to get along in a place that big, but we didn't, we managed to have stupendous war all the time."

I ask Toby, "Where were you when you heard about Zero's death, and did you have any sense he was going to be cremated?"

"Now the day he died I had gotten home from work, I guess—I forget what job I had. And Sam Cohn [Zero's last agent] called up and said, 'Your father's had a heart attack,' or something, they weren't sure, 'he's in the hospital, I'm sending a car, you can drive down to Philadelphia.' So that sounded very bad to me and I changed from my jeans into a pair of dark grey pants, a jacket and a tie. And I had time to call my shrink. So I went over to Kate's. There was a lot of bustling about, and Kate came down and then a call came down to the lobby. It was Sam Cohn again. He says, 'You don't have to go to Philadelphia.' So Kate said, 'What does that mean?' I said, 'It means he's dead, we don't have to go.' We were all terribly shocked, and I was drunk for two years afterwards. And Kate never recovered from it."

"How did the cremation happen?"

"Zero wanted to be cremated. So as soon as we found out he was dead . . . I believe I called . . . one of us called the hospital and said, 'No funeral. Cremate the body.' And we've lost the ashes."

"You've lost the ashes?"

"We don't know where they are—There's the title for your book: *Where Are Zero's Ashes?*"

Toby recalls the night of his father's death:

"I called Milton. He was terribly upset, he howled, almost like those for-hire mourners in the Middle East. Many people were upset. Madeline Gilford—it was the first time I ever heard her not say something in response to a statement. They all came over to the house. Jack Gilford was crying and he ain't the most emotional guy in the world. I had never seen them crying before. It speaks to how close they were to Zero. I thought I killed Sam Jaffe, he started howling on the phone, and Bettye grabbed the phone—'What happened?' I said, 'Zero's dead but I don't want to kill Sam for Christ's sake.' And Sam took to his 'death bed.' He wouldn't get out of bed, he was terribly upset. Everybody was just rocked by it. Like my own grief, which was elemental—I felt like I had been cut in half. In the midst of all this there was a call from some rabbi in Connecticut or Rhode Island who said he was a cousin by marriage or whatever, and he had been appointed by the family to do the honors of the funeral, and I said, 'No you're not,' and he said, 'What do you mean?' and I said, 'He's been cremated already, for your information.' And he's telling me, 'You can't do that! The Jews! The Book! Let us speak to your mother!' I said, 'No—Zero wanted to be cremated and that's what we're doin'. We did it already.'"

Toby tells me about his plans for a book: "I was in analysis for fifteen years and you try to make sense of all that chaos that got you into hot water. At one point you want to get out of the water and go on with your life and in order to do that you have to make some sense of all that stimulus. At one point after Zero died I decided to do a book on him [with editor-publisher Ben Raeburn]—part of it was a way to hold onto him and part was a way of understanding him. Working on it, I'm understanding all kinds of things I didn't know growing up as an object of his hostility and a victim of his madness."

I want to know if this tyrant, this alcoholic, this obsessive eater, this high-stress character on the threshold of genius who in the view of many who were close to him never made it over the threshold, actually left a will.

"Absolutely. He didn't wanna mess around with ceremony."

So, as far as I can determine, for the benefit of those who have a particular interest in questions of estate, the care of the paintings are generally in Josh's hands. Josh oversees the Monhegan house and studio that Herbie and Brian and a handful of Monhegan carpenters slammed together. Toby was presented with the Twenty-eighth Street building, along with the books, the two grand pianos and Kate's asthma.

The mention of ceremony and Judaic practice triggers an image that Toby decides he's going to share with me. And it's a revelation of no small consequence "Let me tell you something. Zero claimed he wasn't religious. I'm giving you a gem that's gonna be in my book."

And it's absolutely a gem among gems.

"My father spent a fair amount of time being Jewish in the best sense of the word. Now in the Belnord my bedroom was next to the room that had previously been Josh's bedroom and Zero took that bedroom and made it his studio, his workroom. And Zero would stay up till four or five in the morning, reading and smoking cigars. Now I'm a night person, I stay up late reading. One night I looked through a crack to see what Zero was doing and I remember seeing him with his yarmulka on reading the Holy Book late at night when he thought nobody was looking. He was sort of *davening* and being religious. I mentioned this story to a couple of his friends and they think I was hallucinating, but I wasn't. I think he was so hurt by his mother that he was questing after a kind of religious or family unity from his childhood. This excluded the living family because we weren't Jews in his Orthodox eyes. But he was terribly hurt by his mother. His mother said he was dead, wouldn't speak to him on her deathbed. He went to the hospital, he even brought Josh, and in everybody's presence, with the other brothers there, she wouldn't talk to him. Not to Josh, not to Zero. She wouldn't mention him. It must have been hell. Even for a regular guy it would be difficult, but for somebody who was as sensitive and crazy as Zero was it must have been terrible."

"I was under the impression that he would still go up to the family on Friday nights."

"My impression is that she never spoke a single word to him again, never looked at him, never said his name again. And Milton corroborated that for me once. He told me some time in the Seventies, 'My mother was terrible to Zero. When she was dying she wouldn't talk to him or look at him.' The thing that made Zero's Tevye different from everybody else's interpretation is that he played the climax of the show roughly two thirds of the way through it, when one daughter married out of the faith, and by the time he got to the last scene things were looking up. Everybody else played it that the last scene, the breaking from the homeland, was the climax. And Zero must have hated Kate at some fundamental level, because that's a hard choice, your mother or your wife. I would pick my wife any day over my mother, but Zero obviously had difficulty."

"You feel that you have a new life, away from all that craziness?"

"Well, I'm away from it by virtue of the fact that they're dead."

"But inside? You're still working it out."

"I work on remembering them as shitheads. I think that's as honest as I can be with them. I don't want to smooth over my memories with a honeyglow of fond remembrance, because it's a lie. They were fuckin' nasty to me. My mother did not like me, she treated me like a goddamned animal all my life. She was just a hostile bitch as far as I was concerned. She loved my wife Aileen, she was a virtuoso, she could sit in the same room with both of us and be very nice to Aileen and very nasty to me, and Aileen would witness this and say, 'Why is she so nasty to you?'"

"And Josh?"

"She loved Josh, she wanted him to be like Zero. This of course made him crazy, he could never be like Zero, and the son has no business being like daddy. The positive stuff I'm thankful for—that I'm bright and well-read has something to do with them. Reading a book was considered an accomplishment. Zero once said to me, 'If you're bored we got five thousand books in the house.' So I read: art, architecture, music, history, literature. Oh, there was competitiveness at the dinner table, we'd play these word games."

"Botticelli?"

"Right. Josh always had obscure chess-players, Zero had obscure everybody-under-the-sun, so I had to have obscure pianists, obscure architects. Having a certain amount of intellectual ability was a valued thing in our family. There were always accomplished, interesting, sometimes brilliant people around, and they're the ones that got me through my troubled time which I became aware of when I was about nineteen. I consider myself lucky that Zero gathered around him a bunch of people who were sensitive to me, and they got me through. Three of them acted as intermediaries when communication had completely broken down between me and my parents. They were marvelous people. Arthur Burntkrant is one, he's dead, his wife Ruthie who's still alive. And there was Herbie Kallem. They taught me warmth and affection. If Zero touched me it was always a pinch. He would raise a strawberry. And Kate was not affectionate, not demonstrative. I learned outside the house that you could touch somebody without hurting them. And I marveled at Ben Raeburn that he could talk so quietly. These people saved my life.

"Zero was never there for us, he'd threaten to break my arm. And you couldn't talk to him about these things, so—we shouted, we ran, I got involved heavily in drugs, I almost killed myself, and there was not one ounce that was perceivable to me as caring on my parents' part. All their friends say, 'They cared about you so much,' but I never saw they cared about me as a human being, not once. They couldn't give either of their kids any love. Look at Josh, he weighs three hundred and twenty pounds, for Christ's sake. Excuse me, three-fifty, and he's got high blood pressure. You know the expression, fat as a house? He says, fat as a housing project.—You've had enough? I can go on like this for weeks."

It was surely midnight. I'd have enough for months, for years. I head upstairs to bed and check out George Bush's victory.

I slept over for two nights, then took to the highway very early the following morning, with navigational help from Aileen and Toby on the previous night, had a good lumberjack-type breakfast on Route One, made it to Bangor Airport without getting lost, flew home with Toby's discourse ringing through the spaces we call the mind, and was consumed by a major headache for the next two weeks.

For the summer of 1994, the Monhegan Historical and Cultural Museum Association chose as its one-person subject, the paintings and drawings of Zero Mostel. Each summer, the Museum at the Lighthouse, as it is formally known, presents the work of a deceased artist who has been intimately connected to the life of Monhegan Island. Previous artists have included Rockwell Kent, who lived on Monhegan for some years and constructed a number of its houses, and Sarah MacPherson, whose Greenwich Village life brought her in contact with the Provincetown Players and other members of the Bohemian tribe in the Twenties, and who summered on Monhegan for many years. Anne Seelbach, curator for the Lighthouse Museum, mounted some half dozen or more paintings and a number of sketches which Josh Mostel had sent up. In conjunction with the Mostel exhibit, I read a few early chapters from the book you are now holding in your hands. The reading was at the Monhegan Library and the four-dollar admission fee was used to benefit both the Lighthouse Museum and the Library.

Zero Dances

a short film

The film is in one solitary shot. Camera in close on Zero. Is this an exterior shot? Interior? Daylight? Night? The sun moves somewhere, it goes about its business. Zero is some age or other, tends toward corpulence. Bearded, clean-shaven, your choice. And smiling. Camera begins its long tracking shot away from the figure. He appears to be standing quietly at rest, a neutral position. Camera continues tracking away. Zero grows visually smaller, exceedingly small. And yet our sense is that Zero is absolutely enormous in his smallness. Larger, as they say, than life. And at the last, last possible second, the last instant, while the figure maintains some visibility through our eyes, Zero appears to be breaking into a little dance. But one can't even be certain.

Dimension, image in space—recurring issues. From time to time the painter, working a flat surface, is hit by the urge to propel the image outward, to drive it off the canvas. In one sense the image, worked, dripped, scraped, glazed, brushed, is never simply maintained. Whether on the canvas, the paper, the wood, the tin, the ceramic, the image instantly appears within our sight. *Within us.* But in another sense the image obstinately maintains its two-dimensionality. Even as if often appears to us in a three-dimensional state, the spectator and the artist both concede that, for good or ill, the image rests in its two-dimensionality.

When the artist recognizes a growing pressure to liberate the image from its two dimensions, a number of strategies present themselves. One is impasto, the piling on of paint, the encrusting. Another is the introduction of the found object, e.g., the auto carburetor slammed tightly against and as if growing out from the traditional surface. In his 1987 show at New York's Museum of Modern Art, Frank Stella offered another way.

Writing in the MOMA quarterly of his visit to Stella's studio, Christopher Lyon speaks of

> paintings that seem about to project themselves from the wall, eccentric metal dancers in the wings waiting to do a stellar turn.

The works almost catapult, or seem to, from the heavy mountings that support their presumptuous journeys four, five, perhaps six feet away into the spectator's domain.

> The issue of whether these works are paintings or relief sculptures is an old one for Stella, whose shaped canvases of the late 1960s were considered by some to be sculptured objects. For the artist, it's a tiresome question. "You see," he explains, leading the viewer toward a stuffed furry head attached to the wall, with work gloves for antlers, "we have this moose here and when we get worried about it, we ask, 'Is this painting or sculpture?'"

Some of Stella's work is reminiscent of the pop-out figures in a child's picture book, wildly, beautifully distorted. The spectator might be viewing hallucinatory dripping settled onto the mangled surface of some giant airplane collapsed in a field. But the drippings are celebratory if frantic; the extension from the surface to spectator is a moment that seems to be courting the ecstatic.

The early Sixties witnessed other approaches. Alan Kaprow, Claus Oldenburg, Dick Higgins, Robert Whitman, and a number of others from the visual arts began experimenting with an event that came to be known as the Happening. The impulse was to create a performance, usually never repeated, in which human beings, often nonactors, and/or various objects, furnishings, and even works of art are situated within some spatial relationship to each other, indoors or outdoors. Something then either happens or doesn't happen. The relationship between the various three-dimensional phenomena is either changed or not, and ultimately, within a few moments, hours or days, the event ceases either to happen or not to happen. One of the Happenings at Judson Memorial Church in Greenwich Village involved people jumping onto a series of mattresses; in London in 1966, as part of a Happenings convention, I witnessed some half-dozen paintings literally being blown up in an empty lot known, if memory serves, as the London Free Playground.

The sculptor Robert Morris experimented with several strategies in the Sixties. He began to dance with the Judson Dancers, particularly in work choreographed by Yvonne Rainer. He created his own Happenings. One involved a living Maja, reclining in the fashion of the Goya painting. So for a time Morris worked on his own body, and for a time he employed objects separated from his body.

The artist searches for a new canvas and sometimes comes upon himself or herself. We are taken back to early tribal rites, to the more sophisticated forms of the Balinese dancers today, and to the Kathakali theatre in Kerambala, India. The performers in the tribal event transform themselves; the Kathakali performers devote hours to the transformation of their faces through a kind of emblematic use of makeup that is more complex than that employed by the Western clown. And there is Kabuki and Noh and Commedia.

I want to relate the issues of dimension, of the image in space, to the painter-performer we knew as Zero Mostel. What I see, if sketchily, is an artist who at a very early stage of his life began to labor at two canvases: one of cloth and paper, the other his very flesh. No, not his flesh but all his living being. He worked one canvas ardently, quietly, with reverence; and he worked the other ardently but noisily, grossly, with as much irreverence as that frame and breath and that spirit which is breath was able to muster. He was the private artist and he was the gross, pain-in-the-ass, public fat-man artist. And he ran from one to the other. From one to the other. And back again. Endlessly.

We hear that he had enough money, that he could have turned his back on theatre, certainly on commercial theatre, that he could have given up acting in films that rarely rose above the level of the potboiler or the gross comedy. Given them up, gone into his studio, and shut the door. Was it Kate driving him? Partially, apparently. But he seemed to have need of that driving

Kate, to want that Kate to drive him. A driven man, who tells us he views money as being of little value, but a man trapped by money. Hal Prince tells us Zero demanded too much. Did Zero-Tevye need a limousine and lots of cash in order to engage *Fiddler* night after night? His beloved Sholom Aleichem needed cash to keep his own loved ones alive, to pay the recurring medical bills, but a fancy limo?

Zero could have directed in theatre, could have directed film. But there appears to have been that need to lock someone else into the role of director so that Zero could then collaborate or undermine or overrule or play bad boy, hurl the blame elsewhere or throw the project over when it got boring. It was fun to steer Buddy Kornbluth's boat but then the fog settled in and navigational skills, rigorously learned, had to take over from spontaneity.

Was Zero religious, spiritual, God-fearing? Above "the superstitions" of the synagogue, of Torah? How does God-fearing man metamorphose, in Barney Josephson's phrase, recalling Zero's performance in *A Funny Thing Happened on the Way to the Forum*, into someone "a little dirty," ogling, pinching, suggesting the prurient, always geared for the next sexual innuendo, for the next moment of *Foreplay*? We understand that the blaspheming fool is the other face of the saint, that the profanity of the Mardi Gras or Halloween is the other, licensed face of the sacred rite. So does that make Zero the holy sinner, the one who stands within the light of the sacred being, the transcendent being who then blasphemes as a way of fulfilling an age-old mandate? Or was Zero simply a lazy, sex-driven creature who craved the condition of an ongoing spirituality but found it too tiresome to pursue the discipline and was too much a slave to his appetites and to the very concept of sexuality to channel his impulses. Perhaps the answer is that he was all of these. I don't know.

Frances Kornbluth recalls: "Zero's pawing of Maria Karnilova in the limo during *Fiddler*? My sense is that he always needed approval, he constantly had to solicit it in one way or another." Which may help explain Zero's constant soliciting of attention, at the Hotel Balfour, at the Monhegan ballfield when he was umpiring, in *Forum* when he began stealing some of Jack Gilford's material onstage, at the hotel in Philadelphia when he was phoning Marian Seldes long past midnight, during the party for Ionesco when Zero was challenging the playwright and announcing to his face that he, Zero, was the real Ionesco, at the Monhegan dock one summer's day when his hand strayed along the backside of an attractive woman who, unbeknownst to Zero, happened to be a Protestant minister. Burgess Meredith, who admired Zero, nevertheless spoke of him as a predator. Andrea Marcovicci noted that during rehearsals of *The Front*, Zero always had to get whatever laughs were available, often in proximity to Woody Allen. Clara Baker was emphatic in her declaration that Zero was always "the life of the party." But doesn't the party ever end? And where does "the life" go when the party ends?

Does this soliciting of attention generate approval? Did Zero believe it did? The marriage to the Gentile Kate certainly got his mother's attention, he took over center-stage in the mind of that beloved being, but the catastrophic degree of Tzina Mostel's disapproval was to haunt him for the remainder of his days. Several of those close to him saw Zero as a silent, absorbed being when he was closeted with himself, painting, studying, praying. Perhaps then the world was an intruder, perhaps the presence of others was a constant challenge, he had to divert these intruders, these others—from what? from their own path?—he had to take them over, to become the life of some party or other in order to do what?—to validate his own existence? To tell himself that the others actually had no path?

I have the sense that Frances Kornbluth, no wallflower herself but hardly an obsessive performer, is onto something, and I prod her for more insights. I ask Frances, "What's your sense of Zero's creativity?" And she tells me that "there have been interesting studies, psychological profiles on shizoid functioning, on creative personalities. The creative person goes into the realm of fantasy and the primitive realm and is able to extract solutions for problems. When the schizophrenic goes into these same modes of thinking, he stays there, while the creative person is able to come back at will."

"So Zero was able to come back."

"Zero would do anything"

"Josh said his father was a child."

"My husband tells me I'm very naïve."

"People think I'm an innocent or a fool."

"Exactly. And what happens? You begin to know who you're safe with."

The many, many facets of Zero. The one hand, the other hand. Does a separation of these diverse Mostels even make sense? Does a man's life add up? I like to believe in a mystery that tells me that no person's life adds up, that the parts don't produce a sum, or if they do it's a sum past all our accounting. And that we are also each other, every one of us, as well as every leaf, stone, dog, star, virus, and constellation. The issues are difficult enough for the critic, the artist, the psychologist, the social and political historian, the aesthetician, the philosopher of whatever competence. But the other face that Zero and all humans present to the world is beyond our comprehension. We attempt painful excursions. We attempt a tunneling into mysteries, and we come up against—bedrock, against a mountainous, impenetrable face. The critical faculties can't help us against such impenetrability. Against this face we have only two strategies: the one is art, the other silence.

Like the Jews of Auschwitz, Zero was consumed by fire. Did he go into the oven alone? Perhaps someone said a prayer for him. And probably *he was no longer there*, in that crematorium out of the city of brotherly love. Perhaps he was already dancing with the angels. Perhaps he is dancing with them now.

NOTES

CHAPTER TWO

1. Much of the information regarding Sholom Aleichem and the Yiddish theatre in New York is taken from three sources: Lulla Rosenfeld's *Bright Star of Exile/Jacob Alder and the Yiddish Theatre*, Thomas Y. Crowell, New York, 1977. *My Father, Sholom Aleichem*, by Sholom Aleichem's daughter Marie Waife-Goldberg, Simon and Schuster, New York, 1968. Nahma Sandrow's *Vagabond Stars/A World History of Yiddish Theatre*, Harper & Row, New York, !977.

2. At the time Zero and Clara were separated the elder Mostels were also living on Kelly Street. This writer was born at 730 Kelly Street, in 1924, some two or three blocks from where Sholom Aleichem saw his last days at 968 Kelly Street. Clifford Odets once lived at 758 Kelly Street.

3. My alert editor informs me there was no February 29th in 1915. To deepen the mystery of Zero's birth—Zero loved intrigue!—I have to report that my research at the Dept. of Health's Bureau of Vital Records in Manhattan produced no record of a Samuel Mostel born on *any* day remotely close to February 29th or 28th, either in Brooklyn or Manhattan, either in 1915, 1914 or 1916. Perhaps he was born outside of New York City. Or are we to conclude that Samuel (Zero) Mostel was never born? It's hard to believe that even Zero could have managed this one.

CHAPTER THREE

4. Irving Howe's *World of Our Fathers,* written with the assistance of Kenneth Libo, was published by Harcourt Brace Javonovich, New York and London, 1976. I am indebted to Howe and Libo for a wealth of material and an insightful view of the Lower East Side at the turn of the century.

CHAPTER FOUR

5. Lewisohn Stadium, located southwest of what was known in the Thirties as City College Uptown, was a popular gathering spot for our "serious" mass culture. General seating was fifty cents, not counting excise tax, and you were encouraged to bring a pillow or blanket to create a buffer zone between the concrete bleachers and your material being. The New York Philharmonic usually performed, normally offering 19th-century symphonic works and concertos and an annual George Gershwin night. The Stadium, a prime piece of real estate, was demolished in the Sixties, apparently considered expendable by those in charge of the wreckers.

CHAPTER SEVEN

6. Charlie Martin, whose life intertwined with that of Zero's over countless years, died June 18, 1995 at the Seaside Nursing Home in Portland, Maine at the age of 85. Charlie was a significant figure in publishing and the political life of the U.S. He drew many covers for the *New Yorker,* was political cartoonist for the newspaper *PM* almost from its inception, worked for the Office of War Information in North Africa and Western Europe following the Normandy invasion, and according to Wolfgang Saxon's *New York Times* obituary of the artist, drew political cartoons for Allied publications airdropped behind enemy lines. Charlie befriended this writer at the time I began working on *Zero Dances.* I last saw him on Monhegan Island during the summer of 1994; he was frail but he would still make his way to the small local post office now located next to the Monhegan Store where all Monheganites, winter and summer people alike, gather to pick up their mail and indulge in daily gossip. I always found Charlie a generous, noble, and compassionate spirit.

7. John Wilson's obituary of Barney Josephson ran in the *New York Times,* September 30, 1988.

8. Funt's interview with Kate Mostel, called "Zero Is a Tough Act to Follow," appeared in the *Los Angeles Times* May 9, 1980, and is excerpted from Funt's book, *Are You Anybody?*, Dial Press, New York, 1979.

9. *170 Years of Show Business* is the work of Kate Mostel and Madeline Gilford, in some collaborative relationship with Jack Gilford and Zero Mostel. We know that Zero did some editing of the manuscript. Random House, New York, 1978.

10. According to Gavin Lambert's 1997 biography, *Nazimova*, published by Alfred A. Knopf, the famed Russian actress was originally named Adelaida (Alla) Leventon. Some time in the Twenties, performing both on Broadway and in silent films, Alla Nazimova—she had invented the last name—purchased an estate on Sunset Boulevard which she duly named after herself. The Garden of Alla, according to Lambert, "became a center of Hollywood's bohemian high life, but in 1926, engulfed by one of her recurring financial crises, Nazimova embarked on a real estate scheme to develop it as a hotel." The property was renamed the Garden of Allah, but Nazimova's business partners, apparently a handful of competent swindlers, saw to it that the star reaped no profits from the transformation "However," Lambert informs us,

> she elected to live her last years in one of the 24 bungalows that were built on the grounds. The Garden of Allah, itself a landmark of the Hollywood glamour of the 30's, was torn down long ago. In the Hollywood of the 90's, it has been replaced by a mini-shopping center.

CHAPTER EIGHT

11 Joseph Tenenbaum's study of the history of Jews in Poland, *Underground, The Story of a People*, goes back to the Ninth Century C.E. where the first traces of Polish Jews, including the legend of a Jewish King, Abraham Prochownik, are to be found. Tenenbaum takes us through the Nazi invasions, the murders, the creation of the death camps, and the development of a Jewish resistance movement in the ghettoes of Warsaw, Lodz and other cities, and of Jewish partisans fighting alongside the Polish underground. Tenenbaum himself was from the city of Lemberg. The Philosophical Library, New York, 1952.

CHAPTER ELEVEN

12. The figure of Victor McLaglen is a paradigm of the fascistic move-
    ment abroad in the City of Angels in the late Forties. McLaglen and
    his motorcycle gang performed at a "Liberal" Harry Truman rally in
    Hollywood during the 1948 Presidential campaign. The emcee of
    the rally was none other than Ronald Reagan, but McLaglen stands
    out in my mind (I witnessed this peculiar rally) as a prototype of
    prideful storm trooper. In their biography *Cary Grant: The Lonely
    Heart*, Charles Higham and Ray Moseley report that McLaglen was
    frequently seen riding through Hollywood on horseback or appear-
    ing at meetings in various parks as commandant of the Hollywood
    Czars, a radically anti-Semitic, pro-Nazi group that was discovered
    more than once beating up Jews. One presumes that in the climate
    of the Nineties, McLaglen would be at home in the right-wing
    world of family values. The Grant biography was published by
    Harcourt Brace Javonovich, New York, 1989.

13. Klaus Volker, a native of Frankfurt, is a theatre director and a co-edi-
    tor of what is designated as the complete works of Brecht. His
    Brecht: A Biography was translated by John Nowell and published by
    Seabury Press, New York, 1978. The original entitled *Bertolt Brecht*,
    was published by Carl Hanser Verlag, Munich and Vienna, 1976.

14. Victor Navasky's *Naming Names*, cited many times in *Zero Dances*,
    is an important study in the development of the blacklist in the
    entertainment industries. First published in the U.S. by Viking
    Press, New York, 1980. First Penguin edition 1981.

CHAPTER TWELVE

15. From Navasky's *Naming Names*.

CHAPTER THIRTEEN

16. Jared Brown's *Zero Mostel: A Biography*, the first book-length study
    of Zero's life, was published by Atheneum, New York, in 1989.

CHAPTER FOURTEEN

17. Elia Kazan's 825-page autobiography, *A Life*, published by Alfred
    A. Knopf, New York, 1988.

18. Michael Ciment's study of Kazan as filmmaker was reprinted by
    the Los Angeles County Museum of Art in 1982.

19. Research material on directorial credits for the Bogart feature *The Enforcer* comes from files at Museum of Modern Art's Film Study Center.

CHAPTER FIFTEEN

20. From Jared Brown's *Zero Mostel: A Biography*.

21 Alta Ashley's *Under the Grey Gull's Wing*, her study of Monhegan Island, issued by Grey Gull Publications, Monhegan, Maine in 1983.

CHAPTER SEVENTEEN

22. See *A Treasury of Yiddish Stories* for works by Mendele Mocher Sforim, I.L. Peretz, Sholom Aleichem, Itzik Manger, the Singer brothers, Zalman Schneour, Jacob Glastein and others. Edited by Irving Howe and Eliezer Greenberg, with drawings by Ben Shahn. Originally published by Viking Press, New York, 1953, 1954, reprinted by Meridian Books, New York, 1958.

CHAPTER NINETEEN

23. Eric Bentley's *The Brecht Memoir*, published by PAJ Publications, 1985.

24. Brecht's collaborators included three women, Elisabeth Hauptman, Margarete Steffin and Ruth Berlau. According to John Fuegi, the three wrote much of what has been attributed to Brecht, including important sections of his plays as well as some of his poems. *Brecht and Company*, Fuegi's 731-page study of Brecht and his collaborators, is subtitled *Sex, Politics and the Making of Modern Drama*. Grove Press, New York, 1994.

25. My principal source regarding Samuel Roth's business dealings with James Joyce through the latter's agent, Ezra Pound, is my cousin Adelaide (Chig) Roth Kugel who uncovered some interesting omissions about her father at the British Museum. Chig claims that Richard Ellmann, one of Joyce's major biographers, conveniently disregarded passages in documents available to him which would apparently support Roth's claim that he indeed paid Ezra Pound for publishing rights to *Ulysses*.

Tom Dardis's biography of the publisher, *Horace Liveright*, Random House, New York, 1995, offers a fascinating view of the fallible eyesight of both Joyce and Roth and how these deficiencies impacted on the *Ulysses* that the Modern Library (Random House) finally published in 1934.

26. Orson Welles had a nighmarish experience with Olivier. In her biography, *Orson Welles*, published by Viking Press in 1985, Barbara Leaming records Welles's belief that Sir Laurence was out to humiliate the American director who was in London to stage *Rhinoceros*. "He behaved terribly," Leaming quotes Welles about the proceedings. " . . . he took every actor aside and told them that I was misdirecting them . . . . Then he did something which he had done to John Gielgud before, when he [Olivier] was playing *Twelfth Night* with Vivien [Leigh}. . . . He told John Gielgud four days before the opening that he shouldn't come for any more rehearsals, he was upsetting them. . . . Then he did the same thing to me. He told me to stay home and I *did*! I was so humiliated and sick about it. . ." And what would Olivier have attempted with Zero, and how would the Prince have responded to the Knight in a clash of three Titans? We'll never know, we only know that Zero's bus accident prevented another battle of egos from playing itself out.

27. The bulk of Ionesco's musings on theatre appear in his *Notes and Counter Notes*, Grove Press, 1964, translations by Donald Watson.

CHAPTER TWENTY-ONE

28. The 92nd St. Y's archivist, Stephen Siegel, tracked down the event for me. *Tartuffe* was given a concert reading in a new adaptation by Miles Malleson. The reading was first scheduled for December 14th, 1955, then postponed to January 9th, 1956. *Tartuffe* appears to have been either a late addition to the regularly scheduled Poetry Series or an out-of-house event, with the Y renting the Kaufman Auditorium to the company

CHAPTER TWENTY-TWO

29. The fragments of dialogue and song from *Fiddler* are all based on Paul Lipson's copy of the original script, including revisions and cuts made during out-of-town tryouts and the first Broadway run.

CHAPTER TWENTY-FOUR

30. My colleague Ann Lauinger of the Literature Faculty at Sarah Lawrence College recorded a videotape of *Mastermind* when the film finally made an appearance on Cable TV.

CHAPTER TWENTY-FIVE

31. Vicki Richman's article in the Feb.-March issue of *Changes* is called "Zero Mostel and Ring Lardner Jr., Two Characters in Search of an Author." The one issue of *Changes* I saw suggests a good-humored, somewhat laid-back Leftist publication.

CHAPTER TWENTY-SIX

32. Landau's concept for American Film Theatre was to sell subscriptions for a series of avant-garde features that he would produce. Sufficient subscriptions apparently were never purchased and the films eventually went into general distribution.

33. I had known Lloyd Gough in Hollywood in 1948-49 when I was involved with a short-lived playrights workshop initiated by and taking place at the Actors Lab. I considered Lloyd and his companion, the actress Karen Morley, friends who seemed to have remarkable patience with my "liberal bourgeois tendencies," tendencies that left me ambivalent even as I put in long, arduous, unpaid days as a political organizer for the Presidential candidacy of Henry Wallace. On Election Day, Wallace garnered fewer than a million votes, and was even beaten out by Strom Thurmond's Dixiecrats, but I always considered the cause of the Progressive Party (the American Labor Party in New York) well worth the effort all of us put in, bourgeois liberals and card-carrying Communist members together.

CHAPTER TWENTY-EIGHT

34. Wesker's play is brilliant and impassioned. His Shylock and Antonio are buddies, they carry on a philosophic discourse over the years, they are chess players who appreciate each other's moves, they stimulate one another, they are just men and gentlemen.

35. Arnold Wesker's *Merchant* journal originally appeared in 1985 in *Distinctions: Collection of Essays and Journalism of 25 Years*. Publisher: Jonathan Cape in London. Marian Seldes's *The Bright Lights* was originally published by Houghton Mifflin in Boston, 1978, and reprinted with a new chapter in 1984 by Limelight Editions in New York.

36. Quite likely this toy bird on Zero's hat is a plastic seagull purchased at Zimmy's Island Spa one idyllic summer's day, and probably purchased by Kate.

PLAYS

In New York City unless otherwise noted.

Cafe Crown, a comedy by Hy Kraft. Sam Jaffe stars, word has it that Zero would make unscheduled appearances, sometimes accompanied by Philip Loeb. The cast includes Morris Carnovsky, Mary Mason, Mitzi Hajos, Lou Polan and Sam Wanamaker. The comedy is produced by Carly Wharton and Martin Gabel. Director is Elia Kazan. Opens at the Cort Theatre on Broadway, January 23, 1942; in May it has moved to the Flatbush Theatre in Brooklyn.

Keep 'Em Laughing, vaudeville production with Victor Moore, William Gaxton, Paul and Grace Hartman, and Jack Cole and his dancers. Opens April 24, 1942 at the 44th Street Theatre.

Top-Notchers, essentially the same vaudeville production, opens immediately after the earlier show closes, Gracie Fields stars, many of the earlier players are holdovers.

Concert Varieties, "an entertainment," with Katherine Dunham, Jerome Robbins and Company (dancers), Imogene Coca, Eddie Mayehoff, Sid Catlett, Albert Ammons and Pete Johnson, Deems Taylor emcees, produced by Billy Rose. Opens June 1, 1945 at the Ziegfeld.

The Milky Way, a comedy, opens in the summer of 1945 at the Long Island Beach Summer Theatre.

Beggars' Holiday, a musical adaptation of John Gay's *Beggars' Opera*, book and lyrics by John LaTouche, music by Duke Ellington, choreography by Valerie Bettis, designed by Oliver Smith. Both John Houseman, early, and George Abbott, later, involved in direction, finally in the hands of Nicholas Ray. Cast includes Alfred Drake as Macheath, Marie Bryant, Bernice Parks, Avon Long and Jet MacDoanld. Zero appears as Hamilton Peachum, Opens December 26, 1946. The work is also known as *Twilight Alley*.

The Imaginary Invalid, Molière's comedy, produced by the Brattle Theatre Company in Cambridge, Mass. Jerome Kilty and Albert Marre are producers. Brian Halliday and Kate Mostel are featured and Kate is listed as director as a way to keep Zero's earnings hidden. The company also presents Molière's *The Doctor in Spite of Himself*. The two productions take place between 1949 and 1951.

Flight into Egypt, George Tabori's drama, produced by Irene Selznick, scenery and lighting by Jo Mielziner, directed by Elia Kazan. Cast includes Paul Lukas, Gusti Huber, David Opatoshu, Jo Van Fleet and

Joseph Anthony. Zero plays Glubb. Opens March 18, 1952 at the Music Box.

A Stone for Danny Fisher, adapted by Leonard Kantor from a novel by Harold Robbins. Cast includes Philip Pine, Sylvia Miles and Bert Freed. Zero plays a mobster named Maxie Fields. The director is listed as Francis Kane, but it's a pseudonym for Luther Adler who replaced the original director. Opens at the Downtown National on October 21, 1954.

Lunatics and Lovers. Zero plays Dan Cupid in the tour of Sidney Kingsley's comedy. Performances are in California sometime in 1955.

Once Over Lightly, a revue, produced and performed by blacklisted artists, with lyrics (apparently) by the blacklisted Yip Harburg. Cast includes Sono Osato, Jack Gilford and Zero. Directed by Stanley Prager. Opens March, 1955 at the Barbizon Plaza.

The Good Woman of Setzuan, the play by Bertolt Brecht, translated and directed by Eric Bentley, produced by T. Edward Hambleton and Norris Houghton for the Phoenix Theatre, sets by Wolfgang Roth from earlier designs by Teo Otto, incidental music by Paul Dessau. Cast includes Uta Hagen, Nancy Marchand, Jane Hoffman, Gerald Hiken, Gene Saks, Logan Ramsey and Albert Salmi. Zero plays Shu Fu. Opens at the Phoenix Theatre December 18, 1956.

Good As Gold, a comedy by John Patrick, based on a novel by Alfred Toombs. Cast includes Edmund Fuller, Roddy McDowall, Dana Elcar and Lou Gilbert. Zero plays Doc Penny. Producers are Cheryl Crawford and William Myers. Directed by Albert Marre. Opens at the Belasco, March 7, 1957.

Ulysses in Nighttown, "dramatized and transposed" [not clear to me what transposed means] by Marjorie Barkentin from James Joyce's *Ulysses*. Original production, with Alexander Cohen as producer, opens at the Rooftop Theatre June 5, 1958. Zero plays Leopold Bloom opposite Pauline Flanagan's Molly Bloom. Kate Mostel records that at one period of the run she played Molly Bloom. Burgess Meredith directs this production, as well as the Broadway revival, again with Zero, which opens at the Winter Garden March 8, 1974. Zero is awarded an Obie by the *Village Voice* for his performance at the Rooftop.

On January 13, 1960, while rehearsing Felicien Marceau's comedy *La Bonne Soupe (The Good Soup)*, which Garson Kanin is directing, Zero has his unfortunate bus accident and spends the next months in and out of the hospital. Jules Munshin replaces him in the play.

Rhinoceros, Ionesco's play, translated by Derek Prouse, features Morris Carnovsky, Eli Wallach, Anne Jackson, Mike Kellin, Michael Strong, Jean Stapleton and Dolph Sweet. Zero wins a Tony for his role as John. Producer is Leo Kerz. Bobby Lewis was to have directed and may have begun rehearsals, but Joseph Anthony takes over. Opens at the Longacre, January 9, 1961.

A Funny Thing Happened on the Way to the Forum, music and lyrics by Stephen Sondheim, book by Burt Shevelove and Larry Gelbart. Choreographer: Jack Cole. Setting and costumes: Tony Walton. Lighting: Jean Rosenthal. Cast includes Jack Gilford, David Burns, John Carradine, Ruth Kobart, Preshy Marker, Eddie Phillips, David Evans and Raymond Walburn. Hal Prince produces, with George Abbott as co-producer and director. Jerome Robbins is brought in as trouble-shooter. Opens at the Alvin on May 8, 1962. Zero, as the slave Pseudolus, wins his second Tony award.

Fiddler on the Roof, a musical based on the stories of Sholem Aleichem, book by Joseph Stein, music by Jerry Bock, lyrics by Sheldon Harnick, sets by Boris Aronson, assisted by Lisa Aronson, costumes by Patricia Zipprodt, lighting by Jean Rosenthal, orchestrations by Don Walker, musical direction and vocal arrangements by Milton Greene, dance arrangements by Betty Walberg, directed and choreographed by Jerome Robbins with Ruth Mitchell assisting, produced by Hal Prince. Cast includes Maria Karnilova, Beatrice Arthur, Joanna Merlin, Austin Pendleton, Bert Convy, Julia Migenes, Michael Granger, Joseph Sullivan, Tanya Everett, Joe Ponazecki and Paul Lipson. Opens at the Imperial on September 22, 1964. As Tevye, Zero wins his third Tony.

The Latent Heterosexual, a comedy by Paddy Chayevsky. Burgess Meredith directs a cast that includes Jules Munshin, Randy Moore and Chris Richard. Zero plays John Morley, a homosexual poet. Opens at the Kalita Humphreys Theater in the Dallas Theatre Center, Dallas, Texas, in early April of 1968.

Another musical that was planned but, according to playwright John Guare, never even got to the rehearsal stage, was a musical version of Brecht's *The Exception and the Rule*. Leonard Bernstein wrote the music, Stephen Sondheim the lyrics, and John Guare the book with choreography by Jerome Robbins. After a four-week period of pre-views in New York, in lieu of an out-of-town tryout, an opening at the Broadhurst was planned for February 18, 1969.

The Merchant, Arnold Wesker's drama, a revisionist interpretation of the material Shakespeare used in fashioning the Shylock and Antonio of *The Merchant of Venice*. The cast as the play finally opened in New York includes Joseph Leon who replaces Zero, John Seitz who replaces Sam Levene, also Julie Garfield, Marian Seldes, Sir John Clements and Roberta Maxwell. New York opening is at the Plymouth on November 16, 1977. "World premiere," as these events are hyped, is in Stockholm at the Royal Dramaten-theatre on October 8, 1976. The U.S. production, under John Dexter's direction, plays a single preview in Philadelphia at the Forrest Theatre with Zero as Shylock. Date is September 2, 1977. More recently Wesker changes the play's name to *Shylock*.

Note: Zero speaks of playing a priest in a production of *Shadow and Substance*. Perhaps high school or college?

FILMOGRAPHY

Zero's feature-length films. Designates performances unless otherwise noted. Opening in Manhattan unless otherwise noted for early films; for later films multiple openings take place.

DuBarry Was a Lady. Screenplay by Irving Becher, adaptation by Nancy Hamilton, based on the play by Herbert Fields and B.G. De Sylva, with songs by Cole Porter. Additional songs: Lew Brown, Ralph Freed, Burton Lane, Roger Edens, E.Y. Harburg. Musical adaptation: Roger Edens. Musical direction: Georgie Stoll. Orchestration: George Bassman, Leo Arnaud, Alec [sic] Stordahl and Sy Oliver. Cast includes Red Skelton, Lucille Ball, Gene Kelly, Virginia O'Brien, "Rags" Ragland, Donald Meek, Douglass Dumbrille, George Givot, Louise Beavers, Tommy Dorsey and his orchestra featuring the Pied Pipers. Zero plays Rami the Swami and Taliastra. Producer: Arthur Freed for MGM. Directed by Roy Del Ruth. Opens at the Capitol on August 19, 1943. 101 minutes.

Panic in the Streets. Screenplay by Richard Murphy, adaptation by Daniel Fuchs from a short story by Edna and Edward Anhalt. Cinematographer: Joe MacDonald. Editor: Harmon Jones. Cast includes Richard Widmark, Barbara Bel Geddes, Paul Douglas, Walter (Jack) Palance, Dan Riss, Alexis Minotis, Guy Thomajan, Tommy Cook and Lenka Peterson. Zero plays Fitch, Palance's sidekick. Produced by Sol C. Siegel for 20th Century-Fox. Directed by Elia Kazan. Released September, 1950. 96 minutes.

The Enforcer. Screenplay by Martin Rackin. Cast includes Humphrey Bogart, Ted De Corsia, Everett Sloane and Roy Roberts. Zero plays "Big Babe" Lazich. Produced by Milton Sperling for United States Pictures and released by Warner Brothers. Bretaigne Windust is credited as director, but according to film material at the Museum of Modern Art, "Raoul Walsh did extensive, if not complete, work on the film." Opens at the Capitol on January 25, 1951. 87 minutes.

Sirocco. Screenplay by A.I, Bezzerides and Hans Jacoby, based on Joseph Kessel's novel *Coup de Grace.* Score by George Antheil. Cinematographer: Burnett Guffey. Editor: Viola Lawrence. Cast includes Humphrey Bogart, Marta Toren, Lee J. Cobb, Everett Sloane, Nick Dennis, Onslow Stevens, Ludwig Donath and Peter Brocco. Zero plays an Arab merchant named Balukjian. A Robert Lord (Santana) production, released by Columbia. Directed by Curtis Bernhardt. Opens at the Capitol on July 2, 1951. 97 minutes.

Mr. Belvedere Rings the Bell. Screenplay by Ranald MacDougall, based partly on the Broadway play *The Silver Whistle* by Robert E. McEnroe and the character "Belvedere" created by Gwen Davenport. Cinematographer: Joseph La Shelle. Editor: William B. Murphy. Cast includes Clifton Webb, Joanne Dru, Hugh Marlowe, Billy Lynn, Doro Merande, Frances Brandt, Kathleen Comegys, Jane Marbury, Harry Hines, William and Ludwig Provaznik. Zero plays Belvedere's sidekick, Emmett. Andre Hakim produces for 20th Century-Fox. Directed by William B. Murphy. Opens at the Roxy, July 1952. 87 minutes.

The Guy Who Came Back. Cinematographer: Joseph La Shelle. Editor: William B. Murphy. Cast includes Paul Douglas, Joan Bennett, Linda Darnell, Don De Fore and Billy Gray. Zero plays Boots Mullins. Produced for 20th Century-Fox by Julian Blausten. Directed by Joseph Newman. Opens in August of 1951. 92 Minutes

The Model and the Marriage Broker. Screenplay by Charles Brackett, Walter Reisch and Richard Breen. Cinematographer: Milton Krasner. Editor: Robert Simpson. Cast includes Thelma Ritter, Jeanne Crain, Scott Brady and Michael O'Shea. Zero plays an optometrist named Mr. Wixted. Charles Brackett produces for 20th Century-Fox. Directed by George Cukor. Opens on or about January 11, 1952, at the Roxy. 103 minutes.

Zero. Screenplay by Samuel Beckett from his mime play, *Act Without*

Words I, or else it's Beckett's play shot without a film script. Produced by Barney Rosset for Eli Landau's American Film Theatre. Zero has the solo role. Directed by Anthony Asquith. The plan was to release *Act* as part of a trilogy, including Beckett's *Film* with Buster Keaton. *Film* eventually released by itself. There's no record that *Zero* was ever released, though it had a screening at the Venice Film Festival in 1960. Under 10 minutes.

A Funny Thing Happened on the Way to the Forum. Screenplay by Melvin Frank and Michael Pertwee. Music and lyrics by Stephen Sondheim. Book by Burt Shevelove and Larry Gelbart. Cast includes Phil Silvers, Jack Gilford, Buster Keaton, Michael Crawford, Annette Andre, Michael Hordern and Patricia Jessel. Zero repeats his role as Pseudolus. Produced by Melvin Frank, released through United Artists. Directed by Richard Lester. Opens in New York on October 16, 1966, at Cinema I and II. 99 minutes.

Monsieur LeCoq. Screenplay by Ian Hunter and Zero Mostel. Cast includes Julie Newmar, Akim Tamiroff and Ronnie Corbett. Zero casts himself in dual role: Monsieur LeCoq and his father Max LeCoq. Carl Foreman is executive producer of Highroad, with Adrian Scott as producer for an anticipated Columbia release. Director is Seth Holt. Production is suspended as of November 15, 1967. Film never completed.

The Producers. Screenplay by Mel Brooks. Cast includes Gene Wilder, Kenneth Mars, Estelle Winwood, Renee Taylor, Christopher Hewett, Lee Meredith, Andreas Voutsinas and Dick Shawn. Zero plays Max Bialystok. Executive producer: Josephh E. Levine. Released by Embassy Pictures. Directed by Mel Brooks. Opens in New York March 18, 1968, at the Fine Arts. 88 minutes.

Great Catherine. Screenplay by Hugh Leonard, based on the George Bernard Shaw one-act play. Music by Dimitri Tiomkin. Cast includes Peter O'Toole, Jeanne Moreau, Jack Hawkins and Akim Tamiroff. Zero plays Prince Patiomkin, the Rabelaisian advisor to the Empress. Jules Buck produces for Keep Films. Distributor is Warner Brothers-Seven Arts. Directed by Gordon Flemyng. Opens late January, 1969, at 20 Showcase Theatres. 98 minutes.

The Great Bank Robbery. Screenplay by William P. Blatty, based on a novel by Frank O'Rourke. Cinematographer: Fred Koenekamp. Editor: Gene Milford. Songs by Sammy Cahn and James Van Heusen. Cast includes Kim Novak, Clint Walker, Claude Akins, Akim

Tamiroff, Larry Storch, John Anderson, Sam Jaffe, Mako, Elisha Cook and Ruth Warrick. Zero plays Reverend Pious Blue. Malcom Stuart Productions, released through Warner Brothers-Seven Arts. Directed by Hy Averback. Opens at various theatres in New York Sept. 10, 1969. 97 minutes.

The Angel Levine. Screenplay by William Gunn and Richard Ribman, based on a story by Bernard Malamud. Cinematographer: Dick Kratina. Editor: Carl Lerner. Cast includes Harry Belafonte, Ida Kaminska, Milo O'Shea, Gloria Foster, Barbara Ann Teer, Eli Wallach and Anne Jackson. Zero plays Morris Mishkin. A Belafonte Enterprises Film, produced by Chiz Schultz and released by United Artists. Directed by Jan Kadar. New York opening at various theatres around July 15, 1970. 105 or 107 minutes.

Mastermind. Screenplay by Terence Clyne and Samuel B. West (together perhaps they're known as William Peter Blatty), from a story by Terence Clyne. Cinematographer: Gerald Hirschfeld. Editor: John C. Howard. Cast includes Bradford Dillman, Jules Munshin, Sorrell Booke and Frankie Sakai. Zero plays Hoku Fat, an Oriental detective. Malcom Stuart Productions with Wordvision for ABC Pictures. Directed by Alex March. A May 1970 release date was planned, but the film was never released; it occasionally shows up on television.

The Hot Rock. Screenplay by William Golden from the novel *The Hot Rock* by Donald E. Westlake. Cinematographer: Ed Brown. Editors: Grank P. Keller, Fred W. Berger. Music: Quincy Jones. Sound track musicians include Gerry Mulligan, Clark Terry, Frank Rosalino, Jerome Richardson, Grady Tate and Ray Brown. Cast includes Robert Redford, George Segal, Ron Leibman, Paul Sand, Moses Gunn, William Redfield, Topo Swope, Charlotte Rae, Seth Allen and George Bartenieff. Zero plays Abe Greenberg. A Hal Landers-Bobby Roberts Production, released through 20th Century-Fox. Directed by Peter Yates. Released in Britain under the title *How to Steal a Diamond in Four Easy Lessons.* Released early March, 1972. 101 minutes.

Once Upon a Scoundrel. Screenplay by Rip Van Ronkle. Cinematographer: Gabriel Figueroa. Editor: Albert Valenzuela. Composer: Alex North. Cast includes Katy Jurado, Tito Vandis, Priscilla Garcia and A. Martinez. Zero plays Carlos del Refugio. A James Elliot Production, executive producer: Felipe Subervielle, anticipated release by Carlyle Films. Directed by George Schaefer. The film was never officially released, though screened at the 2nd Thessaloniki International Film Festival on Octover 30, 1973, and at the Fairfax Theatre in Los Angles during "Zero Mostel Week" in March 1980. 90 minutes in '73.

Marco. Script and lyrics: Romeo Miller. Cast includes Desi Arnaz Jr. and Jack Weston. Zero plays Kublai Khan to Desi's Marco Polo. An Arthur Rankin-Jules Bass production, released by Cinerama for Tomorrow Entertainment. Directed by Seymour Robbie. Opens around December 13, 1973. 109 minutes.

Rhinoceros. Screenplay by Julian Barry from the play by Ionesco. Cinematographer: Jim Crabe. Music: Galt MacDermot. Cast includes Gene Wilder, Karen Black, Robert Weil, Joe Silver, Marilyn Chris, Robert Fields, Melody Santangelo, Lou Cutell, Don Calfa, Kathryn Harkin, Lorna Thayer, Howard Morton and Percy Rodrigues. Zero plays John. Directed by Tom O'Horgan. Opens in various theaters in 1974. 101 minutes.

Foreplay, also *Four Play,* also *The President's Women.* Screenplays: Dan Greenberg, Jack Richardson, David Odell, Bruce Malmuth and John Avildsen. Cast includes Estelle Parsons, Paul Paulsen, Jerry Orbach, Laurie Heineman and Joseph Palmieri. Zero plays the President of the U.S. Executive producers: Carl Gurevich and William Anderson, A Syn Frank Enterprises for Cinema National, re-released by Atlantic Releasing. Directors: John Avildsen, Robert McCarty and Bruce Malmuth. Opens in Los Angeles March 5, 1975. 75 minutes.

Journey into Fear. Produced and adapted by Trevor Wallace from Eric Ambler's novel. Cinematographer: Harry Waxman. Composer: Alex North. Cast includes Sam Waterston, Yvette Mimieux, Scott Marlowe, Ian McShane, Joseph Wiseman, Shelley Winters, Stanley Holloway, Donald Pleasance and Vincent Price. Zero plays Kopeikin, a devious spy. Directed by Daniel Mann. New World Productions. Opens in 1975 with limited exposure and then on Home Box Office January 9, 1976. 103 minutes.

The Front. Screenplay by Walter Bernstein. Cast includes Woody Allen, Hershel Bernardi, Michael Murphy, Andrea Marcovicci, Remak Ramsay, Marvin Lichterman, Lloyd Gough, David Margulies, Joshua Shelley, Norman Rose, Charles Kimbrough, M. Josef Sommer, Danny Aiello, Georgann Johnson, Scott McKay, Julie Garfield, Joey Faye and Marilyn Sokol. A Martin Ritt, Jack Rollins, Charles H. Joffe Production for Columbia Pictures. Directed by Martin Ritt. Opens October, 1976. 95 minutes.

Watership Down. Animated cartoon produced, written and directed by Martin Rosen, from Richard Adams's novel. Animation directed by Tony Guy and supervised by Philip Duncan. Cast (voices only) includes John Hurt, Richard Briers, Michael Graham-Cox, John Bennett, Ralph Richardson and Denholm Elliott. Zero plays Kehaar the seagull. Released in the U.S. by Avco Embassy . Opens November 3rd, 1978. 92 minutes.

Best Boy. Feature-length documentary, directed and produced by Ira Wohl. Zero plays himself. Distributed by Entertainment Marketing Corp. 1979. 111 minutes.

Note: Film Shorts that Zero never managed to appear in include *Freud Strikes Back*, a film created by photographer and illustrator Paul Petrof. Petrof shot some footage of Zero. As we've learned from other events, the man of ample proportions "carried on pretty good," but Petrof found this carrying on not germane to his own purposes.

INDEX

ACKNOWLEDGMENTS

Many many people helped make this book happen. There is Mel Zerman, my editor-publisher, who seems to have found something in it. Phil Turner, editor at Times Books, who ran into Mel at a book fair and told him about *Zero Dances*. My original editor at E.P. Dutton, Meg Blackstone, who was encouraging and wonderfully gentle, but managed to get herself fired along with most of the editorial staff at Dutton one bitter night; this sudden firing sent both Meg, eight months pregnant at the time, and my manuscript looking for new homes. (Images of fire and firings keep turning up in this book.) Dan Strone, my former agent at William Morris who nurtured this book with much patience. My present agent, the indomitable Anne Edelstein, who watches my career with more than a trace of bemusement and has stood by me for several years. Toby Cole, Zero's former agent, still battling for European playwrights from the reasonably peaceful hills of Berkeley, Calif. Julie Gilliam, executive producer of Magnus Films, who housed and fed me and lent me wheels and laughed at my stories while I worked at the Motion Picture Film Academy Library and did my West Coast interviews. Charles Silver who runs the Film Study Center at the Museum of Modern Art. Ed Carter at UCLA's Film Archives.

Kristine Krueger, a young film buff, apprenticing in the late Eighties at the Academy's Film Library. The army of workers at Lincoln Center's Theatre Collection, including my friend Betty Corwin. Old buddies of Sammy Mostel, including Clara Baker, Zee's first wife; the late Nettie Crosley, Zee's first girlfriend; Eeta Linden who learned to ride a bike courtesy of Sam Mostel; the late Aaron Mostel who provided me with another view of the early years; Alex Maltz, one of Zero's first mentors in graphic art; Sig Miller who "discovered" Zero; Himan Brown who took Zee to the late Barney Josephson; Barney Josephson who told me precious and heartbreaking stories; the actress Bettye Jaffe, widow of Sam Jaffe, along with Ian Hunter, Frances Chaney and Ring Lardner Jr., all of whom suffered through the blacklist with Zero. My cousin Viola Harris, who worked in the theatre with Zero and whose late husband, Robert H. Harris, was on a poisonous "greylist." Also, theatre critics and literary scholars Eric Bentley and Irving Howe and producers and public relations people Norris Houghton, Sandy Friedman, Merle Debuskey, the late June Prensky Gitlin and Art D'Lugoff. Performers include the late Paul Lipson, Andrea Marcovicci and Marian Seldes. Directors Elia Kazan, George Schaefer, playwright Arnold Wesker and playwright-director George Tabori. Sam Katz who, in his quietly manic way, introduced me to the mysteries of Word Perfect, and Mary Adelman of Osner's Business Machines who nurses old typewriters, including my ponderous manual that served me faithfully during my early drafts. English Strunsky and Emily Paley who remembered early Mostel stories for me. Gloria Cahill who came upon the enchanting *Zero by Mostel* and made me a gift of it. And Josh and Toby Mostel, who talked to me in spite of their own conflicts, and Elaine Wechsler who reached out to Toby on my behalf. And my friends on Monhegan who loved and were irritated by Zero, and some Monheganites like Charlie Martin and Zimmy and Alta Ashley and Sue Rosenthal who are no longer here. So many are here to help relate this journey, and I believe they are all, the living and the dead, somewhere in the heart of this vast universe, all connected to all.

ABOUT THE AUTHOR

Arthur Sainer was born in the Bronx and studied at New York University and Columbia. He is deeply involved in theatre and, more generally, in the world of literature. He has been awarded playwriting grants from the Ford and Rockefeller Foundations, the University of Minnesota, and, on two occasions, the National Foundation for Jewish Culture. He has also been nominated for several *Village Voice* Obie awards. For two decades he was drama critic for *The Voice* and the paper's book editor in the early Sixties. He has written critical pieces for *Vogue, The Nation, Midstream, Ikon, Bennington Review, Yale Theater, Michigan Quarterly Review*, and *American Book Review*. He has taught at Bennington, Middlebury, Wesleyan, The New School, C.W. Post, Hunter, and the College of Staten Island, and is now on the theatre faculty at Sarah Lawrence. His book *The New Radical Theatre Notebook* was published in 1997, and he is now working on a novel, *The Perfection of Loss*. Mr. Sainer lives in Brooklyn with his wife, psychotherapist Maryjane Treloar.